Christianity, Empire, and the Making of Religion in Late Antiquity

DIVINATIONS:
REREADING LATE ANCIENT RELIGION

Series Editors: Daniel Boyarin, Virginia Burrus, Derek Krueger

A complete list of books in the series is available from the publisher.

Christianity, Empire, and the Making of Religion in Late Antiquity

JEREMY M. SCHOTT

PENN

University of Pennsylvania Press

Philadelphia

Published by
University of Pennsylvania Press
Philadelphia, Pennsylvania 19104-4112

Printed in the United States of America on acid-free paper

10   9   8   7   6   5   4   3   2   1

Library of Congress Cataloging-in-Publication Data

Schott, Jeremy M., 1977–
   Christianity, empire, and the making of religion in late antiquity / Jeremy M. Schott.
      p. cm. — (Divinations)
   Includes bibliographical references (p.   ) and index.
   ISBN 978-0-8122-4092-4 (alk. paper)
   1. Church history—Primitive and early church, ca. 30–600. I Title.
BR165.S398 2008
270.1—dc22

2008007809

To Michelle

For nothing is stronger or better than this:
when two people, united in purpose, make a home together.
It brings much pain to their enemies, but joy to their friends,
and they themselves know the greatest blessings.
—Homer *Od.* 6.182–85

Contents

Identity Politics in the Later Roman Empire

In 299 C.E. things were going well for Diocletian. His political experiment in tetrarchy had paid off. Maximian and Constantius I had defeated the usurper Carausius in Gaul and Britain. Meanwhile, Diocletian's Caesar, Galerius, had defeated the Persians and concluded a treaty that promised to secure the eastern borders. A pious man, Diocletian attended auguries following his recent successes. These sacrifices did not go as planned. Despite repeated attempts, the *haruspices* were unable to read the entrails of the sacrificial victims. Somehow, "either by suspicion or by seeing it himself," the chief *haruspex* identified the problem: "profane people"—the Christians—were interfering with the rites.[1] Diocletian required members of his court and his army to perform a traditional sacrifice; surely this would weed out, or reform, anyone so impious as to disturb the traditional religion of the court. And so the matter stood until the winter of 302–3, when, according to the Christian apologist Lactantius, Diocletian and Galerius summoned "judges . . . and some military leaders who held superior rank" as well as some "friends" of the emperor to court.[2] According to Lactantius, the decision to initiate the Great Persecution came only after a series of consultations and conferences with various advisors. During the winter of 302–3, Diocletian's advisors recommended that the Christians, "as enemies of the gods and hostile to traditional religion, ought to be done away with."[3] By the end of February 303, the Great Persecution was on.[4]

To an empire in control of vast territory and diverse peoples, the Christians could appear threatening—they refused to participate in imperial cult, rejected public amusements, were wary of public office, and were openly critical of traditional religions. Yet while they seemed almost completely antithetical to Rome, Christians could also appear very Roman. Many Christians spoke and thought in Greek and Latin, the two imperial *koinai*, shared the same civic spaces, and even espoused, at least ostensibly, the same desire for the preservation of the empire.[5] Christians could speak of themselves as Romans.[6] The scholar and bishop Eusebius of Caesarea, who had witnessed the martyrdoms of many friends during the Great Persecution, identified the confusion that lay at the heart of anti-Christian sentiment. "In all likelihood," Eusebius reflected, "someone may ask who we are . . . that is, whether we are Greeks or barbarians, or what might there be in-between these?"[7] How appropriate then, that the edict initiating the Great Persecution should have been promulgated in the day of the Terminalia, a festival celebrating boundaries and limits.[8]

Long before Diocletian's edicts, however, earlier persecutions had served as crucibles in which Christians negotiated their identity. Under examination by the Roman proconsul, for instance, the reply of the African martyr Vestia was a two-word confession, *Christiana sum.*[9] The narratives of many early martyr acts hinge on similarly succinct declarations of identity. Indeed, many ancient Christians (as well as modern scholars) claim that the taxonomic classification "Christian" was the central legal grounds for the pronouncement of capital sentences.[10] Despite the clarity with which martyrs declared their identity as "Christians," the meaning of the label often remained unclear to those who passed sentence. When Pliny, the Roman governor of Bithynia, for instance, found himself presiding over trials of Christians he had to ask Trajan for clarification as to "whether the name 'Christian' in itself . . . or the crimes associated with the name ought to be punished."[11]

Martyrdom represented a dramatic and visceral means of establishing one's identity,[12] but a less bloody, though no less agonistic, means of self-definition lay in the composition of literary treatises, or "apologies," in defense of Christianity. The work of Christian apologists was twofold, defining and defending Christianity, on the one hand, and attacking traditional religions, on the other. Beginning in the first century, Christians grappled to fix the boundaries between themselves and others. Paul's letters show him wrestling to define himself in relation to Jews and Greeks, while the author of Acts also presents apologetics as a central component of Paul's mission to the gentiles. Paul's arguments with Epicurean and Stoic philosophers in the Athenian agora and his speech in the Areopagus are often considered the first Christian apologies.[13] By the mid–second century, a number of writers began authoring full-scale apologies for Christianity. Some, such as Quadratus, Aristides, Justin, Athenagoras, and Theophilus, in Greek, and Tertullian, in Latin, addressed themselves to Roman emperors or other imperial officials in the hope that reasoned defenses might dissuade them from persecution. Others, such as Tatian and later Clement of Alexandria, wrote more generally to the "Greeks" in efforts to explicate Christianity and prove its superiority over other traditions in the Greco-Roman world. According to Eusebius, apologetics served as a defensive weapon in the conflict with the persecutors.[14] Eusebius's evaluation of the early apologists has influenced modern definitions of apologetic literature.[15] Frances Young, for instance, stresses what she sees as the inherently defensive character of apologetics.[16] Jean-Claude Fredouille considers the anti-Christian slanders of pagan critics as the main motivation for apologetics.[17] For Michael Fiedrowicz, "apologetic literature originated in the life of the early Church out of the experience of contrast and confrontation."[18]

While many characterize apologetics as a defensive response to the anti-Christian offensive of persecutors and critics, others stress the aggressive aspect of the genre. The vitriol of the apologists' critiques of traditional religion and society in these ostensibly defensive pieces is striking and leaves one to consider the extent to which Christian apologetics *prompted* anti-Christian sentiment. Others stress the constructive aspect of apologetics as an effective tool for conversion. For Robert Grant, apologetics is a matter of cultural translation.[19] Apologists explained their scriptures in terms of the categories of pagan mythology, their god in terms of Greco-Roman theological categories, and their cosmology, anthropology, and soteriology in terms of Greco-Roman philosophy. This process of cultural translation cut both ways. If apologetics was the conduit through which Christianity was made intelligible to the Greco-Roman majority, many argue, it was also the door through which Greco-Roman philosophy entered Christianity. To some, this represents an "acute Hellenization" of Christian theology.[20] For others, apologetics is a catalyst by which the base elements of pagan culture and philosophy were transmuted into Christian gold.[21]

Histories of apologetic literature are also replete with the rhetoric of territorial conquest and expansion. Edward Gibbon, for instance, described Christianity as a "republic which gradually formed an independent and increasing state in the heart of the Roman empire" and consequently portrayed the interactions between Christians and others as a war between sovereign states.[22] Gibbon began what would become a nearly dogmatic practice of describing Christianization as an inevitable, if sometimes glacial, accretion of provinces.[23] Over a century after the publication of *The Decline and Fall of the Roman Empire*, Adolf von Harnack presented a similarly triumphalist account of Christianization in *The Mission and Expansion of Christianity in the First Three Centuries*. As this title suggests, Harnack, like Gibbon, perceived the growth of Christianity as something territorial.[24] Harnack did not stop at recounting the spread of Christianity in terms of geographic territory; he also gauged Christianity's conquest of various segments of society: the wealthy, the court, the military, and women.[25] A territorial framework continues to underlie many recent surveys of the history of Christianity and lies behind the traditional division of the subfields of early Christian studies (Patristics) into Greek, Latin, and "Oriental."[26]

In familiar narratives of the history of Christianity, this battle between

Christianity and paganism for geographic and cognitive territory reaches its climax in the Great Persecution and its denouement in Constantine's victory over the persecutors. If the Christians had confounded the identity politics of the empire at the opening of the fourth century, Constantine represented a triumphant and univocal Christianity that stood in stark contrast to a defeated and discredited paganism. Before Constantine's rise to power, Christians had been a persecuted minority under Roman rule. After Constantine's victories, a Christian held sole rule of the empire. How are we to understand this transformation? Robert Markus observes that "the image of a society neatly divided into 'Christian' and 'pagan' is the creation of late fourth-century Christians, and has been taken at face value by modern historians," but in what ways was this discursive Christian/pagan difference produced.[27]

The battles of the Milvian Bridge and Chrysopolis decided who would wear the purple, but the rise of a specifically Christian form of Roman imperialism was not simply a function of military victories. Because imperial hegemony depends on the construction of difference, it is never based on force alone. Rebellions can be put down and usurpers crushed, but the lion's share of imperialism is rhetorical.[28] Military might cannot successfully maintain empire without a rhetoric of imperial ideology that makes differences between rulers and those they rule seem natural. The formation of Christian identity, therefore, cannot be fully understood apart from the broader politics of ethnic and cultural identity engendered by Roman imperialism. In contrast to traditional narratives that assume the explanatory power of categories like "Christian" and "pagan" or "monotheism" and "polytheism," however, this book suspends such static, essentializing conceptualizations of religious identity to investigate the *processes* through which Christian and pagan identities were constructed by Christian apologists and pagan polemicists in the early fourth century. Situating Christian apologetics within the contexts of imperial power and subjugation reveals the fluidity and complexity of identity formation in the late ancient world. This fluidity should not be taken to imply that identity formation was an irenic process. Quite the contrary. For the Christian apologists and pagan polemicists who are the subjects of this book, identity politics—the often tortured game of establishing oneself or others as Greek, Roman, Egyptian, Jewish, Christian, and so forth—had very tangible, and sometimes violent, material consequences.

As an effective means of establishing and contesting identity, moreover, apologetics also offered a means of accessing and/or subverting power and privilege. Of course, the agonistic process of crafting paganism and Christianity began long before the age of Diocletian and Constantine. Nevertheless, the polemical exchanges that accompanied and immediately followed the Great Persecution mark a crucial moment in this process. By situating apologetic discourse in the context of Roman imperialism, I contend, we can understand more fully the ways in which these conflicts between pagan and Christian intellectuals proved instrumental in the production of Christian identity and, in turn, the construction of a specifically Christian imperial ideology.

Late Ancient Identities: Ethnic, Cultural, and Religious

What do the terms "Christian" and "Christianity" identify? Are ancient Christians best thought of as a belonging to a "religion"? Or did Christians represent a distinct ethnic or cultural group, a "third race," as some early Christian texts appear to intimate?[29] What distinguished Christianity (*Christianismos*) from other morphologically similar terms such as Hellenism or Platonism? The study of identity and identity formation in antiquity is freighted with the modern valences of terms such as "race," "nation," "ethnicity," and "culture." Despite the lack of a clear point-for-point correspondence between ancient and modern vocabularies, however, as Clifford Geary argues, "It's no use trying to invent new terms for past social groups: We are stuck with the vocabulary we have inherited."[30]

In modern usage, the term "ethnicity" designates a "composite of shared values, beliefs, norms, tastes, behaviors, experiences, consciousness of kind, memories and loyalties."[31] A definition of "culture" might be equally broad. The main difference between ethnicity and culture, however, is that "ethnicity" has biological and/or geographical valences that "culture" often does not. Ethnic identities are understood to be inborn—an indelible, physical mark. While ethnicity is often used in contemporary contexts as a positive expression of self-identity in contrast to "race," marginalizing connotations are never far below the surface.[32] Ethnic groups often become visible as minorities within dominant societal groups; hence the prevalence of hyphenate identities such as African American, Hispanic American, Polish American, and so forth in the United States. The second element of each hyphenate contains, controls, and otherwise ameliorates the distinctiveness of each ethnic modifier. "Culture," in contrast, is not considered geographically bound or biologically determined. One may become "acculturated"; that is, one may access a new cultural identity through various performances, such as learning a particular *koinē* (such as American English) and participating in certain ideological expressions (such as "being patriotic"). If ethnicity is considered inherited, culture is perceived as to some extent elective. One may opt in or opt out of a given culture. At the same time, there is a hierarchical relationship between culture and ethnicity. Hence "culture" often designates a privileged set of literary, artistic, and intellectual formations, while "ethnicity," in contrast, is marginalized as a flavorful curiosity. To use a gastronomic metaphor, the distinction between "culture" and "ethnicity" is well illustrated by the difference between the "ethnic food" available in a Chinatown or Little Italy and the haute cuisine enjoyed by cultured elites in the city center.

People in the ancient world made differentiations of identity along lines similar to the modern difference between "culture" and "ethnicity." The English "ethnic" and its derivatives come from the Greek *ethnos*. The term *ethnos* is inextricably connected to ancient traditions of ethnography inaugurated by Herodotus, in which the world was thought to be composed of various *ethnē*, each with its distinctive characteristics. In the ethnographic imagination of classical Greece, particularly Herodotus, for instance, peoples are defined especially by geography, language, and descent from common ancestors.[33]

While ancient Greek did not have a term that corresponds exactly to the English "culture," the term *paideia* approximates it. Often translated as "education," *paideia* refers simultaneously to the act and content of education and may best be rendered "acculturation." The signs of *paideia*, like the modern "culture," are performative: one must learn and practice proper grammar, skillful rhetoric, and philosophy to become a "cultured" member of society. *Paideia* was, theoretically, elective; no matter one's *ethnos*, one could "become Greek" by acculturating oneself through rigorous education and the mimetic practice of Greekness via writing, declamation, and other performances.[34]

Jewish identity, like Greekness, was a fluid category. Late ancient Jews, for example, understood themselves in terms of many of the same ethnological categories as other contemporary groups. The Greek *Ioudaios* and the Latin *Iudaeus* designated an *ethnos*—a people sharing a language and a native land (*Ioudaia*/Judea)—and was analogous to "Greek," "Cappadocian," "Egyptian," and so forth.[35] Like these other ethnological categories, however, *Ioudaios* could also mark sets of practices that individuals could choose to adopt to varying degrees (that is, by "Judaizing" [*ioudaïzein*]) whether or not they had been born with Jewish "blood."[36] The principal ethnological schema of the Hebrew Bible, moreover, is the difference between the people of Israel (*am*) and all other peoples (*goyim*). The Septuagint renders "*goyim*" as *ta ethnē*, while Jerome's Vulgate has *gentes*. For Jewish and Christian readers, of course, the signifiers ethn? and gentes functioned within specific soteriological and theological discourses (easily connoted in English translation when rendered as "gentiles"). As we will see in the chapters that follow, when thus translated (and read by Jews, Christians, and their critics), this biblical terminology was not fundamentally different from and easily dovetailed with broader late ancient discourses of ethnography and universal historiography.

"Constitutional" Roman identity also stood in dynamic tension with ethnic and cultural identity in the Roman world.[37] Romans could define themselves as a people resulting from "a continuous process of political amalgamation."[38] Rome, according to Livy and Virgil, had been founded by a blending of heterogeneous peoples: Trojan, Latin, Sabine, and so forth.[39] Roman citizenship was defined by adherence to common laws and participation in common government. As such it was, theoretically at least, open to all regardless of ethnic origins. Before Caracalla's grant of citizenship to all free residents of the empire in 212 C.E., grants of citizenship were a means of establishing ties of loyalty with provincial elites and investing them in Roman interests.[40] For some provincials, then, Roman citizenship represented a "transnational" identity—in the sense that it cut across individuals and populations from different *ethnē/nations*. Citizenship also conveyed certain legal privileges: lighter sentences, for example, and for those in the provinces, the ability to circumvent local judicial systems.[41] With the *Constitutio Antoniana* of 212 C.E., Caracalla enfranchised all free residents of the empire. What prompted Caracalla's edict is hard to tell precisely; he may have been seeking to extend the tax base.[42] Others have suggested piety as Caracalla's motivation. As Clifford Ando puts it, the emperor may have wished "to lead the people of the empire in a unanimous display of consensual piety, and believing that the *populus* of the empire was most properly constituted by its citizen body, Caracalla granted citizenship to all its residents."[43] By the early third century, there had already been a "decline in the value of citizenship"; although citizenship continued to convey certain legal privileges, in actual practice, however, other marks of status (like wealth and political influence) were more likely than citizenship to get one preferential treatment.[44] The edict had the effect not so much of devaluing Roman citizenship as of marking a revaluation of Romanness. Caracalla's edict can be seen as a legislative expression of a phenomenon that was already, or well on the way to becoming, a reality—the implication (in different ways and to different degrees) of most (free) residents of the empire in a shared "transnational" identification with Rome.

Whether or not we can discern "religious" identities as distinct from ethnocultural, civic, or "constitutional" identities in antiquity is a difficult question, not least because many practices and discourses that stand out to moderns as "religious" were not readily distinguished from other marks of belonging in the ancient world. The myriad Greek and Latin terms—such as *eusebeia, pietas, religio,* or *thrēskeia*—that are often rendered as "religion" when translated for modern readers served as key markers of ethnic and civic belonging. Thus, to be a Jew, Egyptian, or Greek, or an Antiochene, Athenian, or Roman was to practice the traditional rites of one's ancestors. Other discursive forms—such as philosophy—that moderns might identify as "religious" or related to "religion" offered other modes of identification and belonging. While the terminology of ancient philosophical circles and other voluntary associations (such as *collegium, secta, factio, philosophia, hairesis*, and so forth) do not mark the difference between beliefs and practices so characteristic of modern constructions of religion as "belief systems" (to be a philosopher was to cultivate a specific mode of life, for instance), they do indicate modes of identification and belonging that were to a significant extent elective rather than "native."[45]

In addition to shifting inquiry away from the purely taxonomic definition of categories and toward the *processes* of identity formation, scholars such as Denise Kimber Buell and Aaron Johnson have also questioned the value of drawing hard and fast distinctions between constructions of ethnic and cultural identity, on the one hand, and religious identity, on the other, in the study of ancient Christianity. Christians, they contend, do not mean something other than "ethnicity" when deploying terms like *gens, ethnos,* or *natio* to describe Christians and Christianity. Rather, it may be more helpful to examine the ways in which ancient Christians deployed this vocabulary to negotiate their identity in the context of contemporary ethnocultural discourses.[46]

While Christians did, as Buell and Johnson have argued, use the ancient vocabulary of ethnicity *as* a vocabulary of ethnicity, they, like their non-Christian contemporaries, were simultaneously immersed in discursive traditions that sought to privilege the univocity of a unitary, "spiritual," transcendent reality and denigrate difference.[47] Thus a second-century Platonic "handbook" defines philosophy as "a striving for wisdom, *or* the freeing and turning around of the soul from the body, when we turn towards the intelligible and what truly is."[48] Through their figurative reading practices, Christian, Jewish, and pagan exegetes split the letter and the spirit of texts, elevating the latter as transcendent signified and casting aside the former as mere signifier. Late ancient intellectuals also deployed history and ethnography to craft accounts of ethnic/religious origins in which the different cultural expressions of the world's diverse peoples were understood as the products of *human* history rather than as preexistent, timeless givens. Similarly, the many gods and various cultic systems of the world's many peoples were the products of decline, decadence, and conflict within human civilization. Christianity (or, depending on one's allegiances, Judaism or Hellenism), in stark contrast, was understood to be timeless and superior because it was not a product of civilization but a-cultural and inherently nonethnic.

Many late ancient Christians, for instance, thought of themselves as a people united by their *transcendence* of ethnic identity; as the author of the letter to the Colossians puts it, "There is no longer Greek and Jew, circumcised and uncircumcised, barbarian or Scythian, but Christ is all in all."[49]

My examination of the production of "Christian" and "pagan" identities participates in a broad trend away from conceptualizations of identity as fixed and determinative and toward the recognition of identity as the product of constant negotiation and renegotiation.[50] As Buell has demonstrated, "the dynamic interplay between fixity and fluidity," rather than empirical relationships of kinship and descent, is the constitutive feature of ethnic identity.[51] Constructions of ethnic identity, like cultural, constitutional, and religious identities, emerge out of the crucible of social conflict and competition. Ultimately, then, the meaning of ethnocultural terms in ancient texts is situational; that is, their meaning depends more on the specific political situation of a given text than on fixed lexicographical dicta. In much the same way that the unity and permanence of identity are constantly negotiated and renegotiated in contemporary contexts, the ancient world offered a "movable feast" in which identity was always in process.[52] In light of this fluidity, I do not consistently use one English term to translate Greek and Latin terms such as *gens, natio,* or *ethnos* but construe each instance *ad sensu* depending on context.[53] Neither do I attempt to synthesize rigid divisions among ethnic, cultural, and religious identities, preferring instead to highlight the inherent elasticity of the ancient vocabulary. This approach will help bring into better relief conflicts, contradictions, and ambivalences that might otherwise be obfuscated by a synthetic over-schematization.[54] Reading the production of Christian and pagan identities in terms of broader discourses of ethnicity and universalism rather than as purely religious or philosophical debates decenters the a priori explanatory power often accorded to "religion" in studies of the ancient world. Finally, if discourses of ethnicity function strategically within specific political contexts, a more complete understanding of ancient identity politics also requires a theoretical orientation that pays particular attention to the realities of imperial domination and subjugation in which late ancient Christians and pagans lived.

Approaching Roman Imperialism

The theoretical bases of my approach to Roman imperialism lie in the insights of postcolonial theory and postcolonial discourse analysis. Because it insists that identities are produced and deployed in the context of imperial systems of power and control, postcolonial discourse analysis offers a particularly useful theoretical basis for the study of identity in the Roman Empire. Not satisfied merely to analyze imperial systems of domination, many postcolonial theorists argue for an organic connection between the lived realities of subjugation and resistance and the production of theory, and self-consciously take a theoretical position actively *interested* and *invested* in pointing out ways in which such systems have been or may be subverted and resisted.[55] Some scholars, however, have questioned the applicability of postcolonial theory to premodern contexts, contending that the discursive formations of nineteenth- and twentieth-century imperialisms—especially the particular racial theories and economic systems employed by European colonialists—did not obtain in premodern contexts.[56] Some Roman historians, moreover, resist analogies between ancient Roman and modern European imperialisms on the grounds that Rome had no systematic mercantile or capitalistic interest in her territories.[57] Despite such criticisms, in more recent years postcolonial theory, like feminist criticism and theory before it, has been applied beyond these original contexts to become a more broadly applicable form of discourse analysis.[58]

Though there may not be a point-for-point correspondence between premodern and modern varieties of imperialism, these forms of discourse analysis have been fruitfully applied in studies of premodern history.[59] In particular, these theoretical models are a necessary corrective to studies of the Roman world that obscure or ignore the material consequences of domination.[60] Rome, after all, conquered and controlled territory and people, established colonies, and controlled its subjects via provincial bureaucracies. The Roman Empire was a diverse place but not an equal one. The right to rule was based on polarized differences between rulers and the ruled, between the metropolitan center and the provincial periphery. Consequently, establishing oneself or others as Greek, Roman, Egyptian, or Jewish was not an academic exercise. This was just as true under the Julio-Claudians of the first century as it was in the Flavian and Theodosian empire of the fourth century. On both sides of the "Constantinian divide," the game of empire continued to depend on the control of the ethnic and cultural diversity of the provinces. Familiar dichotomies between "civilized" and "savage," and "culture" and "barbarism" remained a critical component of Christian imperial ideology. Indeed, this book argues that the discourse of Christian imperialism was effective precisely because it developed out of, rather than erased, earlier imperial discourses.

There are several factors that recommend postcolonial theory for an analysis of the role of apologetic literature in the production of Christian imperialism. Although many apologies, written as open letters to Roman emperors or officials, speak quite directly to Roman power,[61] scholars often situate apologetics as a genre belonging to the "religious" or "philo-sophical" spheres and disconnected from "unapologetic" political dis-courses. The apologists are often represented as working in an ivory tower, writing esoteric texts that never had an audience beyond other Christian intellectuals.[62] By casting apologetics as a purely academic ex-ercise, scholars marginalize apologetic literature and isolate it from "po-litical" histories of the Roman Empire. It is more useful to see the boundaries between various discursive fields as fluid, or even illusory; fields as seemingly disparate as philosophy, politics, theology, ethnogra-phy, and history interact to produce regimes of knowledge and power.[63]

If postcolonial theory can contribute to understandings of the ways in which academic discourses like apologetics are productive of hegemony, it also reveals instabilities within those systems of power and control. While Edward Said has indicated the ways in which empires established hegemony by establishing knowledge about and power over their sub-jects, subsequent theorists have questioned histories of imperialism that overstate and polarize the rift between master and subject. The differ-ences upon which hegemony depends are always unstable and must be constantly rearticulated and reestablished. In this view, the distinction between metropolis and province is a chimera and imperial territory a constantly shifting desert that needs to be repeatedly reclaimed through acts of differentiation.[64] The game of identity politics does not play out on a clearly demarcated field but within the fissures, gaps, and chasms of imperial discourse.

The arrangement of this book is diachronic. I begin in the contested, in-terstitial spaces between philosophical paganism and Christianity. Chap-ter 1 opens with a consideration of the ways in which Greek philosophers living in the Roman Empire (especially the later Stoics Posidonius and Cornutus and the Platonists Plutarch, and Numenius) deployed the disciplines of ethnography, universal history, and allegori-cal reading to engage in comparative studies of the sacred texts, icono-graphies, and ritual practices of "barbarians." Through these comparative projects, intellectuals sought to distill a universal philoso-phy that transcended ethnic and cultural specificity. The quest for an ec-umenical philosophy, however, was not a purely objective intellectual pursuit or a pluralistic venture in cultural appreciation but a politically interested enterprise. Much as the Roman Empire viewed its provinces as resources ripe for exploitation, philosophers' cross-cultural research served as a means to extract valuable resources from native sources. As an intellectual practice that closely paralleled the relationship between Rome and her provinces, therefore, philosophy was simultaneously a potent discourse of social power and privilege.

The second portion of Chapter 1 examines the ways in which two second-century Christian intellectuals—Justin Martyr and Tatian—imitated and manipulated the cross-cultural practices current among late ancient philosophers. Where Greek intellectuals focused their ecumenical philosophy around a thoroughly Greek center of gravity, Christian apologists anchored their intellectual peregrinations around in set of confessedly "barbarian" texts—the Hebrew scriptures. This disruptive mimesis of late ancient philosophical practice served to destabilize Greek philosophical identity and subvert the always tenuous distinctions between center and periphery upon which Roman imperial ideology depended. I conclude by examining the response of the Platonist Celsus to Christianity, *On the True Logos*, as a reactionary treatise that struggles to reassert Greek cultural privilege and the imperial status quo in light of the Christian threat.

In Chapter 2, I turn to the crises of the turn of the fourth century. Here I examine the anti-Christian polemics of the Platonist Porphyry of Tyre, as represented by the extant fragments of his *Against the Christians* and *Philosophy from Oracles*. Porphyry's interpretive strategies were integrally related to the way in which this Syrian provincial constructed his own identity as a Greek philosopher. The Christian mimesis of Porphyry's interpretive practices, I argue, threatened the stability of the difference between province/metropolis and subjugation/privilege upon which Porphyry's own self-identity depended. Porphyry became an unlikely bedfellow of the persecutors in his efforts to contain the threat Christianity posed to the privilege he enjoyed as a Greek philosopher in the Roman Empire.

Chapter 3 considers the *Divine Institutes* of the Latin apologist Lactantius as a response to Porphyry's polemics. Lactantius imitated Porphyry's own hermeneutical approach to sacred texts to position Christianity as the universal philosophy. In the course of responding to Porphyry, moreover, Lactantius crafted a history of religions and a new imperial geography in which a theological difference between monotheism and polytheism emerges as the central marker of ethnic and cultural distinction. Finally, I consider the ways in which Lactantius subsequently edited the *Divine Institutes* after Constantine's victories, thus lending a new, imperial timbre to his historical geography, in which a univocal Christianity (or "true religion" [*vera religio*], as Lactantius terms it) enjoyed privilege of place over and against the error-ridden religious plurality ("false religions" [*falsae religiones*]) of the world's diverse peoples.

Chapter 4 focuses on Constantine's *Oration to the Saints* and imperial letters as fruitful sites in which to explore cross-fertilizations of apologetic discourse and imperial power. Drawing on the rhetoric of earlier apologists, especially Lactantius, Constantine fashioned an imperial ideology that was based on differences between Christianity and the ancestral traditions of the peoples that made up the empire. Constantine blamed the Great Persecution and the civil wars that followed on irrational devotion to ancestral traditions and portrayed his own reign as a necessary corrective to ancestral error. By deploying apologetic arguments in tandem with strategic material demonstrations of imperial power, moreover, Constantine contributed to the formation of a discourse about traditional religions that correlated with the categories "idolatry" and "polytheism" deployed by Christian apologists. Thus, during Constantine's reign, certain aspects of traditional cult, such as sacrifice and statuary, became visible as a new category—idolatry—that required imperial supervision and correction.

Chapter 5 considers the relationship between Christian apologetics and imperial panegyric in the work of Eusebius of Caesarea. I argue that Eusebius's apologetic in his *Preparation* and *Demonstration of the Gospel*, was goaded by the Great Persecution and Porphyry's attack on Christian identity. I explore Eusebius's complex intertext of universal history, ethnography, and biblical exegesis to craft a history of human civilization in which religious error and diversity figure as the central signs and symptoms of ethnogenesis. After Constantine's assumption of sole rule in 324 c.e., however, Eusebius's historical narrative came to serve as the basis for an effective and durable rhetoric of Christian empire. Focusing on Eusebius's *Life of Constantine* and *Tricennial Orations*, I consider the ways in which Constantine's reign catalyzed the potential energy of Eusebius's apologetics into an effective and rhetoric of power and difference. As ancestral religions (cast now as "idolatry" and "polytheism") became objects of imperial supervision and control, Eusebius's history of religions became a potent narrative of Christian manifest destiny, in which the civilizing power of the one true religion of the one true God was to be spread among all peoples, supplanting the barbarism of ancestral traditions. This new rhetoric did not succeed by displacing earlier rhetorics of difference but by appropriating and recasting them. On both sides of the "Constantinian divide," I conclude, the need to conquer, restrain, and supervise *ta ethnē*, "peoples," remained the central ideological basis for imperial rule of the Mediterranean.

Finally, I offer a brief epilogue that considers the way that these new rhetorics of imperialism developed by Lactantius, Constantine, and Eusebius, grounded as they were in universalizing histories of religion and civilization, informed future conflicts and negotiations between pagans and Christians into the fourth century and well beyond. I also suggest some of the ways in which the histories of religion and comparative practices of Christian apologists served as models for early modern colonial encounters between European colonialists and conquered indigenous peoples. If, as a number of contemporary scholars have noted, the category "religion" emerges largely as a product (and instrument) of the subjugation of native cultures by (Christian) European imperialism,[65] then exploring the interrelationship between Christian apologetic discourse and Roman imperialism suggests that we might locate the seeds of this process in the early fourth century as "religion" was emerging as both the primary marker of ethnic and cultural identity and the central basis for (Christian) Roman imperial power.

Chapter 1
Philosophers, Apologists, and Empire

In the early 150s C.E. the Christian philosopher and teacher Justin responded to the persecution and martyrdom of his fellow Christian Ptolemaeus by penning his *Second Apology*. Justin feared that he too might "be plotted against . . . and fixed to the rack—maybe even by Crescens, that lover of empty chatter and glory-hound" (*2 Apol.* 3.1). Justin's student Tatian would later write that the Stoic Crescens did indeed try to instigate Justin's downfall (*Orat.* 19.2). Whether or not Crescens's machinations were the cause of Justin's martyrdom, it is clear from these accounts that friction between Christian and pagan intellectuals in second-century Rome could have very tangible, even violent, consequences. Why would pagan philosophers have felt such antipathy toward Justin and other Christian philosophers and, moreover, what common concerns might there have been between philosophers like Crescens and the Roman authorities? What was at stake for pagan intellectuals in the "Christian question"?

Irreconcilable theological differences between Christian monotheism and pagan polytheism have often seemed to explain animosity between Christian and pagan intellectuals. Yet Christian and pagan intellectuals were more similar than either would have liked to admit. The recent scholarly interest in "pagan monotheism," for instance, points to a theological and philosophical *koinē* shared among orthodox Christians, philosophical Judaism, Platonists, various Gnostics, and others. For Christian philosophers, as for their non-Christian contemporaries, "philosophy" was as much a way of life as it was an academic discourse. Accounts of Christian philosophical circles—such as those around figures like Justin, Pantaenus and Clement of Alexandria, Origen, and others—look remarkably like the circles of Ammonius Saccas, Plotinus, and the later Platonic schools in Athens and Alexandria.[1] Both based instruction around the exegesis of sets of authoritative, "inspired" texts—Plato, Pythagoras, and inspired "barbarian" wisdom among Platonists, the Hebrew Bible and, later, the New Testament among Christians.[2] For pagans as well as Christians, philosophy was considered a spiritual exercise to be realized through diligent *askēsis*—the disciplinary practice of setting body, mind, and soul in correct relationship.

A great deal of academic energy has been spent categorizing the religious and philosophical literature of antiquity as "Stoic," "Platonic," "Christian," and so forth. This research is important; indeed, understanding the lineaments of ancient philosophy is a necessary prerequisite to any study of ancient intellectual controversy, including this one. Nevertheless, recognizing the intense similarities among ancient intellectuals militates against assuming the fixity and stability of categories like "Stoic," "Platonist," or "Christian." The grounds of the conflict between pagan and Christian intellectuals ought to be sought not in debates over the finer points of metaphysics and theology or in the a priori explanatory power of categories like "pagan philosophy" and "Christianity" or "polytheism" and "monotheism" but in these very similarities themselves. At the same time that this common philosophical and theological discourse enabled debates over the nature of God, the cosmos, and so forth, it also engendered anxiety. To differentiate themselves from others, philosophers and apologists alike resorted to the politics of ethnic and cultural identity as a more visceral strategy of distinction.

The Quest for a Universal Philosophy

What has Athens to do with Jerusalem, or with Rome, Alexandria, Tyre, Carthage, Antioch, or Edessa? What precisely marked the difference between Hellenes and barbarians, between Hellenicity and barbarism? Before Tertullian posed this rhetorical question at the end of the second century, Greeks had been pondering the same problem for centuries.[3] Herodotus's *Histories*, some of the earliest Greek prose, was concerned as much with barbarians as with Greeks. Writing in the wake of the conflict between Persia and Greece in the early fifth century B.C.E., Herodotus sought to explain recent turmoil by writing a universal history, an account that would cover all peoples of the known world. The *Histories* thus had an important ethnographic component, as Herodotus presented accounts of the habits and customs of the peoples he investigated. It would take several centuries, however, and the conquests of Alexander for the notion of universal history to come to full flower.

Scholars often connect imperial expansion, first by Alexander the Great and later by the Hellenistic and Roman empires, with a broadening of cultural horizons across the Mediterranean. In this cosmopolitan setting intellectuals had unprecedented access to other cultures. As Alexander marched toward India for example, several philosophers, ethnographers, and other polymaths accompanied him. According to Diogenes Laertius, for instance, the philosophers Anaxarchus and Pyrrho of Elis traveled in Alexander's entourage as far as India; both were reputed to have been impressed by Indian "gymnosophists."[4] Later, Alexander's Ptolemaic successors in Egypt began to compile the famous library of Alexandria. Under the direction of Demetrius of Phalerum, the library "aimed at collecting, if possible, all the books in the world."[5] The library was to be a repository for all the knowledge of all the peoples of the world—an ancient universal catalogue of the world's wisdom.

While the library at Alexandria aspired to catalogue the world's history and literature, some historians sought to synchronize the histories of all peoples into a single grand historico-ethnographic narrative. Several narrative tropes facilitated the writing of universal history and ethnography. Herodotus had pioneered comparative ethnography by ascribing similarities between the religions of different peoples to migrations and imitation.[6] During the Hellenistic period, Euhemerism—the notion that the deities of the world's peoples were really ancient human beings who had been great rulers or made important contributions to human civilization—became a means to compare and relate seemingly disparate religious traditions. By ascribing various migrations and genealogies to these ancient humans/gods, universal historians could easily connect the histories of seemingly disparate peoples into one seamless narrative. As Raoul Mortley has put it, intellectuals were driven to provide a "sense of unity within diversity."[7] The most developed extant example of this type of history are the first books of Diodorus Siculus's *Historical Library*. Composed at the end of the first century B.C.E., Diodorus's work purports to record the entire history of human development, beginning with comparative accounts of the creation myths of various peoples, and extending to the rise of the Roman Empire in his own day.

This is not to say that every historian in the Hellenistic world was in a cosmopolitan mood. Under the Hellenistic empires some intellectuals began to compose "ethnic histories." By deploying the techniques of universal history and Euhemerism, historians could ascribe the origins of all that was best about human civilization to their own particular ethnic groups. These histories served as a sort of parochial boosterism. The practice of ethnic historiography was not irenic. Rather, these ethnic histories should be seen as repeated attempts at "one-upmanship." Diodorus Siculus, commenting on the variety of sources from which he compiled his *Historical Library*, offers an incisive critique of the genre: "Again, with respect to the antiquity of the human race, not only do Greeks put forth their claims but many of the barbarians as well, all holding that it is they who are autochthonous and the first of all men to discover the things which are of use in life, and that it was the events in their own history which were the earliest to have been held worthy of record."[8] Thus Hecataeus of Abdera and Manetho, each of whom composed his own *History of Egypt*, did not simply inquire into the ancient past but ascribed the origins of all aspects of Mediterranean cultures to the Egyptians. Philo of Byblos's *Phoenician History* and Berossos of Chaldea's *Chaldean History* served the same function for the Phoenicians and Mesopotamians, respectively.[9] It was as part of this rise of ethnic historiography that Jewish historiography had its beginnings with writers like Artapanus and Eupolemus,[10] while Josephus's *Jewish Antiquities* stands as the sole example of an ethnic history from the Hellenistic period that has survived intact.[11] As they praised their own group, ethnic historians also disparaged the histories, myths, and traditions of their neighbors. The result was what Arthur Droge has aptly termed a "war of books" among Hellenistic intellectuals.[12]

There was a similar trend toward universalism among philosophers during the late Hellenistic and early Roman periods. This interest in ancient foreign wisdom is reflected in the many trips to foreign lands that were increasingly ascribed to the scions of classical Greek philosophy. Diogenes Laertius, for instance, reports that Plato visited the priests and sages of Egypt and had hoped to frequent the sages of Persia.[13] Pythagoras was credited with even more exotic travels. In addition to his journey to Egypt, he is said to have met Persian wise men and to have learned arithmetic from the Phoenicians and astrology from Chaldeans.[14] Philostratus adds a trip to India and Iamblichus credits him with visiting the Celts and Iberians as well.[15]

These travel narratives are indicative of a broader reorientation of philosophy that stemmed, in large part, from changes in the way philosophers of the Hellenistic period and early Roman Empire were coming to view the history of philosophy. Philosophers of the classical period tended to view philosophical inquiry as primarily critical and constructive. In the estimation of many Hellenistic and Roman philosophers, by contrast, philosophy had not gotten better over time; instead, time had caused true wisdom to become tainted, corrupted, and devolved. The pursuit of wisdom thus became a project of recovery.[16] In particular, philosophers strove to articulate and defend orthodoxies grounded in the authority of ancient inspired texts. Antiquity guaranteed authenticity; "truth and tradition, reason and authority, were identified with each other."[17]

According to the Stoics, for instance, all humans, both Greek and barbarian, shared in the *Logos*, the divine rationality that imbued the world with order and reason.[18] Thanks to this ubiquitous *Logos*, the Stoics argued, "the first mortals and those who, uncorrupted, were descended from them followed nature."[19] According to Seneca, Stoics believed that the first stage of human development was pre-philosophical; because of their pure, unadulterated connection to the rationality of nature, the first humans had no need for the arts and sciences, including philoso-phy.[20] Rather, Seneca ascribes the most basic technological skills, such as tool making and hunting, to a natural survival instinct (*sagacitas*) rather than to philosophy (*sapientia*).[21] The earliest humans might have seemed "wise" in a philosophical sense, but any likeness is due to the simple fact that these early people lived in accordance with pure na-ture.[22] Philosophy, then, arose in later stages of human development as a corrective to greed and other perversions brought about by technolog-ical and cultural innovations.[23] The goal of the philosopher, then, was to live a life that imitated this original state of nature.

Most Stoics would have agreed with Seneca that the earliest humans lived an idyllic life according to nature and free of moral vice. The ear-liest humans were not philosophers, for philosophy, like other arts and sciences, was something that developed as part of human civilization. Posidonius, in contrast, locates the origins of philosophy precisely in the earliest periods of human development. Posidonius claimed that true philosophy had been present among humans at their origins by virtue of the *Logos*. Later, however, philosophy was altered when it was divided into different branches and corrupted as human vice followed upon the development of human civilization. Seneca reports that Posidonius be-lieved "sovereignty was in the power of philosophers" in the earliest eras of human development.[24] This original philosophy had been obscured by gradual accretions of human contrivance. If the universal philosophy lay at the origins of human history, then philosophers must return to the most *ancient* sources. As a universally present divine rationality, more-over, the *Logos* was present among all peoples.[25] Only through a compar-ative study of the widest possible range of source material—both Greek and non-Greek—could a philosopher mine the pure, original philoso-phy from the centuries of accretion obscuring it. For Posidonius, this meant going beyond Plato, back to the wisdom of the Pythagoreans,[26] but also, for example, to ancient non-Greek sources, such as the Phoeni-cian philosopher Mochus of Sidon.[27]

The philosopher had to become historian and ethnographer. Posido-nius conducted historical and ethnographic research for his *History* while on a number of world tours.[28] Posidonius's *History* covers the pe-riod from 146 B.C.E. to the mid-80s B.C.E., is universal in scope, and dis-cusses the habits and history of peoples from Africa to northern Europe and from the Iberian Peninsula to the Middle East. The extant frag-ments of the *History* provide a wealth of ethnographic details: the crops grown in Dalmatia, banqueting customs of the Babylonians, Romans, and Cimbri, the military habits of the Apameans and Celts, and the po-litical structures of the Parthians.[29] Posidonius may also have studied Jewish traditions while on his world tours. Posidonius's estimation of foreign peoples was not always flattering. According to Josephus, the anti-Jewish polemicist Apion had used the Stoic philosopher as a source for his critique of Jewish exclusivism as well as the Jewish temple.[30]

Posidonius's interest in ethnography and history was intimately connected with his philosophical projects. The first-century C.E. medical writer Athenaeus of Attaleia described Posidonius's history as "composed in a manner consonant to the philosophy he had adopted."[31] In particular, it seems that Posidonius used his vast ethnographic and historical knowledge to buttress his moral philosophy. For Posidonius, human actions could not be explained by reference to their natural environment alone; he believed that "ethnography reveals the character and psychology of a people, and is a descriptive and aetiological key to their actions, and thus historical explanation."[32] Thus he understood the migrations of the Cimbri from northern to more southern climes as the result of particular Cimbri psychology rather than mere reaction to climate change.[33] Through comparative historical and ethnological study, Posidonius hoped to stress the role of psychology and reason in history over physical explanation.[34]

A similar broadening of horizons is also evident in later Stoic allegorical exegesis. If the true philosophy of the earliest stages of human development had been adulterated by the civilizing process, how were philosophers of the present age supposed to access that original philosophy? Some Stoics thought that the answer lay in the proper interpretation of ancient texts. If people had purest access to *Logos* in the earliest stages of human history, the earliest literature was most likely to code philosophical truths.[35] Homer, Hesiod, and other ancient authors, they believed, had concealed kernels of ancient wisdom in their fictions.[36] The drive to interpret Homer and other early Greek poets allegorically was variously motivated. Some have argued that allegory was a way to recover traditional texts by ascribing a philosophical (that is, Stoic) dimension to them,[37] while others claim that Stoics interpreted Homer and Hesiod because these traditional authors could act as authoritative buttresses to Stoic philosophy.[38] Thus Velleius, the Epicurean character in Cicero's *On the Nature of the Gods*, mocks what he considers the circularity of Balbus's Stoic allegorical methods: "[Balbus] seeks to reconcile the fairy-stories of Orpheus, Musaeus, Hesiod, and Homer with his own account of the immortal gods."[39] These reading strategies began with Zeno and were pursued further by Cleanthes and Chrysippus.[40] Zeno, the founder of the Stoic school, wrote a work titled *Homeric Problems*, which was based on the supposition that Homer had coded deeper philosophical truths in his verses. Zeno's main interpretive method was etymology—the names of the gods were thought to encode (Stoic) physics. Thus he decoded the myth of the Titans: "[T]he Titans have al-

ways stood for the elements of the world. He interprets Koios as a quality. . . . Krios is the royal and dominant element; Hyperion (*Huperiana*)
designates the ascending movement because of the expression 'to go
higher' (*huperanō ienai*); finally, because all light things that are let loose
naturally fall upwards (*piptein anō*), this part of the universe was called
Japet (*Iapeton*)."[41] Cleanthes and Chrysippus, Zeno's successors, appear
to have continued this method of interpretation.[42]

Stoic allegory was based on a particular philosophy of language in
which phonetic units were thought to bear a natural relationship to
their referents. Thus, on a fundamental level, the meaning of all languages transcended their particular cultural instantiations. Allegory
could thus be applied comparatively and cross-culturally.[43] In the first
century C.E., the Stoic exegete Cornutus authored a textbook outlining
Stoic allegorical methods. For Cornutus as for his predecessors, allegorical reading served as a tool for "reading through" the artful obfuscation
of the poets to get at the kernels of ancient philosophical doctrine transmitted in poetry. Cornutus's allegorical exegeses were motivated by a
comparative impulse similar to that of Posidonius—read as much as you
can, as widely as you can, to discover philosophical truths.[44] Although
Cornutus's *On Greek Theology* focuses on Greek traditions, he thought
that foreign mythology might be subject to the same analyses as Greek
sources:[45] "Many and various myths concerning the gods arose among
the ancient Greeks," he writes, "just as others arose among the Magi,
others among the Phrygians, and still others among the Egyptians and
Celts, and Libyans, and the other peoples."[46] Cornutus explored the
myths of different peoples to derive a cross-cultural consensus. Because
the *Logos* is ubiquitous, one should be able to find truth among the traditions of all peoples. Consequently, the discovery of similar allegories in
the traditions of a number of different peoples confirmed the universality of the *Logos* as well as the philosophical (that is, Stoic) truths contained within them. Thus, when Cornutus compares the Egyptian myth
of Isis and Osiris and the Phoenician myth of Adonis with the Greek tale
of Demeter's search for her kidnaped daughter Kore, each of these culturally specific traditions reveals allegorical representations of the agri-
cultural cycle.[47]

Though motivated by different philosophical presuppositions, certain
Platonists of the first three centuries C.E. were also interested in comparative ethnography, history, and myth. The Platonist who perhaps best ex-
emplifies the growing interest among first- and second-century
philosophers in cross-cultural research is Plutarch. Plutarch evinces his
greatest interest in foreign religion and philosophy in *On Isis and Osiris*.
The text, addressed to Clea, a priestess at Delphi, takes the form of a

long discourse on the Egyptian myth of Isis and Osiris. What Plutarch in fact delivers is a treatise on Platonic cosmology and metaphysics.

Plutarch's exegetical approach to myth differs from the Stoics' methods in several respects. He entertains but rejects, for instance, just the sort of etymological exegeses offered by Stoics like Cornutus.

Cronus is but a figurative name for Chronus, Hera for Air, and that the birth of Hephaestus symbolizes the change of Air into Fire. And thus among the Egyptians such men say that Osiris is the Nile consorting with the Earth, which is Isis, and that the sea is Typhon into which the Nile discharges its waters and is lost to view and dissipated, save for that part which the earth takes up and absorbs and thereby becomes fertilized. (*On Isis and Osiris* 363d–e).[48]

According to Plutarch, this method of allegory confuses the effects of the gods with their essences, just as the ignorant mistake images of the gods for the gods themselves.[49]

In place of the physical allegories of the Stoics, Plutarch advocates metaphysical interpretations. He likens the exegete to a priest or priestess and the practice of exegesis to participation in mystery cults. Reason, the faculty necessary for interpretation, is "mystagog."[50] Just as the mysteries of Isis and Osiris (mysteries in which both Plutarch and his addressee, Clea, are initiates) celebrate the passage from death to life, the process of interpreting myth correctly is an "epoptic" experience in which "those who have passed from beyond these conjectural and confused matters of all sorts by means of Reason proceed by leaps and bounds to that primary, simple, and immaterial principle" (*On Isis and Osiris* 382d–e).[51] The assimilation of exegesis to the mysteries also helps explain Plutarch's interest in interpreting *foreign* mythologies. Plutarch believed that Egyptian priests had first encrypted philosophy "veiled in myths and in words containing dim reflections and adumbrations of the truth" and cites "the wisest of the Greeks," including Plato and Pythagoras, "who came to Egypt and consorted with the priests" as proof of the antiquity of the practice (*On Isis and Osiris* 354c–e).

Having rejected atomistic (i.e., Epicurean) and Stoic interpretations, Plutarch proceeds to uncover the Platonic cosmology encoded in the Isis/Osiris myth. His main claim is that the world is subject to "two opposed principles and two antagonistic forces. . . . For if it is the law of Nature that nothing comes into being without a cause, and if the good cannot provide a cause for evil, then it follows that Nature must have in herself the source and origin of evil, just as she contains the source and origin of good" (*On Isis and Osiris* 369c–d). Plutarch argues that this dualist cosmology has no identifiable source but that it is "in circulation in many places among barbarians and Greeks alike" (*On Isis and Osiris* 369b). Having identified this *communis opinio*, Plutarch brings in several foreign traditions to support his cosmology. He cites Zoroaster as encrypting a dualistic cosmology, calling one god "Oromazes and the other Areimanius; and he further declared that . . . Oromazes may be best compared to light, and Areimanius, conversely, to darkness and ignorance" (*On Isis and Osiris* 369e). Similarly, he claims that the Chaldeans propound dualism in their astral theology (*On Isis and Osiris* 370c). The intertext throughout Plutarch's comparative exegeses is Plato's *Timaeus* and cosmological passages from the *Laws*.

> And Plato, in many passages, as though obscuring and veiling his opinion, names one of the opposing principles "Identity" and the other "Difference"; but in his *Laws*, when he had grown considerably older, he asserts, not in circumlocution or symbolically, but in specific words, that the movement of the universe is actuated not by one soul, but perhaps by several, and certainly not less than two, and of these the one is beneficent, and the other is opposed to it and the artificer of things opposed. (*On Isis and Osiris* 370f; cf. *Timaeus* 35a and *Laws* 896dff.)

Plutarch can easily read the *Timaeus* as a mythical account like those of the Egyptians, Zoroaster, and the Chaldeans because Timaeus adverts to the "mythical" character of his account of creation at the outset of the dialogue (*On Isis and Osiris* 371a–b). Plutarch proceeds to deploy etymology and figurative interpretation to characterize Osiris as "Intelligence and Reason, the Ruler and Lord of all that is good" in the soul and Typhon as "that part of the soul which is impressionable, impulsive, irrational, and truculent" (*On Isis and Osiris* 371a–b). From the *Timaeus* Plutarch also introduces a triadic aspect to his cosmology: "The better and more divine nature," he writes, "consists of three parts: the conceptual, the material, and that which is formed from these, which the Greeks call the world. Plato is wont to give the conceptual the name of idea, example, or father, and to the material the name of mother or nurse, or seat and place of generation, and to that which results from both the name of offspring or generation" (*On Isis and Osiris* 373f; cf. *Timaeus* 50c–d). The trio of Osiris, Isis, and Horus are, for Plutarch, an obvious representation of this triad: "Osiris may be regarded as the origin, Isis the recipient, and Horus the perfected result" (*On Isis and Osiris* 374a). Plutarch completes his exegesis by comparing Greek and Egyptian iconographic representations of the gods and numerological symbolism, and offers syncretistic *interpretationes Graecae* for the Egyptian gods (*On Isis and Osiris* 380f–381f, 381f–382a, 382e).

Another second-century Platonist interested in barbarian religion and philosophy was Numenius of Apamea. A contemporary of the Christian apologists Justin and Tatian, he flourished in the second half of the second century. He was known to both Clement of Alexandria and Origen and was an important influence on Plotinus and his circle. Sadly, Numenius's work is known only from fragments preserved by later authors. His treatises *On the Good* and *On the Infidelity of the Academy to Plato* are known principally from citations in Eusebius's *Preparation for the Gospel.*[52] Origen mentions additional works titled *Epop, On Numbers,* and *On Places.*[53] Based on the extant fragments of Numenius's works as well as the *testimonia* of Origen, it is clear that cross-cultural research was central to Numenius's philosophical projects.

Plato served as the primary philosophical benchmark for Numenius, but he also believed it necessary to "go back" (*anachōrēsasthai*) to Pythagoras and the traditions of non-Greek peoples. Eusebius preserves an important fragment from *On the Good* that indicates the breadth of Numenius's reading.

At this point, having cited the witnesses of Plato [on the subject of the "good"], it is necessary to go further back and join with them the sayings of Pythagoras, and also to recall the peoples of good-repute (*ta ethnē ta eudokimounta*) and comparing the rites, dogmas, and foundational doctrines in so far as they accord with those of Plato, those which the Brahmins, Jews, Magi, and Egyptians have established.[54]

Porphyry of Tyre preserves another fragment that offers a glimpse of how this cross-cultural imperative played out in Numenius's work. Porphyry reports that Numenius interpreted various textual and iconographic representations of water and moisture as representing the soul's descent into the world of becoming.

In support of this he [Numenius] cites the words of the prophet, "the spirit of God was borne upon the waters"; the Egyptians as well, he says in this connection, represent their divinities as standing not on solid ground but on a boat. . . . We must understand that these represent souls hovering over moisture, i.e., those souls descending into genesis. And he quotes Heraclitus as saying, "It is a delight, not death, for souls to become moist," meaning that the descent into genesis is a pleasure for them; and, in another place, "we live their death, they live our death." And he believes that this is the reason why Homer calls those in genesis "wet," because they have their souls "moist."[55]

Like Plutarch, Numenius's practice is to range "foreign" sources, like the Hebrew Bible and Egyptian iconography, alongside ancient Greek philosophy (Heraclitus) and poetry (Homer). Origen, moreover, notes Numenius's use of the Hebrew Bible in *On the Good*: "Numenius, who writes in the first book of *On the Good* about various peoples (*ta ethnē*) who say that god is incorporeal, ranks the Jews among them, and does not hesitate to mention the words of the prophets in his work and to interpret them figuratively."[56] In other passages, Numenius appears to have used formulations taken from the Septuagint to describe his First God.[57] According to Origen, Numenius did not limit his comparative projects to *On the Good*, but states that he used the Hebrew Bible throughout his works, in the *Epop, On Numbers*, and in *On Places*.[58] Origen's focus on Numenius's use of the Hebrew Bible is due no doubt to his apologetic interest in proving that Greeks recognized the value of Hebrew wisdom. Nevertheless, Origen's account gains veracity because he sets Numenius's use of the Hebrew Bible in the context of comparisons of "many peoples."

Many have read the cross-cultural trend in first- and second-century philosophy in terms of an eclectic "broadening of horizons." Just as the Roman Empire facilitated commerce and contact between disparate peoples, philosophers were seeking to bridge cultural gulfs and cultivate an intellectual ecumenism.[59] Philosophical cross-culturalism is thus seen as parallel to other forms of cultural syncretism in the ancient Mediterranean. Like syncretism, moreover, philosophical eclecticism has also been cast as a disconcerting form of cultural miscegenation.[60] John Dillon, for instance, locates "eclectic" philosophers such as Numenius and their desire to synthesize seemingly disparate traditions in a "Platonic underworld" that stands in the shadow of mainstream, "dogmatic" Platonism.[61] Syncretism indicates neither irenic points of intercultural contact nor instances of cultural imperialism; rather, syncretism is always a locus of consonance *as well as* dissonance. The hyphenate "Greco-Roman philosophy" itself serves to signpost the field of philosophical discourse and the formation of philosophical identities as sites of ambiguity and contestation in the late ancient Mediterranean. "Signs of 'syncretism,' then, always need to be interpreted" in order to understand the complex negotiations of power and resistance that take place at these points of contact.[62]

Plutarch's work is characteristic of this tendency to blur any secure distinctions between Greeks, Romans, and others. Throughout the *Parallel Lives* and the *Greek and Roman Questions*, for instance, Plutarch presents Greeks and Romans as sharing all that is best about civilization.[63] As Simon Goldhill has put it, Plutarch's fondness for parallelism "assimilates Greek and Roman aspiration, expectation, and moral precept."[64] *On Isis and Osiris* similarly reduces the cultural gulf between Greeks and others as Plutarch engages in allegorical exegeses of Egyptian myths. Likewise, Numenius's project of *anachōrēsis* would appear to set Greek and barbarian wisdom on an equal playing field. These blendings of Greeks and others form hybrid texts in which many scholars continue to struggle to separate the "Greek" elements from the "barbarian."

The comparative study of religious and cultural traditions is disruptive of hierarchical systems of power insofar as cross-cultural research sets different traditions side by side in a way that, initially at least, relativizes the differences among them. That is, comparative projects make similarities between ostensibly disparate traditions visible. In the late ancient world, for example, Plutarch's comparison of Egyptian and Greek mythology or Numenius's reading of the Pentateuch alongside Plato brought certain similarities between deities and mythological narratives into better relief. Borders and limits always beg to be crossed. In transgressing boundaries between native and foreign, such syncretistic gestures also threatened to break down any meaningful distinction between "us" and "them."[65] The practice of cross-cultural research thus opened an interstitial space in which distinctions like "Greek" and "barbarian" became highly unstable. If there is little meaningful difference between "Greek" and "Egyptian" traditions, what meaningful difference remains between Greeks and barbarians?

Because the process of comparison threatens the security of distinct identities, cross-cultural research tends, ironically, to prompt reiterations of difference.[66] Philosophers like Numenius and Plutarch resolved these disruptions not by abandoning the search for barbarian wisdom process but by (re)asserting the univocity of that quest. Fleeing the limbo land of true isometric comparison, these philosophers opted for a schema in which a diversity of particular cultural and religious formations orbited a universal (but again, Greek) center.

Despite its egalitarian appearance, Plutarch's and Numenius's complex juxtapositioning of Greek with "foreign" traditions was not an isometric exercise. The very act of setting Greek alongside Roman or Brahmins, Magi, and Jews alongside Plato, in fact, problematized difference. Plutarch's readings of Egyptian and Persian traditions in *On Isis and Osiris*, for example, do not erase distinctions between cultures but instead bring them into stark relief. These cross-cultural projects were centered in the idiom of Greek philosophy. The various texts, myths, oracles, and other pieces of religion and philosophy that philosophers like Plutarch and Numenius use to construct their ecumenical philosophies do not stand freely in their texts like so much flotsam. Instead, we should imagine a mobile in which each piece acts as weight and counterweight around a center of gravity that is thoroughly Greek.

Plutarch's reading of Isis and Osiris resolves differences of identity through a Greek lens. Throughout his exegesis of the Isis/Osiris myth, material that seems straightforwardly Egyptian receives soundly Greek interpretations. Plutarch employs *Greek* etymologies to explain *Egyptian* names, deriving "Isis" from the Greek verb *oida*, "to know," and "Typhon" from *tuphō*, "puff up" (*On Isis and Osiris* 351f). Plutarch interprets the myth of Isis and Osiris as a Platonic allegory: Isis's restoration of Osiris represents the restoration of the *hieros logos*, the sacred truth, which is the possession of those who practice a philosophical life and has as its end "knowledge of the first, the lord, the intelligible one" (*On Isis and Osiris* 2.352a).[67] Likewise, Plutarch introduces Zoroastrian cosmology to support his dualistic cosmology, not to offer an objective account of Persian religion and philosophy. "Zoroaster the magus" serves as supporting evidence that "the majority and the wisest think that there are two opposed divinities—one the artificer of good and the other of evil" (*On Isis and Osiris* 369d). Plutarch uses "Persian" sources to demonstrate the universality of his Platonic allegory, not to present an objective, comparative account of foreign religions. As Numenius engages in *anachōrēsis*, for example, he does not set Greek and barbarian wisdom on the same level. Rather, the traditions of India, Mesopotamia, Judaea, and Egypt are of value only "in so far as they stand in agreement with Plato."[68]

Plutarch and Numenius may have perceived themselves and have wished to have been perceived as philosophers and nothing more. Nevertheless, this does not mitigate against exploring the political and social ramifications of their interpretive methods. While there certainly were dogmatic reasons for cross-cultural interests of philosophers, the very fact of empire itself was crucial in determining the shape of that interest. It is often noted that empire, first that of Alexander and his successors and later that of Rome, facilitated intercultural enterprises. Certainly, ease of travel and increased contact with other cultures was a consequence of world empire. Nevertheless, imperial geography is not neutral but centered—in Rome, Antioch, or Constantinople, for instance. Moreover, intellectuals were not insulated from the political realities of imperial expansion and domination. The ecumenical drive of late ancient philosophers was suspended within and in contact with the political conditions of its possibility. By reading barbarian texts *in Greek* and interpreting them *for a Greek readership*, these philosophers were engaged in a process of intellectual despoliation homologous to the Roman conquest of peoples and territory.

For all their focus on comparison and cross-cultural research, Posidonius, Numenius, and Plutarch construct barbarian wisdom as something other than "Greek." The projects of these intellectuals are not discourses of sameness. Rather, they are based on classical rhetorical constructions of Greek/barbarian difference.[69] Egyptian, Persian, Jewish, or Indian wisdom is valuable only insofar as it can be given an *interpretatio Graeca* and contribute to Plutarch's (Platonic) philosophy. Actual cultural and religious practices, the tangible realities of difference, remain objects of censure. In recounting the myth of Isis and Osiris, for instance, Plutarch exhorts Clea, "Whenever you hear the myths which the Egyptians tell about the gods, their wanderings, dismemberments, and many experiences like this, . . . you must not think that any of these tales actually happened in the manner in which they are related" (*On Isis and Osiris* 355c–d). Egyptian traditions, in other words, are not of value as *Egyptian* traditions but only as a further source of universal—that is *Greco-Roman*—philosophy. In almost the same breath Plutarch can extol the wisdom of Egyptian mythology and theology yet denigrate Egyptians with a stock lampoon of Egyptian religious iconography: "The great majority of the Egyptians, in worshipping the animals themselves and in treating them as gods, have not only filled their sacred offices with ridicule and derision, but this is the least of the evils connected with these silly practices. There is engendered a dangerous belief, which plunges the weak and innocent into sheer superstition, and in the case of the more cynical and bold, goes off into atheistic and brutish reasoning" (*On Isis and Osiris* 379e). As a Greco-Roman polymath who knows the Egyptians better than they know themselves, Plutarch can have it both ways. He can *appropriate* and *allegorize* the venerable lore of Egyptian tradition in order to annex it to the universal (again, that is, Greco-Roman) philosophy.[70] Simultaneously, however, Plutarch positions *Egyptians* as practitioners of superstition and near-atheism, subcivilized objects of Greco-Roman supervision.

It is also important to note that many of the Greco-Roman intellectuals interested in cross-cultural research were neither Greek nor Roman. Several of the most important figures in Greco-Roman philosophy, including Posidonius, Numenius, and, as we will see in the next chapter, Plotinus and Porphyry, were born and raised in the provinces—that is, outside Greece and Italy. Both Posidonius and Numenius hailed from the Syrian city of Apamea, on the Orontes River, for example. Nonetheless, becoming philosophers offered these Syrian philosophers a means of accessing the privilege accorded the Greek intellectual tradition. That intellectuals and other elites were able so seamlessly to access the metropolitan center was due in large part to the tendency of Roman imperialism to annex and assimilate provincial elites.[71] Philosophers' attitude toward barbarian wisdom was similarly "interested." "Egyptian," "Syrian," and other "foreign" voices, like Posidonius or Numenius, were welcome within the Greco-Roman intellectual tradition but only so long as they spoke and thought (or could be made to speak and think) in a Greco-Roman idiom.

Christian Challenge and Pagan Response

Christian intellectuals shared their contemporaries' interest in "barbarian wisdom."[72] Against accusations that their tradition depended on blind faith and ignorance, Christian apologists compared diverse philosophies, mythologies, and cultic practices to prove the superiority of their tradition. In mimicking the discourse of philosophical universalism, the apologists were out to beat the philosophers at their own game. If one investigated the traditions of all peoples, the apologists argued, one could only conclude that *none* of them possessed a universal philosophy. Only Christianity, they asserted, offered an authentic philosophy that transcended ethnic and cultural particularity. Rebecca Lyman thus stresses that Christian apologetics is not merely a reaction to Greek philosophy as something other than and outside itself; rather, at the same time that the apologists "displaced the sole cultural authority of Hellenic philosophy, . . . the truth of [their] own 'philosophy' rested in acknowledged and shared cultural concepts of transcendence and mediation as well as biblical authority or revelation."[73]

But second-century Christian apologetics was more than an imitation of Greek intellectual practice. The work of Jewish historiography also provided important models for the apologists. Jewish historiography emerged out of contact with Hellenistic culture and literature. The extant fragments of the Hellenistic-Jewish historians—figures such as Eupolemus, Artapanus, and others—suggest that Jewish historiography had its origins in Ptolemaic Egypt.[74] As "Hellenistic Jewish" implies, these writers adopted and adapted the conventions and idioms of contemporary Greek historiography—particularly the tradition of universal historiography. The first "ethnic histories" were written in Hellenistic Egypt, where Hecataeus of Abdera was commisioned by Ptolemy I to write a history of Egypt.[75] Hecataeus and, later, Manetho placed the discovery of language, technology, astrology, and religion squarely in ancient Egypt. Later, Philo of Byblos would claim similar cultural precedence for the Phoenicians, while Berossos made the same claims for his native Chaldea. At the same time that ethnic historians extolled their own cultural histories, they often disparaged the histories, myths, and traditions of their neighbors. The result was what Arthur Droge has aptly termed a "war of books."[76]

"Ethnic" historians crafted their competing narratives of cultural precedence using a common set of historiographic tools. One could simply subvert the chronologies of other peoples by claiming exceedingly ancient dates for one's own cultural heroes, gods, and traditions. One could also trace the discovery of science, technology, and language back to one's own cultural heroes (the *Erfinder* motif) and claim that these culture heroes had crossed the Mediterranean and Near East sowing the seeds of other cultures (the *Kulturbringer* motif).[77] In addition, Euhemerism—the notion that the gods and goddesses of mythology had been ancient human culture heroes, subsequently worshiped as deities—served as a useful tool for "demythologizing" the myths of rival peoples, as well as a means to assert the cultural and chronographic precedence of one's own cultural heroes. Thus, the history and development of the cultural field we would term "religion" figured importantly in these historical narratives.

The Ptolomaic historians Hecataeus and Manetho included accounts of the origin of Egyptian religion in their ethnic histories. In doing so, they also offered polemical accounts of Jewish history. Moses, in particular, figured importantly in their accounts.[78] Hecataeus, for example, includes Moses among a list of Euhemeristic "lawgivers who have arisen in Egypt and who instituted customs unusual and strange."[79] According to Hecataeus, the first lawgiver was an Egyptian, Mneves. Mneves realized that people would be more likely to obey laws if they were thought to come from a divine source and "claimed that Hermes had given the laws to him."[80] Hecataeus groups Moses, who "referred his laws to the god who is invoked as Iao," with a number of other foreign lawgivers who imitated the original, Egyptian lawgiver.[81] Manetho claims that the Jews of the Exodus were nothing more than lepers led by a rebellious Egyptian priest, Osarsiph.[82] According to Manetho, Osarsiph (Moses) led his band not out of Egypt but on a campaign to "set cities and villages on fire" and "pillage the temples and mutilate the images of the gods."[83] Manetho's Moses is also a lawgiver, but his laws are "absolutely opposed to Egyptian customs."[84]

The Hellenistic Jewish historians of Ptolemaic Egypt confronted Manetho's and Hecataeus's polemical accounts of the Jews with their own counterhistory. Egyptians, Greeks, and others, they contended, owed the very basis of their societies to the ancient Hebrew patriarchs. This counterhistory, however, was crafted using the same techniques and historiographic tools—especially the *Kulturbringer* and *Erfinder* motifs and Euhemerism—used by Hecataeus and Manetho. Thus Eupolemus credits Abraham with teaching astrology to the Egyptians. Drawing on Euhemeristic theory, he equates the god Atlas with Enoch, whom he argues learned astrology from God's angels.[85] Artapanus also locates Abraham as the source of astrological wisdom for the Egyptians and the Phoenicians.[86] Moses is also cast as a *Kulturbringer* in the narratives of Jewish historians. Eupolemus describes Moses as "the first wise man"—the inventor of the alphabet and the first lawgiver.[87] According to Artapanus, moreover, Moses taught music to Orpheus. Artapanus also equates Moses with the Greek demigod Musaeus and the Egypto-Greek deity Hermes-Thoth. As Hermes-Thoth, Moses was the inventor of writing, philosophy, and Egyptian theology—not to mention the author of technology and the arts, including shipbuilding, masonry, and weaponry.[88]

The chronographic and historiographic tactics developed by the Hellenistic Jewish historians living under the Ptolemies served as an important basis for Jewish intellectuals writing under Roman rule as well. Two of these—Philo of Alexandria and Josephus—influenced and often served as direct sources for early Christian apologists. Euhemerism, the *Kulturbringer* motif, and polemical chronology provided the apologetic arsenal for Philo's *Hypothetica* and Josephus's *Against Apion*. Josephus and Philo, in turn, provided models for the work of second-century Christian apologists. Theophilus's treatise *To Autolycus*, for instance, is a "revisionist" account of universal history.[89] "I hope to provide a more accurate chronology," Theophilus writes, "in order that you may understand that our teaching is neither recent nor mythical, but more ancient and more true than [the teachings] of all the poets and authors, who write uncertainly."[90] Theophilus, like his Jewish predecessors, argues that Moses and the Hebrew scriptures are more ancient than the philosophical and religious writings of all other peoples; therefore, they offer the most accurate and universal philosophy.[91] Clement of Alexandria, too, set out to a counterhistory in his *Exhortation to the Greeks*: "Error seems to be ancient, while truth [i.e., Christianity] seems to be an innovation."[92] In his *Stromateis*, moreover, Clement appeals directly to the Jewish historians of the Ptolemaic period, as well as Philo, to argue for the historical primacy of Moses.[93]

Josephus and, especially, Philo also offered direct comparisons between Moses and Greek intellectuals and between the Torah and Greek literature. Against anti-Jewish critics, Josephus claims that Moses had founded an ideal form of government, better than monarchy, oligarchy, and democracy, which he can describe only by coining a famous neologism—"theocracy."[94] Like the Platonic lawgiver, Josephus's Moses bases his legislation on "first principles"—that is, upon his extensive knowledge of the highest levels of reality.[95] Moses also strives, again like the Platonic statesman, "to be rather than to seem" by "making his actions agree with his laws."[96] In addition, Josephus explicitly compares Moses with Lycurgus and Mosaic legislation with that of Sparta and Crete, which, we have seen already, are the two perennial examples of "good constitutions" in Platonic political theory.[97] Philo's *Life of Moses* is a philosophical *bios* analogous to contemporary lives of Pythagoras, Plato, and other scions of Greek philosophy. For Philo, Moses is the perfect incarnation of the Platonic philosopher-king.[98] Like Pythagoras, Moses legislates for ideal philosophic communities—the Essenes and Therapeutae—the lifestyle of which Philo spends some time elaborating in his *Hypothetica* and *On the Contemplative Life*. But Philo's Moses surpasses any Greek lawgiver—he also embodies the perfection of three other qualities: lawgiving, high-priesthood, and prophecy.[99] Consequently, Moses' legislation is qualitatively better than that of Plato or any other Greek philosopher.[100]

The early Christian apologists, deploying the same tactics as Josephus and Philo, were also involved in a form of writing that challenged Greek philosophical discourse at the same time that it imitated it.[101] One important way in which the apologists disrupted Greek discourses of universalism was by comparing Jewish and Christian philosophers (i.e., Moses or Jesus) to Greek thinkers (i.e., Homer or Plato). The chronological gymnastics of Christian apologists and their polemical *sunkriseis* of Homer and Moses, or Moses and Plato, have long captured the attention of scholars.[102] What has gone largely unnoticed, however, is that comparisons of Plato or Homer with Moses or Jesus depended first on an initial recognition of similarities between them. Thus, Theophilus prefaces his chronological arguments by acknowledging that "there were many . . . among the Hebrews but also among the Greeks . . . who have said things harmonious and in agreement with one another."[103] Justin Martyr's negotiation of the relationship between Greek philosophy and Jewish and Christian thinkers is also predicated on a recognition of similarity: "we say some things like unto those said by the poets and philosophers honored among you."[104] By identifying similarities between Greek philosophical texts and the Bible, the apologists were practicing a form of comparison—much like Plutarchian *sunkrisis* or Numenian *anachōrēsis*—that sought to distill universals from culturally specific expressions. Yet the impulse for universality that drives these comparative projects is also a threat to the distinctness of different peoples. Plutarch and Numenius had safely situated Moses and other barbarian sages in subordinate relation to Plato, but the apologists challenged Greek philosophical hegemony by reopening the question of similarity. By forcing a reentry into these fissures between Greek and barbarian, Christian apologists threatened to reduce the Greek/barbarian dichotomy to absurdity.

Christian apologists, for their part, were as uncomfortable as the philosophers with the ambivalence and ambiguities of the quest for universalism. Like later Stoics and second-century Platonists, the apologists explain the similarities shared by Greeks and other peoples by positing a singular, universal truth that transcends cultural and ethnic particularity. For the apologists, again as for the Stoics and Platonists, this ecumenical drive was simultaneously differential. Like Numenius and Plutarch, the apologists were driven to take their cross-cultural comparisons to a conclusion that reasserted, rather than problematized, difference. Indeed, the apologists were not arguing for the superiority of Christianity over and against philosophy; they were arguing that Christianity *was* the only valid philosophy. The apologists needed a narrative of the history of civilization and an ethnological rhetoric that could contain and control the ambivalence and ambiguity inherent in their universalizing discourses.

Alongside their polemical chronologies, Christian apologists also offered discourses in which they located the origins of human difference in theological and cosmological error. Ethnogenesis was understood to be part of a larger metanarrative that posited an original Ur-theology and a subsequent decline marked by cosmological error and mistaken cultic practices. Perhaps the clearest example of this metanarrative in early Christian apologetic comes from Aristides. Aristides opens with a description of the Ur-theology: there is one God who is prime mover, creator, perfect, immaterial, and so forth. This Ur-theology is natural—in the sense that it is accessible to all through humans' inborn capacity for reasoned contemplation of the order of creation.[105] Aristides divides humanity into five types—barbarian, Greek, Egyptian, Jew, and Christian.[106] He understands these groups to be constituted by the ways they have strayed from (or, in the case of Christians, adhered to) the Ur-theology. The barbarians err because "they worship created things in place of the one who created them"—they deify the elements and famous humans from the past.[107] The Greeks, for their part, went beyond the barbarians by developing blasphemous mythologies that present the divine as imperfect and subject to passions while giving license to adultery, fornication, incest, and other vices.[108] The Egyptians represent a further decline: "they have erred much more than any other people on the earth" by deifying animals.[109] Lastly, the Jews, though they "seem to hold to the truth more than all other peoples," nevertheless err by instituting purely physical practices like circumcision, dietary regulations, and Sabbath observance—practices that Aristides claims involve the worship of angels instead of God.[110] The Christians, however, are a people defined by their adherence to the original Ur-theology.[111]

Similar accounts that link theological and cultic differences with ethnogenesis can be found throughout early Christian apologetics. Minucius Felix's *Octavius*, for instance, connects the origin of each *nation* with the Euhemeristic worship of dead kings and culture-heroes.[112] For Clement of Alexandria, too, ethnic difference can be mapped with reference to cultic practices: thus, "Scythians worshiped their sabers, the Arabs stones, the Persians rivers," and so forth.[113] In (re)discovering and returning to the Ur-theology, the apologists contended, Christians were forsaking the errors of the gentiles—escaping the decline of human history and transcending ethnic particularity. Clement of Alexandria offers a succinct account of this narrative trajectory: "There was an innate original communion between humans and heaven, obscured through ignorance, but which now at length has leapt forth instantaneously from darkness."[114] The advent of Christianity constitutes a disruption of the processes of decline and ethnogenesis. For the apologists, the salvation history is also an ethnographic narrative and a "history of religion" that posits an original, universal, transcendent Ur-theology and its subsequent (perverse) embodiment in various ethnocultural forms.

Christian apologists did not craft these "histories of religion" from whole cloth. Their accounts of an original Ur-theology and its subsequent decline had a biblical precedent in Paul. Two portions of the Pauline corpus proved especially fruitful for the apologists' thinking on ethnic difference, universalism, and the "history of religion." These Christians read Paul's declaration that "There is no longer Jew or Greek, there is no longer slave or free, there is no longer male and female, for you all are one in Christ Jesus" (Gal. 3:28) and parallel passages (Col. 3:10) as an affirmation of Christian identity as constituted by the denial and erasure of ethnicity (and other marks of difference, including sex and social class). At the same time, the first chapter of Paul's letter to the Romans provides an account of the history of civilization and ethnogenesis. Like the apologists—or rather, the apologists, like Paul—can resolve "Christianity" as a transcendence of difference only within and through a working out of ethnicity. Pauline universalism is thus inherently ethno-logical.

The letter to the Romans is protreptic—designed to encourage the forsaking of one way of life in favor of a new one; here, the abandonment of idolatry and its associated ethical lapses in favor of the well-ordered, reasoned life "in Christ." Protreptic often took the form of narratives of cultural decline and associated moral degradation.[115] Romans 1:18–32 narrates human history as decline (both moral and intellectual) from knowledge of and proper worship of God. Paul's decline narrative positions theological and ethical degradation as the origin of ethnic difference and the constitutive feature of gentileness. Exegeses—especially traditional Christian exegeses—that "spiritualize" the contrast between "Israel" and "gentiles" obscure the ethno-logic so crucial to Paul's argument.

This narrative trajectory, in which theological error precipitates both *idolatreia* and *porneia*, represents Paul's own development of a wider Jewish discourse connecting ethnogenesis and the origins of idolatry. Specifically, Romans 1 is an improvisation on Genesis analogous to similar expansions in works like the *Wisdom of Solomon*, *Jubilees*, and Pseudo-Philo's *Book of Biblical Antiquities*. In these works, the Genesis narrative is read as a universal account of human history—specifically as a narrative of the preservation of godliness among the patriarchs and the parallel decline of all other peoples, or gentiles. As an account of the origins of different peoples, then, Genesis also lent itself to interpretation as an ethnographic text. The genealogical lists in chapters 5 and 10 of Genesis, along with the narrative of the Tower of Babel and the fracturing of human languages, in particular, tended to be read ethnographically.

Like the Hellenistic Jewish historians, moreover, these parabiblical texts refract Genesis through the lenses of Greek intellectual idioms like Euhemerism and decline theories (especially Stoic) of the history of civilization.[116]

Paul's narrative connects the transference of God's glory onto "images resembling a mortal human being or birds, or four footed animals or reptiles" and the worship of creature in place of creator (Rom. 1:23, 25) with God's abandoning the errant to their passions and the exchange of "natural intercourse for unnatural" (Rom. 1:26–27). The *Wisdom of Solomon* makes the same connection more succinctly: "The idea of idols was the beginning of *porneia*" (Wis. 14:12). Paul's account also summons a tradition in Jewish discourse that located the origins of idolatry at the nexus of Euhemeristic worship and the development of arts and technology (tools and the plastic arts). The *Wisdom of Solomon*, for instance, explains idolatry as originating in ancestor worship: "For a father, consumed with grief at an untimely bereavement, made an image of his child . . . he now honored as a god what was once a dead human being, and handed on to his dependents secret rites and initiations" (Wis. 14:15). The development of skills like the plastic arts are closely linked with this theological mistake (Wis. 14:18–21). *Jubilees* links the arts with error more explicitly through an expansion on Genesis 4:20–22 (Tubal-cain's invention of bronze and iron tools) as well as a creative etymology of the name of the patriarch Serug to interpolate the origin of idolatry into the genealogical tables presented in Genesis after the fall of the Tower of Babel (Gen. 11:20–22). The Pseudo-Philonic *Book of Biblical Antiquities* draws the same connection between *artes* and the worship of cultic statuary.[117] Thus, as Stanley Stowers has argued, Romans 1 is not an account of the fall of a universal humanity (as it would be read by later patristic exegetes, most notably and influentially Augustine) but an ethnographic and historical account of the origins of the gentiles and cultural difference.[118] Paul's narrative in Romans 1 describes a degenerative trajectory—*technē*, idolatry, ethnogenesis—parallel to those in pseudepigraphical and apocryphal literature. Paul locates the ultimate origin of this decline in a cosmological error. The descent into idolatry, passion, and vice began with a failure to recognize God's power in the created order (Rom. 1:20). Much as Paul describes the way in which humans "exchanged the truth about God for a lie and worshiped and served the creature rather than the creator" (Rom. 1:25), the *Wisdom of Solomon* locates the origin of idolatry in the failure to "recognize the artisan while paying heed to his works" (Wis. 13:1).

Philo also read Genesis as an account of human difference. Philo's reading of Noah and the Flood is ethnological at the same time that it is allegorical, or rather, it is an allegory articulated in ethnological terms.

Before the Flood, humanity had degenerated to such a state that "every region, nation, city, house, and each individual person was filled with evil customs."[119] Noah, Philo explains, was the only person to remain "just and perfect in his generation" (Gen. 6:9); Noah is unlike all other people and peoples—he is not called " 'human' in the common sense, that is, as a rational, mortal animal, but pre-eminently" having tamed all animalistic passions.[120] As the only really authentic "human" living before (and, of course, after) the Flood, Noah was "both the last and first of our race (*genos*)."[121] Abraham, Isaac, and Jacob, for their part, represent a distinct "house and race," distinguished by its devotion to the natural law of God in contrast to other, contemporary peoples.[122] Much as Paul and the *Wisdom of Solomon* drew a contrast between gentile worship of creation and the Jewish worship of the creator, Philo describes Abraham's emigration from Chaldea as a rejection of inferior modes of worship—Abraham sought the true God, while the Chaldeans "honored visible reality" and "liken[ed] creation to the creator."[123]

For Paul and Philo, historic-ethnographic narratives of decline mediated projects similar to the "return to ancient sources" urged by Greek philosophers such as Posidonius and Numenius. Thus, in a manner similar to Stoic historiography, like that of Posidonius, and Stoic exegesis, like that of Cornutus and Heraclitus, "being Israel" also becomes an archaeological process of recovering and interpreting the remains of ancient wisdom—in this case, the Torah of Moses. Thus, the writers renowned among the Greeks, Philo argues, spent their intellectual energies authoring licentious comedies and fables.[124] Moses, in contrast, wrote two sorts of "sacred books": narrative histories, on the one hand, and commands and prohibitions, on the other.[125] Unlike the historians of other nations who wrote history for pleasure or entertainment, Moses provided, first, a true cosmological account and, second, the lives of patriarchs. "These men," Philo writes, "are like ensouled and rational laws" and "followed the unwritten law with perfect ease"; Moses' legislation in turn reflects "natural law" and thus transcends processes of historical becoming.[126] Philo also universalizes the lineage of Abraham—Genesis "seems to speak about holy men" but in fact describes "modes of soul," or ascending stages of psychic accomplishment on the path to the contemplation of God and true being.[127] There is, consequently, a certain multivalence in Philo's ethnological vocabulary. When writing against anti-Jewish polemics in the *Hypothetica* and *Against Flaccus* or offering a more literal account of the patriarchs, Philo defends "the nation" and "the people (*to ethnos/to laos*)."[128] Living in Roman Alexandria, in which the Jewish population was embroiled in conflicts over group identity and the legal privileges and restrictions relating to that identity, Philo was acutely aware of literal kinship. At the same time, for Philo, anyone who cultivates reason and virtue can, in theory, be a child of Abraham—be part of "our race (*genos hemōn*)."[129]

Paul's thinking on "nature" and "law" in Romans is somewhat more opaque than Philo's. Romans 2:14 is a critical passage. The New Revised Standard Version translates: "When Gentiles, who do not possess the law, do instinctively [*phusei*, i.e., 'by nature'] what the law requires, these, though not having the law, are a law to themselves." Early Christian exegetes, like Clement and Origen for instance, read Paul as arguing that righteous gentiles follow the inborn compass of natural law in contrast to the literalism and legalism of the written Torah.[130] Unlike early Christian exegetes, contemporary scholars recognize the esteem in which Paul held the Torah as well as his assumption that the Torah does relate to gentiles.[131] Stanley Stowers proposes that Paul does not argue in Romans 1 that gentiles have access to natural law but that some gentiles know the written Law of Moses. He points to two sources from which Paul might have gotten the idea of gentile knowledge of Torah: passages in Psalms and in the prophets that describe gentiles as hearing God's moral injunctions as well as the *Kulturbringer* motif and Euhemerism used by the Hellenistic Jewish historians.[132] Thus, Stowers suggests a better translation of Romans 2:14: "For when gentiles, not having the law by nature do what the law requires. . . (etc.)."[133] To Stowers's insights I would add that this rereading need not preclude the presence of "natural law" in Paul. Paul, in a manner similar to Philo, is simply equating "natural law" (that is, universal ethical norms) with the Torah. For Paul, the law is not bound by *phusei*—that is, not limited to those who are "ethnic" Jews by physical descent. Knowing and doing Torah, then, is presented as the way for non-Jews to overcome the history of theological error and *porneia* narrated in Romans 1:18–32. Ethnic Jews, for their part, must get beyond the mere "letter" of Torah to its essence—an essence, he drives home, that transcends traditional notions of ethnicity as literal, physical descent.

That both Paul's and Philo's thinking on "law" and "nature" should resemble (if in different ways) the "natural law" theories of later (that is, late Hellenistic and early Roman) Stoics should not be surprising given that all were operating in the context of Rome's conquests and the consolidation of the early empire. Andrew Erskine has described the ways in which later Stoics, such as Posidonius and Cicero, came to equate "laws of nature" with Roman norms.[134] Universal "natural law" thus became a means for imposing imperial unity upon foreign peoples (or foreign elites, at least) with diverse laws and customs. These Philonic, Pauline, and late Stoic discourses of "natural law," concerned as they were to distinguish perennial ethics from mere native "custom," thus always also represented an engagement with homologous discourses of universality and particularity that structured Rome's imperial project.

For Paul, in contrast to the *Wisdom of Solomon*, his contemporary Philo, and Roman Stoics, these ethnological and historiographic discourses serve to disturb the dichotomy between gentiles and Jew, barbarians and Greeks (and Roman intellectuals steeped in things Greek). In Paul's account of the soteriological economy in Romans, the God of Israel has allowed a portion of Israel (the broken olive branches of Romans 11:17) to fall into the same degenerate state as the gentiles. "Israel" is reconfigured in terms of an allegorized ethno-logic in which Jew and gentile (as well as male and female, slave and free) will be reconstituted as Israel "in Christ." Paul's narrative of decline and the difference between Jew and gentile is a means to a soteriological end that effaces, even as it depends on and is articulated through, the logics of universal history and ethnology.[135]

Paul's discourse on ethnicity and universalism is disruptive of the ethno-logic of Greek philosophical discourse *and* Jewish counterhistories of culture in at least two important, interrelated ways. First, Paul's equation Israel = universal humanity = transcendence/authentic being relativizes or, more precisely, subordinates all human difference. All human distinctions (sex and social status as well as ethnicity)—including the dichotomy between Israel and gentile that is the engine of the narrative in Romans 1—are suppressed.[136] This aspect of Pauline universalism would make it highly productive for Christian apologetic discourses that devalorized ethnic identities—whether Greek (apologetic discourse) or Jewish (anti-Jewish polemic and apologetic)—as negative terms in a new universalizing equation: Christian = universal humanity = transcendence/authentic being. Second, this universalizing discourse involved or precipitated a revaluation/reevaluation of cognitive geography. As an allegorized ethno-logic, Pauline discourse is always infected by the "ethnic reasoning" that permeated the comparative discourses of ethnography, historiography, and philosophy. Paul's soteriological economy—the recovery of the gentiles from error and depravity and the reconstitution of Israel—takes place some*where*. To erase ethnicity, to exchange the particularized world of becoming for the transcendence and authentic, universal humanness, is to be in "Israel"—in the Torah and in relationship to the God of Israel.

The tensions within Paul's allegorized ethno-logic also helped drive later Christian discourses. In the pages that follow, we will look at two second-century apologists—Justin Martyr and Tatian—to consider the ways in which discourses of universalism and ethnology functioned within the context of the Roman Empire. For Christian apologists, the ironic construction of Christianity as a people constituted by their transcendence of ethnicity disrupted both Greek intellectual hegemony and Jewish identity. The possibility of a Christian identity emerged in these fissures. By claiming access to a transcendent Christian identity that resided "no-where," the apologists could arrogate "Greek" and "Jewish" idioms for themselves. Under the aegis of universalism, the apologists effaced the "Hellenicity" or "Hebraism" of those idioms in efforts to render "Christianness" as a sui generis category above and beyond any particular ethnic or cultural incarnation.

Justin

Justin hailed from Flavia Neapolis in the Roman province of Syria-Palestine. The city had been established as a Greek city and Roman colony in 70 C.E. in honor of Vespasian's victory in the Jewish War. Justin provides the names of his father and grandfather: Priscus and Baccheius, respectively. The former name is Latin, the latter Greek. Justin's own name, like his father's, is Latin, suggesting that his family may have been among the Roman colonists of Flavia Neapolis.[137] Flavia Neapolis lay in Samaria, and Justin identifies himself as "Samaritan" in the *Dialogue with Trypho*.[138] At the same time, he reports that he was uncircumcised and raised as a gentile; he had a traditional Greek education.[139]

Justin describes his philosophical education in the *Dialogue with Trypho*. He states that he began his quest for the true philosophy with an assumption similar to that of the Greek philosophers considered earlier in this chapter—that a true philosophy is singular, perennial, and universal. Justin's philosophical peregrinations, however, first with the Stoics and then among the Peripatetics, Pythagoreans, and Platonists, led him to realize that the ancient, original philosophy had become "many headed."[140] Justin's account of his own conversion inverts as it imitates the usual philosophical peregrination. Plato and Pythagoras had gone from Greece to the Orient and back again in search of wisdom; Justin toured the schools of the Greeks only to return to the "provincial" wisdom of the Hebrew Bible.[141]

A liminal figure, Justin straddles boundaries between east and west, province and metropolis, barbarian and Greek. All of Justin's extant writings could reasonably be described as projects in boundary identification and maintenance. The *Dialogue with Trypho* works out the difference between Christianity and Judaism. He describes his *Apologies* variously as *prosphōneseis* (speeches of praise for a ruler), *enteuxeis* (pleas or petitions), and *exegēseis* (speeches of explanation or justification).[142] In sum, the *Apologies* seek (ostensibly, at least) to curry the benevolence of the emperor while explaining who Christians are and what Christianity is—all as Christians were facing persecution based solely (as Justin claims) on their identity as Christians.[143]

Christian are persecuted, Justin asserts, "by mere statement of a name." A group is deserving of punishment, Justin counters, only if there are specific crimes associated with membership in that group. Justin does more than pose procedural arguments, however. The surest defense of Christianity, he contends, lies in a thorough inquiry into the nature of Christianity (*1 Apol.* 3). "Reason," Justin continues, "names as truly pious and philosophers those who honor only the truth" (*1 Apol.* 2.1). In locating Christians as "philosophers," Justin acknowledges the privilege accorded "philosophers" and "philosophy." In doing so, he also challenges others' claims to philosophic identity. Justin rails sarcastically to his imperial addressees that even philosophers who propound impious doctrines "are not censored by you; instead you offer prizes and honors" (*1 Apol.* 4.9). It is not the content of philosophy that garners status, Justin charges, but simply one's ability to "pass" successfully as a philosopher—or "assume the name and dress" as Justin puts it (*1 Apol.* 4.7–8). By deliberately pointing out similarities between Christianity and Greek philosophy, moreover, Justin calls both into question: "If we say some things that are similar to the poets and philosophers honored among you, and others that are greater and more divine, and alone speak convincingly, why are we, of all people, hated unjustly?" (*1 Apol.* 20.3). Justin's proprietorial claim on "philosophy" thus forces him to maintain the distinction between Christianity (as true philosophy) and all that merely "passes" for it. Justin does this by drawing on Pauline discourse and coupling it with his *Logos*-theology.

In the *Second Apology*, Justin offers an account of the origins of gentile traditions that, in its broad outlines, parallels the Pauline theodicy in Romans 1. God, as creator, intended humans to be led to true theology through contemplation of the order in creation (*2 Apol.* 5). Justin differs from Paul, however, in ascribing the origins of the gentiles to the work of evil demons. Demons, or fallen angels, figure prominently in the parabiblical books of *Jubilees* and *1 Enoch*. The development of idolatry during the time of Serug is aided, according to *Jubilees*, by "cruel spirits" who "assisted [humans] and led them astray so that they might commit sin and pollution."[144] The apocalyptic *1 Enoch* similarly ascribes the origins of idolatry, as well as other cultural and social ills, to the deceit of a race of fallen angels known as the "Watchers."[145] Justin is here developing another strain of Jewish and Christian improvisation on Genesis.[146] In Justin's account, humans, terrified by the wicked demons, "declared them gods, and called each by the name which each of the demons gave to himself" (*1 Apol.* 5.2). Cultic iconography ("idolatry" in Justin's biblical terminology) is also a demonic product, for craftspeople simply imitate the forms of the demons (*1 Apol.* 9). In addition to explaining the origins of idolatry among the gentiles, Justin's demonology helps him explain similarities between gentile and Christian traditions. Yes indeed, Justin acknowledges, the Sibyl, the Persian prophet Hystaspes, and the Stoics all proclaim the earth's destruction by fire in ways that parallel Christian prophecies. Mythological accounts of Hermes as teacher, Asclepius as healer, Dionysius and Hercules as dying gods, and even the apotheosis of Caesar resemble Christian accounts of Christ. Justin's explanation: "among the Greeks and all peoples" the demons merely mimicked the biblical prophets; of course, the resemblance is only partial, for although they eavesdropped on God's true prophets, "they did not understand accurately" (*1 Apol.* 54.3–4).

To negotiate the similitudes between Christianity and other philosophies Justin turns to the concept of *Logos*.[147] Justin deploys the concept of *Logos* to disrupt the polarity of the Greek/barbarian dichotomy. For Justin, the ubiquity of the *Logos* explains why the same philosophical and religious ideas and forms are found among disparate peoples. As the principle of all rationality and the basis of philosophy, the *Logos* is found wherever there is reasoned expression: "For not only among the Greeks through Socrates were these things revealed by *Logos*, but also among the barbarians" (*1 Apol.* 5.4). But Justin is not in the game of multicultural appreciation. All peoples may manifest the *Logos*, but not all share it equally. As the passage just quoted continues, truth was revealed among the barbarians "by the *Logos* himself, who had taken shape and become man, and was called Jesus Christ" (*1 Apol.* 5.4). Justin's cross-cultural *sunkrisis* of Greek and Christian wisdom is resolved by reaffirming a Greek/barbarian difference. In Justin's schema, however, barbarian Christians replace Greek philosophers at the top of the pile: "the things we say, which were learned from Christ and the prophets before him, are alone true and older than all of the writers who ever were; and we do not ask to be accepted because we say the same things as they do, but because we speak the truth" (*1 Apol.* 23.1). There is an historical component to Justin's argument in that, like Theophilus, he equates antiquity with truth, but the real thrust of Justin's argument is that only Christians have access to *Logos* in its entirety in the person of Jesus. While others, like Posidonius, Numenius, and even Theophilus, believed philosophy to be authentic in direct proportion to how close it could be traced to the origins of humanity, Justin thinks that the *Logos* antedates all creation. Justin describes the preexistence of the *Logos*/Christ: "the only one who is legitimately called [God's] 'Son,' the *Logos* who is with [God] and begotten before all creation, when in the beginning [God] created and ordered all" (*2 Apol.* 6.3). Christianity,

then, "seems greater than all human teaching" (*2 Apol.* 6.3). Christianity
is the only authentically ecumenical philosophy. Christians have access
to the *Logos* himself, obviating any concern for an earthly *diadochē*.

Other peoples, especially the Greeks, offer merely imperfect, culturally specific instantiations of the *Logos*. Without access to the entire
Logos, Greeks and others were destined to fail in their philosophical pur-
suits: "Since they did not know the entire Logos, who is Christ, they
often said contradictory things" (*2 Apol.* 10.3). Justin's understanding of
the relationship between philosophies that are universal, and therefore
authentic, and culturally specific varieties of philosophy is summarized
near the conclusion of his *Second Apology*. According to Justin, the *sunkrisis* of Greek philosophy and Christianity reveals the superiority of the latter "*not* because Plato's teachings are something different from Christ's,
but because they are not in every way *equal*, just as neither are the teachings of others, the Stoics and the poets, and historians" (*2 Apol.* 13.2).
Christians are privileged to know the entire *Logos* and thus enjoy hegemony over other forms of philosophical expression, or as Justin famously puts it, "What has been said correctly among all is ours, the
Christians'" (*2 Apol.* 13.4).

Justin was a Christian philosopher and teacher in Rome; we can imagine him as the focal figure of a small circle of intellectuals. Later sources
report that Justin lived in an apartment "above the baths of Timothi-
nus," and that his circle met in the home of a Martinus.[148] This "school"
would have been one among many in second-century Rome, which
placed Justin into conflict with a number of competitors. Justin himself
speaks of ongoing conflicts with Marcionites, for instance (*1 Apol.* 26).
As we saw at the opening of this chapter, however, Justin also found himself in conflict with the Cynic Crescens. Justin and Crescens, then, were
in competition over the status of "philosopher." In the *Second Apology*,
Justin openly declares Crescens "unworthy of the name of 'philosopher'" (*2 Apol.* 3). Writing later, Justin's student Tatian goes further—
Crescens, the great pederast and money lover, epitomizes all
pseudo-philosophers. Some of these wannabes, Tatian sneers, "receive
from the emperor of the Romans 600 aurei yearly" (*Orat.* 19). Tatian's
allusion to the philosophical chairs established by Marcus Aurelius in
Athens helps point to the ways in which Justin's claims on philosophical
identity presented a challenge to the *imperial* authority. Justin addressed
his *First Apology* to the emperor Antoninus Pius and "to his philosopher
son Verissimus [i.e., Marcus Aurelius], and to Lucius [i.e., Lucius Verus]
the philosopher." Justin is aware of the importance of philosophical
identity to the self-representation of Antoninus Pius's sons. But this *cap-
tatio benevolentiae* is double-tongued. Justin sets out to test these philoso-
pher-kings: "since you are called pious and philosophers and guardians

of justice and lovers of culture, listen in every way, and it will be shown if you are such" (*1 Apol.* 1). Beyond his appeal for justice and "common sense," Justin threatens to expose the would-be philosopher-princes as *poseurs.*

TATIAN

Tatian identifies himself as an "Assyrian," by which he probably means that he came from Mesopotamia, possibly from Osrhoene or its environs (*Orat.* 42). It was in that region that his *Diatessaron*, a harmony of the four canonical gospels, enjoyed currency. Like Justin, Tatian was an eastern provincial whose intellectual career landed him in Rome. Also like Justin, Tatian describes his conversion to Christianity in terms of cultural peregrination. Tatian crossed the Mediterranean investigating different cultic practices and religious texts as well as philosophy, ending in Rome itself. "Having seen these things," he reports, "and having participated in the mysteries, and having examined the religious practices among all peoples, . . . going off on my own, I sought in what way I might be able to discover truth. . . . While I was pondering these serious matters, I happened upon some barbaric writings, more ancient as compared to the doctrines of the Greeks, and more divine as compared to their error" (*Orat.* 29.1–2). Robert Grant points out that the form of the *Oration* is that of a *logos suntaktikos*, or "farewell discourse."[149] The *Oration*, in other words, represents Tatian's bidding adieu to Greek and Roman traditions in favor of "barbaric" Christianity. Thus, where Justin's *Apologies* take the form of open letters to the emperors and the citizens of Rome, Tatian's *Oration* is addressed to an ethnic group—the Greeks. Even more explicitly than Justin, Tatian construes philosophical identity in ethnological terms—to choose Christianity is not merely an intellectual option; it is to forsake Hellenicity as an ethnocultural identity.

To explain why he has abandoned Hellenism to become "Tatian, who philosophizes barbarian-style" (*Orat.* 42.1), Tatian sets up a formal rhetorical comparison, or *sunkrisis*, of Greek and Christian wisdom. As a rhetorical method that plays on the tension between similarity and difference, *sunkrisis* could also be an effective tool for negotiating ethnic and cultural boundaries. Plutarch's *Parallel Lives*, as we saw earlier in this chapter, is an excellent example—in comparing the lives of renowned Greeks with those of famous Romans, Plutarch negotiates the relationships between Hellenicity and Romanness in the context of Roman domination of Greece. *Sunkrisis*, as the second element of this compound word (*sun-krisis*) suggests, also prompts a crisis (*krisis*). Setting Greek and barbarian in comparison destabilizes identity and the differences upon which identity depends.

Where Justin had articulated a nuanced *Logos* doctrine to resolve the threat of Greek philosophy's similarity to Christianity, Tatian opts for a more belligerent comparative method. Tatian argues that Christian literature, in the form of the Hebrew Bible, is more ancient than Greek literature. Indeed, after recounting his conversion experience, Tatian enjoins his audience, "Let them be compared (*sunkrisin paralambanesthōsan*), for we shall find that our teaching is older not only than the teaching of the Greeks, but older than the discovery of letters!" (*Orat.* 31.1). But Tatian's choice of a barbarian philosophy (Christianity) over Greek philosophy is based on something more than chronology.[150] When compared, Tatian asserts, Greek and Christian literature are fundamentally unequal: "I understand that this [Greek] sort of literature leads to condemnation" (*Orat.* 29.3). Tatian does not appeal to a complex *Logos* doctrine to explain any similarities between Greek and Christian wisdom. Instead, he simply resolves similitude by denying that any comparison of such clearly different literatures is valid at all.[151]

Tatian takes his comparison even further, challenging the very integrity of Greek identity itself.[152] According to Tatian, a good comparative investigation reveals that Greek philosophy and culture are little more than poor imitations of various barbarian traditions. "Which of your customs has not originated from the barbarians?" Tatian asks (*Orat.* 1.1). He provides a litany of peoples from whom the Greeks have imitated as they cobbled together their "own" traditions: from the Telmessians, dream interpretation; from the Carians, astrology; from the Phrygians, augury; from the Baylonians, astronomy; from the Persians, magic; from the Egyptians, geometry; and from the Phoenicians, the alphabet (*Orat.* 1). Tatian goes on to question that most fundamental marker of Greek identity, the Greek language itself. The multiplicity of Greek dialects militates against the notion of a Greek language, Tatian argues. Indeed, Tatian argues that there is a civil war (*stasis*) in the Greek language (*Orat.* 1.4). Greek wisdom, like the Greek language, is merely a bricolage of barbarian traditions: "If each city were to take away its own teaching from your own, they would deprive your sophistries of all power" (*Orat.* 26.1). Based on his examination of Hellenicity, Tatian simply jibes, "What I ought to call 'Greek' perplexes me" (*Orat.* 1.4). If Greek identity is a chimera, then Greek chauvinism has no legs to stand on; thus Tatian mocks the Greeks, "Why do you say that wisdom is with you alone; you have no other sun or rising of stars, nor a birth or death more glorious than those of any other people!" (*Orat.* 26.4).

Tatian recognized that he represented a challenge to the privilege of Greek intellectuals and Greek intellectual idioms. He imagines the accusations his critics might level against him: "Tatian innovates (*kainotomei*) with barbarian doctrines over and against the Greeks and the numberless crowd of philosophers" (*Orat.* 35.3). It is not accidental that Tatian places the verb *kainotomeō* in the mouth of his imagined accusers. The term can mean "innovation," but it also connotes the threat of social disruption and rebellion that went along with religious or philosophical novelty; Socrates, for instance, was accused of "innovating with respect to the gods."[153] Tatian, then, recognizes that his claims to be both "philosopher" and "barbarian" represented a disruption of the larger sociopolitical field in which he and other intellectuals competed for status. If the trial and execution to which Justin owes his epithet "martyr" is any indication, philosophers like the Cynic Crescens sometimes shared the concerns of Roman officials about Christians. Not all reaction to Christianity took the form of persecution and martyrdom, of course. If non-Christian philosophers were threatened by Christian philosophy, they could respond in kind with polemical texts of their own.

CELSUS

The only pagan response to Christian apologetics that has survived from the second century is the anti-Christian pamphlet *On the True Logos* by Celsus, a late second-century Platonist.[154] Celsus's treatise survives only in fragments cited in Origen's *Against Celsus*, written over seventy-five years later. [155] When Celsus published his polemic in the late 170s, he had likely read Justin's *First Apology* and chose his title in direct response to Justin's *Logos*-theology.[156] Celsus, in fact, had no objections to barbarians as such, so long as each people consistently adhered to its own traditions. Celsus likes Egyptians who act like Egyptians, Persians who act Persian, and so forth. Christians presented a threat because they refused to fit neatly into this system. Justin and Tatian claimed that Christianity *was* the ecumenical "ancient doctrine" that Celsus argued had achieved its fullest expression among the Greeks. Against Justin's claim that Christians possessed the only authentic philosophy by virtue of the *Logos*, Celsus set out to reassert the Greek center of philosophy by giving an account of the true *Logos*. To do this, Celsus had to renegotiate the relationship between philosophical universality and ethnocultural particularity.

Like his fellow second-century Platonists Plutarch and Numenius, Celsus believed that genuine philosophy transcended ethnic and cultural particularity. Although Celsus criticizes Christianity by deriding it as a "doctrine . . . originally barbarian," Celsus did think non-Greeks possessed wisdom. The universal philosophy was not to be found among any one people; rather, "there is kinship of doctrine among many peoples" (*CCels*. 1.14). Celsus's list of "wise peoples" recalls Numenius's list of the "peoples of renown" but is even more wide-ranging: Egyptians,

Assyrians, Indians, Persians, Odrysians, Samothracians, and Eleusinians. No other philosopher captures the simultaneously eclectic and hegemonic nature of comparative philosophy better than Celsus. "There is an ancient, original doctrine," Celsus elaborates, "which the wisest peoples and cities and wise men shared" (*CCels.* 1.14). Yet, he is quick to remind his readers, "the Greeks are more able to judge, confirm, and virtuously practice those things that the barbarians have discovered" (*CCels.* 1.2).

Celsus is clearly uncomfortable with the similarity of Christian philosophy to his own "true doctrine." He deflects Christian mimesis by turning many of the apologists' own tactics to polemical effect. He levels the charge of plagiarism: Christian "ethics . . . are common and compared to other philosophers have no wonderful or new teaching" (*CCels.* 1.4). Where the apologists accused Plato and Homer of aping Moses, Celsus does the opposite, asserting that Moses stole aspects of the ecumenical philosophy that existed "among the wise peoples and famous men" (*CCels.* 1.21). Neither was Moses' notion of a highest god unique, for "it makes no difference to call the God who is above all by the name he bears among the Greeks, . . . or among the Indians or among the Egyptians" (*CCels.* 1.24). Moreover, the Christian imitation of ecumenical philosophy is a poor one because Christians simply "misunderstand" the doctrines they copy (*CCels.* 4.10). Thus Celsus exploits the instability of Christian philosophy as a hybrid discourse. Justin had deployed the concept of *Logos* to subordinate other traditions to Christianity. Celsus, however, points out the inherently imitative quality of Christian philosophy. Isn't all (from Celsus's perspective) Christian philosophical speculation conducted in Greek? *Logos*, after all, is a Greek term, and Justin's treatise is merely a pastiche of Greek doctrine (*logos*) and Greek terms (*logoi*).

Celsus also compares Christian literature and reading practices unfavorably with those of other peoples. Celsus thinks that the true philosophy is something to be discovered in the most ancient sources and believes that the true *Logos* was preserved textually by "ancient and wise men who helped the people of their time and, through their writings, helped those after them" (*CCels.* 1.16). His list of reliable ancients recalls the sources preferred by Numenius: Linus, Musaeus, Orpheus, Pherecydes, Zoroaster, and especially Pythagoras (*CCels.* 1.16). Origen fumes that Celsus deliberately excludes the Jews from among the "most ancient and wise peoples" and Moses from the list of "ancient and wise men" (*CCels.* 1.14, 1.16). The Alexandrian scholar writes that Celsus rejected Moses and the Hebrew Bible because he denied that the Hebrew Bible could bear figurative exegeses (*CCels.* 1.17). Origen challenges Celsus to compare Moses' writings with those of other sages; if Celsus were to do so, he argues, he would see that Moses was a master allegorist (*CCels.* 1.18). In fact, this sort of comparison is exactly what underlies Celsus's rejection of the Hebrew Bible.

Celsus pursues the issue of Christian texts and interpretation most thoroughly in the fragments preserved in Book 4 of *Against Celsus*. The wise peoples of the world, such as the Athenians, Egyptians, Arcadians, and Phrygians, offer believable accounts of their antiquity. In comparison, Celsus argues, "the Jews, bent low in the corner of Palestine, were completely uncultured and had never before heard the ancient things commemorated in Hesiod and a thousand other divinely inspired men" (*CCels.* 4.36). Not only does the Hebrew Bible fail to meet the criterion of antiquity, it also fails even more fundamentally as good literature. Celsus lampoons the Hebrew Bible on the grounds that it is merely a collection of immoral tales. Celsus reads the story of Adam's disobedience, for example, as an account of a god that cannot control his creation. The tale of Noah's ark is nothing more than a poor copy of the Deucalion myth, and the patriarchs' tremendous life spans are ridiculous (*CCels.* 1.40–43). Not only are biblical narratives poor stories, they are also immoral; Celsus ridicules the many sexual escapades of the patriarchs and levels some particularly scathing comments at the story of Lot's intercourse with his daughters (*CCels.* 1.43, 1.45). Celsus's assumption is that some texts are simply too base to deserve figurative reading. In such cases, allegory is merely a way to obscure the poor quality of the literature. Such is the case with the books of the Hebrew Bible, which "do not admit allegories, but are utterly ridiculous myths" (*CCels.* 4.50). Celsus's treatment of the Hebrew Bible as provincial literature of low quality is part of his larger program of defusing the Christian threat by reasserting the Greek/barbarian and metropolitan/provincial dichotomies. Plutarch's treatises on Egyptian philosophy and religion had provincialized Egypt at the same time that they held up heavily allegorized readings of Egyptian mythology as articulations of ecumenical philosophy. For Celsus, the Christian tradition bears no value as a carrier of the ecumenical philosophy. Drawing on several common ethnographic stereotypes, Celsus shows that Christianity is fit to be ridiculed alongside other strange and laughable provincial practices. Deploying the rhetoric of "superstition," Celsus charges that Christianity is a deception based on an overweening fear of "invented terrors" of divine anger combined with mere pageantry and overstimulation of the senses. Christians "distract people in just the same way as those who whip people up into a Corybantic frenzy with their clamoring" (*CCels.* 3.16). It was commonplace for Greco-Roman intellectuals to cite the processions of the Phrygian goddess Cybele as an example of depraved superstition. Nor are Christians much different from other peoples who honor humans as founders of oracles, like "the Getae who honor Zamolxis, and the Cilicians who honor Mopsus, the Acarnanians Amphilocus, the Thebans Amphiarus, and the Lebadians Trophonius" (*CCels.* 3.34). Celsus uses another common stereotype when he compares Christianity with that most barbaric of all religions in the Roman world, Egyptian animal worship. Just as the Egyptians hide their "superstitious and mysterious religious rites" inside magnificent temple complexes, so too do the Christians hide their absurd worship of a crucified man behind the trappings of religion (*CCels.* 3.17). It is clear from the way Origen couches this Celsian quotation that the thrust of Celsus's argument was not lost on the Alexandrian.

He wishes to equate the elements of our faith with those of the Egyptians. . . . But what is there among us that is analogous to the false wonders the Egyptians offer to those who come to their temples, what is there among us that is analogous to the irrational animals which are worshipped inside? Is Jesus Christ crucified analogous to an irrational animal that is worshipped? (*CCels.* 3.17)

That Christianity is comparable to Egyptian worship is precisely Celsus's intention: Christian teachings about Jesus are "no more worthy of honor than the goats and dogs of the Egyptians" (*CCels.* 3.19).

Celsus's reaction to Christian exclusivity makes it clear that the Christian mimesis of ecumenical philosophy among the early apologists threatened Roman imperialism as well as Greek philosophical hegemony. Christians refused to worship any divine being other than the highest god, but Celsus counters by claiming that Christians misunderstand the divine hierarchy. Since all lesser deities are subordinate to the highest god, those who worship many gods please the highest god (*CCels.* 8.2). Celsus also accuses the Christians of hypocrisy since "they go out of their way to worship this fellow who appeared recently, and do not think they are mistaken concerning the highest god if they worship his servant [i.e., Jesus]" (*CCels.* 8.12). Celsus likens the Christian refusal to worship the traditional gods to a rebellion: to refuse "to serve many masters" is "a rebellious statement (*staseōs einai phōnēn*)" (*CCels.* 8.2). The lesser gods are subordinate to the highest god, but that does not mean they lack power or authority. Celsus uses a political metaphor to portray the divine hierarchy: "The satrap, lieutenant, general, or governor or the Persian or Roman Emperor, or even those who have lesser responsibilities, commissions, or posts, have the power to do harm should they be neglected; would the satraps and ministers of the air or earth do little harm if they are insulted?" (*CCels.* 8.35). Celsus thus elides theological language with the vocabulary of imperial geography and bureaucracy. His theological discourse, in which there is room for myriad local deities, is shaped by the political conditions of its very possibility. At the same time, of course, Celsus's theological discourse reiterates these political conditions. To participate in Celsus's ecumenism is simultaneously to participate in the empire that conditions the very possibility of his theology in the first place.

Christians' antipathy to traditional forms of worship along with their staunch refusal to participate in traditional cults, in particular their refusal to offer sacrifices to the emperor's *genius*, were important factors in their persecution. Celsus's distaste for recalcitrant Christians echoes that of many of the Roman officials recorded in martyr acts and other documents beginning with Pliny's correspondence with Trajan in the second decade of the second century.[157] But Celsus is concerned with more than refusals to participate in imperial cult. In their staunch cultic exclusivism, then, Christians appeared to Celsus as a threat to imperial territory as much as to traditional religiosity. In refusing sacrifice on behalf of the emperor and the empire, he warns, "the things of the earth will come under the control of the most lawless and uncivilized barbarians, with the result that no trace of your religious rites or of the true wisdom will remain among humans" (*CCels.* 8.68). Christians may claim that they pray to their God for the safety of the empire,[158] but history shows the futility of worshiping local deities like the Jewish god—the Jews are without king or country and subject to foreign rule, while Christians hide in the shadows under threat of capital punishment (*CCels.* 8.69).

Celsus sees Greeks, Egyptians, Phoenicians, Thracians, and other *ethnē* as the natural building blocks of the empire. Celsus understands these distinctions to be the consequence of both the natural development of human civilization and divine fiat.

> . . . Each [people, i.e., *ethnos*] honors its traditions, whichever ones they happen to have set up. This seems fitting, not only because it came into the mind of different people to think differently and because it is necessary to protect common custom, but also because it is probable that the regions of the earth were distributed among different overseers and divided among various masters to be governed in this way. (*CCels.* 5.25)

Celsus's second assumption follows from the first: if ethnic and cultural difference are in origin divine and if the (always differential) social order depends on strict adherence to ancestral tradition, then any who choose to deny or reject their ancestry and any who alter ancestral custom are guilty of impiety and treason. As Celsus puts it, "the practices among each people are rightly done when they please those masters, and to undo the customs which have been in place from the beginning is unholy" (*CCels.* 5.25). Jews and Christians, for their part, do not even represent authentic ethnic groups: "The Jews were Egyptians with respect to ethnic origin," Celsus argues, "and left Egypt after revolting

(*stasiasantas*) against the common customs of the Egyptians and despising the religious rites practiced in Egypt . . . and just what they did to the
Egyptians they have suffered from those who followed Jesus and believed in him as Christ, and in both cases the cause of innovation was rebellion (*to stasiazein*) against ancestral custom" (*CCels.* 3.5). Several
scholars have ascribed Celsus's distaste for Christians to their refusal to
reciprocate his "ecumenism."[159] This explanation of Celsus's antipathy
to Christianity misses an important point—Celsus's relationship to barbarian wisdom was not reciprocal. By (re)locating Christians as barbarians, Celsus is able to reassert Greek philosophical hegemony over them.
Christians might have universalizing pretensions of their own, but in reality they are, at best, one more provincial barbarism among many or, at
worst, a group of confused half-breeds. Christians may resemble
philosophers—their doctrines might even resemble the truth—but they
are frauds nonetheless.

In this chapter I have explored the ways in which cross-cultural research
became a means for intellectuals in the Greco-Roman world to negotiate difference in the context of the Roman Empire. These comparative
projects helped establish and support asymmetrical relationships between Greek philosophy and other, culturally specific traditions. By dis-
locating barbarian "wisdom" from its specific cultural expressions,
Greek philosophers situated non-Greeks as objects of intellectual domination. But even as they pursued transcendence, philosophers were not
insulated from the political and social realities of Roman imperialism;
rather, the very pursuit of transcendence was a politically interested venture. Christian philosophers imitated this ecumenical impulse, but their
mimesis challenged the carefully constructed, if always tenuous, dichotomy between Greeks and others.

Apologetics was not simply a form of Christian boosterism. Christian
apologists offered a direct challenge to the cultural hegemony of Greco-
Roman philosophers as well as an oblique riposte to Roman imperial
hegemony. Power and privilege in the Roman Empire was staunchly hierarchical, and philosophy was an effective way to gain access to cultural
and political privilege. Even philosophers from the provinces, like Posidonius and Numenius, could become part of the "metropolis" by living
the philosophical life. Christians, however, exerted pressure from the
periphery in ways that disrupted the boundaries between metropolis
and province. The complex negotiations of identity that are played out
in apologetic texts challenged the logic and stability of imperialism. The
drive to distinguish culturally and ethnically specific expressions and
subordinate them to a transcendent, universal truth was conditioned by,
suspended within, and in contact with the power dynamics of empire.

Thus, the apologists did not offer a discourse that erased the effects of empire. Mimicry reiterates, even if partially, confusedly, and disruptively, the conditions of its own possibility. Apologetics was a discourse of resistance *within*, not liberation from, the asymmetries of power and prestige that helped produce it.

This tension did not end with the second century. Apologists like Tertullian, Clement of Alexandria, Cyprian, and Origen continued to offer a challenge to the privilege of Greek philosophy throughout the third century. The outbreak of the Great Persecution under Diocletian in 303 C.E. and the subsequent rise of Constantine, however, signaled increasing contacts between imperial power and apologetic discourse that would catalyze new rhetorics of difference and social domination. It is to this moment that I turn in the following chapters.

Chapter 2

Porphyry on Greeks, Christians, and Others

At the turn of the fourth century, the philosopher Porphyry was nearing the end of his long career.[1] Born in Tyre in the province of Syria in or around 234 C.E., he had traveled first to Athens, where he studied under the philologist Longinus. He then made his way to Rome, where, at around the age of thirty, he joined Plotinus's circle. After Plotinus's death, he would go on to become one of the most influential figures in later Platonism. Besides authoring numerous works on ethics, physics, and religion,[2] he was responsible for the standard edition of Plotinus's *Enneads* and would exert an influence on both pagan and Christian philosophers for centuries to come. Despite his age (he was in his late sixties at the opening of the new century), Porphyry married Marcella, a widowed Roman matron with several children.[3] Porphyry seems to have reconciled his new role as *pater familias* with his philosophical career.[4] After only a few months of marriage, however, Porphyry undertook a major journey across the empire. Porphyry was leaving wife and family, he recounts in a letter home to Marcella, "because the needs of the Greeks called, and the gods confirmed their appeal."[5]

Porphyry was traveling at or around the same time that Diocletian and Galerius were holding their persecution conferences of 302–3. The Christian Lactantius, who had been appointed Diocletian's court rhetorician, reports hearing presentations by two anti-Christian polemicists during this period.[6] One was Hierocles, a judge and dabbler in religion and philosophy whose polemics against Christianity consisted of attempts to "reveal the falsity of scripture," with a special emphasis on an unfavorable comparison of Jesus with the holy man Apollonius of Tyana.[7] Lactantius writes that a second polemicist "professed that before all things the duty of a philosopher was to cure people of error and to recall them to the true way, that is, to the worship of the gods."[8] Unfortunately, Lactantius leaves this polemicist unnamed, but there is strong evidence that this philosopher was none other than Porphyry.[9] Lactantius's description of this unidentified philosopher's attack on Christianity is markedly similar to accounts of Porphyry's polemics available in other sources.[10] Although previous scholarship tended to date Porphyry's polemics earlier in his career, there is a growing consensus that they belong to the late third or early fourth century.[11] Lactantius also reports that the speaker claimed to be a "priest of philosophy"—precisely the terms Porphyry uses to describe a true philosopher in his *Letter to Marcella*.[12] As will be seen in detail in the next chapter, moreover, much of Lactantius's apologetics seem to be fashioned in direct opposition to known Porphyrian arguments.

Whether we place Porphyry at Nicomedia or situate him more generally in the highly polemicized "atmosphere" of the late third and early fourth centuries, the prominence and threat of Porphyry and his polemics for Christians writing during and immediately after the Great Persecution is beyond dispute. Constantine's order to burn Porphyry's books and his designation of Arius and followers as "Porphyrians" is just one example of how damaging many felt his polemics to be.[13] Porphyry continued to cast a shadow long after the persecution; in the West, for instance, Augustine would expend great energy refuting Porphyry in the *City of God*, while in the East the emperor Julian would draw on Porphyry for his own polemics.[14] As late as the fifth century, Cyril of Alexandria described Porphyry as the "father of the ceaseless babbling against us," while Theodoret of Cyrrus characterized him as "our deadliest and most hated enemy."[15] Thus, more substantial questions remain. *Why* and *how* did Porphyry attack the Christians? What made his polemics so threatening to early Christians? If we consider *Against the Christians* and *Philosophy from Oracles* in light of Porphyry's attitudes toward ethnic and cultural difference, a clearer picture of the motivations behind his antipathy to Christianity emerges.

A repressive streak was certainly a component of Porphyry's anti-Christian polemics: "To what kind of punishments," he wrote, "may fugitives from ancestral customs, who have become zealots for the foreign mythologies of the Jews which are slandered by all, not be subjected?" (Harnack fr. 1).[16] Once the philological, textual, and historical details of Porphyry's relationship with the Great Persecution have been worked out, however, a more substantive question remains: why was Porphyry so antipathetic to Christianity, and why would his distaste for Christians have driven him and the pro-persecution party in Diocletian's court to become bedfellows? It is obvious from Lactantius's summary of the position taken by Diocletian's advisors, as well as from Porphyry's polemics, that both found the Christians to be apostates from tradition. But the answer is more complicated. The Christians were more than annoying upstarts; they threatened the cultural and political privilege that Porphyry enjoyed as a philosopher in the Roman Empire.

Porphyry understood himself as heir to the tradition of Plato and

Pythagoras, as bequeathed to him by his teacher, Plotinus. Following the example of Plotinus's Middle Platonic predecessors such as Plutarch and Numenius, however, Porphyry also researched and wrote about Egyptian, Persian, Indian, Phoenician, and Jewish religious and philosophical traditions.[17] Although not stated explicitly in his extant writings, implicit assumptions about the relationship between cultural universality and particularity undergirded Porphyry's methodology. Porphyry's interest in "barbarian wisdom" has led to his being labeled "eclectic" or even "orientalizing."[18] For all of his interest in other cultures and traditions, however, Porphyry staunchly identified himself as Greek. If he examined other cultures and traditions, it was only insofar as he could mine them for contributions to his own philosophical projects. Thanks to this encyclopedic knowledge, Porphyry believed he was able to distill a philosophy that transcended cultural and ethnic particularity. This philosophy was universal and therefore authentic.

Such radical assertions of universality had a particular tenor in the context of Roman imperialism. In the Roman world, difference was rigidly hierarchical. As we saw in Chapter 1, certain (especially Greek) cultural formations were privileged as universally authentic while other, provincial, "barbaric" literatures, religions, and philosophies were considered ethnically specific, contextually bound by geography and history in a way that Greco-Roman culture was not. In the staunchly hierarchical world of the Roman Empire, to claim that one's religion and philosophy were ecumenical, therefore, was also to assert their dominance.

But the difference between Greeks and Romans, on the one hand, and barbarians, on the other, was not always as secure as it appeared. One of the most potent threats to imperial hegemony is the "mimic man," a provincial subject who imitates the habits, literature, religion, language, or other cultural forms of the metropolitan center.[19] Imperial discourse insists on the fixed, stereotypical difference between ruler and ruled. Straddling this supposedly fixed gulf, mimic men appear almost totally same as their imperial masters at the same time that they seem almost totally different.[20] By revealing inherent weaknesses in the barrier between ruler and subject, these transgressions threaten to reduce the very logic of imperialism to absurdity.[21]

As we saw in Chapter 1, Christian intellectuals like Justin, Tatian, and Theophilus imitated and manipulated the practices of Greek philosophy to argue that their own tradition transcended cultural and ethnic particularity and was, in fact, universal. Porphyry's conflict with the Christians, then, can be read as a dispute between remarkably similar yet competing attempts to negotiate cultural and religious difference within the context of Roman imperialism. Christians imitated Greco-Roman philosophers so well, in fact, that they threatened to turn Porphyry's carefully polarized world upside down. Eusebius of Caesarea summarized the quandary that Christian intellectuals, as liminal figures, presented for Porphyry: "In the first place, one might well raise the *aporia*—who are we [i.e., the Christians] . . . [are] we . . . Greeks or Barbarians, or what could there possibly be in-between these?" (Harnack fr. 1).[22] Christian intellectuals, in their disruptive mimesis of Greek philosophical practice, made the interstitial wasteland between Porphyry's own metropolitan (Greek-philosophical) identity and that of these confused provincials all too visible.

Porphyry at Home and Abroad

Porphyry was heir to the polymaths of the first two centuries C.E., and like them, his intellectual gaze was double. A glance at the *Conspectus Fragmenta* in the Teubner edition of Porphyry's fragments lists treatises covering topics both Greek and barbarian.[23] His contributions to philosophy included commentaries on Platonic dialogues, a work titled *The Agreement Between Plato and Aristotle,* and the *Isagoge,* which remained a standard introduction to logic well into the Middle Ages. Arguably, Porphyry's edition of Plotinus's *Enneads* was his most important and lasting contribution to Greco-Roman philosophy. Porphyry was also interested in the history and development of philosophy; he wrote *Philosophical History,* which surveyed the origins and development of the Greek philosophical tradition, and *Life of Pythagoras,* a hagiographic presentation of the ideal philosophic life. Porphyry was also an adept philologist; he composed a book of *Homeric Questions* as well as an allegorical exegesis, *On the Cave of the Nymphs in the Odyssey.* Treatises on rhetoric, music, and ethics round out his oeuvre.

Alongside this focus on Greek philosophy and literature, Porphyry also looked abroad and was deeply immersed in "barbarian wisdom." We can better appreciate the function of Porphyry's interest in barbarian wisdom within his larger philosophical project by juxtaposing two Porphyrian statements about the relationship between universal truth and cultural particularity. In the nineteenth book of the *City of God,* Augustine of Hippo offers a curious summary of Porphyry's *On the Return of the Soul.* According to Augustine, Porphyry was in search of a universal doctrine for the salvation of the soul.

Near the end of the first book of *On the Return of the Soul,* Porphyry states that there is no tradition in any one particular sect (*in unam quandam sectam*) that contains a universal way for the liberation of the soul—not in any philosophy (in the strictest sense), nor in the discipline and practices of the Indians, nor in the learning of the Chaldeans, nor in any other tradition (*via*), and that this "universal way" had not yet come to his attention through historical inquiry. Yet he confesses without doubt that some such way exists, but that it had not yet come to his attention. (*Reg.* 302F [= Augustine *City of God* 10.32.5–16]).[24]

The passage is important because it shows that Porphyry, like Numenius, Plutarch, and other first- and second-century philosophers, thought that cross-cultural research was an important part of the philosopher's task. Porphyry searched far and wide, from one end of the known world to the other, for the *via universalis*, but Augustine suggests that Porphyry ultimately failed in his quest.

According to Eusebius, Porphyry's *Philosophy from Oracles* also had universal philosophy, or " 'theosophy,' as he liked to call it," as its subject.[25] Porphyry includes an Apolline oracle that suggests an ecumenical approach to philosophy.

The way of the blessed is difficult and rough.
The entrance is through brass gates.
The paths within are beyond number,
which the earliest of humans revealed for eternal use—
those who drink the fine water of the Nile.
Later, the Phoenicians learned the ways of the blessed,
as did the Assyrians, Lydians, and the Hebrew people. (*PO* 303F).[26]

Porphyry glosses this oracle by commenting that "barbarians have found many paths" to the truth, "while the Greeks have strayed." Indeed, this universal "way of the blessed" appears to have been the principal subject of *Philosophy from Oracles*, in which, as the title suggests, Porphyry adduces a universal philosophy from his collation of oracular material. His list of peoples that have known this universal way strongly echoes Numenius's list of the Jews, Egyptians, Indian Brahmins, and Persian Magi as "peoples of renown" to which philosophers must extend their research.[27] Here, in apparent contrast to the doubts expressed in *On the Return of the Soul*, Porphyry clearly claims to have discovered a *via universalis*.

The relationship of these two texts remains a problem for Porphyrian studies. Did Porphyry, as Joseph Bidez argues, write *Philosophy from Oracles*, which extols the wisdom of the barbarians and purports to offer an ecumenical philosophy, during a period of youthful exuberance, only to retract this assertion years later in *On the Return of the Soul*?[28] Or is *On the Return of the Soul* the earlier work and *Philosophy from Oracles* a later attempt to craft a more inclusive philosophical theology?[29] To explain the relationship between Porphyry's apparently contradictory remarks in *Philosophy from Oracles* and *On the Return of the Soul* and to understand fully his quest for a *via universalis*, one must first grasp the complexity of Porphyry's negotiations of Greek and barbarian identity.

The goal of Porphyry's intellectual peregrinations was the discovery of a universal, and therefore truly authentic, philosophy. On the one hand, Plato held a central place in Porphyry's conception of philosophy. Like Numenius and Plutarch, he believed that Plato, in the main, had gotten philosophy "right." On the other hand, Porphyry did not think that truth was to be found in Plato alone. As Porphyry admits in *On the Return of the Soul*, the *via universalis* was not to be found in any particular philosophical school or among any single people (*Reg.* 302F). Wisdom and knowledge were not uniquely Greek. Although Augustine relishes Porphyry's apparent failure to discover the *via universalis*, he seems to have missed the point of Porphyry's remark, or twisted it for polemical effect.[30] The passage points to the importance of universalism for philosophy, not its impossibility. By admitting that the universal way of salvation is not found in any one particular group (*unam quandam sectam*), Porphyry implies that the *via universalis* is only discernible when one's pursuit of philosophy is sufficiently ecumenical. The introduction to *Philosophy from Oracles* confirms this ecumenical imperative. Porphyry tells his readers that "Secure and steady is he who takes his hope of salvation from this as from the only secure source" (*PO* 303F). How is this claim to offer a universal philosophy reconcilable with *On the Return of the Soul*? After his introduction, Porphyry offers verses that alert the reader to his cross-cultural methods: "The way (*hodos*) of the blessed is difficult and rough," but, he notes, "the paths (*atrapitoi*) . . . are beyond number" (*PO* 323F). Porphyry's choice of vocabulary is not simply a function of meter. There is one *hodos*, but it can be known only by investigating the many, ethnically diverse *atrapitoi*.

For Porphyry, even language, that quintessential marker of difference between Greeks and barbarians, is no boundary for ecumenical investigation. At the opening of the third book of *On Abstinence*, Porphyry compares human and animal language to help prove that animals participate in *Logos*. To prove his point, Porphyry mocks classic, chauvinistic Greek attitudes to language. Those who assert that language is solely the province of humans, he asserts, err in the same way as "the people of Attica [who said] that Attic is the only language, and thought that others who do not share the Attic way of speaking lack *Logos*. Yet the Attic speaker would understand a raven sooner than he would a Syrian or Persian speaking Syrian or Persian."[31] Porphyry also places Greeks and barbarians on the same plane in the fourth book of *On Abstinence* when he draws on examples from Greek, Egyptian, Jewish, Syrian, Persian, and Indian sources to argue that all peoples impose dietary restrictions on religious functionaries. Porphyry hopes to prove the general rule by collating specific examples: "[Abstinence] applies whether you consider Greek or barbarian custom, but different peoples have different restrictions; so that if you consider them all together, it will be apparent that those taken from all regions abstain from all animals" (*Abst.* 4.5.5). Porphyry can discern a genuinely universal ethic only by looking beyond Greece.

On Abstinence is an excellent example of Porphyry's cross-cultural project. In Book 4, Porphyry draws from Egyptian, Phoenician, Mesopotamian, and Jewish sources to construct a consensus concerning philosophical asceticism. Porphyry appropriates Chaeremon the Stoic's "account of Egyptian priests" to recount the temperate lifestyle of Egyptian philosophy (*Abst.* 4.6–10). This way of life included periodic sexual continence and a rigorous regimen of bathing and other purificatory rites along with abstinence from animal food. He cites Neanthes of Cyzicus and Asklepiades of Cyprus for material on Phoenician customs. According to Asklepiades, "At first no animate creature was sacrificed to the gods" (*Abst.* 4.15). Although Porphyry's sources for Persian and Mithraic traditions are more difficult to discern, one seems to have been Eubulus (*Abst.* 4.16). In support of vegetarianism, Porphyry describes the importance of animal symbolism in Mithraism: "They symbolize our community with animals by giving us the names of animals: thus initiates who take part in their rites are called lions, and women hyenas, and servants ravens" (*Abst.* 4.16). For information on Indian customs, Porphyry looks to the *Book of the Laws of Countries,* a document from Bardaisan's philosophical circle. The vegetarianism of Indian Brahmins supports the ascetic consensus (*Abst.* 4.17). Porphyry also compares Brahmin asceticism more broadly with the philosophical life practiced by Greek philosophers like the Pythagoreans. Finally, Porphyry draws on Josephus's and Philo of Alexandria's accounts of the Essenes. He is impressed by Essene *sōphrosunē*: "they shun pleasure as vice . . . they despise wealth, and the community of goods among them is remarkable" (*Abst.* 4.11.4–5). More to the main point of Porphyry's argument, the Jews avoid alimentary excess. In one of the few passages in pagan literature in praise of Jewish dietary practices, Porphyry lauds Jewish abstinence from pork, fish without scales, and the meat of animals without cloven hooves (*Abst.* 4.14.1–2).

Porphyry takes a similarly comparative approach to religion and philosophy. In *Philosophy from Oracles* he blends various traditions to offer "an account of many philosophical doctrines that the gods declared to be true" (*PO* 303F). Much of the material seems to have supported theological syncretism. For example, Porphyry quotes from an oracle in which Apollo identifies himself with Osiris, Horus, and Helios. Laying out his demonology, moreover, he equates Sarapis and Pluto, and in analyzing the symbolism of his cult for information on how to drive away evil *daimones* writes that "among the Egyptians and Phoenicians, and among all peoples who are wise concerning divine matters whips are cracked in the temples, and animals are dashed to the ground in the rites of the gods as the priests drive away these demons by giving them the breath and blood of the animals" (*PO* 326F). Whether Porphyry used the *Chaldean Oracles* in his compilation remains in doubt.[32] This collection of oracles had an important role, however, in *On the Return of the Soul*.[33] Summarizing the work, Augustine reports that Porphyry "could not keep quiet about his borrowing of 'divine oracles' from the Chaldeans, those oracles which he refers to so continuously."[34] Several Byzantine sources also credit Porphyry with a commentary on the *Chaldean Oracles*.[35] A cross-cultural impetus also lies at the heart of Porphyry's religious musings in his *Letter to Anebo*. In this text, Porphyry looks to the ancient wisdom of Egypt to find answers to a series of theological questions. He inquires about the nature of the gods, the differences between the gods assigned to various "spheres," and how material objects, like the sun and moon, can be called "gods" if divinity is incorporeal (*An.* 1.1b,1.2b, 1.3c).[36] Porphyry also poses specifically "Egyptian" questions. He asks Anebo to explain the myth of Isis and Osiris and wonders why Egyptian priests keep their knowledge of philosophy and religion secret (*An.* 2.8c, 2.12a). Finally, he inquires after "the way of happiness" (*An.* 2.19a).

Porphyry's copious appeals to foreign theologies, philosophies, and history reveal a Greek intellectual who, like Herodotus, might justly be termed a *philobarbaros*.[37] Porphyry's description of the "many paths" that make up the "way of the blessed" shows a philosopher who found "barbarian wisdom" integral to any authentic philosophy. But if Porphyry thought that the intellectual traditions, myths, and religions of other peoples were *valuable*, did he believe that all peoples were of *equal* value?

Although Porphyry compares Greeks and other peoples in ways that appear, initially, to place them on the same level, he simultaneously works to secure the integrity and superiority of Greek identity. Consequently, he never abandons the classic distinction between Greeks and barbarians. *Barbaros* appears thirty-nine times in Porphyry's corpus, and in at least eighteen of these instances it is set in explicit contrast to *Hellēnes*.[38] While Porphyry draws many favorable comparisons between Greeks and barbarians to bolster his arguments in *On Abstinence*, elsewhere in the same treatise he denigrates barbarians with stock stereotypes. For example, he mocks the masses who take Egyptian animal worship too literally (*Abst.* 4.9.10). Against someone who might claim that abstinence would compromise the practice of divination, Porphyry jibes that "This person should destroy people too, for they say that the future is more apparent in human entrails; indeed many barbarians use humans for divination by entrails" (*Abst.* 2.51.1). By imputing human sacrifice to his opponents Porphyry hoped to make them seem savage, worse, perhaps, than the animals they were wont to consume.

Porphyry also uses the Greek/barbarian distinction to support his arguments against eating animals. "We posit," he writes, "that all human beings are kin to one another, and moreover to all the animals, for the principles of their bodies are naturally the same" and they "have also been allocated the same soul" (*Abst.* 3.25.3). Here Porphyry's reasoning echoes his discussion of genus (*genos*) and species in his *Introduction to Aristotle's Categories.* Porphyry notes that the term "genus" can be taken in three senses. First, it can denote "an assembly of certain people who are somehow related to some one item and to each other"; Porphyry gives as an example "Heraclids," the group taking its name from a shared relationship to the same "one item," Hercules. Second, genus can refer to "the origin of anyone's birth," whether one's parent or one's native land, "for anyone's fatherland is a sort of origin of his birth, just as his father is too." Finally, genus has a particular meaning for philosophers, as "that under which a species is ordered."[39] Following Aristotle, this use of genus hinges in particular on its serving a differential function; it "must separate things from other genera."[40] Even though Porphyry sets off this special "philosophical" sense from the more common, genealogical senses, the latter tend to infiltrate the former quite readily. Reflecting on shared humanness, then, serves to accent, rather than erase, distinctions between Greeks and others. When Porphyry explains that the eating of animals cannot be justified by the necessity of killing certain dangerous animals in self-defense, for example, he draws an analogy between the treatment of savage animals and savage people. The relationship shared between animals and humans as beings endowed with soul "is not severed because some of them are savage. . . . We get rid of them, but we do not break off our connection with those that are civilized" (*Abst.* 3.26.2). Even when he wishes to posit the most basic commonality among peoples—their common humanity—we find Porphyry simultaneously asserting a distinction between Greeks and barbarians: "Thus also we say that Greek is related and kin to Greek, barbarian to barbarian, all human beings to each other" (*Abst.* 3.25.2).

But where does Porphyry situate himself in respect to the Greek/barbarian divide? Porphyry prefaces his cross-cultural examples in Book 4 by stating that he will proceed "people by people: the Greeks, as the most closely related to us among the witnesses, shall lead off" (*Abst.* 4.2.1). Porphyry thus ranks himself (and Castricius, his addressee) among the Greeks. The differences between the locutions Porphyry uses to discuss his Greek and barbarian examples of abstinence also indicate his self-identification with the Greeks. In his account of Greek customs, Porphyry recounts the ethical ideas of individual Greeks—Dicaearchus and Lycurgus. In contrast, when providing Egyptian, Jewish, Syrian, Persian, or Indian exempla of abstinence, Porphyry employs the third-person plural and its derivatives almost exclusively to denote his subjects. Porphyry also employs a partitive genitive to introduce his account of Jewish customs: *tōn de ginōskomenōn hēmin Ioudaioi*... (*ktl.*) ("Of those [peoples] known to us ... [etc.])" (*Abst.* 4.11). This construction draws attention to the differences between the collectivity of ethnic otherness and "us." These grammatical choices help Porphyry construct an ethnographic distance between his own (Greek) perspective and the various barbarian objects of his research.

Other works of Porphyry make it even clearer that his engagement with barbarian wisdom is thoroughly Greek centered. The ethnographic material in Book 4 of *On Abstinence*, for instance, does not come from his own firsthand observations. This is "armchair ethnography"; Porphyry's journeys to Egypt, Palestine, Persia, and India took place in the library. His source material is itself written in Greek: his knowledge of the Jews comes entirely from the Hellenized Greek of Josephus. Chaeremon, his source for Egyptian traditions, was an Alexandrian philosopher of the first century C.E., while his comments on Persian and Indian traditions are so common among Greek ethnography that it is difficult to name a specific source.[41] Gillian Clark astutely notes that an important section of Porphyry's material on animal and barbarian language comes directly from Herodotus, the "father" of Greek ethnography.[42] And although Porphyry asserts that *Philosophy from Oracles* will consider barbarian oracles alongside those of the Greeks, in actual practice his citations of foreign sources are rather limited. The non-Greek oracles that do appear in the extant fragments come from the *Chaldean Oracles*, a compilation that was itself composed in Greek and assumes Greek philosophical (especially Platonic) idioms. Likewise, Porphyry's knowledge of Egyptian tradition in his *Letter to Anebo* seems to derive almost exclusively from his reading of other Greek philosophers—Plutarch, perhaps, or the Hermetic Corpus.[43] Moreover, Porphyry owes his account of Mithraic cosmology in his allegorical *On the Cave of the Nymphs in the Odyssey* to the Greek allegorical tradition rather than to any direct knowledge of Persian religion. Porphyry is immersed in foreign wisdom, but nothing from Egypt, Syria, or any other province is valuable unless it can be filtered through a Greek lens.

Considering Porphyry's own origins, this Hellenocentric approach to barbarian wisdom is somewhat ironic. Although Porphyry's self-identification as Greek is echoed by subsequent tradition, in at least one important respect Porphyry was not a Greek: he was born in the Phoenician city of Tyre, in the Roman province of Syria.[44] In fact, Porphyry was not his given name. For the first decades of his life, this scion of later Greek philosophy was known by his original, Semitic name, Malchus.[45] As Malchus traveled, first to Longinus in Athens and then to Plotinus in Rome, his name began to change. Eunapius reports that it was Longinus who first called Malchus "Porphyry," after the color of royal garments.[46] Such wordplay would be characteristic of this great philologist.[47] After learning philology with Longinus, Porphyry traveled to Rome. Porphyry reports that it was in Rome, the heart of the empire, that his fellow student Amelius translated his name more literally to "Basileus."[48]

These translations of Porphyry's name are indicative of a much deeper transformation, that from Syrian provincial to Greek philosopher.[49] The journey from Tyre to Athens to Rome involved, in fact, an erasure of Porphyry's ethnicity. Porphyry, who famously refers to himself in the third person throughout the *Life of Plotinus*, never calls himself "Malchus." The Semitic name of his birth is simply a palimpsest. Porphyry's transformation echoes that of his teacher, Plotinus. In the *Life of Plotinus*, Porphyry recounts how little he really knew about his teacher's origins: "[H]e could not endure to talk about his race, his parents, or his country of birth."[50] Of Plotinus's life before his teaching career in Rome we are told only that he was born in Egypt and that his first teacher was the Alexandrian Ammonius.[51] We then hear of his urge to learn about barbarian philosophies. He pursued this interest in the Orient by enlisting in the Roman army for Gordian's eastern campaigns.[52] That Porphyry found Plotinus's past impenetrable was due partly to his teacher's design. Plotinus's goal of dissociation from all corporeal particularity included eliminating ethnic specificity. For Plotinus and Porphyry this meant abandoning the culturally specific world of the provinces for the more ecumenical perspective of Rome itself. Becoming a Greco-Roman philosopher entailed establishing oneself within a hierarchical dynamic of power that echoed the hegemonic relationship between Rome and her provinces.

Porphyry's attitudes toward religious texts and religious practices parallel his disposition toward his own origins. The texts that Porphyry plumbed for universal truth—the *Iliad* and *Odyssey*, the oracles compiled in *Philosophy from Oracles*, the myth of Isis and Osiris, Mithraic traditions, and so forth—made no claims of their own to transcend their specific Greek, Egyptian, or Persian contexts. The religious practices that Porphyry considers in texts like *On Statues* or *On Abstinence*, moreover, are equally contextual. Articulating a universal philosophy based on a cross-cultural synthesis of these culturally specific traditions required the application of particular interpretive strategies. Just as Porphyry's journey from Syria to Rome marked a translation from the specific to the ecumenical, his figurative reading of texts and intellectualizations of traditional cult served to establish a hierarchical distinction between that which is universally (and therefore truly) authentic and that which is merely culturally specific.

Porphyry's commentaries on Homer are some of the earliest and best-preserved examples of figurative readings of Greek poetry and myth.[53] Figurative readings of Homer developed largely in response to critics who called the morality of Homer's poetry into question,[54] or as a means of recovering ancient philosophical concepts hidden in the mythical compositions.[55] Nonliteral reading practices, however, were more than academic exercises in interpretation. The quest for meanings beyond the literal could serve important social and political functions. Figurative readings can never be dissociated from historical conflicts and negotiations of identity, authority, and power.[56] Most important for the present study, figurative reading offered a means to differentiate between the apparent, explicit meanings of the text and less evident, but more authentic readings.[57] Under Middle Platonic and Plotinian influence the discovery of these more obscure meanings became equated with the discovery of universal meanings; Homer "the poet" became Homer "the theologian," whose poetry conveyed truths about the human soul and the cosmos.[58] As Porphyry intimates in his treatise *On the Cave of the Nymphs*, the *Odyssey* is more than a Greek epic from the eighth century B.C.E. It was a text with universal implications. Odysseus, for instance, "bears a symbol of the one who passes through the stages of genesis and, in doing so, returns to those beyond every wave who have no knowledge of the sea. . . . The deep, the sea, and the sea-well are . . . material substance."[59] Odysseus's adventure is a representation of the soul's travails in the material world and its ascent to the noetic realm.

Just as Porphyry differentiates the authentic meaning of the *Odyssey* from its Greek context, so too does he subject barbarian myths and texts to figurative readings that serve to sift universal truths out of otherwise culturally specific artifacts. In the course of discussing the significance of caves, for example, Porphyry crafts a figurative reading of Mithraic traditions to support his claim that "caves" signify "the cosmos."

Similarly, the Persians call the place a cave where they introduce an initiate into the mysteries, revealing to him the path by which souls descend and go back again. For Eubulus tells us that Zoroaster was the first to dedicate a natural cave in honor of Mithras, the creator and father of all; it was located in the mountains near Persia and had flowers and springs. This cave bore for him the image of the Cosmos which Mithras created and the things which the cave contained, by their proportionate arrangement, provided him with symbols of the elements and climates of the Cosmos. After Zoroaster others adopted the custom of performing their rites of initiation in caves and grottoes which were either natural or artificial.[60]

Similarly, Porphyry glosses many of the oracles he compiles in *Philosophy from Oracles* with figurative readings in order to draw universalizing conclusions. Explaining an oracle of Apollo concerning the different sacrifices to be offered to different deities, Porphyry explains their symbolic meanings. "Four-footed land animals," he elaborates, are sacrificed to terrestrial gods because "like rejoices in like" (*PO* 315F). The mode in which one sacrifices is also symbolic. For example, sacrifices are carried out in the spheres assigned to different classes of deity; terrestrial gods receive sacrifices on altars set up on the ground, while sacrifices to subterranean deities are performed in trenches (*PO* 315F).

Many later Platonists like Porphyry are characterized as antipathetic to traditional cultic practice. Plotinus, in particular, is often portrayed as an iconoclast when it came to tradition. Porphyry reports that Plotinus's pupil Amelius, who was "fond of sacrifices and traveled around the temples on the new moons and feast days," once asked his teacher to accompany him. Plotinus sternly refused, answering, "It is they who should come to me, not I to them."[61] In contrast, scholars often portray Plotinus's star pupil as much more interested in traditional religion. Although Porphyry certainly did deal with the how and why of sacrificial religion, his main interest was in discovering the more authentic meanings hidden in these "dirty details." Porphyry extended the interpretive strategies he used to understand Homer beyond texts to offer figurative readings of various cultic practices. In his *On Statues*, for example, Porphyry proposes "to teach how to read from statues just as from books the things written there concerning the gods" (*PA* 351F).[62] There was more to statuary than wood and stone: "It is remarkable that the uneducated believe that the statues are nothing but wood and stone, just as the unintelligent see steles as stones, tablets as pieces of wood, and books as nothing other than woven papyrus" (*PA* 351F). This special literacy to which Porphyry lays claim helps him find universal truths in otherwise embarrassing aspects of traditional iconography. Anthropomorphic representations of Zeus, for instance, are not the result of theological immaturity. Instead, the "theologians . . . have made the representation of Zeus anthropomorphic because mind was that according to which he wrought, and by generative laws brought all things to perfection; and he is seated, indicating the steadfastness of his power; and he is naked on top, because he is evident in the intellectual and heavenly parts of the cosmos; but his feet are clothed because he is not evident in the hidden things below" (*PA* 354F).

Yet Porphyry does not limit his reading of iconography to Greek sources. Eusebius preserves a lengthy passage from *On Statues* in which Porphyry distills a late Platonic cosmogony out of Egyptian iconography. Porphyry interprets the Egyptian god Cneph as "the demiurge" because

"They say that this god produces an egg from his mouth, from which a god is born whom they call Phtha . . . and the egg they interpret as the cosmos" (*PA* 360F). Egyptian zoological iconography is also explicable: "they consecrate the hawk to the sun, and make it their symbol of light and breath, because of its swift motion, and its soaring up on high, where the light is. And the hippopotamus represents the western sky, because of its swallowing up into itself the stars which traverse it" (*PA* 360F). Porphyry also interprets this zoological iconography symbolically in *On Abstinence* to buttress his argument that humans should refrain from consuming animals. The Egyptian sages recognized that animals as well as humans had souls and "for this reason they used every animal to represent the gods . . . for they have images which are human in form up to the neck, but with the face of a bird or a lion or of some other animal, or alternatively the head may be human and the rest of the body from other animals. In this way they show that . . . these creatures are in community with each other" (*Abst.* 4.9).

All of these interpretive strategies are intended to reveal universally authentic truths about theology and philosophy. None of these strategies, however, disavows more explicit, literal meanings. The precise relationship between these two levels of meaning is hierarchical; the more authentic meanings of statues, myths, or poems are primary, while the culturally contextual meanings are secondary. Porphyry never denies that the *Iliad* and *Odyssey* contain narratives that are potentially scandalous. Nor does he deny that Greek iconography is anthropomorphic or that animals are central to Egyptian cult. Although these texts, iconographies, and rituals are culturally specific, they yield universal truths if properly excavated. Having sifted his barbarian artifacts, Porphyry removes "universal" meanings from their "native" contexts. Fitting these "universal" elements into his ecumenical bricolage, he leaves behind everything specifically "Greek" or "Egyptian."

Recognizing that Porphyry posits this hierarchical relationship between higher and lower comprehensions of cultural expression helps make sense of his attitudes toward traditional religion. On the one hand, Porphyry never denies the validity of sacrificial religion; in fact, he offers explicit praise of tradition: "For this is the greatest fruit of piety, to honor the divine according to ancestral customs" (*Marc.* 18). On the other hand, an intelligent person, who is able to discern the different levels of signification in ritual acts, recognizes that "The consecrated altars of god do not harm, and if neglected, do not help" (*Marc.* 18). Porphyry draws an important distinction between the cult of the highest, Platonic god and the cults of all other, culturally specific deities. An intelligent person should offer sacrifice. Nevertheless, Porphyry qualifies this: "But we shall make, as is fitting, different sacrifices to different powers. To the god who rules over all . . . we shall offer nothing perceived by the senses, either by burning [i.e., traditional animal sacrifice] or in words [i.e., praying aloud]" (*Abst.* 2.34.2). The intellectual cult of the Platonic One may be found in different instantiations in different cultures. Nonetheless, the universal and therefore singular cult of the One is not to be confused with the plurality of culturally specific cults.

The difference that Porphyry posits between levels of meaning and forms of cult also correlates with a distinction among various peoples. Porphyry does not mince words about those who do not comprehend the deeper meanings within various cultural expressions: such people are ignorant and live in error (*Abst.* 4.9.10). Porphyry's estimation of Egyptian animal worship provides an excellent example of this differentiation between those who truly comprehend Egyptian religion and those who do not.

An ignorant person would not even suspect that they [the wise people among the Egyptians] have not been carried away by the general opinion which knows nothing, and do not themselves walk in the ways of stupidity, but that they have passed beyond ignorance of the multitude which everyone encounters first, and have found worthy of veneration that which to the multitude is worthless. (*Abst.* 4.9.10)

While Porphyry indicates that the more authentic meanings behind zoological iconography signify truths about the relationship between animals and humans, he denigrates a more literal reading of this iconography simultaneously. Here, too, one can see the power dynamic that Porphyry establishes through his readings of cultural artifacts. A true philosopher like Porphyry can see and understand things that the natives cannot. This knowledge grants Porphyry a privileged relationship with Egypt: by so thoroughly and accurately understanding the universal truths behind animal iconography, Porphyry can stake a claim to Egyptian tradition that the mass of ignorant Egyptian natives cannot properly claim as their own. Porphyry's readings of ethnic traditions help him establish mastery over the traditions of various peoples and, by extension, establish power and control over the peoples themselves.

Nowhere does Porphyry assert his rights to possession of local traditions more forcefully than in his *Letter to Anebo*. This treatise is not a letter at all, in fact, but a series of questions about the nature of the gods and their relationship to the human soul. Although the imagined addressee is an Egyptian priest, Anebo, in reality, the "letter" circulated among members of Porphyry's circle and other contemporary philosophers in his network. While Porphyry believed that there was great knowledge to be had from the traditions of Egypt, all of his questions are posed in the idiom of later Greco-Roman philosophy. Porphyry imagines that Anebo will answer in the same idiom. His letter did, in fact, receive a response, but not from an Egyptian priest. The philosopher Iamblichus offered a lengthy response in the form of his long treatise *On the Mysteries*, an account of the nature of the gods and the ways in which the human soul can progress toward the divine. It is significant that this epistolary exchange is between two Greeks, one writing to a fictional Egyptian, the other masquerading as an Egyptian. Porphyry and other Greco-Roman philosophers enjoyed such privilege over the barbarians that they could "pass" as Egyptian in order to work out Platonic metaphysics and theology.

If Porphyry's knowledge brought great privilege and authority, it also brought great responsibility; the authentic philosopher was also a guardian of the truth. Yet even though Porphyry and others looked abroad in their search for a universal philosophy, they did not consider philosophy to be a free-for-all. Wisdom could be found among many peoples, but "truth" was singular. Polemics were part and parcel of a philosopher's training: knowing the truth was not enough; one must be able to defend it as well. Dissension was an integral part of Porphyry's philosophical career; he wrote a polemical critique of Plotinus before he ever became his student.[63] His most famous polemics, however, were those he composed against the Christians. Setting Porphyry's anti-Christian texts in the context of his attitudes toward universalism and cultural difference will result in a more nuanced understanding of his antipathy toward Christianity.

The Christian Menace

AGAINST THE CHRISTIANS

Like so many of Porphyry's treatises, *Against the Christians* survives only in fragments. That so little is left of *Against the Christians* may be due to the issuance of imperial edicts, first by Constantine and later by Theodosius II and Valentinian III, ordering Porphyry's text destroyed.[64] Originally fifteen books, Porphyry's work is known today only from scattered *testimonia* and fragments preserved by early Christian authors, especially Eusebius, Jerome, and the late fourth-century apologist Macarius Magnes. The remains of *Against the Christians* were first collected and edited by Adolf von Harnack in 1916, and his remains the standard edition. Although the exact structure of the text is hard to determine, Harnack's division of the extant fragments into five categories is still a helpful outline of the treatise: 1) criticism of the character and the reliability of the evangelists and apostles; 2) criticism of the Old Testament (including a long fragment on the historicity of the book of Daniel); 3)

criticism of the crime and sentence of Jesus; 4) dogmatic criticisms; and
5) the contemporary church.[65]

Against the Christians was a focused assault on Christian texts and reading practices. Porphyry also deployed literary and textual criticism
against other opponents. In the *Life of Plotinus*, he offers an instructive
portrait of the important place of polemics in Plotinus's circle. Plotinus
did not hesitate to criticize and refute "Christians of many kinds" in his
lectures.[66] Plotinus also offered a textual refutation of gnostics in *Ennead*
II.9, which Porphyry would later title *Against the Gnostics*. Plotinus had focused his polemics on the general doctrines of his opponents, but Porphyry, ever the philologist and literary aesthete, attacks their *texts*.
Porphyry recounts that he and his fellow student Amelius each composed extensive refutations of gnostic texts. Amelius wrote forty books to
refute the book of Zostrianus, while Porphyry, for his part, wrote "numerous refutations of the book of Zoroaster."[67] His polemics were aimed
at "proving the book to be entirely spurious and recent, a fabrication of
those who upheld this heresy to make it seem that the doctrines which
they had chosen to acclaim were those of the ancient Zoroaster."[68] Porphyry's assault on the historicity and literary value of his opponents'
text, along with the aspersions he casts upon the moral fiber of its authors, is remarkably similar to the methods he uses in *Against the Christians*.

The extant fragments of *Against the Christians* reveal a critic who is
quite familiar with the texts of his enemies. In criticizing the gospel writers Porphyry concentrates on discrepancies in individual gospels and
among the gospel accounts. For example, he critiques both Mark and
Matthew for misquoting and conflating citations of the Hebrew Bible
(Harnack frr. 9, 10). He also points out the inconsistencies between the
birth narratives in Matthew and Luke (Harnack fr. 12). Moreover, Porphyry levels an attack against Paul, arguing that the disagreements Paul
reports in Galatians are evidence for both Paul's error and the factious-
ness of Christianity (Harnack fr. 21). Porphyry also chastises Christian
readings of the Hebrew Bible. Although only a few fragments of this portion of Porphyry's work survive, they reveal someone whose critical acumen rivals that of many modern biblical critics. Two of these fragments
concern the date of Moses (Harnack frr. 40, 41). The context of these
passages is difficult to determine, but they likely countered Christian
claims about the antiquity, and therefore primacy, of Moses. By far the
most incisive of Porphyry's critiques, however, concern the book of
Daniel. Porphyry argues very astutely that this prophetic book could not
have been written during the Babylonian captivity, as the Christians
claim, but rather is an example of *prophecy ex eventu* that dates to the time
of Antiochus IV Epiphanes (Harnack fr. 43A). Porphyry based his attack

on careful philological and historical analyses. He realized, for example, that some of the wordplay in the narrative of Susanna works only in Greek (Harnack fr. 43B). Moreover, while Christians interpreted the "four beasts" in Daniel's vision to four world empires (Babylonian, Persian, Macedonian, and Roman), Porphyry argues that they signify only three, for, according to Jerome, Porphyry "assigned the last two beasts to the single reign of the Macedonians, wishing the leopard to be understood as Alexander himself, but the beast different from all the other beasts as the four successors of Alexander" (Harnack fr. 43L).

Reading *Against the Christians* with an eye toward the imperial context in which Porphyry penned his polemics, however, reveals a text concerned as much with issues of power and identity as with matters of history and literary taste. We have already seen Porphyry use figurative reading strategies to take possession of Egyptian tradition while simultaneously positing a hierarchical difference between himself and ignorant Egyptian natives. The philosopher's attack on Christian literature and reading strategies is similar. First, Porphyry counters the Christian threat by eliminating any appeal to the writings of the New Testament. Egyptian, Chaldean, Indian, or Phoenician texts are ancient and therefore worthy to be investigated as potential sources for a universal philosophy. The writings of the evangelists and Paul, however, are new. The sages of Egypt and the Persian Magi were ancient philosophers who carefully veiled the truth so that it could be discovered by educated philosophers like Porphyry. The apostles and evangelists, on the other hand, were "poor country bumpkins (*rusticani et pauperes*)" who performed second-rate magic merely "for profit" (Harnack fr. 4). Similarly, wise barbarians like Philo of Byblos provide philosophers with reliable histories upon which to base their research, but the apostles are guilty of simplemindedness and extreme ignorance when it comes to history (Harnack fr. 6).

Porphyry goes on to castigate his Christian contemporaries for their misguided reading practices. First, Porphyry rejects any figurative interpretations of the New Testament for the same reasons he rejects the gnostic book of Zoroaster—texts that are recent fabrications do not merit figurative readings. Because "the evangelists were such vulgar people, not only in the way they lived, but also in their sacred writings," their texts simply cannot contain anything that is universally authentic (Harnack fr. 9). Christian exegesis of the Hebrew Bible is a different sort of problem for Porphyry. Porphyry had included the Hebrews among those peoples with a knowledge of the *via universalis* in *Philosophy from Oracles*. Indeed, Christians read the Hebrew Bible in much the same way that Porphyry read Egyptian, Chaldean, and Phoenician texts, as sources of universal truth. How could Porphyry criticize Christians for reading texts that he, too, believed contained "barbarian wisdom"?

This similarity lies at the heart of Porphyry's antipathy toward the Christians. Porphyry argued, simply, that Christians did not know how to read the Hebrew Bible properly.

Jerome and Augustine each preserve examples of Porphyry's attack on the Christian interpretation of the Hebrew Bible. In Porphyry's estimation, Christians attempted figurative readings of passages that had overtly objectionable meanings on a literal level. Jerome reports that Porphyry refused to accept a figurative reading of Hosea 1:2, in which God urges the prophet Hosea to marry a prostitute. While exegetes like Jerome could provide figurative exegeses for objectionable passages such as this, Porphyry argues that some texts are not worthy of a true philosopher's attention. Augustine records another Porphyrian objection to Christian exegesis. "What ought one to think of Jonah," the critic asks, "who is thought to have been in the belly of a whale for three days? It is ridiculous and unbelievable for him to have been swallowed with all his clothes and to have been inside the fish. But, if this is to be taken figuratively, then deign to explain it!" (Harnack fr. 46). Porphyry's opposition to Christian reading practices is especially clear in a passage preserved by Eusebius.

Some, being zealous to find a way to exculpate the wickedness of the Jewish writings rather than to simply abandon them, turned to interpretations that are inconsistent and inharmonious with what has been written, and they offer no defense of the foreign aspects of their work, but rather offer approval and praise of their own work. Bragging that the things said plainly by Moses are enigmas and conjuring them up as oracles full of hidden mysteries and enchanting critical abilities with obscurities, they offer their interpretations. (Harnack fr. 39 [= Eusebius, *HE* 6.19.4])

Not all literature should be read figuratively. Some texts, like the more "offensive" parts of the Hebrew Bible, have nothing to offer a philosopher, no matter how hard one may try to conceal the inadequacies of his or her critical abilities. In Porphyry's judgment, a philosopher should use barbarian texts only if exegesis will reveal ecumenical wisdom that can be separated from its "foreign" context. In the hands of Christian exegetes, the Hebrew Bible fails to yield any universal, authentic philosophical knowledge. Among Christians, the Hebrew Bible, like Egyptian animal worship, is simply barbaric.

As we have seen already, Porphyry's readings of various traditions are marked by a process of sifting the wheat of universal truth from the chaff of cultural specificity. Gillian Clark has noted the ambivalent character of Porphyry's attitudes toward cultural diversity: "Porphyry saw in religion both a common philosophical culture uniting all devotees of truth, and a Herodotean display of cultural diversity."[69] Cultural particularity was perfectly acceptable when interpreted correctly and packaged for the consumption of Greco-Roman philosophers. Culturally specific traditions, like Egyptian zoological iconography, or even classical Greek sacrifice, were also perfectly acceptable—provided that the uneducated masses that practiced such traditions made no universalizing claims of their own. The masses should know their place. It was quite unacceptable, however, for the barbarians to make universalizing claims of their own. Christians, who by their own admission claimed to possess a universal philosophy based on a set of barbarian texts from the very edges of the Greco-Roman world, were disrupting Porphyry's carefully constructed, hierarchical world.

Porphyry attacks Christians' rival universalizing claims explicitly in *Against the Christians.* "Why did a compassionate and merciful god," he asks, "allow all peoples, from the time of Adam to Moses, and from Moses to the advent of Christ, to perish through ignorance of the laws and regulations of God?" (Harnack fr. 82). Porphyry impugns Christianity on the grounds that it is not a universal philosophy at all but something novel. A tradition that is newly revealed (or "invented") cannot offer a *via universalis*: "If Christ claims to be the way of salvation . . . what did the people of the world do before Christ?" (Harnack fr. 81). Christianity, moreover, bases its claims on a set of Jewish texts with little or no currency outside of Judaea: "For Britain . . . and the people of Scotland, and all barbarian peoples throughout the entire circuit of the Ocean are ignorant of Moses and the prophets" (Harnack fr. 82). Christians cannot offer a truly universal philosophy because they originated at a specific time in a specific cultural context.

Why did the one who is called "savior" hide himself for so many centuries? But do not let them claim that the human race was saved by the ancient Jewish law, for the law of the Jews appeared only after a long while, and was in force over only a small region of Syria; later it spread across the borders of Italy, after Caesar or during his reign. What then, happened to the souls of the Romans and Latins, which were deprived of the advent of Christ until the time of the Caesars? (Harnack fr. 81)

Unlike Porphyry's own philosophy, which he claims transcends cultural particularity, Christianity belongs to a specific time and place: first-century Judaea, an insignificant region of Syria. Moreover, Porphyry's temporal location of Christianity in the time of the Caesars is an effective retorsion of Christian arguments for the synchrony of Christ's advent and the beginning of the Principate. Porphyry slyly reminds Christians that they are mere provincials subject to Roman hegemony.

Christian assertions of philosophical and soteriological universalism were a direct affront to Porphyry's own ecumenical endeavors. But the

Christian threat ran even deeper. Christians claimed that their faith rendered all cultural and ethnic specificity irrelevant. Always the skilled philologist, Porphyry responded by returning to primary sources. Porphyry attacks this radical challenge to traditional identity by going to its source: Paul's declaration that he "has become everything to everyone in order to surely save some."[70] Porphyry castigates Paul: "How good, or rather how stupid such sayings are! . . . If he was without the Law to those without the Law, as he himself says, and was a Jew to the Jews, and did likewise for all peoples, then he was really a captive of many-faced wickedness and a stranger and foreigner to freedom" (Harnack fr. 27 [= Apocr. 3.30.3]).[71] For further proof of Paul's mendacity, Porphyry looks to Acts. How could Paul declared to the tribune that he was "a Jew born in Tarsus" when later he would declare his Roman citizenship to the same tribune? (Harnack fr. 28 [= Apocr. 3.31.1]). Porphyry's criticism is far from airtight. Paul's declaration of Roman citizenship was in no legal sense a denial of his Jewish identity. Porphyry would surely have known this, if not from a basic knowledge of Roman citizenship before 212 C.E. then from reading the conclusion of the narrative in Acts, when Paul's citizenship is acknowledged by the tribune and later by the governor Festus as he grants Paul a trial in Rome before the emperor.[72] But Porphyry's concern is not with the finer points of Roman enfranchisement; rather, he intends to draw attention to Paul's protean ability to pass as Roman, Jew, or anything else depending on the circumstance. Paul's slippage from Jew to Roman, along with his geographic migration (even though under armed guard) from Caesarea to Rome, may have reminded Porphyry of his own move from Tyre to Rome. Even the geography is similar; Caesarea is just south of Tyre on the Phoenician coast. But where Porphyry erased his provincial origins to become a scion of Rome's metropolitan culture, Paul passed as a Roman only to infiltrate the imperial capital with his barbaric doctrines. For Porphyry, Paul's identity play does not signal a transcendence of provincialism but a dangerous form of miscegenation.

He who says, "I am a Jew," and "I am a Roman," is neither, because he inclines both ways. . . . Wearing a mask of deception, besieging the thoughts of the soul with ambivalence, and enslaving the simple-minded with magical arts he beguiles plain reality and robs the truth . . . .If Paul, playing his roles, is a Jew, then a Roman, someone without the Law, then a Greek, undermined each one when he desired each thing that is foreign and hostile to the other and, taking away the distinct identity of each with flattery, rendered each impotent. (Harnack fr. 28 [= Apocr. 3.31.4])

Paul's mimicry of Roman and Greek threatens renders traditional categories of identity sterile, reducing imperial geography to absurdity. Por-

phyry responds by turning Paul into a joke: "Such acrobatics! These theatrics adorn such laughable scenes!" (Harnack fr. 27 [= *Apocr.* 3.30.2]).
Using theatrical metaphors, Porphyry turns Paul into a fool whose sub-
version is really nothing more than a comic fiction.

To his chagrin, Porphyry saw contemporary Christians engaged in the
same hucksterism as Paul. Eusebius quotes a fascinating fragment of
Against the Christians in which Porphyry denounces the Christian exegete
Origen.[73] Porphyry claims that Origen was a student of Ammonius Saccas, who had also been Plotinus's teacher, and even claims to have met
Origen.[74] Porphyry acknowledges that Origen was highly conversant in
the same philosophical traditions that influenced his own philosophy:

"He [Origen] was always consorting with Plato, and he was conversant in the
writings of Numenius and Cronius, Apollophanes and Longinus and Moderatus,
Nicomachus and the distinguished men among the Pythagoreans; he used the
book of Chaeremon the Stoic and Cornutus, from whom he learned figurative
interpretation, as employed in the Greek mysteries, but he applied it to the Jewish writings" (Harnack fr. 39 [= *HE* 6.19.8]).

It is not Origen's interest in barbarian wisdom, in itself, that is objectionable. What Porphyry found insufferable was Origen's use of Porphyry's
own "Greek" interpretive strategies to replace Greek philosophy with a
"foreign" tradition. Porphyry assures his readers (and himself) that Origen was nothing more than a fool whose research into barbarian wisdom
lacked the necessary critical acumen. Porphyry confronts the problem of
Christian identity by drawing a contrast between Ammonius and Origen.

For Ammonius was a Christian, brought up in Christian doctrine by his parents,
yet, when he began to think and study philosophy, he immediately changed his
way of life conformably to the laws; but Origen, a Greek educated in Greek
learning, drove headlong towards barbarian recklessness; . . . *and while his manner of life was Christian (kata men ton bion Christianōs zōn)* and contrary to the law,
in his opinions about material things and the Deity *he played the Greek, and introduced Greek ideas into foreign fables (Hellēnizōn te kai ta Hellēnōn tois othneiois hupoballomenos muthois).* (Harnack fr. 39 [= Eusebius *HE* 6.19.5–9; tr. Oulton 59])

In Porphyry's account, both Ammonius and Origen straddle the supposedly fixed gulf between Greek and barbarian. In Porphyry's staunchly
polarized world, however, such hybridity threatened the carefully constructed, hierarchical dichotomy between Greeks and others. Ammonius resolved this identity crisis by opting for the better (Greek) option.
It is not accidental that Ammonius's transformation from Christian to
Greek parallels Porphyry's own abandonment of the provinces for
Athens and Rome. Origen, on the other hand, is merely playacting.
Though Origen and other Christians may hide their barbarism behind

the mask of Greek language and reading practices, Porphyry can see through this disguise.

PHILOSOPHY FROM ORACLES

In addition to the biblical and historical criticism of *Against the Christians*, Porphyry also attacked Christianity in his *Philosophy from Oracles*.[75] This book was esoteric; Porphyry warns his readers "not to make these things public, or cast them before the uninitiated" (*PO* 304F). The work was a compilation of oracles glossed by Porphyry's own exegeses and commentary in which he aimed to present a universal philosophy—or, as Porphyry puts it, "our present collection will contain a record of many philosophical doctrines according as the gods through oracles declared the truth to be" (*PO* 303F). In addition to discussing the nature of different classes of divine beings, Porphyry also comments on the forms of cult each should receive.[76] Porphyry's anti-Christian polemics come from the third book, as part of his discussion of heroes and holy men. Augustine preserves three of these oracles, two from Apollo and one from Hecate. Porphyry quotes and glosses these oracles to argue two points: 1) the Jews, like all peoples of good repute, worship that highest god, while Christians mistakenly worship a crucified man; 2) Jesus is a wise, but entirely human, sage. We will see shortly that this oblique attack in *Philosophy from Oracles* was at least as damaging as the philological and historical arguments of *Against the Christians*.

The anti-Christian oracles in *Philosophy from Oracles* are of a piece with the attack on Christian identity presented in *Against the Christians*. The oracles fall into two general categories: comparisons of Christianity with Judaism, and oracles concerning Christian worship of Jesus. The first of these anti-Christian oracles is preserved in the nineteenth book of Augustine's *City of God*. Porphyry reports an oracle of Apollo in response to a pagan man who wishes to know how he should deal with a Christian wife. It is futile to make an apostate of a wife who has turned to Christianity, Apollo prophesizes: "Let her go as she pleases, persisting in her vain delusions, singing in lamentation for a god who died in delusions, who was condemned by right-thinking judges, and killed in hideous fashion by the worst of deaths" (*PO* 343F [= *City of God* 19.23, tr. Bettenson 884–85]).[77] This oracle repeats a stock anti-Christian polemic. Pagan critics of Christianity often denigrated what they saw as the worship of a crucified criminal. But, according to Augustine, Porphyry followed this oracle with a comparison of Christian and Jewish worship. First, Porphyry asserts that the oracle indicated not only the "incurability" of the Christians but also "that the Jews uphold god more than the Christians" (*PO* 343F [= *City of God* 19.23, tr.

Bettenson 885]). Porphyry, it will be remembered, ranked the "Hebrews" among the peoples who had "learned the ways of the blessed" (*PO* 323F). Augustine claims that Porphyry "denigrate[s] Christ in preferring the Jews to the Christians" (*City of God* 19.23, tr. Bettenson 885). Augustine then quotes again from Porphyry's compilation, this time citing an oracle that locates elements of universal philosophy within Judaism: "Truly, at god, the begetter and king before all, the heavens and earth and sea and the hidden places of the underworld tremble and the *daimones* themselves shudder; their law is the father whom the holy Hebrews honor" (*PO* 344F [= *City of God* 19.23, 30–37]).[78] It appears that Porphyry wished to draw a distinction between the Jews, whose traditions contain elements of universal validity, and the Christians, who, in his estimation, worship a mere human. The Jews might be provincials, but the Christians were even worse, for Jewish traditions, at least, evinced some aspects of universal truth. Judaism was perfectly acceptable to Porphyry because it was the ancestral tradition of a distinct people. This sort of locatedness assured that Porphyry could easily "map" Jews into his ecumenical philosophy. Straddling the border between Greek and barbarian, however, Christians disavowed any cultural or geographic rootedness.

If some of Porphyry's oracles of Apollo reiterate standard criticisms of Christianity, Porphyry's second anti-Christian oracle is something quite different among anti-Christian polemics. "That which we are about to say may appear to be paradoxical to some," Porphyry boasts. "For the gods declared Christ to be most pious and to have become immortal, and they remember him with praise" (*PO* 345F [= *DE* 3.7.1]).[79] While "Apollo" had uttered a standard denigration of Jesus, "Hecate" appears to praise Christ as a wise man whose soul has become immortal after death (*PO* 345 [= *City of God* 19.23]). "Hecate's" opinion of Christ is quite different from that of other anti-Christian polemicists, most of whom preferred to disparage Christ in comparison with pagan holy men. Hierocles, for example, focused his *Lover of Truth* around a negative comparison of Jesus with Apollonius of Tyana. Some have argued that Porphyry uses the Hecatean oracle to establish a kind of entente with the Christians, that is, on the condition that they recognize their error in deifying Jesus and recognize that he, in fact, preached the one true religious philosophy shared by all people of good common sense.[80]

Though the oracle is preserved by both Eusebius and Augustine, Eusebius edits the oracle so as to obscure Porphyry's polemical intentions.[81] Eusebius softens the oracle by excising lines that are much more critical of Christ and Christianity. Augustine, however, preserves these important lines.

Now that soul of which we speak gave a fatal gift to other souls, . . . that fatal gift
is entanglement in error. That is why they [Christians] were hated by the gods,
because, not being fated to know god or to receive gifts from the gods, they were
given by this man the fatal gift of entanglement in error. For all that, he himself
was devout, and, like other devout men, passed into heaven. And so you shall not
slander him, but pity the insanity of men. From him comes for them a ready
peril of headlong disaster. (*PO* 345aF [= *City of God* 19.23, tr. Bettenson 886])

In its reluctant acceptance of Jesus as a blessed soul at the same time that
it impugns Christians and Christianity, this was an insidiously effective
polemic. Instead of rejecting Jesus out of hand, "Hecate" usurps the very
object of Christian worship. By assimilating the founder of Christianity
within his universal philosophy, Porphyry makes Jesus innocuous. Christ
becomes one more entry in Porphyry's encyclopedic collection of foreign sages, another example of the liberation of the soul—a path open
to all who can understand the philosophy to be gained from oracles (or
all those who can understand Porphyry's *Philosophy from Oracles*).

It was bad enough that Christians placed their hope of salvation in a
mere human being; it was worse that the Christians claimed this man as
the sole and universal source of salvation. In reality, Porphyry argues,
Jesus was as mortal as any other human being and, like other souls,
Jesus' soul was rewarded with immortality only because it had achieved
wisdom.[82] This misperception about Jesus' true identity was symptomatic
of a confusion Porphyry thought endemic to Christianity, and Porphyry
intended to put Christians back in their place. The Hecatean oracle
helped Porphyry disabuse Christians of their misplaced universal claims
about Jesus. Similarly, if Christians denied that they were reducible to
the hierarchical differences upon which Porphyry's authority and privilege as a Greek philosopher in the Roman Empire depended, if they
claimed to be neither Jew nor Greek, Porphyry took it upon himself to
remind them that they were really nothing other than a group of Greeks
and barbarians confused about their own identities.

Porphyry and the Persecutors

Diocletian was a staunch conservative and his religious policies were
aimed at renewing the state through the revival of "tradition."[83] As he lay
dying in 311, Galerius, now the senior member of the Tetrarchy after
Diocletian's retirement, ordered an end to persecution. His edict confirms that concern for tradition was one of the principal reasons for beginning the persecution eight years earlier: Christians had "abandoned
the way of life of their own fathers."[84] The notion that the safety and success of the empire depended on the traditional worship of the traditional gods was shared by emperors and intellectuals. An anonymous

panegyricist captured this sentiment in an oration in praise of Diocletian's co-Augustus, Maximian: "You have earned, best of Emperors, that
felicity of yours by your piety."[85] Porphyry, however, was a philosopher
and man of letters whose polemics are focused on philological and historical critiques of Christian texts. If Porphyry had anything in common
with the persecution hawks in Diocletian's court, some argue, it was only
this shared distaste for the Christian neglect of tradition.[86] In his *Letter
to Marcella*, Porphyry echoes Maximian's panegyricist: "This is the greatest fruit of piety—to honor the divine according to ancestral custom"
(*Marc.* 18). According to Eusebius, moreover, Porphyry's rationale for
the forced repression of Christianity stresses the relationship between
the social good and traditional piety: "How are those who reject the ancestral gods, *on account of whom every people and every city has endured*, not
in all ways impious and atheists?" (Harnack fr. 1 [= *PE* 1.2.2]). Porphyry,
of course, had his own rationale for supporting tradition. While the sim-
pleminded might cultivate piety to avoid the wrath of neglected gods,
Porphyry thought that traditional religion was of beneficial to the wor-
shiper.[87] By adhering to tradition, the human soul progresses in virtue
and becomes more like God;[88] this is the sort of cultivation that makes
cities and peoples endure.

While there was not a point-for-point correlation between the "official" grounds for persecution and any given individual's reasons for supporting the persecution, we must be wary of the tendency to distinguish
between "pure" academic or religious discourses and overtly political
discourse of imperial edicts. To do so ignores the political reality in
which an intellectual like Porphyry operated.[89] That political reality was
empire. Porphyry and the emperors perceived the Christians as a threat
to imperial order, an order that depended on stark contrasts between
ruler and ruled, metropolis and province. Christians, so Greco-Roman
at the same time that they seemed so entirely barbaric, transgressed
these boundaries.

In repealing the edicts of persecution, Galerius reveals the anxiety behind their original promulgation: Christians throw the hierarchical geography of Roman imperialism into disarray by "assembling in different
places people of different nationalities."[90] If Christians claimed to be
neither Jew nor Greek, provincial officials would put them back in their
place. As Lactantius saw it, officials such as Hierocles persecuted the
Christians "as though he had subjugated a barbarian people" (*DI*
5.11.15). It seems that at least some officials continued to struggle with
Christian identity after the Edict of Toleration in 311. Eusebius, moreover, preserves a letter of the prefect Sabinus to his governors describing
the new policy: "If a Christian is found taking part in the rites of his own
people (*tou idiou ethnous tēn thrēskeian metiōn*) release him from danger

and harassment" (*HE* 9.1.5). Sabinus seems to describe a return to the tried and true Roman practice of allowing provincials to practice ancestral rites as long as they do not interfere with Roman authority. Sabinus's use of the category *ethnos* represents another attempt to relocate Christians as merely one more governable *ethnos* among the many peoples under imperial rule.

In Porphyry's estimation, Christians had done more than reject tradition; they had abandoned their ancestral gods in favor of barbaric traditions.

> To what punishments may fugitives from ancestral customs, who have become zealots for the foreign mythologies of the Jews which are slandered by all (*othneiōn kai para pasi diabeblēmenōn Ioudaikōn muthologēmatōn genomenoi zēlōtai*), not be subjected? How is it not extremely depraved and reckless to exchange native traditions (*to metathesthai . . . tōn oikeiōn*) casually and take up, with unreasonable and unreflective faith, those of the impious enemies of all peoples? (Harnack fr. 1 [= *PE* 1.2.3])

Porphyry has chosen his words carefully. The antonyms *othneios* and *oikeios* stress the differences between the traditions of one's home city and those of outsiders. Not a common word, *othneios* connotes an otherness that is hostile and dangerous as well as "foreign." Porphyry had ascribed the same sort of foreignness to Paul's masquerade and Origen's misguided interpretive practices.[91] Porphyry can tolerate a Jewish Paul or a Greek Origen, but he cannot abide either's attempts to pass as something else. Porphyry's vocabulary betrays his anxiety over Christian transgressions of identity at the same time that it reasserts a difference between center and periphery. As Christians "cut some sort of new directionless desert path, keeping neither to the ways of the Greeks or the Jews" (Harnack fr. 1), Porphyry welcomed the use of imperial force as a means to reestablish imperial geography in the face of its desertification at the hands of Christians.

Chapter 3

Vera Religio and *Falsae Religiones:* Lactantius's *Divine Institutes*

Porphyry's erudite and spirited anti-Christian polemics did not go unanswered. According to Jerome, Methodius of Olympus countered with a work, *Against Porphyry,* in the early fourth century.[1] Eusebius of Caesarea, for his part, wrote a twenty-five-book response *Against Porphyry,* now lost,[2] while his apologetic masterwork, the *Preparation/Demonstration of the Gospel,* was also written largely as a response to Porphyry. Other Grecophone Christians wrote against Porphyry later in the fourth century, including Apollinaris of Laodicea, who penned thirty books *Against Porphyry* around 370.[3] Unfortunately, none of these Greek works (with the exception of Eusebius's *Preparation/Demonstration of the Gospel*) has survived.

One of the earliest respondents to Porphyry, however, was not a Greek-speaking Christian but Lactantius, a Latin rhetorician in Diocletian's court. The source material for a thorough biography of Lactantius is, unfortunately, very limited.[4] Lactantius was born somewhere in Africa in the mid–third century. Nothing is known of his youth except that he studied rhetoric with Arnobius of Sicca.[5] Arnobius wrote his own apology, *Against the Nations,* in the early fourth century, though neither apologist seems aware of the other's efforts.[6] Lactantius eventually followed in his teacher's footsteps, becoming a successful teacher of rhetoric, and surpassed him, gaining a teaching position in Diocletian's court at the turn of the fourth century.[7] Lactantius's life after the outbreak of the Great Persecution is difficult to reconstruct. Some scholars suggest that he spent several years in North Africa, while others posit a stay in Italy.[8] Lactantius fared better after the persecution, when he was named tutor to Constantine's son Crispus at Trier.[9] He may have later returned to his position in Nicomedia, this time as part of Constantine's court.[10] In addition to the *Divine Institutes,* Lactantius wrote *Symposium, Travels* (an account of his journey from Africa to Nicomedia written in verse), the *Grammarian,* the two-book work *To Asclepiades,* and four books of letters to Probus. All of these works are lost, but Lactantius's well-known *On Deaths of the Persecutors,* the treatise *On the Anger of God,* the treatise *On the*

Workmanship of God, as well as a poem, *On the Phoenix,* survive along with the *Divine Institutes.*[11]

Lactantius knew that he stood upon the shoulders of earlier giants of Latin apologetic.[12] He acknowledges Minucius Felix, Tertullian, and Cyprian as his predecessors, but his estimation of their work is mixed. Minucius Felix and Tertullian receive praise as skilled defenders of the faith. Lactantius, however, wishes they had provided more lucid and thorough accounts of Christian doctrine itself, rather than simply responding to pagan attacks. Tertullian is criticized for rhetoric that "is overly simple and less ornate, and leaves much obscure" (*DI* 5.1.23). Lactantius thinks Cyprian a better rhetorician and theologian than either Minucius Felix or Tertullian (*DI* 5.1.24, 5.4.3). But Cyprian erred, Lactantius claims, by trying to convince pagans of Christian doctrine by arguing from scriptures that pagans refuse to accept. What Cyprian should have done (and Lactantius aims to do) is "reveal the principles of light to them little by little, lest it blind them by casting all its light at once" (*DI* 5.4.4–5).

The *Divine Institutes* marks a watershed in Latin apologetic literature. Not only does Lactantius respond to pagan critics, he also provides the first attempt at a systematic presentation of Christian theology in Latin patristic literature. In length the *Divine Institutes* equals Origen's *Against Celsus* of a half century earlier. In more than one respect the *Divine Institutes* is the forerunner of Augustine's massive apologetic project in the *City of God.* Like Augustine, Lactantius writes for an educated audience familiar with all that is best in arts and letters and combines a skillful critique of traditional religion and philosophy with an apologetic presentation of central Christian doctrines. Books 1 and 2 constitute an attack on traditional religion, or *falsae religiones,* while Book 3 offers a critique of philosophy, or *falsa sapientia.* In Books 4 through 7 Lactantius shifts his emphasis from polemic to an elaboration of Christian doctrines for his pagan audience. Book 4 offers a defense of Christianity as the one true religion and philosophy. Book 5 reacts directly to the events surrounding the persecution. Book 6 concerns "true worship" and is an apologetic presentation of the Christian life. In the final, seventh book, Lactantius presents his eschatological vision: the final judgment will take place after a cosmic battle between good and evil that will ensue following the dissolution of the Roman Empire.

Lactantius likely began writing the *Institutes* immediately before or soon after leaving Diocletian's court when the persecution began.[13] In a rare autobiographical section in the *Institutes,* Lactantius indicates that he was prompted to write by Diocletian's anti-Christian measures, the first of which were going into effect as Lactantius arrived in Nicomedia to take up his appointment as court rhetorician.[14] The persecution itself, however, was not the only reason Lactantius wrote in defense of Christianity. He was also reacting directly to the anti-Christian polemicists he had heard in Nicomedia in the lead-up to the persecution. He wrote, he asserts, not to refute "those who harassed us in earlier times" but to counter two contemporary anti-Christian polemicists who presented their views at the court.[15] Though neither polemicist is named in the *Divine Institutes*, Lactantius identifies one in *On the Deaths of the Persecutors* as Sossianus Hierocles, governor of Bithynia.[16] As we saw in the previous chapter, the other polemicist was likely Porphyry.[17] The *Divine Institutes* constitute Lactantius's reaction to what was, in his view, a dangerous combination of philosophical critique and imperial rhetoric. Lactantius felt compelled to respond to Porphyry because his attack on Christianity left him all too aware of the need to reestablish Christian identity against Porphyry's withering assault.

Lactantius countered Porphyry and the persecutors with a two-pronged counteroffensive. First, he imitated Porphyry's own uses of oracular sources to argue that Christianity, not Porphyry's philosophical paganism, is the one true religion and philosophy. Second, by constructing a universal history of religions, Lactantius crafted a new geography in which Christianity enjoyed privilege of place over and against the error-ridden religions of the world's many peoples, or *gentes*. Lactantius wrote the *Divine Institutes* in response to persecution, but he lived to see Constantine's rise to power and his victories over Maxentius and Licinius. Lactantius produced a new edition of the *Institutes* during this period and dedicated it to the new emperor. At the end of this chapter I will explore the implications and timbre Lactantius's apologetics had in the Constantinian empire.

Divina Testimonia and the Cross-Cultural Consensus

Although he rarely quotes biblical passages in the *Institutes*, Lactantius takes scripture as the benchmark of genuine wisdom and the "font from which the sacred religion originates" (*DI* 4.5.9).[18] He declares that the Bible contains in and of itself a sufficient validation of Christianity. At the same time, however, he bases his apologetic arguments on extrascriptural sources, *divina testimonia*, as he terms them, including Greek and Roman poets and philosophers, the Sibylline Oracles, Apollo, and the Hermetic Corpus.[19] His reasons for preferring these non-Christian sources over biblical texts are twofold. First, he argues that his pagan audience is too innocent of the truth to handle a full helping of Christianity; instead, like young children they must be fed the truth slowly and gently, using familiar tastes (*DI* 5.4.6). His second, more important reason for appealing to nonbiblical texts is the hostility of pagan polemicists to Christian scripture. Lactantius imagines he is writing for an audience of educated pagans who would reject biblical proof texts. According to Lactantius, pagan critics reject the divine inspiration of the Hebrew prophets and mock them as hucksters out for monetary gain.[20] These polemicists (and again, Lactantius almost certainly has Porphyry and his *Philosophy from Oracles* in mind) also deploy oracular texts to refute Christianity. Thus, Lactantius will craft his rebuttal from the very texts that are used against the Christians (*DI* 1.4.2, 5, 1.5.1–2). Using the texts of one's enemies as defensive weapons was a common form of retorsion argument in Christian apologetics,[21] but Lactantius's selection of sources also has a more specific purpose.

Chapter 2 considered the ways in which Porphyry constructed a universal philosophy based on cross-cultural readings. Jewish, Persian, Phoenician, and Egyptian wisdom, if read properly, all contributed to Porphyry's universal philosophy. Lactantius mimics the very same tactic as his opponents, quoting Greek, Roman, and "barbarian" sources to prove Christianity the universal philosophy. At the same time that Lactantius deploys his consensus theory to challenge Porphyry, however, he depends on interpretive strategies that were themselves based on similarly polarized and hierarchical conceptions of difference.

To introduce his consensus theory, Lactantius draws on the Stoic concept of *communis opinio* as it is articulated in the second book of Cicero's *On the Nature of the Gods*. Lactantius states that he will demonstrate cross-cultural consensus concerning two fundamental propositions: 1) that the world is governed by divine providence, and 2) that the world is governed by one god, not many.[22] To prove the first proposition, Lactantius appeals again to Cicero's *On the Nature of the Gods*, in which the Stoic character Balbus argues that all who look at the world and observe its ordered motion and beauty cannot but acknowledge that a greater intelligence lies behind its design. Central to Balbus's argument is an appeal to "the testimony of peoples (*populorum*) and races (*gentium*) who do not differ in this one topic" (*DI* 1.2.4–5, paraphrasing *On the Nature of the Gods* 2.73–153). Lactantius develops his consensus theory further as he pursues the second proposition (that the world is governed by one god rather than many), basing his argument on a comparison of Hebrew prophets, pagan poets and philosophers, and oracular testimony.

Lactantius begins with the testimony of Greek and Roman poets. He quotes Orpheus as a witness to the highest God. Lactantius's evaluation of Orpheus is worth quoting at length, for it reveals the interpretive methods he applies to nonbiblical sources.

The tradition is that he sailed among the Argonauts with the Tyndarii and Hercules. He calls the true and great God "first-born" (*prōtogonon*), because nothing was created before him, but all things were created by him. He also names him "the appearer" (*phanēta*), because when nothing existed, he appeared first and existed in infinity. Because it was impossible to comprehend his origin and nature, he said he was born from the broad air: *prōtogonos Phaethōn perimēkeos ēeros huios*. He had no better way to describe it. He says that he is the parent of all the gods, for whose purpose he set up the heaven and looked-out for his children, so that they could have a little place of their own in common: *ektisen athanatois domon aphthiton* (he set up an eternal home for the immortals). Thus, led by nature and reason, he understood that he was greatest in power, maker of heaven and earth. (*DI* 1.5.4–6)

Like the Stoics and Platonists discussed in Chapter 1, Lactantius uses two criteria to evaluate the authenticity of his sources. The first criterion is antiquity: the older a source is, the more reliable it is as a source of universal philosophy. Here, Orpheus has a particularly exalted status as "oldest of the poets and equal in age to the gods themselves" (*DI* 1.5.4). The second criterion is the extent to which a source measures up to Christian doctrine. Lactantius concedes the deficiencies in Orpheus's theological language; nevertheless, he can make fruitful use of Orphic material for his consensus by reading the text figuratively. Just as Porphyry had used figurative interpretation to offer Platonic readings of Egyptian and Persian myths, so too does Lactantius employ figurative interpretations to reveal the universal (that is, Christian) doctrines coded in non-Christian texts. Thus, the Christian God is not literally "first-born," as Orpheus seems to say, but without beginning in time. Similarly, God did not "appear" out of nothing, but was eternally existent.

This does not mean that all non-Christian texts merit figurative interpretation. The Bible, or Hebrew "oracles" as Lactantius terms them, are the gauge by which all other texts are evaluated for inclusion in the cross-cultural consensus. Homer and Hesiod, for instance, are rejected by Lactantius because they do not measure up: "Homer was able to give us nothing that might relate to the truth, for he wrote about human rather than divine matters. Hesiod was able . . . but nonetheless offered nothing, because he begins not with God the creator, but with chaos" (*DI* 1.5.8). In contrast, Virgil and Ovid do convey universal doctrines. Virgil "was not far from the truth" when he "named the highest god 'mind' (*mentem*) and spirit (*spiritum*)" (*DI* 1.5.11, quoting *Aeneid* 6.724–27 and *Georgics* 4.221–24).[23] Ovid, moreover, acknowledges God as creator of the world, "whom he calls 'framer of the world' and 'maker of things'" (*DI* 1.5.13, quoting *Metamorphoses* 1.57, 79). These non-Christian writers express the truth "not because they have an understanding of the truth, but because truth itself is so powerful that no-one is so blind that he does not see divine clarity when it pours into his eyes" (*DI* 1.5.2).[24] If they had only heeded their natural inclinations, the poets "would have comprehended the same doctrine we follow and would have held on to truth" (*DI* 1.5.14).

After the poets, Lactantius turns to the testimonies of philosophers. While the poets had expressed pieces of truth inadvertently by virtue of natural inclinations, pagan philosophers "are thought to have studiously investigated the truth" (*DI* 1.5.15). The same nonliteral reading strategy used for the poets helps Lactantius construct agreement among philosophers. Thus he argues that Thales, Pythagoras, Anaxagoras, Antisthenes, Cleanthes, and Anaximenes concur in positing a singular providence in the cosmos, thus "whether you call it 'nature,' 'aether,' 'reason,' 'mind,' 'the necessity of fate,' or 'divine law,' it is the same as that which is called 'God' by us." Plato, in particular, bolsters Lactantius's consensus theory because he "simply and openly maintains that God is 'monarch,' not naming him 'aether,' 'reason,' or 'nature,' but 'God,' as he is" (*DI* 1.5.23). Cicero joins Plato (and hence Christians) in calling God the governor of the universe and acknowledging God as incomprehensible and as creator of the world. Like the poets, the philosophers had the natural ability to understand truth, but because they were immured in the worship of many gods, "habitual belief in depraved opinions dragged them down" (*DI* 1.5.24–28).

Lactantius considers oracles even more reliable than the poets and philosophers. Like the poets, oracles are reliable by virtue of their antiquity, but in contrast to poets, who write "vain fictions," and philosophers, who "can err," oracles are revelations direct from the gods (*DI* 1.6.1, 4). Four sources figure in Lactantius's consensus theory: the Hermetica, the oracles of Apollo, the Sibylline Oracles, and the prophetic dreams of Hystaspes, purportedly an ancient Median king.

HERMETICA

In Lactantius's day, Hermes, who had been equated with the Egyptian god Thoth since the time of the Ptolemies, was considered a divine sage from the deep recesses of Egypt's past. Hermetic wisdom was thought to be a source of the universal philosophy. The Platonist Iamblichus of Chalcis considered Hermes a source of Plato's doctrines. Hermes Trismegistos's wisdom was believed to have been transmitted in esoteric texts. Several of these circulated in a collection known today as the *Corpus Hermeticum*. Lactantius quotes from or alludes to several texts included in the *Corpus Hermeticum* as well as the *Asclepius*, a Hermetic text preserved in Latin but which Lactantius knew in its Greek original. It is not certain how Lactantius came by his knowledge of the Hermetica. His teacher, Arnobius, appears to have been steeped in Neopythagorean and Neoplatonic theologies in which Hermetic texts played a role.[25]

This suggests, at a minimum, that Lactantius would have had access to some Hermetic texts while in Africa, and one might speculate that he was influenced by his teacher. Cicero's list of various "Mercuries," the *interpretatio Romana* of Hermes, in *On the Nature of the Gods* provides Lactantius with additional historical and ethnographic information about the "historical Hermes" (*DI* 1.6.1–4).[26] Lactantius hedges somewhat over whether to classify Hermetic texts as oracles or as the work of a wise, but human, sage. He settles on a status somewhere in between. Hermetic texts are reliable, "like a divine testimony," because they meet the criteria of antiquity and because their author, unlike the poets and philosophers, "has been translated from humanity to the gods."

Lactantius points to the similarity of Hermetic and Christian doctrines. Hermes, he contends, concurs with the Christian doctrines of God's oneness and namelessness; Lactantius quotes directly from the Greek of the Hermetic Corpus: "God is one, and the One needs no name, for he is nameless" (*ho de theos heis, ho de heis onomatos ou prosdeetai, esti gar ho ōn anōnumos*) (*DI* 1.6.4). In support of the doctrine of God's uncreatedness and eternity, Lactantius notes that Hermes calls God "fatherless (*apatora*) because he has no origin anywhere" (*DI* 1.7.2).[27] Hermetic material also supports Lactantius's Christology. Drawing on a passage that is extant in the Latin *Asclepius* but which he knows in Greek by the title *Teleios Logos*, Lactantius cites Hermes as testifying to the nature of Christ's sonship.

> The lord and creator of all, whom we are accustomed to call God, made a second god, visible and sensible (by "sensible" I do not mean "passable," whether or not he "senses" I will talk about later, but rather I mean that he made him visible and able to be sensed); and since he created him first and alone, and one, and he appeared beautiful and full of every good, he loved and adored him as his only offspring. (*DI* 4.6.4)[28]

Hermes also confirms Christ's role in creation, designating him "God's craftsman (*dēmiourgon tou theou*)" and "Word (*Logos*)" (*DI* 4.6.9, 4.9.3).[29]

In Book 2, Lactantius uses Hermes to corroborate his anthropology. Arguing for the immortality of the soul later in the *Institutes*, Lactantius quotes another lengthy Hermetic passage: "The same [power] made a single human nature out of two different natures, the mortal and the immortal, making this creature both immortal and mortal and placing it in the middle between the divine immortal nature and the mortal and changeable nature, in order that human nature would see everything and wonder at it" (*DI* 7.13.3).[30] A trademark of Lactantius's anthropology is the emphasis he places on humans' upright stance. Humans walk upright, according to Lactantius, so as to naturally gaze upon the heavens and, in doing so, achieve a natural knowledge of God through the providential design of nature. Trismegistos confirms Lactantius's anthropology, calling the gaze of upright humans *theoptia* (*DI* 7.9.11, cf. *Corp. Herm.* vol. 4, fr.15).[31] For Lactantius, in fact, the entire human form contains an image of God's rationality and providence in microcosm. Hermes, in Lactantius's estimation, confirms this, saying "not only that humans were created in the image of God, but [he] also attempted to explain how subtly he formed the parts of the human body, since there is no part of it that is not praiseworthy for its usefulness as well as its beauty" (*DI* 2.10.14). Lactantius may have in mind *Corpus Hermeticum* 1.12, in which "Mind, the father of all," begets a son "having the image of the father."[32] If this is the case, Lactantius has engaged in some interesting exegesis. In its original context, the "son" created in the image of Mind is not a human being but the "second god" or demiurge, creator of the visible universe. By paraphrasing the Hermetic passage rather than quoting it directly, Lactantius has transformed a cosmological passage into a statement about anthropology.

Lactantius's creative interpretations are also evident when he deploys Hermetic passages in support of a soul/body dichotomy. He quotes a Hermetic passage describing human bodies as composites, made up of "something of fire, something of air, something of water, something of earth, without being fully fire, air, water, or earth" (*DI* 2.12.4–5).[33] The way in which Lactantius uses this Hermetic quotation offers a good example of his interpretive approach to non-Christian sources. In its original context, the passage asserts that the "composite" nature of humans is an impediment to direct knowledge of the divine.[34] Lactantius, on the other hand, deploys the passage in order to stress the "dual" nature of human beings, who are composed of material bodies and an immaterial, immortal soul.[35]

Finally, the Hermetic Corpus provides fuel for Lactantius's demonology. According to Lactantius, Hermes testifies that humanity is harassed by a cohort of demons led by the devil, the "leader of demons," and warns that "demons are the enemies and harassers of humans," calling them "wicked angels" (*DI* 2.14.6, 2.15.8).[36] Even so, Hermes announces that the true worship of God is an effective deterrent to demons. Lactantius quotes at length in Greek: "The one defense is piety, for neither bad demons nor fate has any power over the pious. God protects the pious person from all evil, for the one and only goodness among humans is piety" (*DI* 2.15.6).[37]

Lactantius treats Hermes as a genuine source of universal wisdom. The high esteem in which he held the ancient Egyptian sage may be inferred from Augustine, who, upon reading Lactantius's account of Hermes, felt the need to temper what he saw as an overly keen interest in pagan literature.[38] Hermes represented a source of ancient wisdom that anchored and validated Lactantius's universalizing pretensions as well as those of contemporary Platonists. Consequently, it has appeared to some that Lactantius uses the Hermetica to plant "common ground" between Christians and other philosophically minded intellectuals, especially Platonists and Neopythagoreans wont to use Hermetic texts in their theologies.[39] But Lactantius's interpretive methods are more hostile than such a characterization might imply. He removes Hermes' words from their original contexts and his exegesis often changes the text in important ways in order to make Hermes agree with Christian doctrines. Lactantius read many of the same texts that Porphyry and other philosophers did, but his bookshelves must have been arranged quite differently. Platonists like Porphyry's younger contemporary Iamblichus of Chalcis portrayed ancient sages like Hermes as a source of Plato's wisdom, but their exegeses of "foreign" sources are always focused through a Platonic lens.[40] By reading Hermes with the Bible, rather than with Plato, Lactantius shifts the polarity of the intellectual landscape.

Apollo

It may be surprising to find Apollo included in Lactantius's consensus theory in the first place, given the prominent role the god's oracles played in both the outbreak of the persecution as well as in Porphyry's anti-Christian polemics. According to Lactantius, Diocletian remained reticent to institute a full persecution even after the anti-Christian conferences of 302–3. He decided to resolve the issue by consulting Apollo "and sent a *haruspex* to Apollo at Miletus, [who] responded as an enemy of the divine religion" (*Mort.* 11.7). The importance of Apollo's oracles in the persecution is corroborated by Constantine in an imperial letter of 324. This letter will receive more detailed attention in Chapter 4. For the moment, however, it is important to note that Constantine reports that the persecution was precipitated by an anti-Christian interpretation of the Pythian Apollo's declaration that "the just people of the earth were an impediment to accurate prophecy and that it was on account of this that false oracles came from the tripods."[41] At several points in the *Divine Institutes*, moreover, Lactantius blames anti-Christian sentiment on Apollo's demonic influence. For example, he mocks the second anti-Christian polemicist (Hierocles) in Book 5 by implicating Apollo: perhaps, he gibes, "some Apollo pronounced [the anti-Christian charges] to him in a dream" (*DI* 5.3.5).

Apollo's oracles could be interpreted for anti-Christian purposes, but this necessity for interpretation also made the oracles fruitful tools in the hands of a Christian apologist. Lactantius imitates the persecutors' own uses of Apollo, quoting his prophecies in ways that support his cross-cultural consensus theory while simultaneously inverting the meanings of anti-Christian oracles. He thinks that this will be a particularly effective response to pagan critics, for "Apollo is esteemed more divine and prophetic than all others" (*DI* 1.7.1). Apollo participates in the monotheistic consensus.

When the question of who or what is in all respects God was put to him, he responded in twenty-one verses, of which these are the first: "Self-born, untaught, motherless, impassible, impossible to name with words, abiding in fire, this is God, and we are messengers [or: "angels"], small portions of God." (*DI* 1.7.1)

Apollo cannot be referring to Jupiter, Lactantius argues, because Jupiter has a mother and a name. Rather, Apollo agrees with Hermes, who, like Apollo, calls God "motherless" but adds "fatherless" as well (*DI* 1.7.2). Lactantius interprets these oracles in the same way he does other pagan sources: by trying to uncover the universal doctrines veiled in Apollo's enigmatic utterances. Thus, Hermes and Apollo use apophatic language "because his origin is not in another, for it is impossible for he who himself generated everything to have been generated from another" (*DI* 1.7.2–3).

Lactantius quotes two additional oracles of Apollo that probably also appeared in Porphyry's *Philosophy from Oracles*. The first is found in Lactantius's *On the Anger of God*, a short treatise that, like the *Institutes*, deploys a number of non-Christian texts. As proof that even demons like Apollo "tremble . . . at his command," Lactantius quotes Apollo's testimony to the power of the God of the Hebrew Bible.

The Milesian Apollo, when consulted about the religion of the Jews, put this in his response [Lactantius quotes the Greek]: "God, the king and creator of all, at whom even the earth, heaven, and sea tremble, whom the recesses of Tartarus and the demons fear."[42]

Augustine preserves the same oracle in Latin and explicitly ascribes it to Porphyry's *Philosophy from Oracles*.[43] According to Augustine, Porphyry had given an anti-Christian spin to this oracle; the Jews possess some wisdom, for they place the one highest god at the center of their religion, in contrast to the Christians, who mistakenly worship a crucified man. Lactantius, however, simply "lifts" this Apolline oracle and spins it as Apollo's own (unwilling) admission of his subservience to and fear of the one true (Christian) God.

Augustine cites a second Apolline oracle from Porphyry's collection that impugns Jesus as a crucified criminal, unworthy of worship: "a god rightly condemned by the decisions of judges, killed by a humiliating death, bound in iron."[44] Lactantius quotes a very close Greek parallel to this oracle in Book 4 of the *Institutes*. After quoting passages from Isaiah, Jeremiah, and the Psalms in support of Jesus' dual nature as God and human, Lactantius adds an oracle of Apollo.

> On this very matter, when Apollo of Miletus was consulted as to whether he was a god or a man, replied in this way. "He was mortal with respect to the flesh, wise with marvelous deeds, but condemned by Chaldean judges and nailed to trees, he met a bitter end" (*DI* 4.13.11).

This oracle, in fact, seems to blend polemical notions of two Porphyrian oracles quoted by Augustine: the Apolline oracle just discussed as well as the Hecatean oracle, discussed in the previous chapter, in which Hecate describes Jesus as a wise, but human, sage.[45] In fact, Lactantius inverts the polemical intent of this oracle to attack Apollo and Porphyrian polemics based on it. Again, despite his best attempts at deception, Apollo unwittingly testifies to the truth of Christianity: "What he said in the first verse is true, but he has subtly deceived the person asking the question, who does not know the mystery of the truth, for he seems to deny that he [Jesus] is God. But when he confesses that he was 'mortal according to the flesh,' just as we say, it follows that he was God according to the spirit, as we affirm" (*DI* 4.13.12). Lactantius also deflects Apollo's (and Porphyry's) denigration of Jesus as a mere "wise man"; if Jesus' wisdom is agreed upon, what business do critics have accusing Christians of being ignorant? Likewise, why do critics impugn Jesus' miracles, when Apollo himself allows that Jesus performed miracles (*DI* 4.13.15)?

Although Apollo contributes to Lactantius's cross-cultural consensus, his prophecies have a very different status from the Hermetica. Hermes consciously testified to the one true God, even if he had been misunderstood by most interpreters through the centuries. Apollo, in contrast, confesses the truth about God unwittingly as a result of his own hubris.[46] In praising himself, Apollo in fact evidences the inferiority of his own status within the supernatural order. He adverts to his true, demonic identity and his future fate at the hands of God.

> In other oracles he confessed that he was a demon. When he was asked how he wanted to be supplicated he responded: "All wise, completely-taught, many-faceted *daimōn*, listen." And again, when asked for a prayer to Sminthian Apollo, he answered, and began with this verse: "cosmic harmony, lightbearer, all-wise daimon." What remains, then, except that by the words of his own confession he subjects himself to the eternal punishment of the true God? Thus in another oracle he said, "The *daimones* who roam around the earth and sea are overpowered by God's untiring whip. . . . Although he hopes to honor himself and to place himself in heaven, he nevertheless has confessed, as is the case, in what manner one ought to name those who eternally serve at God's side. (*DI* 1.7.9–11)

Hermes was an ancient sage who later achieved divine status, but Apollo is an inimical demon out to dupe humanity into error.

Most interpreters (again Lactantius has Porphyry and his *Philosophy from Oracles* in mind) do not understand the difference between demons, like Apollo and the other traditional deities, and angels, the true servants of the one God. They have been duped by Apollo's oracles. Lactantius chastises these misguided interpreters: "Let them know by what name [their gods] ought to be called, lest they offend the true God, whose name they apply when they attribute it to many gods. Let them believe Apollo himself, who by his own oracle, when he denies primacy to Jupiter, so too he denies the name 'god' to the other gods. The third verse shows that the true ministers of God ought not to be called 'gods,' but 'angels'" (*DI* 1.7.7–8). The accusation that traditionalists confuse lesser divinities with the highest God would have been a particularly effective rejoinder to a philosopher like Porphyry, who claimed to differentiate clearly between the highest God and lesser divinities.[47] Apollo's oracles, the centerpiece of Porphyry's own *Philosophy from Oracles*, have become fodder for Lactantius's cross-cultural consensus.

Sibylline Oracles and Hystaspes the Median Sage

Lactantius quotes from the Sibylline Oracles more than any other *divina testimonia*. The Oracles held an important place in the history of Roman religion; according to a tradition preserved by Dionysius of Halicarnassus, the mythical king Tarquin acquired this collection of prophetic texts in the late seventh or early sixth century B.C.E.[48] These prophetic texts (or, more accurately, their interpretation) played an important role as vehicles for innovation in Roman religion, particularly with respect to the introduction of new cults. The disruptive, revolutionary aspect to the *Oracles* made them useful material for Jewish and, later, Christian apologetic and apocalyptic, including the composition of collections of so-called Jewish and Christian Sibylline Oracles.[49] Thus, despite Lactantius's claims for their antiquity, his Sibylline Oracles were rather late compositions and probably come from a collection made in the third century C.E.; many of the oracles betray clear Christian or Jewish influence.[50] Lactantius, in fact, was aware that critics impugned these oracles as forgeries. As far as Lactantius is concerned, however, these texts are genuine divine revelations. He anticipates the accusation that his Sibylline collection is merely prophecy *ex eventu*, much as Porphyry critiqued the authenticity of the book of Daniel. In response, Lactantius appeals to Cicero and Varro, noting that their discussions of Sibylline Oracles antedate Christ's advent (*DI* 4.14.26–27).

Just as he mined Cicero for ethnographic information about Hermes,

Lactantius appeals to Varro's *On Divine Matters* as offering historical and geographic contexts for the Sibyls. According to Varro, there were ten Sibyls.

the first was Persian . . . the second Libyan . . . the third was from Delphi . . . the fourth was from Cimmeria in Italy . . . the fifth was Erythraean . . . the sixth was from Samos   the seventh was Cumaean, named Amalthea or by others, Herophile or Demophile . . . the eighth was born in Trojan territory in the Hellespont, in the town of Marmessus near the city of Gergithium . . . the ninth was a Phrygian who prophesied in Ancyra . . . the tenth was a Tiburtine by the name of Albunea. (*DI* 1.6.8–12)

Though there are many Sibyls, their prophecies "are believed to be from one, because all are inscribed with the name 'Sibylline'" (*DI* 1.6.13). As a group, therefore, the Sibyls contribute to Lactantius's broad consensus through their geographic ubiquity. Because the Sibyls are not particular to any specific people they represent a single, coherent authority.

According to Lactantius, the theology of the Sibylline Oracles concurs with that of the Hebrew prophets, ancient poets, philosophers, and Hermes Trismegistos. On one particularly fruitful sortie to Erythraea, Lactantius recounts, the Romans obtained a number of Sibylline testimonies to the one true God (*DI* 1.6.14–15).[51] Lactantius quotes directly from the Greek: "God is one, who alone rules, supermajestic and uncreated" (*DI* 1.6.15). He glosses the verse with his own commentary coupled with a second Sibylline verse, again in Greek: "This is the one highest God, who made the heaven and adorned it with stars, 'God is single, one, and highest of all, he who has made heaven, the sun, stars, and moon, and the fruitbearing earth and wave-swollen waters of the sea'" (*DI* 1.6.15). The Erythraean Sibyl also testifies that worship of the highest God is exclusive: "Worship him who is the only truly existent, the governor of the cosmos, who alone exists for ever and ever" (*DI* 1.6.16). Finally, he cites the testimony of another Sibyl: "I am the one God and there is no other God" (*DI* 1.6.16).

Lactantius also combines Sibylline Oracles with Hermetic texts and passages from the Hebrew Bible to construct a wide Christological consensus. The Sibyl supports Jesus' title "Son of God," while a second confirms his role as demiurge: "the Sibyl calls him 'advisor' because God instructed him in so much wisdom and virtue that he used his counsel and hands in the creation of the world" (*DI* 4.6.5, 9). This oracle, along with the phrase "demiurge of God" taken from the Hermetic *Asclepius*, is placed alongside Proverbs 8:22–31 ("God made me the beginning of his ways in his work, before the ages he founded me . . . (etc.)" (*DI* 4.6.6–9).

Lactantius's Sibylline quotations also serve as an apologetic response to accusations that Christianity was based on uncritical "blind faith." In his anti-Christian pamphlet *The Lover of Truth*, Hierocles, the other polemicist who prompted Lactantius's apologetics, had "attacked Jesus' miracles" and argued that Christians "have believed him to be a god based on meager fictions" (*DI* 5.3.7, 5.3.16). Lactantius corrects Hierocles, noting that Christians do not believe in Jesus' divinity simply because he performed miracles "but because we have seen everything predicted to us by the prophecy of the prophets fulfilled in him" (*DI* 5.3.18). Lactantius deploys a set of Sibylline quotations that corroborate the gospel narratives. Jesus healed with his word, not by sleight of hand, just as the Sibyl predicted: "Doing all by his word and healing every illness" (*DI* 4.15.9). The prophet Isaiah predicted that Jesus would heal the blind, deaf, lame, and mute (Is. 35:3–6), and the Sibyl prophesied the same thing in Greek: "There will be a resurrection of the dead, and the lame will run fast and the deaf will hear and the blind will see, and those who cannot speak will speak" (*DI* 4.15.13–15). He also juxtaposes Sibylline verses with the "suffering servant" passages in Isaiah 53:1–6; the Sibyl states, "He is pitiable, without honor and unsightly, so that he may give hope to the pitiable" (*DI* 4.16.15–17). Likewise, the prophet Micah "announced that he would give a new law" (Mic. 4:2), and the Sibyl also testifies to Jesus' abrogation of the ancient Jewish Law: "When all these things I say are completed, then the whole law is undone in him" (*DI* 4.17.3–4). The Sibyl also agrees with Isaiah and David in predicting Christ's passion. It will be useful to quote this passage at length, as it more clearly shows the way that Lactantius interweaves Sibylline and biblical prophecies.

David, in Psalm 34 says: "They gathered their whips against me and did not know me . . . they put me on trial and derided me, they gnashed their teeth at me." The Sibyl showed that the same thing would come to be [Lactantius quotes again in Greek]: "Later, he will come into lawless and unbelieving hands. They will give lashings to God with unclean hands and with polluted mouths they will spit poison. They will simply give his clean back to whips." Isaiah spoke similarly about his keeping silent until death: "He was led like a sheep to the slaughter and like a lamb without a voice among shearers he did not open his mouth." And the Sibyl says [again in Greek]: "Though buffeted he will be silent, lest someone know who the Word is or whence he came, in order that he may speak with the dead and wear his crown of thorns." About the food and drink they gave before they fixed him [to the cross], David in Psalm 68 says: "They gave me gall as food and in my thirst they gave me vinegar as drink." The same Sibyl again says that this will come to be [again in Greek]: "They put gall in my food and vinegar in my drink; they will reveal this inhospitable table." And another Sibyl impugns the land of Judaea with these verses [again in Greek]: "Your meanness did not see that your God was playing with mortal thoughts, but crowned him with a crown of thorns and mixed frightful gall." But this prediction that the Jews would lay hands on their god and kill him surpasses even the testimonies of the prophets! (*DI* 4.18.14–21)

Lactantius virtually inundates his readers with proof texts, blurring distinctions between biblical and Sibylline prophecies and between Greek and Latin. The Psalms, which Lactantius gives in Latin, serve almost as translations of the Sibylline material, which he quotes in Greek. At the same time, the Greek oracles grant the biblical material a sense of legitimacy beyond the immediate context within the Hebrew Bible. The Sibylline Oracles are not mere parallels with the Hebrew prophets but genuine testimonies of the true religion in their own right.

Lactantius posits the same relationship between the New Testament and the Sibylline Oracles. Summarizing the miracle of the loaves and fishes (Mark 8:5; Matt. 14:16), Lactantius quotes the Sibyl: "From five loaves of bread and fish of the sea he will feed five thousand people in the desert and taking the leftovers he will fill twelve baskets for the hope of the peoples" (*DI* 4.15.18). For Lactantius, the relationship between the New Testament and the Sibylline Oracles is the same as, or nearly the same as, that between the Hebrew prophets and the New Testament, for both preceded the events of Jesus' life and accurately predicted them. For instance, Lactantius remarks that some critics of Christianity may disbelieve the "holy texts (*litterae sanctae* [i.e., the New Testament])" when they describe Jesus' ability to calm storms and walk on water, but "what about the fact that the Sibyls taught this earlier in their songs?" (*DI* 4.15.23–24).

Lactantius makes several suggestions as to how the Sibyls managed to prophesy accurately. He describes the Sibyl as a conduit for the voice of God and writes that "Visions were offered before their eyes by the divine spirit and they saw these things with their own eyes just as if they had been completed already" (*DI* 1.6.16, 7.24.9). Yet, if the Sibylline prophecies were accurate and enjoyed currency in the centuries before Christ's advent, why had their prophecies gone unrecognized? Lactantius anticipates this critique by arguing that previous generations lacked the critical acumen to interpret the Oracles properly, leading many to consider the prophetesses mad (*DI* 4.15.28). Lactantius's own interpretive approach to the oracles is identical to the reasoning behind his interpretation of biblical prophecies. To a native Latin speaker like Lactantius, the Hebrew Bible could seem an odd collection of strange, Jewish texts, much as the Sibylline Oracles could appear to be a bizarre collection of Greek mumblings. But this cloud of misunderstanding has been lifted for those living after Christ. Just as the Hebrew prophets, "though they had been read for more than fifteen-hundred years, were nevertheless impossible to understand until after Christ interpreted them by his word and deeds," so too are the Sibylline Oracles intelligible only after Christ's advent (*DI* 4.15.30–31). Lactantius situates himself in an era in which there has been a sea change in the hermeneutic landscape.

Thanks to the advent of Christ, linguistic barriers have been eliminated to reveal the universal doctrines contained in otherwise obscure, exotic texts.

The Sibyllines also figure prominently in Lactantius's eschatology. The apologist believed that the final millennium before the end of all time would begin after six thousand years, corresponding to the six days of creation in Genesis (*DI* 7.14.6–11).[52] Drawing on "those who have written about chronology, gathering together their material from sacred literature and from various histories," Lactantius concludes that "the expectation of all of them seems to be that [the last millennium will begin] in no more than two-hundred years" (*DI* 7.25.5).[53] Lactantius's eschatology is a complex mix of Christian apocalyptic traditions, including Revelation, and other, non-Christian apocalyptic traditions. As he puts it, the "earthly prophets" (*saeculariae prophetae*)—that is, the Sibyls, biblical prophets, and other human vehicles of God's revelation—agree with "heavenly prophets" (*caelestibus*)—that is, Hermes, Apollo, and other divine and demonic testimonies—about the events of the final millennium (*DI* 7.14.16). The millennium will begin with global disorder and the fall of Rome (*DI* 7.15.11).

The Sibylline Oracles were an ancient part of Roman religion; one of the "colleges" of Roman religious officials was concerned solely with interpreting the Sibylline books.[54] Despite their antiquity and their status as a venerable fixture in Roman religion, the Sibylline books were also disturbingly foreign. They were written in a strange language (Greek), and when consulted in times of crisis, the interpretation of the Sibylline verses could open the door to the introduction of new, foreign cults, like those of Asclepius and Magna Mater, into the city.[55] In a world in which cult and territory were inextricably linked, the Sibyllines offered a potent site in which to challenge the imperial landscape. As literature written from the margins, apocalyptic was a way to challenge imperial power. Lactantius draws on a number of Sibylline passages that threaten the dissolution of the empire. According to Lactantius, the *Oracles* predict that "Rome will be annihilated . . . because it remained hostile to [God's] name and as an enemy of justice massacred the people who were disciples of the truth" (*DI* 7.15.18). The passage Lactantius quotes comes from *Sibylline Oracle* 8, a lengthy oracle redolent with anti-Roman sentiment. Lactantius quotes another verse from the same oracle that promises freedom from "the yoke of slavery that lies upon our necks" while in another verse, which Lactantius does not quote directly but which undoubtedly informs his eschatological vision of Rome's demise, the Sibyl threatens Rome: "No longer will Syrian, Greek, or foreigner, or any other nation place their neck under your yoke of slavery. . . . You will be a triumph-spectacle to the world and a reproach of all" (*DI* 7.18.8).[56]

The end-times, in other words, will be ushered in with an inversion of that most visible and theatrical demonstration of Roman imperialism—the triumphal procession. The Romans, who once paraded captives from exotic lands, will be humiliated as they are subjected to the gaze of their former subjects.

Christopher Frilingos has shown how the viewing of such spectacles served as sites in which imperial subjectivities were simultaneously constructed and contested. In early Christian apocalyptic literature, these theatrics are fetishized. At once revolting and seductive, participating in the "spectacles of empire" offers subjects neither a univocal demonstration of imperial power nor a secure site in which to challenge it.[57] Frilingos's observations help elucidate the ambivalence of Lactantius's apocalyptic vision, which for all of its anti-Roman and anti-imperial sentiment reiterates the asymmetries of power that it seeks to challenge.[58] Mimicry, while disruptive of imperial discourse, is limited as a means of resistance precisely insofar as it is always a partial representation of that discourse.[59] The post-imperial world of the eschaton is no isometric paradise. In the Sibyllines and in the prophecy of Hystaspes the polarity of Roman power has simply been reversed—"The name of Rome . . . will be lifted from the earth, and imperial power will return to Asia, and East will again be master and West servant" (*DI* 7.15.11). Lactantius also cites the apocalyptic dreams of Hystaspes, who, like Orpheus and Hermes, is reliable because of his antiquity; according to Lactantius he was an ancient Median king who antedated the foundation of Troy (*DI* 7.15.19). The end of the Roman Empire, however, does not entail the eradication of difference. The world will end with an ultimate distinction. According to Hystaspes, "The pious and faithful will be separated from the guilty . . . Jupiter [whom Lactantius claims Hystaspes has mistaken for the true God] will look down on the earth and will hear the voices of humanity and he will extinguish the impious" (*DI* 7.18.2). God once freed his people from bondage by humiliating the Egyptians; "now, however, the people of God are a congregation drawn from all languages and dwelling among all peoples (*gentes*)," and God can free his people and establish his kingdom only by imitating Rome's conquests: "all nations (*nationes*), the whole world (*orbem totum*) that is, must be beaten by heavenly blows in order to liberate the people . . . who worship God" (*DI* 7.15.5). The coming Kingdom of God is not written on a blank slate but inscribed upon empire's palimpsest.

Lactantius believed that he had discovered the universal philosophy in the sacred texts of the Hebrew Bible. But it is really the consensus among the traditions of disparate peoples that proves the truth of Christianity to Lactantius. This leaves one to wonder whether Lactantius owed his own conversion to a similar demonstration of the "consensus theory." He does not quote *divina testimonia* as a mere demonstration of erudition for his educated pagan audience, even though he self-consciously strove to impress his audience with his rhetoric and knowledge.[60] Rather, Lactantius takes it for granted that philosophically inclined pagans will be looking for just this sort of cross-cultural proof.

Porphyry took the initiative in deploying comparative religion and philosophy to attack the Christians, and the consensus that Lactantius offers in the *Divine Institutes* is a deliberate defense of Christianity using similar methods. Lactantius's consensus theory is based on the same assumptions as Porphyry's ecumenical philosophy: no single *ethnos* monopolizes truth and authentic philosophy has no borders. But Lactantius's interpretive practices, like Porphyry's, were politically interested. Like Porphyry, Lactantius's consensus theory established asymmetrical relationships between a (biblical/Christian) center and a periphery populated by a variety of peoples with their respective *falsae religiones*. The prophecies of Hystaspes, Hermetica, and the Sibylline Oracles, therefore, are not valuable as Egyptian, Persian, or Median, but only to the extent that they can bear a Christian interpretation. Lactantius, like Porphyry, subordinates the "foreign" contexts of wisdom to the universal philosophy he constructs from his consensus theory. For Lactantius, foreign texts like the Hermetica and Sibylline Oracles are of no value as such; rather, they are authentic only when extracted from their native contexts, glossed with biblical parallels, and run through the mill of Lactantius's interpretive practices. This sort of textual archaeology offered Lactantius a means to reshape the intellectual landscape and establish his place within it. Lactantius's hermeneutics do not erase or ameliorate cultural and ethnic distinctions; rather, his reading strategies articulate distinctions along different, though no less stark, lines.

Lactantius's History of Religion and Religions

Lactantius's reading strategies were integrally related to his understanding of history.[61] The apologist understood all of history in terms of a grand "history of religions" in which the natural, ancient cult of the one true God stands in stark contrast to the kaleidoscopic variety of the erroneous religions of the world's diverse peoples. The basic outline of Lactantius's history of true religion and false religions is a familiar one— like other apologists, Lactantius improvises on the Pauline theodicy of Romans 1, positing an original and authentic Ur-monotheism that was subsequently lost and obscured in the course of human history. For Lactantius, the same comparative project that reveals cross-cultural consensus of Roman, Greek, Egyptian, Median, and Hebrew prophets simultaneously schematizes a historical distinction between this original, pure monotheism, or *vera religio*, and the plurality of ancestral cults, or *falsae religiones*. The former is ancient and timeless, while the latter are contrived, the product of cultural and ethnic difference.

Lactantius begins elaborating his history of religions in the middle of Book 1, as he levels a series of Euhemeristic attacks on traditional gods and goddesses (*DI* 1.11.33–34).[02] The deification of great rulers and culture heroes, Lactantius asserts, is not natural but cultural development. The distinction between the states of nature and civilization is Stoic. Quoting Balbus, the Stoic character in Cicero's *On the nature of the Gods*, Lactantius positions traditional cults as the negative by-product of human civilization: "Human life and the *habit of civilization* allowed men of excellence and who had provided benefits to the community to be elevated into heaven" (*DI* 1.15.5, quoting *On the Nature of the Gods* 2.24.62, emphasis added). As an explanation for the origins of the gods, Euhemerism also applies cross-culturally; as Lactantius puts it, Euhemerism explains why "the Romans treated their Caesars as holy and so did the Moors their kings" (*DI* 1.15.14).

Since traditional religions began after humans had begun to form distinct communities with their own particular rulers and culture heroes, all false religions are ineluctably "ethnic," though some cults subsequently gained wider currency while others remained local.

> Thus, little by little, religions began to exist, during the time when those who first knew them began to instruct their children and grandchildren in the rite, and later all their posterity, and in the end these great kings were celebrated in all the provinces (*provinciis*) thanks to the renown of their names. Individually though, specific peoples (*singuli populi*) in tribes (*gentis*) and cities (*urbis*) worshiped their own founders, either men distinguished for their fortitude or women remarkable for their chastity: thus Egypt worships Isis, the Mauri Juba, Macedonians Cabirus, Punic people Urania, Latins Faunus, Sabines Sancum, Romans Quirinus, and in the very same way the Athenians worship Minerva, Samos Juno, Paphos Venus, Lemnos Vulcan, Naxos Liber, Delos Apollo. *Thus, throughout different peoples and regions (populos atque regiones) various rites are instituted*, when people desired to give thanks to their rulers and are unable to find other honors to confer on the dead. (*DI* 1.15.7–10, emphasis added)

Lactantius thus posits a crucial link between ethnogenesis and the origins of religion. Indeed, for Lactantius, to be a distinct people is to develop a new religion, and vice versa. Religious differentiation and ethnic differentiation are indistinguishable. Consequently, to write a history of religions is simultaneously to conduct an ethnographic survey. Lactantius had an ethnological vocabulary ready at hand in the language of Roman territory and administration. Thus, the language of imperial geography and administration (*provincia, populum, gens, urbs*) provides the lineaments for Lactantius's account of the origins of religions. To do the history of religion, then, Lactantius finds himself rehearsing imperial geography.

Yet at the same time that Lactantius deploys the vocabulary of imperial geography and bureaucracy, he also challenges Roman hegemony. Though the Romans often argued that it was their special piety that gave them control over such a vast empire and had helped them conquer so many peoples,[63] Lactantius implicates Romans in the same processes of error and deception. He quotes Aeneas's prayer to his father, Anchises ("Let us ask for winds, and, once the city is founded, may he allow that these rites be performed yearly in a temple dedicated to him"), as proof that Roman religion is based on the same fallacious deifications (*DI* 1.15.12, quoting *Aeneid* 5.59–60). By singing the praises of heroes and kings, the poets are complicit in the perpetuation of false religions. Finally, Lactantius implicates the persecutors themselves in this history of religious error and deception: "Those who now praise bad kings with deceitful panegyrics do the very same thing" (*DI* 1.15.13).

Though all peoples are guilty of deifying their culture heroes, Lactantius lays special blame at the doorstep of the Greeks, who, he claims, subsequently handed the custom on to other peoples. He deploys Rome's foundational myths to construct a genealogy that situates the origins of Roman religion in Greece. He follows traditional accounts by making Numa the founder of Roman religion and draws on Varro and another late Republican scholar, Gavius Bassus, to trace the foundations of Roman religion back further to Faunus of Latium (*DI* 1.22.1, 9). Finally, Lactantius connects the origins of Roman error to Greece by arguing that Faunus was influenced by Orpheus, who "first brought the rites of father Liber to Greece" (*DI* 1.22.15). This anti-Greek polemic is an example of classic Greek-bashing on the part of Roman intellectuals. Lactantius may well be imitating the type of anti-Greek slur practiced by Cicero, who, for all his interest in Greek philosophical and intellectual traditions, lampoons Greek intellectuals in the prefaces to his philosophical treatises. Such insults served to distance Cicero from charges of an overfondness for things Greek. Lactantius, in fact, praises Cicero for privileging Roman statecraft over Greek intellectualism (*DI* 3.16.2). Lactantius's own anti-Greek sentiment may be a similar attempt to lay claim to Romanness despite his clear interest in Greek philosophy and other "foreign" traditions. At the same time, Lactantius's placement of the Greeks as key players in the history of error can be read as an oblique attack on Porphyry and other Hellenists who backed the persecution. Lactantius may wish to imply that Diocletian has allowed Roman statesmanship to be polluted by Greek intellectualism.

Toward the end of Book 1, Lactantius extends his historical research further into the recesses of history to uncover the ultimate origins of Euhemeristic worship. Lactantius knows of two contradictory accounts, both of which confirm the centrality of the Greeks in the development of false religions. According to the first-century Alexandrian exegete Didymus, false worship began with "Milisseus king of the Cretans," while Ennius reports that Euhemeristic worship began with Jupiter, originally a Greek king, who established his own cult "in many places" (*DI* 1.22.19–21). Lactantius goes on to date the precise origins of Euhemeristic worship: "in his history Thallus says that Belus, whom the Babylonians worship, is found to have been 322 years older than the Trojan War, and that Belus was a contemporary of Saturn, and that both grew up in the same time-period" (*DI* 1.22.27, 1.23.2).[64] Lactantius places the fall of Troy 1,470 years before his own time and dates Saturn, father of (the human) Jupiter, about 1,800 years prior to his own time. Thus Lactantius undercuts any pagan claims to possess an ancient tradition: "those people are not glorified by the antiquity of their sacred rites, the origin and causes and dates of which are so easy to discern" (*DI* 1.23.5). Though traditional religions are ancient, they are only relatively so.

Having shown in Book 1 that "the various and different cults founded throughout the whole world were based on a stupid human consensus," Lactantius announces that Book 2 "will make plain the very source of the errors and will explain all the reasons by which humans were deceived" (*DI* 2.1.1). To do this, Lactantius has to return to the very beginning of time itself. In practice, this means offering an apologetic synopsis of the first chapters of Genesis. After recounting God's creation of his Son and the world, Lactantius comes to the Flood and Noah, who "though all other people were corrupt, survived alone as an example of justice" to become the progenitor of all contemporary humans (*DI* 2.13.1). Error began, however, not long after the Flood, when Noah's son Ham was disinherited after seeing his father naked. The inheritance that Ham lost was none other than the Ur-monotheism God had planned to preserve in Noah. Ham's descendants formed a new people, the Canaanites. According to Lactantius, "this was the first people (*prima gens*) that was ignorant of God, because their leader and founder, cursed by his father, did not accept the cult of the true God from his father, passing on an ignorance of divinity to his descendants"; thus, all other *gentes* derived from this original ignorance (*DI* 2.13.7–8).

Next, the Egyptians inaugurated a new form of error when they began to worship the stars and planets. Worship of the elements and natural phenomena spread: "The other peoples, who were spread throughout the world, admired the elements, the sky, the sun, the earth, and the sea, worshiping them without any images or temples and celebrating these sacrifices in the open" (*DI* 2.13.12). Lactantius had not mentioned this stage of nature worship in his Euhemeristic account of religions in Book 1, but this interim period does make sense within his conception of religious development. Humans were created as upright beings in order to observe the heavens and in so doing to *recognize the creator god.* Thus the Egyptian recognition of order in the cosmos represents an improvement over the pure ignorance of Ham and his descendants, yet it is abortive, nothing more than a perversion of humanity's natural ability to recognize the creator behind creation. Nature worship was merely an interim stage on the way toward full-blown Euhemeristic worship. While the Egyptians were the first to recognize the order in nature, they soon replaced the worship of the stars with animal iconography. Other peoples went on to deify human beings and make "temples and statues for their most powerful kings and began to worship them with victims and incense" (*DI* 2.13.11–12).

This period of *human* history from Noah to the institution of Euhemeristic cults, Lactantius explains in the subsequent chapter, is integrally related to the origins and activities of *demons.* Lactantius interprets the offspring of "the sons of God" in Genesis 6:1–4 as referring to the origin of demonic activity among humans (*DI* 2.14.3). The most objectionable religious practices developed among the *gentes* in the generations after Noah are the result of demonic influence.

Astrology, haruspicy, augury, those things called oracles, necromancy, magical arts, and anything else evil that humans practice in the open or in secret are their [i.e., the demons] inventions. . . . It is they who taught how to fashion images and statues, who, in order to turn people's minds away from the cult of the true God, caused effigies of the faces of dead kings to be set up with exquisite beauty and consecrated, and assumed their names for themselves, just like actors put on masks. (*DI* 2.16.1–3)

Thus Lactantius goes beyond a basic Stoic dichotomy between the state of nature and the contrivance of human civilization. Traditional cults are not only products of human history, they are also a demonic masquerade.

Lactantius situates the origins of true religion outside of time, beyond the ken of historical inquiry and within the processes of human civilization and demonic subterfuge. The origin of true worship, therefore, cannot be found in the annals of history but only through a careful consideration of human anthropology. If *falsae religiones* are the products of human machinations, then *vera religio,* in stark contrast, is not of this world; it is a divine, not ancestral, tradition.[65] According to Lactantius, human nature desires two inextricable things: religion and wisdom (*religio et sapientia*). The great majority of people, however, commit one of two forms of error: "they abandon wisdom which is able to teach them that it is impossible that there be many gods or they are eager for wisdom, but for false wisdom, which omits the religion of the highest God, which is able to lead them by instruction to the true wisdom" (*DI* 3.11.3). The surest indication of this natural condition is the upright stance of the human animal: "Thus the Greeks use the term *anthrōpos* because a human 'looks upward'" (*DI* 2.1.16). Some of the earliest humans, however, abandoned this natural state, and "the division of the human race followed" (*DI* 4.1.4–5). Christians, therefore, as the devotees of the true highest God, are the only authentic humans. The devotees of the *falsae religiones*, however, are troglodytes bent under the weight of cultural detritus and demonic oppression.

THE FAILURE OF THE PHILOSOPHERS

Porphyry would have agreed with Lactantius that truth was accessible only if one transcended culturally specific and intellectually inferior traditions in favor of the timeless worship of the One. Porphyry believed that philosophy and religion were integrally connected; only the philosopher is a true priest, he claimed.[66] The Christians, in Porphyry's estimation, were both impious and lacking in any sort of intellectual rigor. For Porphyry, the true philosopher enjoyed a position of privilege; engaged in the pure, noetic worship of the One, only true philosophers transcended the materiality and intellectual poverty of traditional religions. Lactantius turns Porphyry's own assumptions back upon him. He argues that philosophers are not privileged at all; rather, philosophy can be located as one more event within the history of human civilization. For Lactantius, however, no philosophy can claim wisdom. The history of philosophy, like the history of religions, is fraught with multiplicity; where there is multiplicity there can be no truth.[67]

Philosophers, Lactantius contends, advert to their inability to discover true wisdom by their very self-identification as "lovers of wisdom," that is, "philosophers": "they believed the name 'wise' too haughty, and they called themselves not 'wise,' but 'eager for wisdom'" (*DI* 4.1.13). Recognizing that wisdom was not their special province, some Greeks began to look for it abroad. Despite this impetus to look beyond their own borders, the Greeks failed terribly. In Lactantius's opinion, this failure was the result of not going far enough afield: "Therefore I tend to marvel," he writes, "that Pythagoras and later Plato, although they were so enflamed with a love for exploring the truth that they penetrated as far as the Egyptians, Magi, and Persians so that they might learn the rites and religious traditions of those peoples (for they suspected that wisdom depended on religion), never went as far as the Jews, even though truth was only with them at the time and it was easier to travel to them!" (*DI*

4.2.4). The Greeks need not have traveled to Judaea had they simply read Jewish texts. Moses, after all, "antedated the Trojan War by about 900 years," and the antiquity of the Hebrew narratives is corroborated by Greek and Roman chronography (*DI* 4.5.6–8). By ignoring the Hebrew Bible, however, the Greeks had no way of knowing "in what ways wisdom had become depraved" (*DI* 3.16.16). Lactantius's denigration of Greek interest in "barbarian wisdom" is a criticism of Porphyry's own cross-cultural project. Porphyry and other Greek philosophers might claim privileged knowledge of Egyptian, Persian, and "Chaldean" wisdom, but, Lactantius retorts, this sort of Greek chutzpah is really hubris. In their hunt for wisdom, the Greeks had simply overextended themselves; Lactantius's metaphor, *extra fines suos quaesierunt*, connotes an extension beyond one's intellectual faculties as well as beyond one's borders, and suggests that the Greeks might actually have been better-off keeping to their own territory (*DI* 4.2.2).

Philosophers like Porphyry fail to recognize the universal validity of Christian wisdom because they have not interpreted the biblical narrative correctly. In the first place, Lactantius points out, philosophers do not correctly understand the relationship between the Old and New Testaments. While Porphyry distinguishes between the Hebrew Bible (a provincial text that nonetheless contains some "barbarian wisdom") and Christian literature (which is altogether lacking in any value, the product of illiterate country bumpkins), Lactantius argues that they are ineluctably intertwined. The Hebrew oracles cannot be properly interpreted without the Christian scriptures, or as Lactantius puts it, "they are not different, because the new is a fulfillment of the old, and the witness, Christ, is the same in both" (*DI* 4.20.5). According to Lactantius, Porphyry and other philosophers do not understand that the hermeneutical "key" to unlocking the wisdom in these Jewish texts lies in the crucifixion of Jesus, an event Porphyry and other critics reveled in mocking. Lactantius relies on some wordplay on the Latin *testamentum*.

That is why Moses himself along with the prophets call the law which was given to the Jews a "testament" (*testamentum vocant*), because unless the person making out his last will and "testament" is dead, it is not possible to confirm the "testament/will" nor to know what he wrote in it, because it is closed and sealed. Thus, if Christ had not submitted to death, it would not have been possible for the "testament/will" to be opened (that is, "revealed") and the mystery of God to be understood. (*DI* 4.20.2–3)

The first step toward understanding the mystery of God, Lactantius goes on to argue, is to recognize that the writings of Moses and the prophets only seem "Jewish"; in reality, God simply used the Jews and their literature as a carrier or cipher for true wisdom and religion. Porphyry had attacked Christians by arguing that their universalizing claims about the Hebrew Bible were bogus because it was a provincial, Jewish text. Lactantius acknowledges that the Hebrew Bible is a Jewish text, but only in the most pedestrian sense. God had allowed wisdom to be preserved in these foreign books because "it was not yet right for the religion and justice of the true God to be known among foreign people" (*DI* 4.2.5).

Even the manner of Jesus' death shows that Christianity transcends linguistic and ethnic specificity: "The principal reason why God chose a cross," Lactantius explains, "was that it was necessary that he be raised up and that the passion of God be recognized by all peoples. . . . Thus in his passion he extended his hands and encompassed the world, so that he could show that a great number of people from among all languages and tribes, from the sun's rising to its setting, would gather under his wings" (*DI* 4.26.33–36). Upon Jesus' death and resurrection, moreover, the disciples spread this ecumenical philosophy "through the provinces" (*DI* 4.21.2). Lactantius does not often quote from scripture, but here he offers two proof texts from Jeremiah (Jer. 31:31–32, 12:7–8) to prove that God disinherited the Jewish people and that his promises of salvation for "Judah and Israel" are really meant for Christians, who "were called by him from among the peoples" to transcend ethnic particularity and cultivate the universal philosophy (*DI* 4.20.11).

Lactantius goes on to draw a specific contrast between Christians as an a-cultural tradition and the multiplicity and geographic specificity of traditional religions. He does this by stressing again the role of demons in the genesis of religions: "[The demons worshiped by the persecutors] are the same ones who established *various* cults for themselves in *different* regions for the purpose of casting humans down, taking false names in order to deceive. Because they were not able to assume divinity by their own merit, they took the names of powerful kings as their own, so that, under these false names, they might win divine honors for themselves" (*DI* 4.27.17). Lactantius is alluding directly to his own Euhemeristic account of the history of religion in Books 1 and 2. In Book 1, Lactantius argues that "various sacred rites are established among different peoples and in different regions" when humans began to worship dead rulers and culture heroes. The parallel locution in these two passages is important. The shared vocabulary and syntax serve to reinforce the contrast between the univocity and universality of Christianity and the diverse cults practiced by different peoples in different regions (*per populos atque regiones varia sacra suscepta sunt; varios sibi cultus per diversa regionum condiderunt*) (*DI* 1.15.10, 4.27.17). Here, too, the vocabulary of religious difference (*varia sacra, varii cultus*) is intertwined with the language of imperial geography (*populi, regiones, diversae regiones*). Because they worship the demons responsible for instigating false religions and the fracturing of original cultural and ethnic unity, the persecutors (and their philosopher allies) are confused, fractured, and "ethnic." Christians, in contrast, abandon the *religiones* of their respective peoples and transcend the mire of the demon-deceived gentile world.

The persecutors and their philosopher allies argued that the Christians were destroying traditional piety. Lactantius retorts this accusation back upon his accusers: "Those who destroy religions ought to be punished, right? Then do we really do more damage than the Egyptian people, who worship the most unseemly representations of beasts and domestic animals, and adore as gods things one ought to be ashamed to mention? Are we worse than those who, when they claim to worship the gods actually mock them rudely in public, the gods about whom they allow mime-shows with laughter and frivolity?" (*DI* 5.20.12). Lactantius here musters familiar and powerful stereotypes. In Porphyry's *On Abstinence*, the superstition of Egyptian natives served as a cipher for natives who do not understand the deeper meanings within their own mythologies and iconographies. This insult worked because it paralleled the closely related stereotype of Egyptians as "superstitious provincials" in need of Rome's corrective governance. This stereotype lay behind Diocletian's own edict of 297, in which Egyptian customs were said to be based on "the monstrous laws of the barbarians."[68] Lactantius, in stark contrast, breaks down the distinction between rulers and provincials: the emperors, judges, and philosophers who support persecution are really no better than the provincials over whom they claim the authority to rule. According to Porphyry, the "Christians" were nothing more than a confused rabble. If one investigated their history and literature, he had argued, one would find them to be a group of barbarizing Greeks, like Origen, and Hellenizing Jews, like Paul, who tried to mask their worthless doctrines in Greek dress. Lactantius turns the tables on Porphyry by equating Porphyry and other philosophers with Egyptians, those licentious provincials who stood most in need of Rome's paternalism.

Lactantius also links philosophers with the Jews. While Lactantius does claim that "the religion of God persisted" among the earliest Jews (or "Hebrews" as he terms them) even as the rest of humanity split into a variety of peoples following false religions,[69] he sees later Judaism as yet another form of error. According to Lactantius, once the early Hebrew population began to grow, many dispersed throughout the world. As a result, "they abandoned the holy root-stock and set up whatever new mores and institutions they wanted" (*DI* 2.13.9). Thus the Jews are like any other *gens* in their preference for arbitrary and fictive religion instead of the original Ur-monotheism of their ancient ancestors. Philosophers like Porphyry claimed that the "barbarian wisdom" found in ancient Jewish texts revealed aspects of universal, ancient truth. In contrast, summarizing this portion of the *Institutes* in his *Epitome*, Lactantius argues that philosophers and Jews both commit the same mistake—by claiming that they, rather than the Christians, practice true religion and philosophy by rejecting Christ and worshiping only the highest god as truly divine.[70] Thus the philosophers, like the Jews, do not escape from the history of religious diversity and error. Rather, they remain ineluctably trapped among the variety of false religions that have been arising among the *gentes* since the time of Ham. Pagan intellectuals like Porphyry might deploy their figurative reading strategies to differentiate between ancient barbarian "wisdom" recovered from foreign texts (e.g., Hebrew "wisdom") and contemporary barbarian provincials (e.g., the Jewish people) themselves, but Lactantius argues that such intellectuals are really no better than the Jewish provincials over whom philosophers like Porphyry asserted their superiority.

The greatest error of the philosophers lies in their inability to distinguish between true religion and false religions. Lactantius points to Cicero's famous etymology of *religio* as characteristic of this error. According to Cicero, *religio* is derived from *relegere* (to reread), and the religious are those who carefully reviewed and investigated their ancestral traditions. *Religio* also stands in diametric opposition to *superstitio*, an overweening interest in prayer and sacrifice with a view toward ensuring the survival of one's children (*superstites* = "survivors"). Instead, Lactantius claims that *religio* comes from *religare* ("to tie back"). Thus, *religio* is "the bond of piety by which we are joined and 'linked back' to God" (*DI* 4.28.3). Where Cicero's etymology locates religion as a culturally specific practice, Lactantius's casts religion as inherently a-cultural. Indeed, for him the cultivation of true *religio* is precisely that which enables the transcendence of ancestral traditions. Lactantius also sets *religio* in opposition to *superstitio*. While Cicero portrays *supserstitio* as "too much *religio*" or "misdirected *religio*," Lactantius describes the superstitious as those who worship images of the deceased to preserve their memory (*DI* 4.28.13–14). Lactantius has reversed the polarity of Cicero's dichotomy; for the Christian apologist, *superstitio* consists precisely in the cultivation of cultural memory and tradition that was for Cicero the mark of *religio*. Moreover, Lactantius argues, because he has shown that *all* traditional *religiones* are really forms of ancestor worship, *all* ancestral cults are actually *superstitiones* (*DI* 4.28.16). Lactantius thus insists on a univocal Christianity as the one transcendent (and therefore authentic) *religio* of the one true God. The privilege of Christianity is constructed in hierarchical opposition to the diverse *religiones* of the world's peoples.

Lactantius's redefinition of *religio* marks an important moment in the emergence of "religion" as a distinct category in the Western intellectual tradition. With its characterization of *religio* as an act of cultural memory, Cicero's etymology reflects a thought-world in which cultic practices, texts, and mythologies were not distinguished from other cultural forms. Lactantius, in contrast, defines true *religio* as a set of theological propositions (in particular the worship of one god) that are authentic precisely because they transcend culture. *Religio* has emerged as a universal category, and true *religio*, that is, Christianity, has become a "normative paradigm for understanding what a religion is."[71] Lactantius's definitions represent an important milestone on the path toward the eventual construction of "religion" as theistic and theological ("those who worship quantities of false gods are 'superstitious,' but we who pray to the one true God are 'religious' ")[72] that is of such great consequence in the history of Europe (as well as its encounters with various global "others"). Jonathan Z. Smith is correct when he writes that "the most common form of classifying religions . . . is dualistic and can be reduced, regardless of what differentium is employed, to 'theirs' and 'ours.' "[73] These differences, however, do not exist apart from the material realities of the specific political circumstances in which they are constructed and deployed. Lactantius's distinction between *religio* and *superstitio*, the true religion of the one true God and the many false religions of the world's peoples, is a difference inscribed in imperial space. At the same time that his etymologies situate religion as an a-cultural, universal category, Lactantius's dichotomy between true and false religion is one that is manifested in the cultural and ethnic diversity of the empire. For the apologist, religions are false because they are the visible signs of ethnogenesis. Thus, to talk about religion is always also to engage in an ethnographic and territorial discourse.

Lactantius and Constantine

Lactantius was the first early Christian writer to have been personally embroiled in court politics.[74] As Diocletian's court rhetorician and later in his new office as personal tutor to Constantine's son Crispus, Lactantius's contact with the centers of imperial power was both personal and official. It is odd then that some scholars have argued that Lactantius had little political investment in Constantine's rise to power other than his role in ending the persecution.[75] Lactantius wrote the *Divine Institutes*, however, during one of the most politically fraught decades in Roman history. When Lactantius began writing the *Institutes*, the persecution had just begun. He completed the first edition of the *Institutes* before 310 C.E.[76] Persecution had ended in the West by the time he was first called to Constantine's court, but at least a decade of intermittent civil war remained before Constantine would wrest control of the East from Licinius.

At some point during this period, Lactantius inserted several dedicatory passages to Constantine into the *Divine Institutes*.[77] The vocabulary and tone of the first long dedication inserted in Book 1 suggests a *terminus post quem* between 310 and 313.[78] Because the dedication encourages Constantine to continue his fight against "the evil ones who persecute against justice in other parts of the world," Eberhard Heck suggests that Lactantius made these additions during Constantine's conflict with Licinius between 321 and 324.[79] The rough, slipshod nature of the additions, he argues, hint that Lactantius must have died around the time of Licinius's defeat, before he could polish his revisions.[80] More recently, Elizabeth Digeser has challenged Heck's late date and argues that Lactantius added the dedications at Constantine's court in Trier between 310 and 313.[81] Moreover, Digeser has identified marked parallels between the *Divine Institutes* and Constantine's Letter to Arles in 314. These verbal and thematic parallels would make sense if the emperor had imbibed some instruction from Lactantius while the rhetor was tutoring Crispus in the preceding years.[82] Finally, to explain the haphazard manner in which the dedications are inserted into the text, Digeser suggests that Lactantius added them "on the fly," in the course of presenting his work publicly at the court in Trier between 310 and 313.[83] Whether the dedications date to the 310s or the 320s, they mark and facilitate an important textual transformation—a shift from apologetic to panegyric and between philosophical treatise and imperial propaganda. The *Institutes* are the earliest extant Christian text to be produced in Constantine's court.

The dedications in Books 2–5 are brief vocatives added to the existing introductions.[84] These minor additions convey honor and respect toward Constantine as Lactantius's new patron. The bulk of the first long dedication in Book 1 reads like standard panegyric: Lactantius expresses hopes for Constantine's long life and his dynasty, and praises him as a restorer of justice (*DI* 1.1.14–16). Though they are brief, these passages imbue Lactantius's apologetics with a particular resonance given the context of the ongoing civil war between Constantine and the other members of the Tetrarchy. Lactantius's pairing of "wisdom" with "justice" in the final line of the dedication points to the importance of Constantine's knowledge for Lactantius. The invocation in Book 4, in particular, asserts a shared wisdom between apologist and emperor: "When I consider the earlier state of humanity and ponder in my soul, O Emperor Constantine, it often seems equally marvelous and ridiculous that the stupidity of one age founded the various religions" (*DI* 4.1.1). The overall purpose of the *Institutes* is to establish the difference between true religion and philosophy (as contained in the Hebrew scriptures and in the consensus of other oracular and prophetic sources) and the variety of false religions and philosophies (resulting from historical processes as humans began to establish various cultures and societies). In his invocations, Lactantius addresses the emperor as a man "in the know," a wise emperor who himself has privileged knowledge of the difference between *vera religio* and *falsae religiones*: "I dedicate this work to you, Constantine, greatest emperor, who are the first emperor of the Romans to have repudiated errors and to have recognized and honored the majesty of the one true god" (*DI* 1.1.13). Lactantius's invocations suggest that Constantine has performed just the sort of comparative, historical research described in the *Institutes* and owes his success to his knowledge of the truth that "is thought to lurk in darkness" (*DI* 3.1.1).

The difference between the tone of Lactantius's original edition of the *Institutes* and the timbre it would have had in the context of Constantine's court is best evidenced by the placement of the second long invocation to Constantine at the close of Book 7. Lactantius's eschatological vision culminates in a final judgment in which "the entire throng of the impious will be burned forever in eternal fire in the sight of the angels and the just" (*DI* 7.26.7). The final vindication of Christianity is far off, however, and Christians must patiently endure persecution. Just as true religion remained hidden within Judaism until revealed by Christ, God urges that persecuted Christians "keep calm and silent keeping his mystery hidden within our consciences, and not contend with stubborn contention . . . against the profane" (*DI* 7.26.8). The *Institutes* ended here in the pre-Constantinian edition of the text, followed only by a short exordium urging readers "to take up wisdom along with true religion" and "to follow the true path" (*DI* 7.27.1, 4). In the Constantinian edition, however, a final long invocation to the emperor intervenes between Lactantius's final eschatological statement and the exordium. While the original text concluded with encouragement to preserve true religion by silently suffering persecution, this new dedication assumes a dramatic change of fortune: thanks to God's propitious selection of Constantine, persecution has ended and the persecutors are being punished for their crimes.[85] The situation Lactantius describes is that of 313, immediately after the "Edict of Milan" and Licinius's defeat of Maximinus. True religion "has emerged and been made known."[86] In language that recalls his history of religions, the end of persecution reveals the contrast between Christianity and the errors of the *gentes*: "we alone of all people are religious because, having scorned images of the dead, we worship the true and living God," in contrast to the persecutors who tried to suppress true religion "in order to defend impious religions."[87] Here in the final dedication Lactantius does not miss the opportunity to stress the difference between the singular *religio* of the true God and the multiplicity of *impiae religiones*. Constantine has been chosen by God to restore the ancient and natural Ur-monotheism forgotten since the development of different Euhemeristic cults among various peoples. Thus Constantine's reign and the success of the empire hinge precisely on the difference between the ancient religion preserved in the Hebrew Bible and the many false religions of the *gentes*.

Chapter 4

What Difference Does an Emperor Make? Apologetics and Imperial Ideology in Constantine's *Oration to the Saints* and Imperial Letters

In 312 C.E., Constantine defeated Maxentius at the Milvian Bridge to become sole ruler of the Western provinces. According to legend, Constantine owed his victory to a conversion experience: a vision (or dream) of the cross (or *Chi Rho*) and the instruction "by this, conquer."[1] Whatever the exact nature of Constantine's conversion experience or his personal religious commitments, his support and preferential treatment of Christianity became well-known quite soon after his victory. Within months of defeating Maxentius, he was involved in the Donatist controversy and admitted Christians such as Lactantius and Ossius of Cordoba to his court. When Constantine defeated Licinius at Chrysopolis in 324, the empire had been through twenty years of imperial rhetoric charged with traditionalism and the renewal of ancestral traditions. For centuries, Roman piety had meant the preservation (and sometimes despoliation) of the traditions of conquered peoples as well as ancestral devotion to the Roman gods. For Diocletian, Galerius, and Maximinus, the adherence of local populations to ancestral traditions was the guaranty of stability in the empire.[2] The new emperor needed to explain how his immediate predecessors and centuries of Roman rulers had gotten it wrong. The ancestral traditions of *ta ethnē*, or "peoples" of the world, Constantine would argue, threatened the stability of the empire. All ancestral cults, including Constantine's own native Roman customs, were fundamentally invalid. The real difference between piety and impiety, the real fulcrum on which the empire swung, Constantine claimed, was not loyalty to tradition but the recognition of the true worship of the one true God. This was not the province of any one people but had been best expressed in the ancient texts of the Hebrews. The emperor's role was no longer to safeguard tradition but to facilitate the renewal of this ancient and universal, but long forgotten, devotion. In the months following the defeat of Licinius, therefore, Constantine took advantage of public speeches, official letters, and the strategic use of force to articulate his vision for the empire.

Constantine's *Oration to the Saints*

Eusebius reports that Constantine enjoyed giving theological addresses.[3] Unfortunately, however, only one of the emperor's speeches survives. In the *Life of Constantine*, Eusebius promises to include a speech that Constantine called "To the Assembly of the Saints" as an example of the emperor's oratorical habits, and the text of this speech is appended as a fifth book to several manuscripts of Eusebius's *Life of Constantine*.[4] Some have questioned whether the text is a genuine Constantinian document. Suspicion stems from a tendency, inherited from Jacob Burckhardt's highly influential and highly negative study of Eusebius as historian, to cast extreme doubt on nearly all of Eusebius's claims about Constantine.[5] Some have gone so far as to accuse Eusebius of outright forgery, or at least of tampering with the text.[6] Over the past several decades, however, the pendulum has swung firmly in the direction of authenticity.[7]

The opening sentence of the *Oration* indicates that it was written to be delivered on Good Friday.[8] Determining the exact date and venue depends on an interpretation of two passages that allude to Constantine's victories over persecuting emperors.[9]

Some have argued that Constantine delivered the speech fairly early, seeing these allusions as references to the defeat of Maxentius in 312 and Maximinus Daia in 313.[10] It is more likely, however, that Constantine delivered this particular speech in the months following Constantine's final conflict with Licinius. As a rule, the Constantinian documents that Eusebius includes in the *Life of Constantine* are those to which he would have had access as a metropolitan bishop in the East, such as open imperial letters, letters to councils, personal correspondence, and, in the case of the *Oration*, a speech edited for subsequent publication and distribution.[11]

Robin Lane Fox has argued that the *Oration* is very similar in tone and style to other letters issued by Constantine in late 324 and 325[12] and that he presented it in Antioch in 325. Constantine, Lane Fox argues, must have received word of the Arian crisis en route to Egypt, as evidenced by Constantine's disappointed missive to Alexandria in the *Life of Constantine*.[13] According to Lane Fox, the title "To the Assembly of the Saints" suggests that Constantine delivered his address before a gathering of Christian bishops and clergy; therefore, he argues that Constantine spoke at the Council of Antioch convened by his "advance man" Ossius of Cordoba in the spring of 325.[14] Others place the speech in Nicomedia. Given the attention Constantine pays to the effects of persecution in Nicomedia in *Or.* 25, Bruno Bleckman concludes that the "great city" in which Constantine is speaking must be Nicomedia.[15] Taking his cue from Bleckman, Timothy Barnes has retracted his earlier dating and now advocates Nicomedia as the venue. According to Barnes, moreover, the heterodox Christology of *Or.* 9 could not have been used by the emperor after the Council of Nicaea in 325.[16] Constantine could only have given *this* speech, he concludes, in Nicomedia after liberating it in the autumn of 324 but before summer 325—that is, during Holy Week 325.[17]

The persecution had been pursued with particular venom in Nicomedia and Antioch. The first executions of the Great Persecution took place in Nicomedia, and it was there that the first Christian church was razed by Diocletian's orders. Under Galerius and later under Maximinus (and their hawkish governor Theotecnus), moreover, Antioch had been the site of some of the most renowned martyrdoms of the persecution. Either city would have been a fitting place to deliver a speech extolling the suffering of the martyrs and celebrating their victory over the persecutors. In addition, the stress Constantine lays on parallelism between God's sole rule of the universe and his own reign strongly suggests that Constantine delivered his speech as sole ruler of the empire.

Constantine deploys common apologetic topoi throughout the *Oration*. The Emperor's use of Euhemerism, his mockery of traditional mythologies, and the association of traditional religions with human sacrifice are stock themes within the Christian apologetic tradition. Though some have taken the use of topoi as a sign that the *Oration* is a forgery, it is more accurate to take this as indicative of Constantine's facility with the genre. I am not concerned to identify all of Constantine's *fontes*. This would be an impossible task given the commonness of these tropes. Nevertheless, Constantine's similarity with one apologist stands out: Lactantius. The Latin apologist has almost certainly influenced Constantine in several passages. In his *apparatus criticus*, Ivar Heikel identifies ten parallels between the *Oration* and Lactantius's *Divine Institutes* and one with *On the Deaths of the Persecutors*. Lactantius and Constantine argue similarly in support of God's sole rule of the cosmos: if the elements in the cosmos were ruled by many instead of one disorder would ensue, just as if soldiers or imperial officials had to obey the orders of more than one commander. Both accuse pagans of theological error by ascribing sex and generation to the gods, characteristics inappropriate for the divine. Moreover, the emperor and the apologist both use the idea of a "double-birth" to explain the coexistence of divinity and humanity in Christ's incarnation. In addition, both offer similar accounts of the demise of the persecuting emperors. Finally, Constantine and Lactantius both appeal to pagan poets as sources of universal truth, and, in particular, both appeal to the authority of the Sibylline Oracles.[18] These parallels will receive more detailed attention later in this chapter.

Was Lactantius whispering in the emperor's ear as he composed the *Oration*? If the *Oration* dates to 325, it is not impossible that Lactantius was still alive to give the emperor advice; however, it is not certain that Lactantius was present in the East when the *Oration* was composed and delivered. As we saw in the previous chapter, it is more likely that Constantine became familiar with Lactantius while still in the West, perhaps at the court in Trier. Focusing too much on the issue of influence obfuscates another important line of investigation. In terms of understanding the transformation of Roman imperialism under Constantine, it is more fruitful to examine the ways in which Constantine appropriated apologetic arguments (whether from Lactantius or others) and put them to use in actively crafting an ideology of Christian imperialism.

The History of Religion in the *Oration*

In Constantine's anthropology, God "made humans rational animals and gave them knowledge of good and evil" (*Or.* 13). Humans are naturally inclined to know the one true God via the observation of the natural order. In the remote past, however, human reason failed, and people saw in creation not God's providence but mere fortune. Despite the failure of rationality, people still had access to the knowledge of God via the prophets of various nations, who proclaimed the truth about God and the world among all peoples (*Or.* 1.2–3). God's prophets, however, were rejected and a cosmic conflict ensued: "Wicked injustice contrived all sorts of schemes, and having slandered the light of truth, welcomed the darkness which is difficult to refute" (*Or.* 1.3). This passage captures *in nuce* the tension between the true religion of God and the error of ancestral customs that Constantine sees as the central driving force in history.

Like earlier apologists, Constantine links theological and moral error with historical processes of ethnogenesis. "Where does the difference of customs come from?" Constantine asks—the conscious rejection of good in favor of evil, which manifests itself in the forms of worship adopted by various peoples throughout history (*Or.* 13). In particular, these include sacrifice, both animal and human, and idolatry. Constantine adduces specific historical examples, claiming that "according to Egyptian and Assyrian laws, people used to sacrifice just souls to statues of bronze and clay" (*Or.* 16.1). People also insulted the nature of the divine by concocting impious mythologies in which the gods marry, have intercourse, and commit adultery and incest (*Or.* 4). Rejecting the knowledge of God also led people to develop Euhemeristic religions by confusing the worship of the divine with honor for the dead, "for the gods were really human beings, when they were participants in the life of the body" (*Or.* 4.3).

As we saw in Chapter 1, Christian apologists looked to Paul's account in Romans 1 of an original Ur-monotheism and its subsequent perversion among gentiles. For Constantine, too, the differentiation of human customs began when people ignored their inborn knowledge of good and evil and established the trappings of superstition. Superstition, for Constantine, consists in the establishment of the culturally and ethnically specific religious traditions of individual peoples. The great plot in history, the great conflict, is between those who adhere to the natural religion of the one true god and all other, erroneous traditions. Constantine corroborates difference by connecting the persecuting emperors whose defeat he has just brought to completion with famous gentile antagonist empires from the Hebrew Bible.

Approximately halfway through his speech, Constantine provides specific historical examples of the conflict between true religion and *ta ethnē*. Though most often rendered as "pagans" or "heathens" in English translations of the *Oration, ethnē* is the standard Greek translation for the *goyim* of the Hebrew Bible, commonly translated as "gentiles." Thus, Constantine's use of terms such as *ethnos* resonates with the ethnological vocabulary of the Hebrew Bible. The difference between the people of Israel and the idolatrous *ethnē* also served to schematize biblical history. The emperor's *exempla* are well chosen; Egypt and Babylon are the quintessential gentile kingdoms in the biblical narrative. According to Constantine, they enshrine human sacrifice and idolatry, stereotypical markers of *deisidaimonia*, or "superstition," in their laws (*Or.* 16.1). These gentile empires epitomize the sort of misplaced adherence to ancestral custom that Constantine sees as the cause of conflict in history. Their adherence to ancestral customs is the cause of their destruction. Not leaving his audience to rely on historical reports alone, Constantine assures his audience that his own eyewitness account confirms the biblical narrative.

Memphis and Babylon have received the fruit appropriate to such worship—to have been desolated and left uninhabited with their native gods. I do not say these things from hearsay, but I tell it as one who was himself present, who became an eyewitness of the lamentable fortune of these cities. Memphis is a desert, in which Moses, according to the divine plan, shattered Pharaoh's arrogance, then the most powerful ruler in the world, and destroyed his army, which was well-armed and had been victorious over many great peoples, not by shooting arrows or throwing javelins, but by holy prayer and gentle entreaty alone. (*Or.* 16.2)

Constantine may well have seen the ruins of Memphis and Babylon while a young officer in Diocletian's army.[19] To guarantee the authenticity of ancient narratives that he felt might otherwise be doubted by opponents, the emperor was interested in presenting as reliable a reading of Hebrew sources as possible. Constantine's assertion that he has seen the destruction of Babylon firsthand may represent an effort to deflect literary and historical criticisms of the sort leveled by Porphyry, who had criticized the reliability of Moses and the Pentateuch on historical grounds. The emperor's subsequent defense of Moses as a liberator and philosophical guide and the source of Pythagorean and Platonic wisdom may also be a reaction to similar criticisms (*Or.* 17.1–2).

Constantine continues to illustrate the difference between ancestral customs and true religion using *exempla* drawn from the book of Daniel. Constantine contrasts Nebuchadnezzar's devotion to native traditions with Daniel's faith in the one, universal religion of the one true God. "The wealth of the tyrant was famous and is so even now, as is his inappropriate concern for incorrect worship . . . and the horrible laws of worship established with cruelty," Constantine intones, before setting this savage religiosity in contrast to Daniel, who, "despising all these things on account of pure piety towards the true God, prophesied that the inappropriate devotion of the tyrant would be the cause of some great evil" (*Or.* 17.3). Unable to persuade Nebuchadnezzar, Daniel is thrown to the lions; Constantine takes this as proof of the "savage, uncivilized character of his own mind" (*Or.* 17.3). In Constantine's estimation, rulers who are myopically committed to native piety fall, and according to Constantine, God destroyed the Babylonians with thunderbolts (*Or.* 17.4). Constantine takes the second *exemplum* from Daniel as well. After surviving persecution under Nebuchadnezzar, the prophet was subjected to persecution under the Persians. Here, the antagonist of true religion is not the Persian ruler but the religious professionals of his court, the Magi. Though a member of the court himself and an asset to the state, "the magi . . . slandered the power of his prayers in envy, slandering his power as a great danger to the ruler" (*Or.* 17.5). Cambyses, however, recognized his error in heeding the Magi's erroneous accusations and sentenced the Magi to death (*Or.* 17).

These *exempla* are thinly veiled allusions to the events surrounding the Great Persecution and Constantine's own rise to sole rule. The connections between biblical tyrants and the persecutors are made clearer in the final portion of the *Oration* in which Constantine turns his attention to the recent persecutions. Constantine characterizes the ferocity of the persecutors as insanity (*mania*) and savageness (*hōmotēs*) (*Or.* 22.2). This vocabulary resonates with the terms used to characterize Pharaoh's arrogance as well as Nebuchadnezzar's "untimely overeagerness" for inap-

propriate forms of worship, the savage purposes of his religious legislation (*pros hōmotēta hoi tēs thrēskeias . . . nomoi*), and the "savage
character" (*to agrion*) of his mind (*Or.* 16.2, 17.3). The executions of
Christians are likened to human sacrifices, and the phrase Constantine
uses here to describe the execution of martyrs (*dikaiōn andrēn sphagas
adikōs eparantōn*) is a deliberate verbal echo of the phrase *sphagiazontōn
psuchas dikaias* used earlier to characterize the unholy religious laws of
the Egyptians and Babylonians (compare *Or.* 22.4 and 16.1). The persecutors base their injustice on the same misguided devotion to tradition
as did the biblical tyrants. Constantine inverts the traditionalist rhetoric
of Diocletian's court. In a passage that recalls Porphyry's description of
Christian apostasy (*hoi tōn partoōn theōn apostantes*)[20] and Galerius's description of the Christians as "those who have abandoned the traditions
of their ancestors" (*hoi Christianoi, hoitines tōn goneōn tōn heautōn
kataleloipasin tēn hairesin*),[21] Constantine proclaims the insanity of the
persecutors' adherence to native customs: "What caused you to lose your
mind? You say that it was on account of honor towards the gods. . . . Or
you might also say that it was on account of the traditions of your ancestors (*ereis isōs dia ta hupo tōn progonōn nomisthenta*) . . . I agree! For these
traditions accord with recent events, and derive from the same insanity"
(*Or.* 22).

Constantine follows this by recounting the "bad emperors" of the
third and fourth century: Decius, Valerian, and Aurelian. This portion
of the *Oration* almost certainly owes something to Lactantius's *On the
Deaths of the Persecutors.* Lactantius and Constantine identify the same set
of emperors (though Constantine omits the pre-Decian persecutors)
and point to their ignominious destruction as evidence of God's retribu-
tive justice. Constantine diverges from Lactantius, however, by drawing
connections between the persecutors and biblical tyrants. Just as
Pharaoh's invincible army was destroyed by Moses' prayers, so too did
God subject the persecutors to humiliating defeats. Decius "fell with his
whole army on the Scythian fields and led the famed power of the Romans to humiliation against the Getae," Valerian was taken prisoner by
the Persians and his skin kept as a trophy, and Aurelian had his reign cut
short when he was killed on campaign in Thrace (*Or.* 24.1–3). The *Oration* reaches a climax as Constantine narrates the follies of Diocletian
and his successors. Constantine alludes to a fire in the imperial palace
that some believed helped precipitate Diocletian's decision to initiate
the persecution. Mocking Diocletian's hubris in attacking the Christians,
Constantine jibes,

What use was it to have declared a war against our God? I think perhaps passing
the remainder of his life fearing the thunderbolt. Nicomedia speaks of it, and

those who tell it are not silent, of whom I myself happen to be one. For I saw him, when his mind was gone and he was frightened by every sight and sound, lament that the cause of the evils surrounding him was his own thoughtlessness when he called upon God as ally of the just. Nevertheless, his palace and home were utterly destroyed when the thunderbolt struck from the fire of heaven. (*Or.* 25.2)

According to Lactantius, the fire broke out in Diocletian's palace immediately after the first persecuting edicts were issued in February 303. The conflagration was blamed on Christians in Diocletian's household and led to an intensification of the persecution. More than a rebuttal to the now two-decades-old charge of arson, however, Constantine's repeated reference to Diocletian's fear of thunderbolts also recalls the biblical *exemplum* of the Babylonians' destruction by thunderbolt. Similarly, Constantine describes how Licinius's army "was obliterated in a series of battles," recalling the total destruction of Pharaoh's army in *Or.* 16.

Constantine's message is clear: devotion to the savagery of traditional religions leads to war and destruction. The verbal and narratological parallels Constantine draws between Pharaoh and Nebuchadnezzar and the persecutors go beyond historical parallelism; because they are guilty of exactly the same insane devotion to ancestral custom as these biblical tyrants, Diocletian, Galerius, Maximinus, and Licinius can be ranked with them among *ta ethnē*. Thus, at the same time that Constantine's rhetoric resonates with biblical categories, it also resonates with the ethnological vocabulary of Roman imperialism. By connecting biblical history to current events, Constantine weaves biblical and Roman history into a single narrative of territorial conquest and ethnic difference in which he plays the decisive role. Constantine's speech elides the rhetorics of Roman and biblical territory. Roman *imperium* and biblical interpretation represent analogous territorial practices.[22] To read the difference between Israel and the gentiles, between true piety and idolatry, becomes an act homologous to soldiering on behalf of the empire and securing Rome's borders. In the Oration, to point to the there and then of the biblical past is simultaneously to map the here and now of imperial geography.

READING WITH THE EMPEROR

Constantine's historical arguments are coupled with a particular understanding of the authority and interpretation of texts. The emperor views Christianity as a revealed *paideia*. Unlike Greek *paideia*, which is the province of philosophers and intellectuals, the Christian *paideia* has been made available for all people (*Or.* 11.5). It serves as a unifying force that transcends ethnic and cultural boundaries and is "the victorious sign . . .

the rule of self-control that brings harmony to all peoples" (*Or.* 11.6).
Constantine indicates that he is addressing this portion of his speech to
"the uninitiated" (*Or.* 11.1). When delivered before a Christian audience,
this meant catechumens; to a wider audience that included non-
Christians (that is, after the text was published more widely), this could
indicate anyone not fully initiated into Christianity. God is in the process
of spreading his word to all peoples via the apostolic mission. In addition
to the Hebrew prophets and Christ's apostles, moreover, other wise people have had an accurate knowledge of God before the advent of Christ;
Constantine remarks, "Is not this the very God who is honored appropriately among the wisest and most thoughtful peoples and communities?"
(*Or.* 11.7). Constantine's phrase recalls the comparative projects of pagan
philosophers. There are particularly clear echoes of Numenius's imperative to seek wisdom among "the peoples of good-repute (*ta ethnē ta eudokimounta*)."[23] These parallels are deliberate; Constantine aims to accuse
contemporary pagan philosophers, such as Porphyry, of failing at their
own game. Despite their universalizing pretensions, philosophers are
stuck in the error of tradition.

The philosophers fail to know God either through the natural order
or through the wisdom of wise peoples. He apostrophizes those philosophers who persist in denying God: "Go impious ones! . . . to the slaughters of your sacred rites, banquets, and great festivals" (*Or.* 11.7). For all
their pretensions, the philosophers fail thanks to the same overweening
attention to ancestral custom that led to the downfall of biblical tyrants
and the persecutors. In order to implicate philosophers in the timeless
conflict between piety and impiety, Constantine posits a causal connection between the intellectual failures of philosophers and the policies of
oppressive rulers: "They come to believe contrary things and to make
war on each other's doctrines, though they pretend this is wisdom. This
leads to revolts of the people and to harsh judgments from those who
hold power, when they think ancestral customs are threatened" (*Or.*
9.1). Constantine is almost certainly alluding to the role of philosophers
like Porphyry and Hierocles as the intellectual wing of the persecution
faction in Diocletian's court.

Constantine challenges Greek philosophers' claims to universalism as
well. Philosophers like Socrates, Pythagoras, and Plato have expressed
certain truths (often thanks to their plagiarism of the Hebrew
prophets), but they remain fundamentally "local" and "particular"; they
never transcend to grasp universal truth in its entirety. Plato, in fact, contributes to error, for he invented "a throng of gods and gave a form to
each of them" (*Or.* 9.5). People used Plato's philosophy, the emperor
says, to bolster their own anthropomorphic and zoomorphic theologies
and his teaching "became a cause of greater error among unintelligent

people who worship images of them transformed into human form or the forms of other animals" (*Or.* 9.5). The charge of animal worship was a stock insult based on the stereotypical representation of native (especially Egyptian) religions as base and degenerate. Constantine's criticism of Plato thus serves as a criticism of late Platonists like Porphyry who, as we saw in Chapter 2, claimed to discern Platonic cosmology and in Egyptian myth and iconography. By accusing Plato of animal worship, Constantine is indirectly accusing Porphyry of complicity in the lowest, most "native" forms of religious error.

Constantine goes on to criticize the figurative reading practices of the philosophers. Plato had expressed a belief in the afterlife and eternal punishments based on one's merits in this life, yet "when they [the philosophers] happen upon these ideas they are not converted nor do they feel fear, but they mock and laugh at them as if hearing some made-up myths" (*Or.* 10.1). At the same time that they reject these accounts as mere myth, however, Plato's heirs take a highly uncritical attitude toward their own ancestral mythologies, which assign human emotions to the gods, passions to the impassible. Constantine is subtly criticizing the sorts of reading strategies practiced by Porphyry and other late Platonists. According to the *Oration*, these uncritical readers deduce demonologies from traditional mythology (*Or.* 10.2). Philosophers are poor readers; they ignore the appropriate sources of wisdom among the world's peoples, cast aside good ideas as mere myth, and misapply figurative strategies to texts that do not bear them out. The emperor, however, can demonstrate the truth of his position through appropriate readings of appropriate sources. Immediately after presenting the stories of Pharaoh, Nebuchadnezzar, and Cambyses magi, Constantine proceeds to "to mention foreign (*allodapōn*) accounts of Christ's divinity" (*Or.* 18.1). The sources he subsequently enumerates come from venerable Roman sources: the Erythraean Sibyl and Virgil. Since Constantine was a "native" Latin speaker, in what way were these texts "foreign"? "Foreign" is the most common translation of *allodapos*, but in context it also means "extrabiblical." Constantine identifies the Hebrew Bible as a distinct and privileged source of truth, but he fears that this preferred source of wisdom may be rejected as authoritative by critics of Christianity. Therefore, Constantine offers his own version of Lactantius's "consensus theory," arguing that the most Roman of texts in fact contains the same fundamental doctrines and prophecies as does the Hebrew Bible.

In much the same way that Lactantius sought to prove the validity of Christianity from classical sources, Constantine argues that extrabiblical texts prove "that even those who blasphemed him [Christ] knew him to be God and child of God, if, that is, they believe their own texts" (*Or.* 18.1). He begins by quoting an apocalyptic oracle of the Erythraean

Sibyl (*Or.* 18.3–4). Terrifying signs will herald the coming of Christ, who will judge the righteous and the impious. Even emperors will be subject to God's judgment. Lactantius may well have influenced Constantine's choice of texts. Although he does not produce the entire acrostic, Lactantius quotes several lines of the oracle in the *Divine Institutes*.[24] Like Lactantius, Constantine is compelled to comment on the authenticity of the oracle. Some critics, he notes, claim that the oracle is a forgery composed after Christ's death. Christians, he claims, have a much more accurate account of chronology; moreover, Cicero, who died before Christ's advent, translated the oracle into Latin (*Or.* 19.3).

While the most renowned philosophers were mere plagiarists of Moses' wisdom, the Sibyl, in contrast, is the "genuine article," a true prophetess of the one true God. Constantine's understanding of the Sibyl's inspiration is similar to Lactantius's: both argue that the Sibyl, like the biblical prophets, was a knowing conduit of God's foreknowledge (*Or.* 19). The guarantee of the Sibyl's authenticity is that the text bears out a particular reading, that is, it can be interpreted in accordance with Christian teaching. Perhaps even more important, the poem can be interpreted in line with current events. The acrostic is concerned as much if not more with difference as it is with Christ's divinity. The scene is one of judgment, in which the long-suffering righteous are justified and emperors are brought to pay for their crimes (*Or.* 18). In other words, the Sibylline acrostic is genuine for the same reason that the *exempla* taken from Daniel are valid: they bear interpretations that accord with Constantine's understanding of universal history as a cosmic confrontation between the righteous and impious.

One important point of all this quotation and exegesis is, as it was for Lactantius, to prove the veracity of Christian philosophy via the "consensus theory." If one can quote enough nonbiblical texts that bear out an interpretation in accord with Christian doctrine, the sheer volume of the material helps prove the universality of Christian teaching. At the same time, Constantine's figurative interpretations of these texts reinforce the difference between the ecumenism of Christianity as the universal philosophy and the geographic and cultural specificity of native traditions.

Constantine explains that allegorical reading is necessitated by the historical conflict between true and false religion. Constantine's reading of Virgil's *Fourth Eclogue* offers a good example of his exegetical strategy. The poem, he claims, agrees with the Sibyl in prophesying the rise of Christianity in the reign of Tiberius:[25] "We understand that these things were said allegorically, at once openly and secretly, because Christ's divinity brings the power of the words into view for those examining them more deeply. But lest any of those who ruled in the capital city be able to accuse the poet of writing against ancestral custom and overthrowing ancient ancestral doctrines concerning the gods, he hides the truth" (*Or.* 19.8–9). Constantine can assume a middle ground, halfway between the outright denial and veneration of his "native" traditions because he believes that the *Fourth Eclogue* is itself a liminal text. In Constantine's estimation, the *Fourth Eclogue* was intentionally composed as an allegory because Virgil needed to avoid persecution. While the *Eclogue* may conceal the truth, it is manifestly and undeniably Roman. Virgil couches the entire *Eclogue* in the trappings of traditional Roman religion. Constantine explains that this was merely a ruse on Virgil's part in order to avoid persecution. Knowing the difference between truth and native custom, he clothes the true meaning of the *Eclogue* in the trappings of Roman religion. Here again, Constantine reiterates the vocabulary of savagery and insanity to impugn devotion to native religions: "In order to avoid the savagery of their insane anger (*to agrion tēs ōmotētos*), he led the thoughts of those who heard him to their own customs, and says that it is necessary to set up altars, and build temples, and perform rites for the newborn one" (*Or.* 19.9). Thus, Constantine sweeps away any impediment to a Christian exegesis of the *Fourth Eclogue.* Anything Roman in Virgil's poem can be explained as a defense against Roman leaders prone to insane devotion to tradition.

As a herald of the truth, Virgil is privileged to know the difference between native error and the truth that will be revealed at Christ's advent. Ironically, therefore, the seamlessness with which Virgil writes of Christianity in thoroughly Roman idioms indicates not that he accepts native custom but his transcendence of it. He has so outstripped the overweening faith of his contemporaries in ancestral custom that he can deploy it to great effect. Virgil's allegory is doubly important to Constantine, for the ability to understand the allegory is a key marker of difference. Because it requires an act of interpretation that can be accomplished only by those with knowledge of the truth, the act of reading Roman classics becomes a litmus test of identity. Virgil's poem is a razor that separates the righteous from impious Romans who are too mired in ancestral error.

Since Augustus, Roman emperors had been using new interpretations and manipulations of traditional Roman religion to support their imperial ideologies. Diocletian's adoption of "Jovian" and "Herculean" nomenclature to ground the Tetrarchy in a putatively divine genealogy had been another such use of tradition. Constantine's quotations of Sibylline Oracles and Virgil are also an appropriation of tradition, though one that radically transforms his traditional Roman sources. By placing the Sibyl and Virgil in the same category as the Hebrew Bible, Constantine relativizes Roman tradition. More than that, Constantine's figurative approach to texts, whether Roman or Hebrew, reinforces the subordination of native traditions to Christian ecumenism. "Roman" artifacts like the Sibylline texts and Virgil's poetry are valuable *only* insofar as they transcend Romanness. Piety consists not in overweening devotion to one's ancestral traditions but in "reading through" native traditions to discover the universal (that is, Christian) doctrines contained within them. The pious are those, like Constantine, who reject cultural specificity in favor of universal, a-cultural truth that is neither Hebrew nor Roman but consists of the ancient worship of the one true God.

Constantine's *Oration* could be written off as preaching to the choir, simple propaganda targeted at Christian bishops and intelligentsia. Yet Constantine espouses the same ideas in nearly the same language in several edicts and imperial letters that are contemporaneous with the *Oration*. These texts provide an opportunity to consider the extent to which the emperor's apologetic discourse related to more overtly political forms of discourse.

Constantine's Letters to the Palestinians ("On Piety") and Eastern Provincials ("Against Polytheism")

Not long after his final victory over Licinius, Constantine dispatched two versions of an imperial letter to the Eastern provinces outlining his policies and ideology. The first was addressed "to the churches of God" and the second "to the non-Christian population in each city" (*VC* 2.23.2). Eusebius reproduces the latter in the *Life of Constantine*, where it is glossed by a chapter heading that describes it as "On Piety."[26] The authenticity of this and other Constantinian documents in the *Life of Constantine* has at times been called into question; nevertheless, the discovery of a papyrus containing fragments of the letter has helped confirm its authenticity.[27] On a practical level, the letter officially ends any of Licinius's persecuting measures, but goes a step further as well to declare that Christianity will receive Constantine's special favor. After praising the fortitude and perseverance of the martyrs, Constantine proceeds to retract and remedy his predecessors' persecuting measures. All exiles are recalled and those sentenced to the mines or as public slaves are freed and given their former status. Those purged from the army may return or choose retirement with full veterans benefits. Constantine also restores property to all those from whom it was confiscated or to their heirs, or if these cannot be identified, to the local church. Any who have received property confiscated from the martyrs are granted amnesty as long as they forfeit all claims. The imperial fisc will also restore confiscated property. Finally, sites associated with martyr-cult are to become church property.

According to Eusebius, this letter constituted the emperor's first official communication with his newly conquered provinces (*VC* 2.43). Several "practical measures" followed.[28] In keeping with his declaration of preferential treatment for Christians, Constantine favored them for positions in the imperial administration, including governors and prefects (*VC* 2.44).[29] According to Eusebius, Constantine also forbade pagan officials to engage in sacrifice or to worship images. In addition, the emperor urged the construction of new churches and church buildings. Eusebius also reports that the emperor issued a law that "ended the abominations of the works of idolatry in every city and region, so that no one dared to make statues, not to practice divination or other such arts, and no one sacrificed anywhere" (*VC* 2.45.1). Unfortunately, this law is no longer extant, and debate continues over the authenticity of Eusebius's claim. While some argue that Eusebius is accurate (namely, that Constantine issued a law that universally proscribed certain aspects of traditional religion), others believe that Eusebius is either wholly mendacious or has cast as universal what were otherwise specific and local measures. In favor of authenticity is the specificity with which Eusebius identifies the supposed law; the phrase *duo kata to auto epemponto nomoi* parallels the phrase he uses to distinguish the two versions of Constantine's letter "On Piety" (*duo d' en tauta*) (compare *VC* 2.23.2 and 2.45.1). Moreover, a law of Constantius II and Constans from 341 banning certain aspects of traditional religion alludes to the authority of a previous Constantinian ban, which may be a reference to the lost Constantinian document.[30] Against authenticity, one can cite Libanius's claim that Constantine did nothing to curb traditional religion.[31] Some who argue against authenticity also note that Eusebius records only a few instances of specific repressive actions taken against either sacrifice or idolatry, all of which were local and specific. Others cite Constantine's second imperial letter "To the Eastern Provincials" as indicating a policy of tolerance on the part of Constantine.[32]

The "Letter to the Eastern Provincials" (or "Against Polytheism," as it is titled in the chapter heading that preceeds it in manuscripts of the *Life*) was probably issued after Constantine's initial letter but before the Council of Nicaea.[33] The language of Constantine's second major communication to his new Eastern subjects is even more theologically and ideologically charged than the first; Timothy Barnes has remarked that "Constantine writes much of it as if addressing a prayer to God."[34] The letter's content bears out Barnes's remarks. Constantine begins by praising the order and rationality of the universe as a path to "the knowledge of God" (*VC* 2.48.1). After this opening, the letter falls into three main sections before delivering its effective legal content. In the first section, Constantine recalls the horrors and injustices that Christians were made to suffer under the persecutors. In the second section, Constantine reminds his provincials of his special role in ameliorating the civil strife of the past two decades. Finally, Constantine expresses his desire for peace and concord in the East: "I firmly hope that your people enjoy peace and remain unrebellious, for the good of the whole empire and of all people" (*VC* 2.56.1). Constantine seems to have felt the need to clarify his religious policies after his initial letters and edicts; thus he concludes his call for concord with a legal clarification: "I hear that some say the customs of the temples and the power of darkness has been set aside, which I might have advised to all people, if it were not for the fact that the violence and rebelliousness of worthless error had been overly fixed in the souls of some to the detriment of common good" (*VC* 2.60.2).[35]

While scholars agree that Constantine's letters are crucial statements of his imperial policies and ideology, there are marked differences of interpretation. Timothy Barnes and, more recently, Harold Drake represent two current, competing interpretations of these texts. Barnes reads Constantine's letters as unabashed public proclamations of his new faith. Setting the letters alongside the reputed "universal" law against sacrifice and idolatry, Barnes reconstructs a clear pro-Christian program that included equally clear anti-pagan measures. In Barnes's estimation, the first letter ("To the Palestinians/On Piety") was an initial statement of belief and policy preceding a general ban on sacrifice, while the second letter ("To the Eastern Provincials/Against Polytheism") is a "justification of his policy" issued in response to "complaints and protests" of pagans.[36]

In contrast to Barnes, Harold Drake interprets Constantine's letters as documents espousing religious toleration. In Drake's estimation, Constantine's rule was based on "consensus politics," that is, the fostering of a tenuous entente among various Christian factions and more tolerant pagans. In this reading, the emperor seeks concord above all and solidifies his power by establishing a broad-based coalition of Christians and other, non-Christian, monotheists.[37] This consensus is grounded in a policy of religious toleration.[38] In this reading, Constantine's first letter ("To the Palestinians/On Piety") is a statement of generic, inoffensive monotheism along with a conception of his role as liberator and peacemaker. Drake is suspicious of Eusebius's report of a general law against sacrifice and idolatry, preferring instead to see a policy of toleration for the sake of concord.[39] The second letter ("To the Eastern Provincials/Against Polytheism"), he argues, reasserts Constantine's policy of toleration and reiterates his "official" generic monotheism. It is an exhortation to hawkish Christians to refrain from attacking their non-Christian neighbors.[40]

Both of these readings have merit. Barnes's interpretation takes account of Constantine's preferential treatment of Christians in the form of exemption from public service and financial and material support for the construction of monumental Christian architecture, as well as his known anti-pagan actions. It also helps explain the more vehement anti-paganism of his immediate successors. Drake's reading is more attuned to the subtleties of Constantine's rhetoric and helps explain several seeming anomalies in the historical record: the lack of evidence for a serious anti-Constantinian reaction on the part of pagans and the dearth of evidence for a universal ban on sacrifice and idolatry, for instance. Though Barnes and Drake represent two opposing camps in contemporary Constantinian studies, they share the same methodological and historical concern for the legal "realities" or "effects" of Constantine's policies. Methodologically, they agree that the rhetoric of Constantine's letters is to be "read through" in order to reconstruct the policies "behind it." The gauge of change, the mark of the empire's Christianization, is the degree to which the Christian emperor sought to eliminate (or did not seek to eliminate) paganism. Barnes's account of a clear policy of conversion is grounded on the assumption that the emperor inherited already-drawn battle lines between Christian and pagan. Against this overly polarized view, Drake's account pits a less monolithic monotheistic coalition against hard-line traditionalists. Although Drake's Constantine pursues a policy of slow, tolerant change, it is a narrative of conversion nonetheless. It is not clear, however, that the rules of engagement, or even the battle lines, between Christians and pagans had been clearly delineated before Constantine. Unfortunately, this focus on the erasure of traditional religions and their supercession by a "new" Christian religion obfuscates a more fundamental function of Constantine's texts. Instead, I suggest, it is helpful to consider the ways in which Constantine's particular view of the history of religions, a view he adopted from the Christian apologetic tradition, contributed to an imperial rhetoric and motivated actions that were instrumental in establishing the differences between "pagan" and "Christian" that defined religious conflict in the ensuing decades.

The ideology of Constantine's letters is based on the same ideas he articulates in the *Oration*. Constantine is often seen as a military genius with little interest or facility in philosophical or theological issues.[41] Yet when Constantine's letters are read alongside the *Oration*, we can see an emperor actively creating an ideology of empire based on arguments drawn from Christian apologetics.

Constantine's letter "To the Palestinians" opens with a ringing declaration of difference. The parallels with the *Oration* are striking and worth quoting at length. Having just defeated Licinius, Constantine greets his subjects by keying his readers into his particular conception of history: "Since ancient times, the difference (*hē diaphora*) between the accurate observance of the most august rites of Christianity and those who have waged war and have contemptuous wishes against has been clear and indisputable to all those who hold correct opinions about the supreme [God]" (*VC* 2.24.1). The word Constantine uses to denote "difference" (*diaphora*) connotes enmity as well. Not only is the difference between true religion and its enemies great, it is ancient and has been evident to all right-thinking peoples throughout history. Present events confirm an ancient historical pattern evident to anyone conducting thorough research.

If one runs through in his mind the course of time from antiquity to the present and carefully considers all the deeds done in history, he will find that those who based their deeds in justice and goodness bring their exploits to a good end . . . But, in contrast, those who dared to commit injustice, either by raging irrationally against the supreme, or by not taking holy consideration of the exiles, disgraces, confiscations, slaughters, and many similar things, and who neither repented nor turned their minds to good things, justly received retribution. (*VC* 2.25)

Although he does not list specific *exempla* here as he did in the *Oration*, the thrust of Constantine's rhetoric is the same: history is a story of a conflict between true and false religion, and Constantine has been chosen as the most recent champion of true religion "in order that the human race might recall the worship according to the most reverend law by the service of my instruction and, at the same time, that the most blessed faith might grow under the guidance of the supreme" (*VC* 2.28.2). Roman emperors had often cast themselves as restorers of piety, but Constantine here casts his role in pedagogical terms. He will not renew ancestral customs but teach people the folly of their native traditions and recall them to the natural religion of the one true God. Constantine closes the letter in a pedagogical tone, reminding his subjects of the lesson they should take from history and current events: "If they emerged as if from a deep darkness and clearly understood events, they would show him fitting worship and appropriate honor" (*VC* 2.42). He is an "apologist," teaching his subjects the difference between ancestral custom and true religion in his instructive words and by his victorious deeds.

Constantine's second letter ("To the Eastern Provincials/Against Polytheism") has even more in common with the *Oration*. The emperor begins, much as he did in the *Oration*, with the argument from design, claiming that all right-thinking people should arrive at knowledge of God through the contemplation of this natural order (*VC* 2.48.1). Then, in a prayer-like apostrophe to God, Constantine assures his subjects that his piety is not an innovation or revolution by offering a short version of the historical arguments elaborated in the *Oration*: "There is nothing new or revolutionary in our religion, rather, we believe that since the very creation of everything you have demanded this most appropriate and august worship, but the human race fell, having been led into many errors, yet you, through your son, lest evil bear down further, holding up a pure light, recalled all to knowledge of you" (*VC* 2.57). The outlines of Constantine's history of religions are clearly evident in this passage: the original, natural religion of the one God was subsequently perverted, to be returned to the light recently by Christ. The letter reiterates the *Oration* again as Constantine contrasts the unity and order of true religion with the fragmentation and disorder of error. At the cosmic level, the order of the universe and its elements stands in contrast to the disorder that would ensue without the providence of the one true God (*VC* 2.58.2). Constantine draws parallels between this cosmic monarchy and his own rule of the empire. As he stated in the *Oration*, Constantine viewed the one religion of the true God in opposition to the plurality and confusion of ethnically specific ancestral traditions. Constantine reiterates this difference in the letter: "For just as much as humanity is found to have different desires, to the same degree the doctrines of the divine word are confirmed among those who think correctly and concern themselves with true virtue" (*VC* 2.29). Human diversity parallels the diversity of elements that make up the material world, and just as God brings order to the chaos of the elements, Constantine, as God's agent, controls the diversity of humanity.

The emperor's letter concludes with an ambivalent statement of his religious policy: he wishes that all people would abandon error, but he discourages the use of coercion to effect this conversion (*VC* 2.60.2). Drake reads this as a statement of Constantine's toleration.[42] On one level, Drake is certainly correct; Constantine would have recognized the dangers of instituting a policy of bloody, enforced religiosity. Drake's reading of the rest of the letter, specifically Constantine's philosophical and historical arguments, is more problematic. Noting that much of Constantine's religious language would make sense in the context of (pagan) philosophical monotheism as well as Christianity, Drake sees the letter as a public statement of Constantine's generic monotheism.[43] It is better, I would argue, to read Constantine's gestures toward philosophy as retorsion arguments. Much like Lactantius, Constantine is taking the arguments of Christianity's philosophical opponents and using them to polemical effect. But, as emperor, Constantine had tools at his disposal that Lactantius and other apologists did not—the ability to issue law and the power (military and judicial) to alter the physical and intellectual landscape. This marriage of rhetorical and legal/penal arguments made for a particularly effective discourse of power and subjugation. Constantine's justification for sole rule was based on the difference between the timeless, natural religion of the one God and the manifold ancestral traditions of error and vice. Overweening devotion to ancestral custom had led to persecution and civil war. Constantine had defeated the persecutors and restored the ancient Ur-monotheism of the one true God. But Constantine's victory was not as secure as the certainty of his rhetoric may suggest. The successful maintenance of power depended on the repeatability of this victory. The emperor needed a story that would stand the test of time. Constantine's imperial ideology depended on coupling carefully crafted rhetoric with strategic applications of imperial power.

An "Anti-Pagan" Program?

There are eight known instances of imperial intervention that might be termed "anti-pagan" during Constantine's reign: 1) in Jerusalem, Constantine ordered a cult site of Aphrodite cleared for the construction of the Holy Sepulcher; 2) at Mamre, unidentified cult sites were razed for the construction of a basilica on the putative site of God's promise to Abraham of "many nations"; 3) a site of supposed ritual prostitution was ordered closed in Aphaca in the mountains of Phoenicia and likewise; 4) a shrine of Aphrodite in Heliopolis in Phoenicia was closed for similar reasons; 5) at Didyma prophets of Apollo were tortured; 6) at Antioch the governor Theotecnus and accomplices who had used the statue of Zeus Philios to render anti-Christian oracles were arrested and tortured; 7) at Aigai in Cilicia a shrine of Asclepius was closed; and 8) Constantine ordered Porphyry's polemical works burned.[44]

While some have taken these episodes as evidence for a grand and systematic anti-pagan program, others observe that each is a "special case."[45] Four of these instances represent actions taken as reprisals for the Great Persecution. It was at Didyma that Diocletian and Galerius had sought an oracle that proved instrumental in their decision to begin the persecution.[46] Oracles from Didyma also figured prominently in Porphyry's *Philosophy from Oracles*. As for Antioch, Eusebius recounts how the governor Theotecnus erected a statue to Zeus Philios, from which he then claimed to receive an oracle that Christians should be cast out of the city. Eusebius also reports that the officials who oversaw this new cult site were tortured into confessing their lies, surely an effort on the part of Constantine to discredit the persecuting emperors of the East, Maximinus and Licinius, and to demonstrate his power to the Antiochene population.[47] The shrine of Asclepius at Aigai was closely associated with Apollonius of Tyana, the holy man to whom the governor Hierocles had unfavorably compared Jesus in his polemical tract *The Lover of Truth*, which was presented at the persecution conferences of 302–3. Finally, the order to destroy Porphyry's books was clearly owing to the philosopher's role as a key polemicist in the lead-up to the persecution. The four remaining examples of repression fall into two categories. At Mamre and in Jerusalem traditional religious sites were eliminated to clear the way for Christian structures built on sites associated with biblical theophanies: God's revelation to Abraham and Jesus' resurrection. The cult sites at Aphaca and Heliopolis, for their part, were associated with licentious behavior and sexual deviance.

Setting aside quantitative evaluations of the decline of paganism, I suggest instead a qualitative assessment of the ways in which these specific material deployments of imperial power dovetailed with the rhetoric of Constantine's *Oration* and letters. Unfortunately, the sole source for the majority of these cases is Eusebius's *Life of Constantine*, an account highly colored by Eusebius's own preoccupations. Eusebius's interpretation of Constantine's actions will be considered in the next chapter. Fortunately, however, Eusebius does preserve two of the letters by which Constantine ordered the use of force against traditional religions: one to Macarius, bishop of Jerusalem, ordering the construction of the Holy Sepulcher and a second to Macarius and the other Palestinian bishops laying out his orders for the site at Mamre. These letters parallel the *Oration* and the imperial letters in espousing a coherent and consistent ideology based on Constantine's specific historical conceptions of religious history.

Constantine writes to Macarius concerning the Holy Sepulcher like a patron to an architect.[48] He informs the bishop that he is to work in conjunction with the prefect of the East and the governor of Palestine to ensure the timely completion of the new basilica. Macarius must design the building as he sees fit and inform the prefect and governor of his requirements. Though given carte blanche, he should inform Constantine about his plans for the dome of the church. As in the imperial letters considered earlier in this chapter, however, these practical orders are prefaced by a flourish of highly charged rhetoric. Constantine uses the letter as an opportunity to restate the significance of the discovery of the Sepulcher. For Constantine, the miraculous discovery of the tomb after the destruction of the Aphrodite shrine is another example of the revelation of Christian truth, long hidden and unrecognized for centuries. He connects this revelation directly with his victory over the persecutors: "Such is the favor of our savior that there seems to be no words fit for the latest marvel. It exceeds comprehension that the signs of his most holy passion, though hidden under the earth a long time ago, were forgotten for so many years, that is until it was ready to be revealed to his worshippers, once they were freed by the destruction of the common enemy of all" (*VC* 3.30.1). By stressing this important difference in times, the letter recalls the same themes as those in the *Oration* and the letters to Palestine and the Eastern Provincials. The time before Constantine was plagued by an ignorant, overweening devotion to ancestral customs that culminated in the hubris of the persecutors. Now, in contrast, the world is illuminated by the light of truth.[49]

The recovery of ancient wisdom also involves a refashioning of the landscape. In the *Oration* and in his imperial letters, Constantine had argued that the religions of the *ethnē* were the accretion of centuries of error, hiding the universal truth of Christianity by masquerading as ancestral custom. The site of Christ's resurrection was similarly burdened by the detritus of ancient error. Before construction could begin on the site, the temple to Aphrodite, "which smothered it like a heavy weight," had to be cleared (*VC* 3.30.4). If the *Oration* represented Constantine's differential reading of history, the erasure of the temple of Aphrodite and the construction of this new Christian *topos* served to inscribe the difference between the pagan past and the Christian present into the provincial topography of Palestine itself.

The Oak at Mamre, where many believed God had contracted his covenant with Abraham, offered another opportunity to rework the ideological geography of the Eastern provinces. The letter to Macarius and the other bishops of Palestine ordering the construction of a new basilica on the site was prompted, ostensibly, by a report from Constantine's mother-in-law, who, touring the region, had been appalled to discover that "pagan religious sites shared the same ground" (*VC* 3.52.1).[50] Constantine informs the bishops that he has instructed the *comes* Acacius to destroy all vestiges of traditional religion on the site. Once the site has been cleared, the bishops should consult their counterparts in Phoenicia and together provide instructions to Acacius as to the construction of the new basilica. To ensure that the new site remains unpolluted by idolatry, Constantine promises to punish any who attempt to reestablish their traditional practices on the site.

The letter describes the "idols" and "foul sacrifices" established by the "superstitious" at Mamre as a "miasma" (*VC* 3.52.1, 3.53.3). Already in the *Oration*, Constantine had identified idolatry and sacrifice as the characteristic marks of the impiety of the *ethnē*. Like the site of the Holy Sepulcher in Jerusalem, then, Mamre offers Constantine a ripe opportunity to act out the differences between his own reign and all that has gone before. Thus of the pagan rites practiced at Mamre he remarks, "This appears to be both alien to our times and unworthy of the sacredness of the site" (*VC* 3.53.2). Constantine casts his interventions at Jerusalem and Mamre as metonyms for the new era inaugurated by his defeat of Licinius and his assumption of sole rule.

Taking the bishops to task for allowing pagan rites to foul Mamre, the emperor says that he must take "the appropriate corrective and ameliorative measures" (*VC* 3.52.1). The new basilica should reflect the "antiquity and majesty of the site," and Constantine takes it upon himself to explain its meaning.

You are not ignorant that there it was that God the Lord of all first revealed himself to Abraham and spoke to him. And thus it was there that the true religion of the holy law first took its beginning, and there first that the Savior himself with the two angels bestowed the revelation of himself to Abraham, and there that God began to be revealed to humanity, there that he gave his promise to Abraham about his future generations and immediately fulfilled his announcement, there that he predicted that he would be the father of so many peoples. (*VC* 3.52.2–3)

Mamre, like the Holy Sepulcher, memorializes a divine epiphany. Constantine reads the site as more than just a manifestation of the one true God, however; it also marks a promise of universal mission—a mission that is being fulfilled in his own reign. Constantine is referring to Genesis 18:18–19, when God's messengers promise that "Abraham shall become a great and mighty nation and all the nations of the earth (*panta ta ethnē tēs gēs*) shall be blessed in him." Clearing the site of traditional cults to make way for a Christian colonization serves as a metonymic performance of this universalizing mission. Constantine could argue in ways that apologists could not. By wielding the authority of the state he could physically and materially demonstrate the difference between Christians and others. Constantine's support of monumental Christian architecture thus contributed to the formation of a knowledge about pagans that correlated with biblical definitions of idolatry posited by Christian apologetics.

That the emperor felt obliged to promote piety was not in itself a new idea. Since Augustus all emperors had been expected to act as guardians of religion to ensure the safety and success of Rome by maintaining a proper relationship with the gods. Though Constantine sought to characterize his reign in diametric opposition to that of Diocletian and the Tetrarchy, he shared his predecessors' notion that emperors were responsible for policing tradition. For Diocletian, however, this guardianship consisted first in ensuring that the traditional religion of Rome was practiced correctly, and second that Roman piety was not polluted by "barbarian" mores and religion. Such an ideology lay behind Diocletian's repression of both the Manichaeans and the Christians. In Constantine's imagination, local customs remained threatening, but rather than characterizing the threat in terms of a barbaric infiltration of the Roman center, his interventions were conditioned by (at the same time that they helped condition) a dichotomy between the singular, ancient religion of the one true God and the multiplicity of ancestral superstitions. The similarities and differences between Constantine's and Diocletian's understanding of the emperor's religious role is best evidenced by comparing and contrasting the ways in which each justified repressive action.

In 297, Diocletian and Maximian issued an edict outlawing certain traditional Egyptian marriage practices.[51] The edict prohibits marriages to one's own child, parent, grandparent, grandchild, great-grandchild, aunt or uncle, sibling, niece or nephew, in-laws, and stepchildren. Like Constantine's letters and edicts, however, Diocletian's decree is couched in highly charged religious rhetoric. The emperor cites his "deep sense of religion" and "the spirit of our times" (*disciplina nostrorum temporum*) as motivations for his crackdown on immorality. The issue requires swift, severe action because the gods will only continue to support Rome "if all who live under our rule shall be observed by us to lead pious and religious lives."[52] The edict characterizes the native practices of the Egyptians as "the monstrous laws of the barbarians," but the Egyptians can hardly be blamed for their errors, for they are led to such incest by their "execrable lust" and act "after the promiscuous manner of cattle and wild beasts"; they have no "regard for decency and religion."[53] The edict is intended to be corrective of this barbaric mentality, and Diocletian hopes that "all shall remember that they live under the Roman laws and institutions."[54]

Constantine's anti-pagan actions share several characteristics with Diocletian's edict on marriages. First, both emperors respond to specific situations in specific places. Imperial edicts were rarely issued unilaterally; rather, emperors legislated in response to specific requests, at specific times, in specific places, and often at the request of imperial officials in the field.[55] In the case of Diocletian's marriage law, for instance, the focus on the legitimacy of offspring and inheritance rights suggests that the emperor may have been trying to ameliorate inheritance disputes raised by native marriage practices. Constantine also responds to specific local situations. His intervention at Mamre, for instance, was prompted, ostensibly, by his mother-in-law (*VC* 3.52). The local bishops of Palestine may have played a role as well. Macarius of Jerusalem, for instance, may have served as a personal guide for Constantine's mother, Helena, on her journey through Palestine.[56]

Constantine's actions in Phoenicia may have been similarly prompted by local pressure, either from Phoenician Christians or perhaps, given Eusebius's investment in the accounts, pressure from Palestinian bishops hoping to gain influence further north and east. According to Eusebius, Constantine targeted these Phoenician cults as loci of sexual deviance. Eusebius labels Aphaca "a school of wicked deeds . . . [where] some womanlike men . . . appeased the *daimōn* with their feminine sickness, and illegal intercourse with women," and designates Heliopolis as a site of ritual prostitution (*VC* 3.55.3, 3.58.1). At Heliopolis, Constantine followed his usual epistolary habit, sending a letter that legally proscribed ritualized prostitution at the same time that it offered moral instruction. As Eusebius puts it, "A new, sensible law from the emperor appeared, proscribing the ancient customs as illegal, and he sent his teaching in writing, to the effect that he had been brought forward by God in order to instruct all people in the laws of self-control. . . . and urged them to be eager for knowledge of the supreme" (*VC* 3.58.2). As we saw in the *Oration*, the emperor conceived of himself as having a specifically pedagogical duty.[57] In Eusebius's account, Constantine's goals seem quite similar to Diocletian's goals in the edict of marriages in that both emperors urge a common set of sexual mores on residents of the Roman Empire. In addition, both emperors elide sexual deviance with barbarity, and the suppression of sexual deviance is undertaken as ameliorative of barbaric practices. Eusebius's account of Aphaca, for instance, seamlessly connects "unmentionable and infamous practices" with "some lawless, rebellious territory" (*VC* 3.55.3) in the same way that Diocletian had equated incest and barbarism in his edict on marriage.

Thus, despite changes in the rhetoric of empire, there were important continuities. Although Constantine conceived of difference in terms of a dichotomy between Christianity and all other tradition, his reign did not erase the classic distinctions between Rome and her provinces upon which Roman imperialism had been based for centuries. Christians did not have an entirely new vocabulary: *ta ethnē*, or *gentes*, in Latin, was the same terminology used by Romans of previous centuries to classify the peoples they ruled. Constantine, for his part, still characterizes the threat posed by the religions of the *ethnē* in terms of "foreignness." Older strategies of distinction did not disappear in Constantine's rhetoric but blended with them almost seamlessly to create an especially effective discourse of power and subjugation.

Christian apologetics, or more specifically the understanding of history and philosophy developed by Christian apologists in response to anti-Christian polemics, provided Constantine with a new way of conceptualizing the empire. Constantine and Diocletian both felt a need to safeguard piety against the threat of unchecked local customs. For Diocletian, this meant maintaining boundaries between the mores of provincials, like the Egyptians, and those of the Romans. No barbarian deviance could be allowed to disrupt Rome's relationship with the gods. For Constantine, however, difference was conceived in more sweeping historical terms. In his imagination, certain local customs were not merely a contemporary threat to stability but indicative of a grand and cosmic dichotomy between the one true religion and the plurality of human error. In the empire of Diocletian, policing religion meant securing the boundaries between Rome and her conquered peoples, both by reaffirming Roman piety and lambasting provincial animality. In Constantine's world, the security of the empire depended not on a renewal of Roman mores but on righting the errors of history, showing the people of the empire the error of their traditional religions. To rule the empire effectively, therefore, one must be historian, philosopher, and teacher.

In addition to defining and reifying ancestral religions as objects of imperial supervision and control, Constantine's interventions in Phoenicia also contributed to the elaboration of a potent narrative of Christianization. If Christian apologists saw all of history in terms of a conflict between the gentiles and God's people, they also claimed to know how the story should turn out: the one true religion of the one true God was to be spread among all peoples, supplanting ancestral traditions. Under Constantine, certain practices, such as sacrifice and statuary, became visible as a new category—idolatry—that required imperial supervision and correction.[58] By repressing certain traditional cults like those in Phoenicia, Constantine buttressed the efforts of Christian apologists to cast contemporary differences in biblical terms.[59]

Imperialism is a spatial practice, and Constantine's interventions in Palestine and Phoenicia inaugurated a new way of "doing" the imperial landscape. The repurposing of Mamre and the site of the Holy Sepulcher as Christian complexes as well as the (putative at least) eradication of certain traditional cultic practices at Aphaca and Heliopolis provided stages for the production of new imperial subjectivities. The new basilicas, as well as the conspicuous absence of previous cultic structures and practices, were tangible reminders of the power of a distant emperor present in his effects on the local topography. Constructing new monumental architecture (and demolishing old) was also a way to negotiate the expanse between the *here* of a triumphal Constantinian present and the *there* of a scriptural past at the same time that it opened a chasm between a pagan past and a Christian present. These were also sites of dislocation and disorientation. To be at Mamre, the Holy Speulcher, Aphaca, or Heliopolis and to participate in this dizzying strophe and anti-strophe between past and present was to transcend the particularity of local space and to find oneself suspended in a new narrative of Christian manifest destiny.

Constantine's new imperial ideology did not require an empire-wide anti-pagan program. Paganism, or "error" as Constantine puts it in the *Oration*, was the foil to true piety. As such, its existence was vital to the stability of Constantine's empire. More accurately, the continuous threat of a descent back into the chaos of "tradition" was crucial to Constantine's reign. For him, the difference between ruler and ruled could be discerned in the patterns of the past as well as the present. Though the one timeless religion had been revealed and the persecutors destroyed, the empire needed constant vigilance of the sort practiced at Mamre, Aphaca, and Heliopolis. A few specific instances in which Constantine could reenact his victory and the revelation of truth were sufficient to maintain and propagate his ideology.

Much of the power behind Constantine's rhetoric, then, was its repeatability. Imperial hegemony requires a clear, fixed gulf between ruler and ruled. But imperial power is not as secure as it might appear. Regimes based on polar, stereotypical differences succeed only insofar as stereotypes are reiterated.[60] Christian imperial power was maintained not by destroying traditional religion but by strategically reminding imperial subjects that they needed Constantine to contain the threat posed by the errors of traditional religions. After all, he could remind them, had not overweening devotion to ancestral tradition brought on the persecution and the civil wars that followed? As Constantine's speeches, letters, and actions reenacted this story, the differences between Christians and others played out again and again. The formation of the Christian empire was an ongoing process. After Constantine, Christian emperors and the Christian empire needed pagans. At any time, in any place, emperors could reassert Christian hegemony by bringing a knowable and governable paganism into existence.

This chapter has examined Constantine's rhetoric within a specific time frame: the *Oration* and letters all date to the mid- to late 320s, immediately following Constantine's rise to sole rule. Though Constantine deployed this new rhetoric to solidify his reign, panegyricists and polemicists would take it upon themselves to explain Constantine in subsequent decades. Of his panegyricists none was more crucial and influential in propagating a new rhetoric of empire than Eusebius of Caesarea, whose apologetic response to the persecution and panegyrics of Constantine will occupy the final chapter.

Chapter 5

From Hebrew Wisdom to Christian Hegemony: Eusebius of Caesarea's Apologetics and Panegyrics

Born in the 260s C.E., Eusebius was just beginning his literary career when the Great Persecution broke out in 303. Straddling the Constantinian divide, he lived through the persecutions under Galerius and Maximinus Daia as well as Constantine's final victory over Licinius. Eusebius would go on to become the principal historian of both the persecution and the Constantinian revolution. Eusebius's earlier literary efforts, however, and in particular his longest production, the apologetic diptych of the *Preparation* and *Demonstration of the Gospel* (*PE/DE*), were written under the duress and immediate aftermath of the Great Persecution and the anti-Christian propaganda that accompanied it. I begin this chapter by examining the ways in which Eusebius challenged Porphyry's anti-Christian polemics. Though Eusebius's particular narrative of cultural and religious history was crafted in response to Porphyry and the persecution, it would come to serve as the basis for an ideology of Christian empire for future generations.

The *Preparation* and *Demonstration of the Gospel*: Eusebius's Response to Porphyry

Throughout his career, Eusebius's work had a strong apologetic and polemical aspect. One of his earliest compositions, the *Prophetic Extracts*, is a collation of biblical proof texts accompanied by exegesis designed to serve as a catechetical text for new converts. Eusebius focuses especially on passages in the Hebrew Bible interpreted as predicting the advent of Christ and the spread of Christianity among the gentiles: two sets of arguments that, as we will see, Eusebius would go on to deploy to great effect in his later apologetic works.[1] Eusebius is also credited with a work titled *Against Hierocles*, a rejoinder to Hierocles' anti-Christian pamphlet *The Lover of Truth*. Recent philological research has, however, brought Eusebius's authorship of this work into question.[2] Eusebius was also embroiled in intra-Christian disputes. When Eusebius's mentor Pamphilus was imprisoned during the persecutions, Eusebius helped him compose the *Apology for Origen* in response to the anti-Origenist critics.[3] He would figure prominently in the theological controversies leading up to and following the Council of Nicaea.[4]

The great thorn in Eusebius's side, however, was Porphyry.[5] According to Jerome, Eusebius wrote a twenty-five-book work titled *Against Porphyry*, which is no longer extant.[6] This work is usually dated fairly early in Eusebius's career, likely in the early years of the fourth century.[7] This long work must not have been enough to exorcise Eusebius's Porphyrian demons,[8] for approximately ten years later Eusebius developed his greatest apologetic project—the massive *PE/DE*—as a response to Porphyry. There is general consensus in dating its composition to approximately 312-24.[9] Based on internal evidence, it appears that Eusebius began writing while persecution was still in force in Palestine but completed the project after Constantine's victories.[10] Eusebius advertises the work as a response to any and all critics of Christianity, or "To show what Christianity is to those who do not know," as he puts it in the work's opening clause (*PE* 1.1.1). Eusebius goes on to distinguish between two categories of opponents: Greeks and Jews (*PE* 1.1.11). The *PE*, as the first volume of Eusebius's apology, is directed toward the former, while the *DE* is conceived as a response to the latter.

Nevertheless, it becomes clear quite early in the *PE* that Eusebius's main target is more specific. In the second chapter of Book 1, Eusebius imagines the questions "someone" may put to the Christians.

In all likelihood someone may first ask, who are we who propose to take up the pen, that is, are we Greeks or Barbarians, or what might there be between these? And what do we call ourselves, not with respect to our name, because that is evident to all, but with respect to our manner and choice of life; for they see that we neither think like Greeks nor adhere to the practices of the Barbarians. Now what is foreign about us and what innovative about our way of life? . . . To what punishments may fugitives from ancestral customs, who have become zealots for the foreign mythologies of the Jews which are slandered by all, not be subjected? How is it not extremely depraved and reckless to exchange native traditions casually and take up, with unreasonable and unreflective faith, those of the impious enemies of all peoples? (*PE* 1.2.2-3 [= Porphyry, Harnack fr. 1])

As has been discussed in detail in previous chapters, this passage is not the flight of Eusebius's apologetic fancy but reflects Porphyry's attack on Christian identity.[11] Porphyry was threatened by what he perceived as a dangerous form of hybridity. Christians read Jewish books, worshiped a Jewish God and an executed Jewish criminal, yet simultaneously disavowed Judaism. At the same time, Christians engaged in philosophical speculation and discourse that bore a strong resemblance to Porphyry's own philosophical practice. Yet Christians eschewed Hellenism with the same vehemence with which they rejected Judaism. Porphyry demanded clarity: adhere to either Judaism or Hellenism. The dual structure of the *PE/DE*, therefore, responds to Porphyry's twofold accusation. By devoting one tome to explaining the Christian disavowal of Hellenism and a second to differentiating Christianity from Judaism, Eusebius sought to provide definition to the "trackless desert" that Christianity represented to Porphyry (*PE* 1.2.4).

Eusebius exploits the very limbo land between Hellenism and barbarism, Greek and Jew, that Porphyry found so unnerving.

> Despite being Greeks with respect to our ethnic origins, and thinking like Greeks, and being gathered from all peoples like the picked men of a newly called army, we have come to abandon our ancestral superstition . . . but also that, though we rely on Jewish books and take the majority of our teaching from their prophets, we nevertheless similarly do not believe it right to live in a manner agreeable to those of the circumcision (*PE* 1.5.10).

According to Eusebius, Christianity is precisely what Porphyry fears most—a people identified not by their ethnicity but by the explicit rejection and erasure of ancestral identity. In contrast to native identity, Christian identity is elective, and the Christian choice consists precisely in the rejection of one's former allegiances. Thus Eusebius stresses Christians' deliberate choice to "put aside the beastliness of irrationality" and "take up philosophy" (*PE* 1.4.13). Eusebius's repeated identification of Christianity as a "true theosophy" (*alēthēs theosophia*) and "philosophy" in contrast to the "beastliness of irrationality" (*alogou thēriōdias*) characteristic of traditional religions sets Christianity off as distinct from all other native traditions (*PE* 1.5.12, 1.4.13). Setting Christian truth in opposition not to falsehood but to inhuman irrationality and animality, Eusebius fixes Christianity as the mark of civilization. With his explicit rejection of all ancestral traditions, Eusebius sought to establish Christianity as a white space, a pure spiritual and intellectual locus devoid of any ethnic or cultural colorings.

GENEALOGIES OF RELIGION

To carve out a space between Hellenism and Judaism, Eusebius appeals to history. He devotes the first six books of the *PE* to countering the first of Porphyry's criticisms: that Christians have illegitimately rejected their ancestral traditions. Eusebius's response is to construct a history, or rather a genealogy, of religion that traces the emergence of traditional cultic practices and mythologies and their subsequent dissemination and transformation among various peoples. A return to primary sources is imperative; one must begin with "the most ancient theologies" and trace their development into the present to understand why Christians have rejected ancestral traditions (*PE* 1.5.13): "We must necessarily recall the histories of all peoples so that the test of the truth may be demonstrated by the juxtaposition of the doctrines honored everywhere and so that what we have abandoned and what we have chosen instead may become evident to those who inquire" (*PE* 1.6.7). Eusebius's methodology was not groundbreaking. His cross-cultural method draws on and develops the comparative projects of his Christian predecessors. Eusebius's cross-cultural methodology is also conspicuously similar to Porphyry's comparative readings of foreign traditions. The excavation of the sacred traditions of foreign peoples had provided an important basis for Porphyry's own radical reinterpretations of traditional cultic practice. In works like *On Abstinence*, for instance, figurative readings of Greek and barbarian mythologies served as important support for Porphyry's rejection of animal sacrifice and for the ancient origins of the intellectual cult of the One. Furthermore, in works such as *Philosophy from Oracles* and *On Statues*, Porphyry offered figurative exegeses of barbarian oracles and iconography alongside those of the Greeks as part of his archaeological recovery of ancient, universal wisdom.

Lest he incur charges of fabricating a partisan history, Eusebius explains, he will craft his account from non-Christian sources (*PE* 1.5.14). Eusebius incorporates long sections from Porphyry's *On Abstinence, Philosophy from Oracles, On Statues*, and *Against the Christians* punctuated with his own glosses to produce a complex intertext. Eusebius does not accomplish this sleight of hand by altering the letter of Porphyry's works.[12] Instead, by selectively quoting from other Porphyrian texts, he makes Porphyry appear to contradict himself. When Eusebius subjects Porphyry's texts to this textual sausage grinder, the resultant mystery meat represents a disruption of Porphyry's texts. To understand better the ways in which this bricolage functions in Eusebius's response to Porphyry, it is helpful to look more closely at the ways in which he deploys his source material.

In the crucible of the *PE*, Eusebius's quotations of Porphyry are constantly manipulated. Porphyry claims that Phoenician and Egyptian traditions provided evidence that the most ancient forms of cult were purely intellectual. Eusebius, on the other hand, refracts passages from Porphyry's works to locate the origins of error in the same Phoenician and Egyptian sources. Similarly, where Porphyry believes that his allegorical reading practices offered the key to unlocking the wisdom coded in the sacred mythologies and iconographies of the ancients, Eusebius dismantles and manipulates Porphyrian exegesis to resituate Greek philosophical practice as merely another native barbarism among the many that stand in contrast to the true universal philosophy, Christianity.

According to Eusebius, the earliest cults, which consisted in the adoration of the natural world, developed among the Egyptians and Phoenicians before spreading to other peoples.[13] The selection of Phoenicians and Egyptians as the fonts of ancient theology is no accident, of course; both peoples figure prominently in Porphyry's comparative projects. According to Eusebius, the primitive Phoenicians erred in worshiping creation instead of the creator. "You have in the Phoenician theology as well," writes Eusebius, "that the first of the Phoenicians knew only physical gods—the sun, moon, the rest of the planets and stars, the elements, and things connected with them" (*PE* 1.9.5). Locating the origin of false religion in nature worship helps Eusebius establish that traditional religions had their beginning in human error rather than divine wisdom. For the history of nature worship among the Phoenicians, Eusebius relies on Philo of Byblos's *Phoenician History*. Eusebius quotes Philo: "These ideas of worship were of a piece with their feebleness of mind and their backwardness of soul at that time" (*PE* 1.9.6).

Eusebius has not read Philo firsthand but in excerpts preserved in Porphyry's *Against the Christians* and *On Abstinence*. Philo claims to have based his history of Phoenician religion on the work of Sanchuniathon, whom he claims antedated Moses (*PE* 1.9.21). In the former, Porphyry uses Philo to challenge claims about Jewish antiquity. In *On Abstinence*, moreover, Porphyry uses Philo as a source for examples of inappropriate sacrifice in support of his claim that the earliest religion was a form of nature cult, in which no animal sacrifices were practiced (*Abst.* 2.5.56). Porphyry, in other words, was interested in ancient theologies to the degree that they support his specific arguments against animal sacrifice, not, as Eusebius implies, as part of a thorough investigation of the history of religion. Like Porphyry, Eusebius deploys Philo's chronological arguments concerning Sanchuniathon to argue for the reliability of Philo's history. In *On Abstinence*, Porphyry reads primitive nature cult as a purer form of religion. Eusebius, however, takes the Pauline account in Romans 1 of an original Ur-monotheism and its subsequent perversion as the starting point for his genealogy of religion. In Eusebius's estimation, the worship of nature is evidence of error, of worshiping creation in place of the creator, of offering perishable sacrifices instead of looking for the immortal and living God (*PE* 1.9.5).

An "idolatrous turn" in religion occurred when humans began to worship culture heroes and rulers as gods. Eusebius turns to Philo of Byblos (again, via Porphyry) and Diodorus Siculus to flesh out this genealogy. According to Philo, the Egyptians and Phoenicians are "the most ancient of barbarians . . . from whom the rest of humanity took [their theology]"

(*PE* 1.9.29). Later generations of Phoenicians, Philo writes, "worshipped as the greatest gods those who had invented things necessary for life or in some respect aided their respective peoples thinking them benefactors and the causes of many good things" (*PE* 1.9.29). Eusebius goes on to offer extensive quotations from Philo's account of Phoenician mythology (*PE* 1.10.1–55). In the first chapter of Book 2, Eusebius adds the testimony of Diodorus Siculus by including a long quotation from his Euhemeristic interpretation of the Isis/Osiris myth (*PE* 2.1.1–50).

Eusebius presses his attack on Porphyry further in Books 3 and 4 as he traces the spread of idolatry and Euhemeristic religions from the Phoenicians and Egyptians to the Greeks. Euhemeristic interpretations of the gods had long been a means to connect the ancient histories of various peoples. With creative etymologies of the names of gods and goddesses and describing the migrations of these ancient culture heroes-become-gods, the writers of universal history had used Euhemerism to weave a complex web of shared Mediterranean and Near Eastern history. Eusebius draws on this type of history to propel his history of religions further. Specifically, Eusebius draws on the Euhemeristic history in the first book of Diodorus Siculus's *Historical Library* to argue for the Egyptian and Phoenician origins of error.[14] Eusebius summarizes the complex lineaments of Diodorus's account of the spread of religion and culture from Egypt to Greece: "With the Egyptian and Phoenician theologies promiscuously coupled, the superstition of ancient error has come to hold sway among most peoples" (*PE* 2.2.52). In *On Abstinence*, Porphyry wished to draw a contrast between ancient (non-animal) and contemporary (animal) sacrifices. Eusebius, in contrast, quotes Porphyry in order to cement his genealogy of religion. "The polytheistic error of all peoples," Eusebius argues, "has come to light only many ages later, having originated from the Phoenicians and Egyptians, it passed from them to the Greeks themselves" (*PE* 1.9.19). Eusebius supports this claim with a passage from Wisdom: "The idea of idols was the beginning of fornication" (*PE* 1.9.18 [= Wis. 14.12]). With this intertext of Porphyry's own historical research and biblical injunctions against idolatry, Eusebius makes an important transition in his narrative of religious development. Once the nature worship of Phoenicia and Egypt, he argues, it was transformed by the Greeks into polytheism and idolatry. Greek religion is a tertiary form, a perverse miscegenation of Phoenician and Egyptian errors.

Eusebius's narrative posits an important distinction between "theology"—sets of theistic and cosmological beliefs—and cultic practices—"idolatry" in his terminology. "Theology" has been constructed as a transhistorically identifiable phenomenon manifested in, but distinct from, the mythologies and cultic practices of specific peoples. The divorce of "theology" from cultic practice, of course, depends on and reflects a logocentric metaphysics that differentiates an ideal, authentic, transcendent realm of true intellectual being from a derivative realm of embodiment and becoming. Theologies are thus authentic to the extent they transcend embodiment in specific cultural forms; likewise, theologies are false to the degree to which they are entangled in the processes of ethnogenesis and civilization. Thus in Eusebius's narrative, terms such "theology" and "idolatry" are also ethnological categories—a tool for thinking through peoplehood and ethnic difference. To compare the theologies of different peoples, as Eusebius has set out to do in the *PE*, is also to schematize the relative value of different peoples.

The transhistoricity of Eusebius's category "theology" anticipates the category "religion" in modern academic discourses. In these modern, anthropological discourses, "religion" depends on and reinforces the partition of "secular" and "religious" fields, which, in turn, is determined by and determines the power dynamics of liberal democracy.[15] As Talal Asad warns, rhetorics that position "religion" as something essential and sui generis "invite us to separate it conceptually from the domain of power."[16] It is crucial to recognize, then, that Eusebius's valorization of "theology" at the expense of "cult" (i.e., "idolatry"), which also maps the difference between the universal and the particular, is conditioned by and conditions the power disparities between center and province characteristic of imperial politics. Eusebius's genealogical account thus summons, at the same time that it subverts, the asymmetries of imperial geography. The partitioning of ancestral traditions into theology and cult structures a subject-object relationship in which Eusebius enjoys power as a privileged observer. With his cross-cultural survey of the expanse of human history, Eusebius has constructed a panoptic vantage point from which to surveil contemporary cultural and ethnic difference.

This privileged vantage point serves as a useful site from which to challenge Porphyry's critique of Christian identity. Porphyry had made an aporia of Christianity by arguing that Christians adhered to no native traditions of their own but had merely blended those of the Greeks and Jews to form an illegitimate hybrid. Eusebius's historical account similarly bastardizes Greek identity by locating the origins of Greek culture in the miscegenation of Egyptian and Phoenician traditions. He also stresses the derivative and borrowed character of Greek religion: "They introduce nothing in their own writings concerning the gods that comes from native sources, but rather fall in with foreign mythologies" (*PE* 2.1.54-55). Eusebius reinforces this concept by twice interrupting his long quotations from Diodorus to remind his readers that the Greeks have "borrowed" their ancestral customs (*PE* 2.2.35, 51).

By situating all deities, ritual practices, and mythologies as the historically contingent products of human civilization, Eusebius was able to gain leverage against the metaphysical assumptions that lay behind Porphyry's interpretive methods. As we saw in Chapter 2, Porphyry challenges Christian interpretive methods by arguing that the Hebrew Bible and New Testament were texts unworthy of figurative readings. Eusebius, however, turns Porphyry's criticism on its head. He again looks to Philo of Byblos, the very source that Porphyry uses to "historicize" Moses and the Hebrew Bible. In the course of quoting a long Euhemeristic passage from *Phoenician History* (which, again, he has lifted from Porphyry), Eusebius interjects a gloss: "he casts blame on more recent thinkers for violently and falsely converting the myths about the gods into allegories and physical statements and theories" (*PE* 1.9.25). Eusebius construes Philo's reference to "recent authors" as indicating Porphyry and those of his ilk, who are inclined to offer figurative readings of traditional mythologies. As we saw in Chapter 2, Porphyry's figurative readings in texts like *Philosophy from Oracles* and *The Cave of the Nymphs* consist of drawing out readings that support his Platonic cosmology and soteriology. By crafting his historical arguments from one of Porphyry's own sources, Eusebius undermines Porphyry's historical and interpretive methods. According to Eusebius, Porphyry should never have attempted to read Phoenician, Egyptian, or Greek mythologies figuratively because these religions can be traced directly to their historical (and very human and pedestrian) origins. The ancient mythologies and religious iconographies are not a Platonic roman à clef. The gods were mere mortals, their cults nothing but the mistaken devotion of their peoples; they are the creation of particular peoples in specific times and places, and therefore do not warrant figurative interpretation.

In Book 3, Eusebius attacks Porphyry's figurative reading strategies: "It is time to look at the embellishments of the more recent of those who profess to do philosophy in our own day. They intertwine doctrines concerning the creative mind of the universe, incorporeal intelligible ideas, and rational powers (doctrines which had been discovered much earlier by Plato and conceived with correct reasoning) with the theology of the ancients" (*PE* 3.6.7). Eusebius's characterization of Porphyry's interpretive methods, though polemical, is apt: Porphyry did indeed read myths and iconography in order to discover Platonic cosmologies and soteriologies he believed were coded within them. Eusebius proceeds by systematically deconstructing two of Porphyry's works: *On Statues* and *Philosophy from Oracles*.

As we saw in Chapter 2, *On Statues* aims to teach people how "to read from statues just as from books the things written about the gods" (*PE* 3.7.1). After quoting Porphyry's introduction, Eusebius quotes several of

Porphyry's exegeses at length, including his figurative readings of Zeus and Hera, Hestia, Rhea, and Demeter, and Apollo, as well as Egyptian gods such as Cneph, Isis, Osiris, Typhon, and Horus.[17] Porphyry's exegeses include "physical allegories"; Hestia, Rhea, and Demeter, for instance, can be read as representations of the powers of the earth (*PE* 3.11.15). In addition to discussing these physical allegories, Porphyry offers exegeses based in Platonic cosmology. Thus Zeus is interpreted as "the whole cosmos, animal of animals, god of gods, and as Zeus, where he is the mind from which it brings forth all things" (*PE* 3.9.3).

Porphyry was quite comfortable offering several possible figurative interpretations of a given text or iconography. Pluralism was inherent in Porphyry's allegorical method, though he did differentiate among the relative values of different exegeses.[18] Eusebius, however, draws freely from Porphyry's text in order to portray Porphyry as self-contradictory. He quotes from the philosopher so as to make his intellectual project seem absurd.

Let it be that "Zeus" is no longer the fiery and aetherial substance, as was thought among the ancients . . . but that he is the transcendent mind, the demiurge of the universe, the generative cause of everything, then how will the father of this one be Kronos, whom they say is time, and Rhea his mother, whom the exegete [i.e., Porphyry] said was the rocky and mountain power; for I do not know how, when he called her air and aether, he likewise says that she is the sister and wife of the mind that created the cosmos, the generative cause of everything. (*PE* 3.13.11)

Eusebius ascribes both physical and Platonic allegories to Porphyry, when in fact Porphyry offers the former in order to present as full an exegesis as possible.

In addition to the logical inconsistencies he claims to find in Porphyry's work, Eusebius also challenges the metaphysical assumptions behind Porphyry's exegesis. As we have seen, the Platonist's figurative reading was based on a hierachical dichotomy between authentic, transcendent realities and the particular cultural and ethnic forms in which they had been coded, or embodied, by ancient poets and sages. According to Eusebius, however, ancient Greek poets had grasped nothing of transcendent reality, while the ancient Egyptian sages had "interpreted everything with reference to natural phenomena" (*PE* 3.9.14–15). In other words, Eusebius accuses Porphyry of "discovering" a Platonic system in ancient myths and iconographies when these ancient artifacts do not in fact merit such an interpretation. To further accuse Porphyry, Eusebius brings in Plato, quoting from the Cratylus: "the first Greeks, just as many of the barbarians do now, believed only the sun, moon, earth, stars, and heaven to be gods" (*PE* 3.9.14). Eusebius does not, in principle, disagree with the fundamentals of Porphyry's cosmology. Rather, he impugns Porphyry for trying to recover and rehabilitate otherwise bankrupt religious traditions by retrojecting his cosmology back into ancient sources.

> If they claim that they do not make the visible bodies of the sun, moon, stars, and the sense perceptible portions of the cosmos into gods, but rather in them the invisible powers of the one who is above all . . . why then do they not mock the disgraceful and inappropriate myths about the gods as unlawful and atheistic and hide the books about them as containing impiety and licentiousness, and praise the one and only invisible God plainly and purely, without any disgraceful entanglements? (PE 3.13.22)

Eusebius argues that Porphyry is guilty of hypocritically promoting the vulgar forms of superstition that figurative readings were supposed to transcend. Though Porphyry claims to transcend the embodied, "ethnic" aspects of traditional religions, he and those like him have become "mixed up in the polytheistic error of the ancients" (PE 3.14.1). Although Porphyry appears to understand the origins of ancient myth, he refuses to reject it and instead "beautifies disgraceful things by the perversion of the truth with his words, and by his deeds actually affirms the mythological error and vulgar superstition" (PE 3.14.2). For Eusebius, the ultimate example of Porphyry's hypocrisy is the philosopher's *Letter to Anebo*. Quoting in extenso from Porphyry's *Letter to Anebo*, Eusebius suggests that Porphyry's overweening interest in Egyptian religion involves an implicit approval of Egyptian barbarism: "It seems to him that they have correctly deified animals" (PE 3.5.1). In seeking the wisdom of Egypt, Eusebius suggests, Porphyry has become just like the objects of his inquiry; in his quest for barbarian wisdom, Porphyry has descended into barbarism.

ORACLES AND DEMONS

Eusebius divides Greek theology into three types: mythical, physical, and the political. According to Eusebius's preface, Books 1 and 2 constitute a refutation of mythical theology, Book 3 a response to the physical allegories of the philosophers, while Book 4 considers the "third part" of theology, which "is called 'political' by the Greeks and which is protected by the laws as both ancient and ancestral" (PE 4.1.2). Eusebius further distinguishes three aspects of political theology: 1) traditional statuary and myth, 2) the allegorical interpretation of statuary and myth, and 3) "the powers inhabiting the statues" (PE 4.1.7). Since he has proved the folly of idolatry and myth in Books 1 and 2 and dispensed with physical allegoresis in Book 3, Book 4 focuses on these "powers."

Oracles and their interpretation represent the primary manifestation of these powers. Eusebius's singling out of oracles as the most visible (to him) aspect of political theology is not accidental. Like Lactantius and Constantine, Eusebius was keenly aware of the prominent role that Apollo's oracles had played in the persecution. It was thanks to the interpretation of oracles, Eusebius argues, that the persecutors became convinced that Christians should be punished for "openly breaking the law that each person ought to revere his or her ancestral customs" (*PE* 4.1.3). Eusebius also reports that Theotecnus, the *curator* of Antioch under Maximinus, established an oracle of Zeus Philios, which conveniently began to offer anti-Christian oracles.[19] In Eusebius's mind, philosophers and imperial officials had been allies in the persecution, and Porphyry, as author of *Philosophy from Oracles*, stood as the great theorist of oracular interpretation (*PE* 4.6.2). Eusebius sets out to prove that oracles and their interpretation were nothing more than demon worship in philosophical dress.

Again, Eusebius proceeds to attack Porphyry by playing selected quotations from Porphyry off one another. He begins by paraphrasing Porphyry's account of the divine hierarchy and the forms of worship accorded to different types of divine beings: "First, distinguishing the first God, they say that he is the first over them all . . . after him there is the second class, the gods, the *daimones* follow, and the heroes are fourth. . . . Having made this distinction, they say it is necessary to worship the heavenly and aetherial gods first, the good *daimones* second, the souls of the heroes third, and fourth, to expiate the foul and evil *daimones* (*PE* 4.5.2). Although Eusebius attributes these notions to Greek theologians generally, the striking parallels between this passage and similar accounts of the divine hierarchy in Porphyry's *Letter to Anebo* and *On Abstinence* (both texts Eusebius had at hand in composing the *PE*) make it clear that Eusebius has the philosopher in mind.[20] For Porphyry, this theological model served as a means to reconcile traditional, or "civic," cults with the intellectual cult that philosophers render to the utterly transcendent One.[21]

The figurative interpretation of oracles in *Philosophy from Oracles* is of a piece with this schematization of the divine hierarchy. On the subject of cultic practice, Porphyry quotes and interprets an oracle of Apollo concerning sacrifices. According to Porphyry's exegesis, the oracle explains not only "the manner of the sacrifices" but, more important, "that they are performed according to the aforementioned categories of the gods" (*PE* 4.9.3). Porphyry's figurative exegesis mollified the more intellectually offensive, corporeal aspects of ancestral tradition and offered a way to subordinate them to the purely intellectual, universal cult of the One.

Eusebius appropriates this Porphyrian passage and casts Porphyry's exegesis as a resounding approval of base forms of sacrificial religion. Immediately after quoting Porphyry's exegesis of the Apolline oracle from *Philosophy from Oracles*, Eusebius inserts a series of passages from *On Abstinence* in which Porphyry explains the differences between the forms of cult offered to different classes of deities. The only cult accorded to the highest God, Porphyry writes (and Eusebius quotes), is the philosopher's "pure silence and pure thoughts about him" and the "*apatheia* of the soul" through which he or she achieves "likeness to God" (*PE* 4.11.1 [= *Abst.* 2.34]). To the intellectual gods, moreover, one offers the "good thoughts about them" but may also add "vocalized hymns" (*PE* 4.12.1 [= *Abst.* 2.34]). True sacrifice must "harm nothing," and the shedding of blood represents the ultimate form of harm (*PE* 4.14.3 [= *Abst.* 2.12.3]). Animal sacrifice is thus inappropriate for the gods; it is a degenerate mode of worship that developed as humanity experienced famine, war, and violence (*PE* 4.16.1-10 [= *Abst.* 2.54-56, 2.27.2]). Animal sacrifices are only offered to (bad) *daimones*, not to gods (*PE* 4.15.1-2 [= *Abst.* 2.36.5, 2.58.1]).

In juxtaposing *Philosophy from Oracles* and *On Abstinence*, Eusebius claims to have caught Porphyry in a contradiction. How could Porphyry, Eusebius argues, decry the vulgarity of sacrifice in one text, yet approve (at least as Eusebius presents it) animal sacrifice in another? Indeed, Eusebius jibes, if the Porphyry of *On Abstinence* thinks animal sacrifices are only to be offered to *daimones*, then the Porphyry of *Philosophy from Oracles* is "accusing his own god." Apollo is a demon, "for he just said that the oracle prescribes animal sacrifice" (*PE* 4.10.2). Relishing the "contradiction" that he has uncovered in his close reading (or, rather, polemical intertexting) of Porphyry, Eusebius presses his argument further. Not only has Porphyry unwittingly admitted that Apollo is a demon, "but also all those who have been thought to be gods among all peoples, those gods to whom entire peoples, both rulers and subjects, in both cities and in the countryside, offer rites in the form of animal sacrifices" (*PE* 4.10.3). According to Eusebius, Porphyry's contradiction proves that every ancestral cultic system is fundamentally invalid.

Eusebius's polemical reading of Porphyry depends on a critical (and intentional) misreading of Porphyry's theological vocabulary. Catalyzed by the Eusebian intertext of the *PE*, Porphyry's terminology undergoes a semantic shift that fundamentally alters the meaning of his texts. Among the philosophers for whom Porphyry wrote *Philosophy from Oracles* and *On Abstinence*, *daimones* were simply another category of divine being that occupied the lowest rung of the divine hierarchy. Ambivalent creatures, they are either "maleficent" or "good" (*Abst.* 2.58.2). Good *daimones*, if "well-disposed by prayer and supplication and sacrifices," benefit humanity, while bad *daimones*, in contrast, are the cause of natural disasters, plagues, and so forth (*Abst.* 2.37.5, 2.40.1). Worse, they fan the flames of human passions. Masquerading as true gods, they deceive people as to the true nature of divinity and, "draw[ing] power from the smoke that rises from blood and flesh," they dupe people into blood sacrifice (*Abst.* 2.40.2, 2.42.2–3). The wise, therefore, avoid animal sacrifices, lest they become associated with maleficent *daimones* (*Abst.* 2.43.1). Porphyry does concede that some may believe that sacrifices to *daimones* are necessary for civic cult, but he encourages the philosophically minded to avoid such practices, as they are conducive to corporeal concerns rather than the care for the soul (*Abst.* 2.43.2–5).

Porphyry ranks Apollo among the higher, intellectual gods, not the *daimones*. In *On Abstinence*, moreover, Porphyry states explicitly that Apollo *never* enjoins animal sacrifice. "When Apollo advises sacrifice according to ancestral tradition," he writes, "he seems to encourage us towards the ancient custom. The ancient custom, as I have shown, was of cakes and crops" (*Abst.* 2.59.1). Elsewhere in *On Abstinence*, Porphyry tells two stories in which the oracle at Delphi declared inanimate sacrifices preferable to animate (*Abst.* 2.16, 2.17). Porphyry, in fact, cites a wide range of native traditions to support his arguments against animal sacrifice. If Syrians, Hebrews, Phoenicians, and Egyptians recommend abstinence from fish, pork, and beef, respectively, neither should philosophers "choose to break the laws of nature and the precepts of the gods" concerning the preference for inanimate sacrifices (*Abst.* 2.61.1–8).

Eusebius, of course, neglects to preserve the nuances of Porphyry's argument. Through his choice of quotations and his mode of presentation, Eusebius has transposed Porphyry's texts. Porphyry's concern with *daimones* is relatively minor, a necessary, though certainly not the central, component of the theological system underpinning his understanding of cultic practices in *On Abstinence*. In the *PE*, however, the Platonic *daimones* have become the demons of Eusebius's Christian cosmology. Eusebius transforms *On Abstinence*, originally an argument against the slaughter and consumption of animals, and *Philosophy from Oracles*, originally an allegorical reading of oracular texts, into a systematic *demonology*.

Eusebius accomplishes these semantic acrobatics by running Porphyry's theological vocabulary through a biblical filter. Eusebius quotes from the Psalms ("All the gods of the gentiles are demons") and 1 Corinthians ("That which they sacrifice, they sacrifice to demons and not to God") (*PE* 4.16.20, quoting Ps. 95:5 [LXX] and 1 Cor. 10:20). In Eusebius's exegesis, which is also his summary of Porphyry, "the idolatrous fabrication of gods among the gentiles (*tōn ethnēn*) came from demons, and not good demons, but totally hateful and wicked demons" (*PE* 4.16.20). Nowhere is the depravity of ancestral custom more evident than in *human* sacrifice.[22] In *On Abstinence*, Porphyry cites cross-cultural examples of human sacrifice in support of his argument *against* traditional sacrifice.[23] In Porphyry's text, the practice of human sacrifice stands in dramatic opposition to true, intellectual cult. Texts that had originally constituted a rather complex and sophisticated reinterpretation of ancestral traditions have become, in Eusebius's reading, evidence for "the extent to which the plague of polytheistic error ruled humanity before the coming of our savior" (*PE* 4.15.6). Eusebius overwrites and recasts Porphyry's language and arguments, fixing his selection of Porphyrian quotation within a biblical matrix in which gentile idolatry is the foil to the genuine monotheism cultivated by God's people. Subjected to Eusebius's intertextual practices, Porphyry's theology has become nothing more than window dressing for demonolatry. "All the gods of the gentiles are demons," and Porphyry, despite his pretensions, is just another gentile.

JEWS OR HEBREWS?

The second half of Porphyry's challenge to Christian identity concerns the relationship of Christianity and Judaism.[24] If Christians refused to adhere to the customs of their respective native peoples, why did they not then follow the customs of the Jews? After all, Christians based their teachings on a set of Jewish texts. Why did the Christians not adopt Jewish practices as well? Eusebius counters this second component of Porphyry's polemics beginning in Book 7 of the *PE* as he goes on to explain "the reason for our pretensions to the Hebrew teachings." Had not "the most renowned Greek philosophers crafted their philosophical doctrines from those of barbarians?" (*PE* 7.1.3). Eusebius thus acknowledges the similarity of the Christian appropriation of the Hebrew Bible to Greek philosophers' borrowings from barbarian wisdom. The Greeks, however, had sought wisdom among the wrong peoples, for "nothing has ever been discovered among any of the world's peoples as good as that which has been passed to us from the Hebrews" (*PE* 7.1.3).

To prove the special status of Hebrew wisdom, Eusebius must differentiate the Hebrews from all other peoples—including contemporary Jews.[25] The difference between Hebrews and gentiles figures the difference between the transcendence and embodiment, between universality and particularity. While all other peoples lived "according to the senses of the body," the Hebrews are sui generis because they were the only people to understand that the "true person" is found in the soul (*PE* 7.2.1, 7.4.1). Moreover, the Euhemerism and nature worship devised by other peoples was hopelessly diverse, "like a hydra with many necks and heads" (*PE* 7.2.5). In contrast, the Hebrews stood alone as the sole island of true religion in this sea of error. While the Phoenicians and Egyptians were worshiping the stars and natural phenomena, the Hebrews correctly inferred the existence of the creator through observation of the order in creation (*PE* 7.3.2). Likewise, the Hebrews were the only people to differentiate soul and body (*PE* 7.4.1).

Although Eusebius does not name Porphyry in this portion of the *PE*, it is easy to find him "between the lines" of Eusebius's argument.[26] As we saw in Chapter 2, Porphyry's figurative readings of barbarian religions were facilitated by the manner in which he differentiated the universal philosophical "meanings" of myth and iconography from their native contexts. This strategy parallels Porphyry's late Platonic notions of the difference between body and soul. Porphyry argues, for instance, that native Egyptians understood the myths of Isis and Osiris in a purely literal, or "bodily," manner. A skilled exegete, however, was able to peel away the "flesh" of the myth to bear its soul, or true meanings. Porphyry's interpretive method was based on the assumption that ancient sages had coded these philosophical truths in clothing fitted to the limited intellectual capacity of the masses. By making the Hebrews the sole proprietors of "psychic" meaning and the Hebrew Bible the lone conduit of ancient wisdom, Eusebius subtly undercuts the historical assumptions behind Porphyry's figurative readings. In addition, Eusebius elevates the Hebrews at the expense of the Egyptians and Phoenicians—two of Porphyry's favorite sources. Finally, the elevation of the Hebrews as the only wise barbarians is the linchpin to Eusebius's explanation as to why Christians do not adopt the traditions of the Jews.

Eusebius designates all pre-Mosaic patriarchs as "Hebrews." The "Jews," by contrast, have their origins in a specific historical moment. According to Eusebius, the Jewish *ethnos* began in Egypt, when Joseph's descendants forgot the religion of their ancestors and began to assume Egyptian customs. The Jews were so miscegenated that "their manner of life appeared to differ in no way from the Egyptians." God sent Moses, however, as a lawgiver to rein in the wayward Jews. The Torah "was appropriate to the mores of those receiving it" (*PE* 7.8.37–38). That is, the legal regulations in the Torah were intended as a concession to Jewish licentiousness, a crutch to help the Jews climb out of the mire into which they had descended while in Egypt.

Though Moses had to accommodate the Jews, the texts he composed for them were not themselves of low religious or philosophical value. Moses was, after all, not a Jew but a "Hebrew of Hebrews" steeped in the theological wisdom of his ancestors. Thus, rather than authoring a purely physical law code that would curb the wayward Jews, Moses included narratives of the most famous Hebrew patriarchs as models for imitation and an accurate account of the creation of the cosmos (*PE* 7.7.1–2). Eusebius describes the book of Genesis as a prolegomenon to Hebrew theology. Unlike the mythologies of Egypt and Phoenicia, Moses' account is accurate and worthy of interpretation (*PE* 7.9.1–2).

Critics of Christianity, however, were not so eager to accept this explanation for Christian adoption of the Hebrew Bible. If, as Eusebius argues, Moses' composition was of such high quality, why, as Porphyry objects, did Christians not adopt all of the legal and ethical measures contained in it? Eusebius leaves this objection unanswered in the *PE*, but does offer an explanation in the first book of the *DE*. Here, much as Porphyry distinguishes between ancient Egyptian *sages* and Egyptian *natives* in texts like the *Letter to Anebo* and *On Abstinence*, Eusebius differentiates ancient Hebrew wisdom from Jewish practice. The Jewish Law does not apply to Christians, he argues, because it is ineluctably bound by geography and history. The Jewish Law enjoins festivals and sacrifices that can be performed only in Jerusalem; therefore, Eusebius continues, the Law was only ever applicable to Jews living in Palestine, not for non-Jews, and not even for Jews living in the Diaspora (*DE* 1.3.1). *A fortiori*, the Law is not applicable to Christians, who come from "all peoples, in the most far-flung regions of the earth" (*DE* 1.3.3).

The same interpretive strategies that help Eusebius differentiate the "Jewish" body of the Hebrew Bible from its spiritual and universal content also help him explain the unique character of the Christian relationship to the Hebrews. While Jewish identity is marked by a physical sign (e.g., circumcision) and adherence to physical regulations (e.g., keeping kosher), the ancient Hebrews had no need for this second-rate moral code. The Hebrew polity, Eusebius argues, was based on the purity of their souls, which led them to establish a polity based on natural, not human, law (*PE* 7.6.3). Eusebius's Hebrews are, in effect, proto-Christians; or rather, Eusebius's Christians are modern-day Hebrews who espouse a timeless, universal monotheism unfettered by the error and false religion rampant among the other peoples of the world.

In the opening of the *PE*, Eusebius describes Christianity as an elevated middle ground, above both the polytheistic error of the Greeks *and* the laughable and anachronistic cult of the Jews. Likewise, Eusebius's Hebrews reside in the space between Jew and gentile: "Among all of [the Hebrews] there was not one mention of bodily circumcision, nor of the Jewish proclamation of Moses; therefore, it is not correct to call them Jews, but neither it is correct to call them Greeks, because they did not believe in many gods like the Greeks or the rest of *ta ethnē* (*PE* 7.8.20). The neutral zone inhabited by the Hebrews/Christians is not the abyss that Porphyry implies it is. Rather, this middle road is a path that leads directly out of the mire of this physical world to the contemplation of the one true God. Thus, Eusebius argues, "More appropriately, they would be called 'Hebrews,' either from 'Eber' or rather from the interpretation of his name. For, when interpreted, they are 'wanderers' sent on a journey from the things of this world to the contemplation of the God of all" (*PE* 7.8.21).

Christian and pagan philosophers were invested in the ethnography of ancient peoples: Porphyry as part of his effort to recover wisdom from the sages of Egypt and Phoenicia, Christians because they claimed the ancient wisdom of the Hebrews as their patrimony. Porphyry challenges the legitimacy of Christian claims upon Hebrew wisdom. By recasting the ethnographic landscape, that is, by distinguishing Hebrews from Jews in the *PE*, Eusebius lays the groundwork for a subtle but effective genealogical argument. Porphyry's charge that Christians forsook their native traditions for the "foreign mythologies of the Jews" was based on the notion that group identity is grounded in *physical* descent from common ancestors (*PE* 1.2.3 [= Porphyry, Harnack fr. 1]). Because the Hebrews occupy the limbo land between Jew and gentile, Eusebius argues that traditional notions of descent and ethnicity do not apply to the relationship between the Christians and the ancient Hebrews. Christian descent from the Hebrews is of an entirely different variety.

How were "all peoples" and "all the tribes of the earth" (Gen. 18.17–18) going to be blessed in Abraham unless there was some kinship with him, either of a spiritual type or bodily kinship? Then explain what kinship of the flesh there was between Abraham and the Scythians, or Egyptians, Ethiopians, Indians, Britains, or Spaniards. How were these peoples and those yet more remote going to be blessed by virtue of kinship with Abraham according to the flesh? But neither was it probable that all peoples would share Abraham's blessing according to the spirit? Some peoples were defiled by marriages with mothers, incest with sisters, and intercourse between men; others established human sacrifice, the deification of irrational animals, statues of soulless matter, and the superstition of deceitful demons as piety; others burned their elders alive, while still others thought it good and pious to give their loved ones to the fire and eat the dead. How were those used to such an uncivilized way of life supposed to participate in the blessing of the friend of God? Unless, that is, they were going to turn away from savagery and take up a way of life similar to the piety of Abraham. (*DE* 1.2.15)

The intertexts in Eusebius's account of Christian/Hebrew kinship are two key Pauline passages: Colossians 3:11 ("There is no longer Greek and Jew, circumcised and uncircumcised, barbarian and Scythian") and Paul's figurative reading of Abraham's conversion in Galatians 3:6–9. Pauline claims to transcend traditional categories of identity was, for Porphyry, emblematic of the disruption that Christianity presented to the status quo.[27] For Eusebius, however, Paul, like Moses, is a "Hebrew of Hebrews" (2 Cor. 11:2) and the fluidity of "Hebrewness" a mark of strength and superiority.

The potency of Eusebius's narrative of descent lies in its simultaneous *affirmation* and *denial* of ethnicity. It is this ambivalence that permits Eusebius to position Christianity as an *ethnos* descended from the Hebrews and membership in that group as the *transcendence* of ethnicity and embodiment.[28] Becoming Hebrew—or, rather, becoming Christian— represents an ascent, or an escape, from the cacophony of ethnic particularity. Thus, as Andrew Jacobs has argued, it is precisely the "terminological slippage" of Eusebius's distinction between Jews and Hebrews that makes it an effective strategy. Eusebius's narratives of descent represent "a 'frontier zone' in which 'Hebrew,' 'Jew,' and 'Christian' all mingle to produce the triumphant Christian self."[29] To Jacobs's analysis I would add that this terminological vacillation is effective because it is coupled with, or rather refracted through, the desire to negotiate the metaphysical tension between transcendence and embodiment. Thus, the equation of "Hebrewness" with transcendence mitigates the simultaneous claims of ethnic descent on the part of Christians. Because "Hebrewness" is defined precisely by an absence of traditional markers of ethnocultural identity, it can contain and control the threat of embodiment. Thus in claiming "Hebrewness" a Christian like Eusebius can safely "play the Jew" in the face of Porphyry's criticisms.

Eusebius refuted Porphyry's first accusation—apostasy from tradition— by demonstrating that ancestral traditions had no divine origins but were errors that developed among specific peoples. Thus Eusebius implicates Porphyry himself in the genealogy of error that began with the nature worship of the Egyptians and Phoenicians. Porphyry had simply given a thin coating of philosophical jargon to myths and practices that have entirely human origins and are devoid of deeper, figurative meaning. The Christians, unlike Porphyry, recognize that there is no wisdom to be found among the *ethnē*. Eusebius counters Porphyry's accusation that the Christians had wantonly adopted a barbaric philosophy by arguing that Christianity represented a rediscovery and renaissance of the only true barbarian wisdom. The Christians were correct in laying aside the religions of their forebearers and adopting Hebrew wisdom. As Constantine emerged as the church's benefactor in the years after Eusebius completed the *PE/DE*, however, what began as a response to Porphyry's attack on Christian identity became the basis for a potent rhetoric of Christian imperialism. As Eusebius came increasingly to consider the relationship between Christianity and Rome, his historical narrative of the Christian appropriation of Hebrew wisdom and the rejection of ancestral traditions would metastasize into a narrative of conversion and conquest.

Imperial Conquest and Christian Mission

Eusebius was not the first early Christian to point to the synchrony of Christ's advent and the beginning of the Principate under Augustus. In the *Ecclesiastical History*, Eusebius preserves a portion of a second-century apology written by Melito of Sardis that points to the synchrony of the incarnation and the rise of the empire. Melito argues that Christianity "became a good omen to your Empire" and claims that emperors who do not persecute this "philosophy" are successful, while those who persecute, such as Nero and Domitian, gain ill repute (*HE* 4.26.7-9). The connection Melito posits between Rome and Christianity is a loose one; his argument hinges on fairly traditional notions of the relationship between Rome and native religions. Melito urges the current emperor, Marcus Aurelius, to respect Christianity as he would other cults within the empire (*HE* 4.26.7). If it is beneficial for Rome to honor the religions of her subject peoples, then *a fortiori* it is beneficial to respect the cult that began, auspiciously, when the empire began. He concludes by exhorting a return to the less aggressive policies of Hadrian and Trajan (*HE* 4.26.10).

In *Against Celsus*, Origen also uses the coincidence of Christ's earthly sojourn and the rise of Rome as an apologetic argument. Melito's concern was to convince Marcus Aurelius to abandon persecution based on an appeal to traditional Roman notions of piety and laissez-faire policy toward the religions of conquered peoples. Celsus, however, accuses Jesus as an obscure nobody; a true son of God, he argues, would have proclaimed himself far and wide, like the rising of the morning sun.[30] Origen argues that this is precisely what Christ did, though by proxy in the form of the mission of the apostles. It was according to God's providential arrangement that "Jesus was born in the reign of Augustus, who reduced the many peoples of the earth into one empire."[31] By eliminating the plurality of rulers and governments, Rome paved the way for apostles to spread Christianity to all peoples.[32]

Eusebius's early views about the relationship between empire and church bear a close affinity to Origen's ideas. In the *DE*, Eusebius uses the "synchrony argument" to answer Porphyrian criticisms of Christ. After quoting a portion of Porphyry's Hecataean oracle, Eusebius sets out to prove that Jesus was not a "charlatan" (*DE* 3.7.3). The miraculous spread of Christ's teaching throughout the world, he argues, is proof that he was no mere magician. Finally, Eusebius urges his readers to consider the miraculous coincidence of Rome's attainment of a world em-

pire and the success of the mission to the gentiles. According to Eusebius, Augustus's victory over "Egypt" at Actium marked a dramatic alter-
ation of political geography (*DE* 3.7.31). The Jews, Syrians,
Cappadocians, Macedonians, Bythinians, Greeks, "and in a word all the
other peoples" are now subject to Rome (*DE* 3.7.32). With the "varieties
of government" eliminated and ancient divisions between peoples re-
moved, the apostles were able to accomplish their mission more easily.
In addition, Rome had helped quash some of the more objectionable
and militant forms of traditional religion, in turn ameliorating some of
the animosity faced by the apostles as they spread the gospel among the
gentiles. Had Rome's paternalism not been a "hindrance to those enflamed by polytheistic error to make war against the teaching of Christ,
you would have seen civil rebellions in cities and the country" (*DE*
3.7.33–34). Like Origen, Eusebius views the empire as an aid to the
Christian mission, a proof of God's providential plan for the growth of
the church (*DE* 3.7.30–33). The coincidence of empire and church,
therefore, does not indicate an alliance between them; their parallel
growth is a miracle to wonder at as well as a powerful argument against
those, like Porphyry, who deny the divine origins of the gospel.

By destroying and dispersing the Jewish nation, moreover, the empire
also serves as God's instrument in effecting salvation history. The defeat
of the Jews during the Jewish War and, especially, the destruction of the
Jerusalem temple were crucial to Eusebius's understanding of history.
The demise of the temple visibly marked, in his opinion, an end to the
Jewish polity established by Moses' law and in turn aided Eusebius's
claims about the difference between Jews and Hebrews. Before the incarnation and the destruction of the temple, the Jews had followed the letter of Moses' law legitimately. After the advent and the destruction of the
temple, the Jews were merely persisting in error by refusing to acknowledge these two events as the fulfillment of Moses' prophesies and the predictions of the prophets. In Book 6 of the *DE*, Eusebius looks to
Zechariah as a proof text for his argument. Eusebius reads Zechariah
14:2-3 ("For I will gather all the nations against Jerusalem to battle. . . .
And the Lord shall go out and join in battle among the nations") as a reference to Rome's siege of Jerusalem. He interprets "nations" (*ta ethnē*) as
a reference to Rome and argues that God led the siege of Jerusalem (*DE*
6.18.14–17). Again, the apologetic thrust of Eusebius's exegesis is on the
role of Rome as a miraculous instrument of God's providence. He
focuses on God's providence, not Rome's imperial aspirations.

Eusebius wrote the *PE/DE* during the reign of Licinius and completed
it immediately prior to Constantine's victory at Chrysopolis. As Constantine emerged as the champion and patron of the church, Eusebius's
ideas about the relationship between church and empire began to shift.

Four texts that date to the end of Eusebius's career (his speech at the dedication of the Holy Sepulcher [*SC*], his oration in honor of the thirtieth anniversary of Constantine's reign [*LC*], the *Life of Constantine*, and Eusebius's last apologetic work, the *Theophany*) reveal an ideology of empire that equates Roman imperial expansion with the mission to the gentiles.[33] Each of these compositions dates to the mid-330s, around the time of Constantine's Tricennalia. Eusebius's panegyric for the occasion is easy to date; it was read in Constantinople on 25 July 336.[34] The speech on the Holy Sepulcher was given in September 335.[35] Eusebius also delivered a speech on the Sepulcher in Constantinople in Constantine's presence.[36] Eusebius promises to include the *LC* and *SC* as appendices to the *Life*. The extant manuscripts of the *Life*, however, contain only a single document titled *eis Kōnstantinon ton basilea triakontaetērikos* ("For Constantine's Tricennalia"), known also by the Latin title *Oratio de laudibus Constantini*. This text is very long, however, and contains a clear break after chapter 10.[37] Thus, most scholars now agree that that text appended to the *Life* is actually two works—chapters 1–10 are the *LC*, while chapters 11–18 are a version of the *SC*.[38] Eusebius began the *Life* immediately before or immediately after Constantine's death in May 337.[39] Eusebius may have died before completing the *Life*, leaving it to his successor to edit the text and add chapter headings.[40] The *Theophany*, the last of Eusebius's apologetic treatises, is preserved complete only in a Syriac translation and is difficult to date precisely. The *Theophany* bears a close relationship to Eusebius's panegyric for Constantine and the speech for the Holy Sepulcher; almost all of the *SC* is included in the *Theophany*, for instance.[41] Some argue that the *Theophany* served as a source for Eusebius's speeches while others argue the opposite.[42] In terms of the present study "the significant fact is that the work was written in the latter part of Eusebius's life, after Constantine had undertaken the great transformation of the imperial order."[43]

Although the nucleus of Eusebius's description of the relationship between empire and church in the *Theophany*, *LC*, and *SC* comes from the *DE*, the later works differ markedly from the earlier text. Eusebius reiterates Rome's role in eliminating local governments and replacing them with one unified monarchy (*SC* 16.304). As in the *DE*, empire facilitates travel and international intercourse, but the accent of Eusebius's argument has shifted to the shared mission of empire and church (*SC* 16.7). He now emphasizes the alliance of Roman imperial expansion and the mission to the gentiles in striking parallel phrasing and a repetitive vocabulary that insists on the unity of church and empire.

At the same time, one empire also flowered everywhere, the Roman, and the eternally implacable and irreconcilable enmity of nations was completely resolved. And as knowledge of One God was imparted to all men and one manner of piety, the salutary teaching of Christ, in the same way at one and the same time a single sovereign arose for the entire Roman Empire and a deep peace took hold of the totality. Together, at the same critical moment, as if from a single divine will, two beneficial shoots were produced for mankind: the empire of the Romans and the teachings of true worship. (SC 16.4)[44]

In Eusebius's pre-Constantinian work, the empire is simply propitious, a tool in God's hands, a useful but ancillary aid to proselytism. In these later works, by contrast, empire and church proceed in lockstep. The imperial conquest of peoples and the conversion of the gentiles have become two prongs in the same offensive against native error and barbarism. Through Rome's conquest and the apostles' dissemination of Christ's teaching "at one and the same time that the error of the demons was refuted, the eternal enmity and warfare of the nations was resolved." Finally, Eusebius deploys biblical proof texts to suture church and empire.

Thus the predictions of the ancient oracles and utterances of the prophets were fulfilled—countless of them not time now to quote, but including those which said of the saving *Logos* that "He shall have dominion from sea to sea, and from the rivers unto the ends of the earth" (Ps. 78.2). And again, "In his days shall the righteous flourish and abundance of peace" (Ps. 72.7). "And they shall beat their swords into ploughshares, and their spears into pruning hooks: nation shall not lift up sword against nation, neither shall they learn war any more." (Is. 2.4) (*SC* 16.7)

In Eusebius's reading of these passages from the Psalms and Isaiah, the vocabularies of Christian mission and imperial expansion are nearly identical. Both Roman Empire and Christian church insist on the catholic scope of their territory and accent peace and concord as the goal and justification of unity. Moreover, the elimination or sublimation of local identities is the means to peace and unity for both church and empire.

The mission to the gentiles and Rome's imperial aspirations cohere in Constantine's *imperium*. The parallels Eusebius draws between Constantine's sole rule and the monarchy of God have been studied exhaustively.[45] More fundamentally, however, empire consists in the control of different territories and peoples. Thus, Eusebius draws a further, less noticed but equally important parallel between the hegemony Constantine enjoys over the empire's peoples and the conversion of the gentiles. In the *LC*, Eusebius draws this connection by metonymy. The human body is representative of the imperial body.

Two kinds of natures have been entangled in us, I mean the spiritual and the physical. . . . And against these were drawn up two barbarian and hostile breeds, the one invisibly, the other openly. Thus, while one attacked the body physically, the other assaulted with incorporeal armaments the naked soul of man itself. Now the visible barbarians . . . no different from wild animals, roamed wildly about the domesticated flocks of man, laid fields to waste, and reduced cities to slavery. (*LC* 7.1.2)

The demons, on the other hand, had allied themselves with the world's peoples to propagate error and "establish in every corner sanctuaries and temples of a theology falsely named" (*LC* 7.5). This demonic invasion had culminated in the recent persecutions, when "those who were thought to rule . . . were so enslaved to the falsehood as to make sacrifice to the gods by the slaughter of their fellow citizens and point their sword at the champions of truth" (*LC* 7.6). God put an end to this conflict when he "put forth an invincible warrior as his attendant," that is, Constantine, who waged a multifaceted offensive. On the one hand, he waged a spiritual battle against error by teaching his subjects "how to live piously" (*LC* 7.12). Constantine's military victory over the persecutors is also the earthly instantiation of Christ's simultaneous victory over the demons. Eusebius again deploys symmetrical constructions and repetitive vocabulary to link Constantine's earthly conquests and the heavenly victories of Christ: "For while the Common Savior of the Universe punished the invisible beings invisibly, [Constantine] as the prefect of the Supreme Sovereign proceeded against those so vanquished, stripping their long and utterly dead corpses and distributing the spoils freely among the soldiers of the victor" (*LC* 7.13). Eusebius unites Constantine's imperial aspirations and the church's proselytizing desires most powerfully when he describes the cross as symbolic of their dual victory: "[To Constantine] He has revealed even His own Saving Sign, by which He prevailed over death and fashioned a triumph over His enemies. Setting this victorious trophy, apotropaic of demons, against the idols of error, he has won victories over all his godless foes and barbarians, and now over the demons themselves, which are but another type of barbarians" (*LC* 6.21). Constantine defeated the persecutors through force of arms, but Eusebius insists that the greater victory that should be celebrated is the elimination of ancestral customs in favor of the true religion conveyed by Christ the *Logos*.

Though Eusebius's speeches were delivered more than a decade after the defeat of persecutors and more than thirty years after the outbreak of the persecution itself, he still feels the need to explain why Christianity ought to be preferred over ancient parochial religions. There are clear echoes of Porphyry's "apostasy charge," for instance, in the opening of the *SC*: "Would it not be better, such a one might say, to preserve the ancestral rites and to propitiate the heroes and gods that are worshiped among each several race, and not to spit on them and desert them on account of some misfortune or other? . . . These things one of them might say, dramatically knitting his brows and proudly displaying his folly with the conceit he calls wisdom" (*SC* 11.4). Eusebius's imagined critic is propounding a more traditional model of Roman imperialism, in which the stability of empire depends on the inclusion and maintenance of native customs. As we saw in previous chapters, this is precisely the model of imperialism advocated by Diocletian and Porphyry.

In the body of the *SC*, Eusebius counters this criticism by portraying Constantine's Christian empire as the perfection of Roman imperialism. Again, Eusebius interweaves Rome's conquest of peoples and territory with the Christian mission to convert the gentiles. To argue his case, Eusebius deploys his history of religious and cultural development. According to Eusebius, "the reason why so great a *Logos* of God made the descent to humans" was to turn humanity away from the many erroneous cults various peoples had developed in the course of human history (*SC* 13.1). Eusebius expounds at length on the diversity of these false religions. He singles out the deification of nature (Demeter, Kore, Dionysius) and the subsequent worship of emotions and rational faculties (Mnemosyne, the Muses). He notes the different Euhemeristic cults "differing from nation to nation," including Heracles, Asclepius, and Apollo among the Greeks and Horus, Isis, and Osiris in Egypt (*SC* 13.4). He lambastes the Egyptians for introducing animal worship and criticizes the Phoenicians, Arabs, Getae, Cilicians, and Thebans for deifying men of ill repute (*SC* 13.5).

Eusebius deploys another ethnographic catalogue to recount the objectionable religious practices of various peoples. So many are these illicit practices, Eusebius argues, that he will single out only the most dramatic—human sacrifice. Drawing on many of the same sources he had used in crafting the historical arguments of the *PE/DE*, Eusebius offers a litany of human sacrifices among various peoples.

What could be more maniacal than to sacrifice human beings and to defile whole cities and one's own household with fraternal gore? Yet do not the Greeks themselves testify to these things? Is not every history book filled with such records? For the Phoenicians used to sacrifice annually to Kronos their only and sole-born children, while on Rhodes they used to slaughter men for the same god. . . . And on Salamis a given man . . . used to run three times around the altar, and then the priest would strike him on the stomach with a spear and roast him whole on the piled pyre. In Egypt used to occur the greatest number of human sacrifices—three a day at Hera at Heliopolis. . . . On Chios they used to sacrifice a man to Omadian Dionysius by tearing him to pieces, as likewise on Tenedos, while in Lacedaemon they honored Ares with human sacrifices. In Crete they did the same things, sacrificing men to Kronos. To Athena a virgin used to be sacrificed annually in Syrian Laodicea. . . . For a certainty both the Libyans and the Carthaginians used to propitiate their gods with human sacrifices, and the Dumatenoi of Arabia annually sacrificed a youth whom they buried under the altar. History teaches that all the Greeks in common performed human sacrifice before going to war, as did the Thracians and the Scythians. (*SC* 13.7).[46]

Human sacrifice is symptomatic of the violence and conflict endemic to humanity. Under the influence of demons, humanity was afflicted with a terrible "disease," the inability to communicate and carry on fruitful intercourse. Again Eusebius uses the metaphor of the human body to accentuate his argument: "Everywhere the great body that is naturally unified was torn asunder" (*SC* 13.9).[47] The *Logos* had become human, Eusebius argues, precisely to ameliorate the "beast-like existence" into which humanity had descended (*SC* 13.14–15). Eusebius was a skilled rhetor with a masterful sense of staging. Preaching before the new Church of the Holy Sepulcher, which housed the reputed sites of Jesus' death, burial, and resurrection, Eusebius uses metaphors with particular resonance. He argues that Christ's death and resurrection served as a "victory trophy (*tropaion epinikion*) over death and the demonic host" (*SC* 15.13). Though not as explicit as his references to the Labarum in the *LC*, Eusebius uses the same wordplay on *tropaion/apotropaion* to accentuate Christ's role as victor over demons. The resurrection also heralded the end to the false religions that gripped humanity, for in addition to victory over death and demons, it was also "a safeguard (*apotropaion*) against the human sacrifices" that were the quintessential mark of the dissent and diversity of the world's peoples (*SC* 15.13).

At the same time that Christ achieved this victory over the demons and had begun to facilitate a turn away from ancestral error, Roman conquest had united formerly diverse peoples into a new political body. Eusebius makes the connection between Christ's victory and the Pax Romana explicit by again using vivid parallel constructions and a repetitive vocabulary of unity.

For while the power of Our Savior destroyed the polyarchy and polytheism of the demons and heralded the one kingdom of God to Greeks and barbarians and all men to the farthest extent of the earth, the Roman Empire, now that the causes of the manifold governments had been abolished, subdued the visible governments, in order to merge the entire race into one unity and concord. Already it has united most of the various peoples, and it is further destined to obtain all those not yet united, right up to the very limits of the inhabited world. (*SC* 16.6)

Critics like the one Eusebius imagines at the opening of his oration charged that this new political vision was a break from Roman tradition.

Indeed, Eusebius himself tended to view the Constantinian empire as dramatically new. His repeated crasis of Pax Romana and the conversion of the gentiles, however, reveals important continuities between classic Roman imperialism and the new Christian variety being crafted by Eusebius. In both older Roman imperialism and its new Christian form, peoples—*ta ethnē*—were the constituent elements of the empire. Old ethnographic categories such as Greek, Scythian, Egyptian, and Phoenician have not disappeared in Eusebius's narrative of conquest.

Conquest, however, is only half of imperialism. The empire, both pre- and post-Constantine, absorbed difference through the acquisition of peoples and territory. Yet, despite Eusebius's rhetoric of assimilation, the process of Romanization/Christianization is never total. Empire does not eliminate difference, it merely controls and contains it. Rome sought to contain the threat of diversity by incorporating otherness within its borders, not through its elimination. Only by the amoeba-like absorption of other peoples, only by ever expanding her borders could Rome abate the threat of otherness. Eusebius envisions Christian imperialism in cognate terms. In the same way that Rome incorporated conquered peoples rather than destroying them, Christ's miraculous death and resurrection does not eradicate the gentiles but convinces them to abandon tradition and become part of the body of Christ.

For all Eusebius's rhetoric, however, there is an irony to his insistence on the achievement of unity and peace among different peoples. Though he proclaims that the empire is as "one people," difference remains a crucial component to the maintenance of Christian hegemony. Imperial power depends on the continual production and maintenance of difference, not its obliteration. There is a certain ambivalence endemic to imperial discourse. On the one hand, empire seeks to erase and domesticate native identities. On the other hand, this process of reformation is never complete. Because imperial power produces the very differences upon which hegemony depends, the irony to the imperial order is that the threat of difference is contained within, not excluded from, empire. In the case of Christian imperialism, this irony is manifest in the latent fear that conversion will miscarry, that subjects will return to their native traditions or, worse, that some more threatening hybrid will emerge in the form of "pagan survivals" and "crypto-pagans."[48] Consequently, the maintenance of hegemony requires that the process of (re)education and conversion be constantly reenacted.

The previous chapter indicated the importance of repeatability to Constantine's own rhetoric of empire. By rescuing Christianity from paganism at sites like Jerusalem, Mamre, Aphaca, and Heliopolis, Constantine was able to reassert his right to rule by reenacting his victory over the persecutors. The same is true of Eusebius's imperial rhetoric. To serve as an effective imperial rhetoric, Eusebius's narrative of conquest and conversion had to be anxiously repeated. Eusebius's narrative of conversion insists on the permanence of difference and the completedness and coherence of the transition from animality to civility, idolatry to Christianity. Conversion, however, is always in process.[49] The power of Eusebius's rhetoric, therefore, lies in its ability to be continually productive of difference. The *Life of Constantine* and the *SC* illustrate well the agonistic character of Christian imperial rhetoric.[50] They both carry the narrative of Christian empire into iterations beyond Constantine's own reign.

The dedication of the new basilica in Jerusalem was a poignant backdrop as Eusebius recounts the dual victory of Christ and Constantine for his audience. As he nears the end of his speech, Eusebius brings back his imagined critic. In the opening of the speech, Eusebius's imagined critic recalls Porphyry's anti-Christian polemics; here, the critic serves more as a cipher for doubters, crypto-pagans, and other threats to the univocal Christian empire of Eusebius's imagination. Eusebius counters this critic by pointing, perhaps quite literally as he spoke before Constantine's new church, to the changed urban space in Jerusalem as a physical manifestation of the conversion of the empire.

Come, let us address our detractor's hardened intellect along this line of interrogation, inquiring of him in this way. . . . Who has ever wrought such swift vengeance for the crimes committed against Him? Or was not the entire Jewish people scattered by an invisible power simultaneously with their impiety against Him, and was not their royal seat completely lifted off its foundations, and the temple itself, together with the sacred objects in it, brought down to the ground? Who, like Our Savior, having uttered clear predictions concerning both these impious men themselves and the establishment by Him of a universal church, made good these pledges with deeds? For He said about the temple of the impious ones, "Your house is left unto you desolate" (Mt. 23.38), and, "There shall not be left one stone upon another in this place that shall not be thrown down" (Mt. 24.2). And about His own church, "on this rock I will build my church, and the gates of hell shall not prevail against it." (Mt. 16:18) (*SC* 17.7–8, cf. *Th.* 24–27)

The juxtaposition of temple ruins and the new Christian basilica serves to justify the Christian colonization of Jerusalem. Constantine's monumental building project constructs imperial presence in Jerusalem and visibly and materially conquers and replaces Jerusalem's native Jewish past with a new Christian present.[51] The contrast between temple ruin and new church "marks the intersection and collusion" of the ecumenical aspirations of Rome and the Christian church.[52]

At the same time that Constantine's new church serves as a visible sign of the supercession of Judaism, however, it is more broadly suggestive of the rejection and defeat of *all* ancestral traditions and their replacement by Christianity. The speech builds to a crescendo as Eusebius recounts Christ's victory over the persecutors and the universal penetration of Christianity.

> What think you of the fact that He summoned originally simple and rustic men and changed them from fishermen into lawgivers and teachers of the law for the whole world? Or that He should . . . provide them with such ability and power as even to compose writings and hand down books that have prevailed throughout the whole world to such an extent that they have been translated into every kind of language, both barbarian and Greek, to be studied among all peoples . . . ? (*SC* 17.9, cf. *Th.* 3.28)

Eusebius directs this apostrophe against his imagined critic, again likely a cipher for Porphyry; criticism of the apostles had been part of his critique of Christianity.[53] Eusebius makes his narrative doubly productive, however, by urging his audience to consider Christ's victory as an imminent and ongoing reality: "Who else continues to command after death, to raise trophies over his enemies, and to subordinate every land and country and city, both Greek and barbarian?" (*SC* 17.11). The two main subjects of the speech—Christ's resurrected body and Constantine—are notable for their physical absence from Jerusalem. Thus, at the same time that Golgotha and the empty tomb reveal the reality of Christ's victory over death and demons, the new basilica that houses these signs serves as visible proof of Constantine's *imperium* (*SC* 18.3). Eusebius accents the omnipresence of Christ and Constantine as he encourages his audience to reexperience the dramatic change in times brought about by the dual victory of church and empire. Thus, the new church is built triumphant over two pasts, Jewish and gentile, and serves as a single sign of the univocal Christian imperial present.

Like the *SC*, the *VC* celebrates the absent presence of Christ's body in order to accentuate the new Christian imperial body born out of Christ's victory over ancestral error and the incorporation of the gentiles. Like the resurrected body of Christ, moreover, the dead emperor has become omnipresent. "Wherever I earnestly investigate," Eusebius intones, "whether to the sun's rising or its setting, or over the whole earth, or to heaven itself, I see the blessed one being present in everything and everywhere in the empire" (*VC* 1.1.2). The omnipresence of the now-deceased emperor helps Eusebius ameliorate anxiety over the persistence of native religion. Ever alert to the persistent threat of error, the emperor embarked on a campaign to remove the remains of traditional religion (*VC* 3.54.4). Eusebius portrays the emperor's subsequent proscription of native practices at sites like Aphaca and Heliopolis as a general campaign against paganism. These rather limited and specific instances of imperial repression thus become an opportunity to experience vicariously the conversion of these spaces from sites of native error to spaces that reveal (Christian) imperial power.

So immanent is the emperor's authority and false religions so weak that a few unarmed officials sufficed for the despoliation of the temples.[54] Like "an eagle soaring the heavens," Constantine "surveyed all with his ruling gaze lest some hidden remainder of error go unnoticed" (*VC* 3.55.1). Constantine's supervision extends even into the most remote mountains of Phoenicia as well as "every dark cave and every inmost hidden passage" (*VC* 3.55.2, 3.57.4). Like Jerusalem, Aphaca, Heliopolis, and Aigai were fruitful sites in which to inscribe the power of Christianity and the frailty of native religions. According to Eusebius, the emperor's order to raze the Aphrodite complex at Aphaca taught locals " to practice self-control" instead of ritual prostitution (*VC* 3.55.5). Curtailing the cult of Asclepius in Aigai taught that "the successes of the emperor were granted by God and no mere myth" (*VC* 3.56.3). At Heliopolis in Phoenicia, moreover, the "city of superstition" became a new Christian community when Constantine banned ritual prostitution associated with Aphrodite, built a new church, and installed clergy (*VC* 3.58.1–4). By these regional actions, Constantine gives an encore performance of his role as universal pedagogue "so that it was visible and clear to all where the perverted ideas that had long held sway over all peoples had come from" (*VC* 3.57.4). In Eusebius's narrative, the displacement of native traditions by Christian teaching, buildings, and officials is demonstrative of the manifest destiny of the Christian empire.

For Eusebius, the most fecund site in which to demonstrate the difference between ancestral traditions and Christianity was, perhaps, Constantine himself. Though Constantine materially supported the church and, as we saw in Chapter 4, developed his own ideology of Christian empire, the lineaments of his identity were far from certain during his reign. Alongside his monumental Christian building program and his curtailing of certain traditional practices, the emperor continued, at least nominally, to preside over Roman religion as *pontifex maximus*, built pagan temples in his new Christian capital, and kept pagans in the court and the imperial service.[55] This ambivalence has led many to consider Constantine the greatest of all "crypto-pagans."[56]

Eusebius negotiates the ambivalences in Constantine's identity by recounting the emperor's deathbed baptism. Realizing that the end was near, Constantine resolved to seal his conversion. Eusebius imagines the emperor's proclamation: "Let there be no ambiguity. . . . It is decided that I will be declared a member of the people of God" (*VC* 4.62.3). More than establishing Constantine's identity, however, Eusebius's narrative of the emperor's baptism and death is demonstrative of the conversion of the empire itself. Constantine's disavowal of any ambivalence in his own self-identity obscures the persistence of ethnic and cultural diversity within the larger imperial body. Constantine dies, propitiously (or conveniently) for Eusebius, on the last day of Pentecost, which celebrates "the ascension of the universal savior into heaven and the descent of the Holy Spirit to humanity" (*VC* 4.64.1–2). By accenting the significance of Pentecost, Eusebius affirms Constantine's place in his narrative of religious history. The two pentecosts—the first, at which the apostles received the gift of languages, and the second, which celebrates the clarity of Constantine's Christian identity—are bookends to the story of Christianity's triumph over ancestral customs—a story that overwrites the ethnic and cultural diversity that is always latent in the empire and evident in the glossolalia with which the mission to the gentiles began.

Empire's Palimpsest

I have argued for a consideration of pagan polemics and Christian apologetics not simply as sites of "religious conflict" or the production of "self-definition" but also as discourses both *constituted by* and *constitutive* of Roman imperialism. Universal history, ethnography, and figurative reading strategies—the tools of philosophers and apologists alike—owed much of their shape to the specific political context in which they were practiced. The leverage of these universalizing discourses lay not in "pluralism" or "inclusivity," as has sometimes been suggested; rather, the political potency of universalism resided in its simultaneous demand for comprehensiveness and difference. The distinction between universality and particularity that grounded these intellectual discourses closely paralleled the asymmetrical relationship of Rome and her provinces, which therefore made them effective discourses of social privilege and social control. Ethnography and universal history sought a comprehension of diversity homologous to the imperial desire for control of diverse territories and peoples. Likewise, much as the empire viewed its provinces as resources ripe for exploitation, intellectuals deployed figurative reading practices as a means to extract valuable resources from native sources. In response to persecution and anti-Christian polemics, the earliest Christian apologists disturbed the imperial order and destabilized the authority and privilege of Greco-Roman intellectuals by manipulating these discourses of universalism and difference. Apologetic discourse did not displace earlier rhetorics of difference, but imitated and disrupted them.

The early fourth century marked a critical moment. The persecutions under Diocletian, Galerius, and Maximinus were the most systematic attempt by the Roman imperial authorities to contain and control Christianity. Simultaneously, polemicists like Porphyry offered sophisticated and incisive challenges to Christian identity. Lactantius and Eusebius imitated and inverted Porphyry's own historical and exegetical arguments, redrawing historical geography by locating Christianity as transcendent, beyond the cacophony of ethnic diversity. Constantine's reign catalyzed the potential energy of Christian apologetic discourse into an effective rhetoric of power and difference. Under Constantine and his heirs the apologists' rhetoric came to map new imperial subjectivities based around the distinction between an a-cultural, transcendent Christianity and a "paganism" embodied in the ethnic diversity of the empire's peoples. For Lactantius, Eusebius, and even Constantine himself, the foundation myth of Constantine's empire was a narrative of "conservative" revolution—the *new* Constantinian empire was based on the "rediscovery" of a putatively *ancient* (Christian) Ur-theology that stood in contrast to all other historically contingent traditions. Although Christian-centered geographies challenged earlier Greek- and Roman-centered conceptualizations of the Mediterranean, *ta ethnē*, "peoples," remained the objects of imperial rule and supervision.

Throughout this book I have also suggested that early Christian apologetic discourses represented a mode of comparative practice analogous to, and in some ways a basis for, certain early modern and modern discourses of "comparative religion" and the "history of religion(s)." While I cannot pretend to anything like a systematic history in this brief conclusion, I would like to suggest some important points of contact between late ancient and early modern and modern thinking on religion. Recent analyses of the history of these academic discourses often acknowledge a kind of origin in the Latin signifier *religio*—particularly in Lactantius's improvisations on Cicero's famous etymology. In the hands of Christians, *religio* begins to assume some of the semantic range of the modern "religion." We have seen this semantic shift in the case of Lactantius, for whom *religio* marks sets of theological propositions and is theoretically identifiable transhistorically among all peoples.

Others are more reticent to trace the history of early modern and modern comparative religion and history of religions scholarship to antiquity. Instead, they contend that "religion" and the discursive systems in which it functions are conditioned by and responsive to distinctly modern, as opposed to premodern, geopolitical situations. I have argued that we should locate the ethnological and historical rhetorics of Christian apologetics in the political context of (Roman) imperialism. The practices and rhetorics of empire were certainly not identical in late ancient Rome and, for example, the late nineteenth-century British or French empires. Late ancient Roman imperialism did, nevertheless, consist in the conquest and control of diverse peoples and territories, and we have seen, especially in Chapter 1, that academic discourses under Rome were conditioned by the power dynamics of imperialism. Early modern and modern colonialists, moreover, often turned to the example of the patristic past in their own encounters with "others." These homologies, I would contend, point to more than simple parallelism between late ancient and modern thinking on "religion" and "religions."

David Chidester proposes a threefold typology of "phases, or domains, or epistemes in the history of comparative religion" that is useful for exploring points of contact between late ancient and modern discourses on religion. Chidester locates the first type, "frontier" comparative religion, at the point of contact between colonizer and colonized. This is the mode of comparative practice characteristic of "travelers, missionaries, and colonial agents."[1] A second type, "imperial" comparative religion, is that practiced in the metropolitan centers of European empires. The academic discourses of the nineteenth- and early twentieth-century European academies are of this type, which tends toward diachronic and geographic comprehensiveness. These discourses offer totalizing historical and evolutionary schemata that provide comprehensive knowledge for the control of subalterns in the metropolis as well as in the provinces.[2] Finally, Chidester describes a third type, "apartheid" comparative religion. Chidester focuses specifically on the role of comparative religion in structuring the apartheid systems of South Africa, but he intends the term to refer more broadly to comparative religion as a science of local control, in which imperial officials in the field deploy the terms and categories of "imperial" comparative religion as a means to structure their governance of subject territories and peoples.[3]

Early Christian apologetic discourse, as practiced in the literary work of Lactantius, Eusebius, and Constantine, is a species of and a precursor of the mode of comparative religion Chidester identifies as "imperial." The comparative religionists of the nineteenth century "arranged disparate evidence from all over the world into a single uniform temporal sequence, from primitive to civilized, that claimed to represent the universal history of humanity."[4] As we saw in Chapter 1, comparative practice and its schematization in totalizing, universalizing histories of religion is predicated on the control of disparate territories and peoples. As such, these totalizing discourses were not a uniquely Victorian creation, nor even a uniquely Christian rhetorical strategy. Empire is the Foucauldian *episteme* that grounds both ancient and modern comparative practice.[5] Conditioned as it was by the context of empire in which it emerged, Christian apologetic discourse was always already a fertile vehicle for the production of imperial knowledge and power.

Comparative religion and the history of religions are disciplines that appear along the event horizon of ethnocultural contact at the edges or *limes* of empire. They are driven by the engine of conquest and fueled by the cross-cultural data that conquest produces. The *limes* upon which the ethnographic and historiographic discourses of Christian apologetic functioned could be literal geopolitical boundaries. The terms of Christian apologetics—idolatry, for example—served the interests of early medieval and Byzantine missionaries as they sought to convert new gentile populations in northern and eastern Europe. The forty or so years between the turn of the fourth century and the death of Eusebius in 339 C.E.—the period I have been considering in this book—was not, however, a time of great territorial expansion for Rome.[6] Nevertheless, the borders between Christians and the *ethnē* could just as well be notional. Terms like *Christianismos, Hellenismos, ethnē, gentes,* and *nationes,* as well as a host of heresiological appellatives, served as signifiers in a science of local and global control. Working within such a system of knowledge, bishops and imperial officials living well inside the borders of Roman territory could find themselves on the frontier between Christians and others. The discourse of apologetics provided a system of knowledge that structured contact between Christians and the *ethnē.* These frontier encounters were also crucial sites for the production of imperial subjectivities.

The rhetoric of Christian imperialism also came to mediate new subjectivities on the part of non-Christians, structuring the ways in which they resisted Christian hegemony. Beginning already in the fourth century, many non-Christians began to understand themselves in the terms set out by Christian imperial discourse. Thus, the reign of Julian "the Apostate" was shaped as much by his uncle Constantine and his cousin Constantius II than the venerable traditions of "pagan" Greece and Rome that he cherished so dearly. Julian's letters and treatises present a world divided into Hellenes and "Galileans," his polemical term for Christians. This polarized landscape looks more like the world of Eusebius's panegyrics than it does the empires of Augustus and Marcus Aurelius, whom Julian so admired.[7] Much of Julian's brief reign focused on self-consciously challenging the narrative of Christianization. Julian's anti-Christian measures, including his attempt to rebuild the Jerusalem temple, his ban on Christian teachers from teaching the "classics," his efforts to renew the oracle at Daphne at the expense of the martyr-cult of St. Babylas, and his polemical *Against the Galilaeans* were attempts to undermine the supercessionist core of the Christian narrative.[8] His abortive efforts to rehabilitate "Hellenism" reflected, at the same time that they resisted, new imperial subjectivities.

In the last quarter of the fourth century, the urban prefect of Rome, Symmachus, also worked to thwart the demise of tradition. Faced with the removal of the Altar of Victory from the senate house in Rome, Symmachus appealed on behalf of the senate to the emperor Theodosius: "That is why we ask you to give us back our religious institutions as they used to be when for so long they were of value to the state. Of course, we can list Emperors of either faith and either conviction: the earlier Emperors venerated our ancestral religious rites, the later did not abolish them."[9] In Diocletian's court a century earlier, Symmachus's rhetoric would have resonated as an appeal to the stability and certainty of a shared Roman identity. In the empire of the late fourth century, however, the prefect casts identity as an either/or proposition as he cites the example of "emperors of either faith and either conviction" (*principes utriusque sectae utriusque sententiae*) who have preserved ancestral tradition. The prefect's argument for toleration assumes a political geography familiar from Christian apologetics—Romans are simply one of the many peoples in the (now Christian) empire. Though perhaps more politically savvy than Julian, Symmachus's resistance affirms the narrative of Christianization upon which Theodosius's reign depended. Ancestral tradition, like the Altar of Victory itself, has become a venerable antique worthy of preservation only as the visible sign of a disappearing past.

Christian hegemony did not go unchallenged by "pagans." Because Christian imperialism emerged out of the inherent instabilities within Roman imperial discourse, the maintenance of Christian hegemony required repetitions of difference. Unfortunately, the only access to much of this "pagan resistance" is that afforded by Christian texts. Augustine, for instance, describes the riots that erupted in Sufes and Calama when traditional religionists celebrated native festivals in defiance of laws banning aspects of traditional religion.[10] Rufinus recounts similar violence in Alexandria that developed in reaction to the despoliation of traditional religious sites.[11] Any resistance on the part of traditional religionists, however, fueled the penetration of Christian imperialism by reifying "pagans" as a threat to order and a legitimate target for imperial supervision.

Pagan resistance also confirmed apologists' characterizations of gentile intransigence and barbarism, which in turn pointed to a need (in the view of Christian intellectuals) for further iterations of apologetic discourse. The durability of apologetic discourse represents the development of a "textual attitude," a preference for "the schematic authority of a text to the disorientations of direct encounters with the human."[12] Apologetics could thus be summoned to *produce* strategically useful encounters between pagans and Christians. One could fashion himself or herself as "Christian" by staging cognitive border disputes. Apologetic discourse thus became ossified as writers like Theodoret, Cyril of Alexandria, and Augustine continued the apologetic tradition of Lactantius and Eusebius well beyond the fourth century.

Early Christian apologetics—as an historical-ethnographic discourse—also proved useful well beyond late antiquity. In the early modern period, in particular, the European "discovery" of new lands and peoples prompted new deployments of these late ancient rhetorics. In her history of the study of "world religions," for example, Tomoko Masuzawa notes that early modern taxonomies of the religions of the world were closely linked to, and were often indistinguishable from, ethnological classifications of the "peoples of the world."[13] As European explorers and colonizers encountered strange new peoples in the Americas, Africa, Asia, and Oceania, they had a discourse at hand that served to structure cross-cultural encounters and a historical-ethnological schema in which to arrange their newfound data.

Spanish conquistadores, missionaries, and colonial officials looked to the example of the Constantinian and Theodosian empires in their encounters with the peoples of Central and South America. Ancient Christian discourses provided conceptual categories and models for the management of newly conquered peoples. In Peru, for instance, colonial administrators modeled their efforts to restrain native "idolatry" on the fourth- and fifth-century legislation preserved in the *Theodosian Code*.[14] A Spanish chronicler describes how by destroying and despoiling an Incan sacred site "the Christians explained to the Indians the great error in which they had been enveloped. . . . [Pizarro] broke the idol in the sight of everyone, told them many things about our holy catholic faith." Just as we have seen Eusebius read Constantine's attacks on certain traditional religious sites and practices as a form of argumentation, Spanish colonialists interpreted their own strategic acts of religious violence as an extension of the "instructive" discourse of apologetics.[15]

European intellectuals also looked to the patristic past as they set out to include the "new gentiles" of the Americas in their globalizing ethnographic and historical texts. José de Acosta's *Natural and Moral History of the Indians*, for instance, was structured around the same basic historical-ethnological narrative that we have traced from Paul through to the apologists of the early fourth century. Acosta argues that all humans have the capacity for natural religion, though the idolatrous nations have devolved from this Ur-monotheism to worship creatures rather than the creator. Like the apologists, Acosta draws on Romans 1 and the *Wisdom of Solomon* to ground his taxonomies of native error and makes explicit morphological comparisons between Greek and Roman "idolatry" and that of the indigenous populations of North and South America.[16] The identification of the indigenous peoples of the Americas as "new gentiles" authorized the militant, often violent, extirpation of traditional religions as "idolatry." Certain colonialists, such as Juan Ginés de Sepúlveda, went so far as to deny that natives possessed the capacity for natural religion at all; as such, they were subhuman and could be exploited as slaves.[17] At the same time, however, others located native cultures along a spectrum of "civilization." Early Christians had linked the development of arts and natural sciences with the projection of natural religious instincts onto inappropriate objects and forms of worship. Even the basest forms of idolatry, in such a reading, evince the innate human drive to worship the creator God. Some New World missionaries, taking a cue from patristic precedent, read the presence of *false* religions among natives as a mark of a universal human capacity for *true* religion. Thus Bartolomé de Las Casas, writing his *Defense of the Indians* in reaction to Sepúlveda, drew upon Romans 1 and patristic authorities to argue that the traditions of the peoples of the Yucatan represented incomplete, yet nevertheless real, expressions of an original, universal monotheism.[18]

These modes of interpreting non-European peoples come from a script now familiar from the preceding chapters. Early ethnographies of New World peoples are marked by a tension. On the one hand, early comparative religionists describe indigenous religions as products of historical processes—especially the Euhemeristic worship of culture heroes and ancestors and the anthropomorphizing of natural forces. On the other hand, there is often also an insistence in the capacity of "natives," whether the "gentiles" of the New World or the *gentes* of early Christian apologetic, for natural, authentic religion. As we have seen, this tension made it possible for Lactantius to extract natural theology from "gentile" sources and allowed Eusebius to devalue traditional religions while presenting classical culture as a preparation for the gospel. These historical-ethnographic narratives were also teleological, culminating in Christian manifest destiny ("making disciples of all nations") and thus conducive to a specific mode of praxis—conversion. Whether newly discovered peoples were positioned as noble savages or savage idolaters, they were being fitted into different object positions in the same totalizing historical-ethnographic narrative. Las Casas, for instance, argues against violence, but the terms of this argument are those of the late ancient apologists. Las Casas and those he critiques, then, though they position indigenous peoples somewhat differently, are working to the same ends—both engage in comparative religion to arrive at the most effective strategies for handling these conquered and about-to-be-conquered peoples. Similar scripts were enacted on other colonial frontiers. In seventeenth-century North America, Jesuit missionaries looked to early Christian histories of religion as they interpreted the practices and mythologies of the Hurons, Iroquois, and Algonquins. As part of his evangelization of the Hurons of upper Canada, for example, Jean de Brébeuf looked for homologies between indigenous mythologies and those of Greece and Rome. "As these poor Indians are men, they have not been able to deny the existence of God altogether," but like the gentiles of Romans 1 (which Brébeuf quotes at length), they worship creation rather than the creator.[19]

In the colonies, the terms of Christian apologetic served as the basis for the efficient conquest and governance of new "gentile" populations.

But early Christian apologetic discourses also functioned productively for Europeans "at home." The discovery of new indigenous populations goaded a renewed interest in universal history and ethnography.[20] Missionaries and colonial officials, like Las Casas or the Jesuits of New France, deployed concepts of natural religion and perennial philosophy that had been rehearsed in the late fifteenth century by Renaissance Neoplatonists like Marsilio Ficino, Pico de Mirandola, and Nicolas Cusanus.[21] Reniassance intellectuals drew on the same panoply of classical theories of religion—Euhemerism, the *Kulturbringer* motif, and so forth—that the early Christian apologists had deployed against "paganism." The work of Renaissance humanists is sometimes read as a return to the classical, pre-Christian past. In fact, Renaissance scholars returned to classical sources in large part *through* the works of patristic authors. Humanists' questioning of what constituted humanness and the limits of "religion" and Christianity involved as much a reworking of late ancient *Christian* discourses on the history of religion and culture as it did a return to classical sources. In his *On the Peace of Faith*, for example, Cusanus (Nicholas of Cusa) argues for an essential unity within the diversity of the world's traditions. The work consists of a set of dialogues between representatives of various peoples: Greek, Italian, Arab, Indian, Chaldean, Jew, Scythian, French, Persian, Syrian, Turk, Spaniard, German, Tartar, Armenian, Bohemian, and English. Cusanus's ethnographic catalogue bears the marks of an ancient (and perhaps also Pauline) ethnographic imagination (Greek, Chaldean, Jew, Scythian) at the same time that it is attenuated to the national identities emerging in early modern Europe. Cusanus, in fact, understands his project as a natural extension of classical and early Christian comparative practice, as he makes clear in his conclusion.

After these topics were discussed in the foregoing way with the wise [men] of all nations, there were exhibited very many books authored by those who had written about the observances of the ancients—excellent books, indeed, in every language (as, for example, among the Latins, Marcus Varro; among the Greeks, Eusebius, who gathered examples of the diversity of the religions; and very many others). After these [writings] were examined, it was ascertained that *the entire diversity [among the religions] lay in the rites rather than in the worship of one God.* From all the writings, which had been collected into one, it was learned that since the very beginning all [men] have always presupposed God and worshiped Him in all their religious practices.[22]

The universal religion that Cusanus extracts from all culturally specific modes of practice is, of course, as it was for Lactantius and Eusebius before him, Christianity. Cusanus's comparison of the world's religions was an extension of the late ancient quest for the universal truth that transcended ethnic particularity and was sanctioned, in effect, by patristic precedent. Renaissance Neoplatonists, moreover, were "authorized" to return to Plato, Plotinus, Porphyry, and Iamblichus precisely because early Christians like Lactantius, Eusebius, and Augustine had adopted and adapted them. Thus, explaining why one must look beyond Scholastics like Aquinas and Duns Scotus to the esoteric wisdom of the Hermetica, Chaldean Oracles, and Platonists, Pico de Mirandola echoes the attitude of apologists like Justin Martyr and Eusebius: "All wisdom flowed from the barbarians to the Greeks, and from the Greeks to us."[23]

Tomoko Masuzawa has traced the emergence of nineteenth-century comparative religion and "history of religions" scholarship from these early modern ethnographic discourses. In the seventeenth and eighteenth centuries, the comparative history and ethnography of religion also came to serve the interests of theologians working to recenter Christianity amid the new cacophony of religious and cultural diversity in the colonies. This project of cross-cultural comparison bore more than a passing resemblance to the work of the early apologists. Indeed, comparative theologians looked directly to patristic precedent in their own work. The ambitious title of Samuel Purchas's 1613 work *Purchas His Pilgrimage, or Relations of the World and the Religions Observed in All Ages and Places Discovered, from the Creation unto This Present* suggests the link between early Christian apologetics and heresiology and Purchas's own project. His preface lays explicit claim to biblical and patristic precedent.

Now if any man thinke, that it were better these rotten bones of the passed, and stinking bodies of the Present superstitions were buried, than thus raked out of their graves . . . I answere, That I have sufficient example in the Scriptures, Which were written for our learning to the ends of the World, and yet depaint unto us the ugly face of Idolatry in so many Countries of the Heathens, with the Apostasies, Sects, and Heresies of the Jewes, as in our first and second booke is shewed: and *the Ancient Fathers also, Justin, Tertullian, Clemens [of Alexandria], Irenaeus, Origen, and more fully, Eusebius, Epiphanius, and Augustine, have gone before us in their large Catalogues of Heresies and false Opinions.*[24]

This structuring of discourse on religion and religions is not distinctly modern. It is based, rather, on the same dichotomies between the particular and the universal that drove late ancient thinking on philosophical and religious universalism. The "ethnic reasoning" of early Christians, refracted as it was through the prism of a polarized metaphysics that privileged the universal over the particular, cast a long shadow over the nascent disciplines of comparative religion, the history of religions, and religious studies. Masuzawa points out that late nineteenth- and early twentieth-century "world religions" curricula and textbooks (and some contemporary ones as well), for example, were structured by a dichotomy between universal religions and "national" religions.[25] The scientific study of religion, in other words, even as it decentered Christianity in important ways, depended on systems of classification that stemmed from early Christian apologetic arguments that set the traditions of *ta ethnē, gentes,* and *nationes* in contrast to the transcendence and universality of Christianity.

The disciplines of comparative religion and the history of religions tend to obscure their implication in imperial conquest and administration.[26] In the nineteenth and twentieth centuries, couching the comparative and historical study of religions as an objective *sciences religieuses* or *religionsgeschichteschule* served to insulate it from implication in the conquests that provided the data for analysis. Such a move in turn acquired for practitioners a privileged epistemological position. Like Porphyry's comparative search for the perennial philosophy, Lactantius's quest for *vera religio* and *vera sapientia,* or Eusebius's historical ethnography, such a move is politically implicated. Like the late ancient intellectuals who surveyed "barbarian wisdom" in order to extract a universal philosophy, mid-twentieth-century historians of religion mined myths and rituals cross-culturally in order to produce an account of "religion" as a sui generis, transhistorical, and transcultural "essence" freed from the messy realm of historical becoming.[27] If early Christian apologetic emerged out of and as a means of negotiating the power dynamics of imperialism, the latter move—based on a similar dichotomy between being and becoming, the universal and the culturally particular—grounds the power dynamics of late nineteenth- and early twenty-first-century geopolitics in which cross-cultural knowledge of "religion" became (and remains) a basis for praxis at the local and global levels.

In the early fourth century, the symbiotics of empire and Christian mission were obscured by appeals to "providence."

For while the power of Our Savior destroyed the polyarchy and polytheism of the demons and heralded the one kingdom of God to Greeks and barbarians and all men to the farthest extent of the earth, the Roman Empire, now that the causes of the manifold governments had been abolished, subdued the visible governments, in order to merge the entire race into one unity and concord. Already it has united most of the various peoples, and it is further destined to obtain all those not yet united, right up to the very limits of the inhabited world. (*SC* 16.6)

Where Eusebius finds the guiding hand of divine providence, modern scholars find "political theology." But this "providential" relationship between monarchic empire and monotheistic theology also shows that to understand the place of late ancient Christian apologetic discourses in the "history of the history of religions" we need to look beyond semantic shifts in terms like *religio*. It can be all too easy to read the lineage of *religio* in terms of the penetration of a Christian mentalité marked by faith and monotheism into an otherwise fairly delimited Latin term.[28] Christian apologists, notably Lactantius, as we saw in Chapter 3, deploy *religio* to signify the difference between Christians and others. Yet the polemical situations in which apologists found themselves transposing traditional vocabularies onto "globalized" histories were occasioned by an imperial politics that valued such hierarchical dichotomies in the first place. Indeed, the very possibility of these semantic shifts was conditioned by the material realities of empire, acknowledged (if opaquely) by Eusebius and Constantine: the penetration of territories, the domination and administration of peoples, and an umbrella of military force–protection making possible global travel and communication. Western discourse on "religion," ancient and modern, is written on empire's palimpsest.

Porphyry's Polemics and the Great Persecution

The Date and Attribution of Porphyry's Anti-Christian Fragments

The remains of *Against the Christians* were first collected and edited by Adolf von Harnack in 1916, and his continues to be the standard edition. Harnack ascribed ninety-seven fragments to *Against the Christians*, most taken from the late fourth-century apologist Macarius Magnes, Jerome, and Eusebius. Based on a reference in the *Suda*, Harnack argues that the text consisted of fifteen books, which references the work as *Kata Christianōn logoi ie* (Harnack, *testimonium* III); however, the extant fragments do not provide enough information to reconstruct the text with absolute certainty. Aside from the discovery of several "new" fragments, Harnack's edition remained largely unchallenged for over half a century.[1] A particular point of contention has been, and remains, Harnack's inclusion of fifty-one fragments from the *Apocriticus* of Macarius Magnes. The *Apocriticus* is written in the form of responses to the anti-Christian polemics of an anonymous "Hellene." Harnack argues that Macarius took the "Hellene's" polemics from an epitome of Porphyry's *Against the Christians*.[2] In the early 1970s, however, Timothy Barnes called for a more rigorous approach to the fragments, arguing in particular for the rejection of those Harnack took from the *Apocriticus*; if the *Apocriticus* preserves anything of Porphyry's polemics, he contends, it does so "only indirectly, from a later writer or writers who used Porphyry."[3] Others contend that the polemics of Hierocles or Julian are Macarius's source.[4] In his recent critical edition of the *Apocriticus*, however, Richard Goulet argues convincingly for the authenticity of the fragments.[5] The anonymous Hellene's arguments, Goulet argues, represent a coherent set of polemics that focus on contradictions and inconsistencies in Christian scriptures, criticism of the apostles (especially Peter and Paul), the absurdity or embarrassing character of biblical passages when read literally, and the inadequacy of Christian exegesis. These represent an ensemble of polemics that the anonymous Hellene and Porphyry share.[6] Goulet also suggests a fair degree of lexical similarity between the Hellene's polemics and other extant fragments of Porphyry.[7]

Joseph Bidez dates the work to circa 270 C.E. based on Eusebius's testimony that "Porphyry, who settled in Sicily in our time, issued treatises against us, attempting in them to slander the sacred scriptures," along with Porphyry's own testimony that he traveled to Sicily to recover from a bout of depression circa 270 C.E.[8] Noting Porphyry's use of Callinicus Sutorius's *History of Alexandria* (a text known to have been written in the early 270s), Alan Cameron has argued for a *terminus post quem* of 271–75.[9] W. H. C. Frend situates Porphyry's polemics within a "propaganda war" between Christians and conservative pagans at the end of the third century, pointing especially to Diocletian's and Galerius's consultation of the oracles in the lead-up to the persecution as evidence for the influence of *Philosophy from Oracles* and to the wide influence of *Against the Christians* in subsequent anti-Christian polemics.[10] Barnes, however, pushes for a still later date. He asserts that scholars have misread Eusebius's reference to the composition of *Against the Christians.* According to Barnes, Eusebius's phrase *ho kath' hēmas en Sikelia katastas Porphurios* does not refer to the time or place of composition but is a descriptive phrase intended to insult Porphyry for living in an "intellectual backwater."[11] He has also pointed to a fragment in which Porphyry refers to Britain as a "fertile province for tyrants"; according to Barnes, this phrase only makes sense if it was penned in the years following Carausius's usurpation of 286–93 C.E.[12] Barnes goes further, identifying Harnack's fragment 1, in which Porphyry calls down "just punishments" on apostates from ancestral traditions, as a summary of Porphyry's argument. This intolerant tone, in Barnes's estimation, makes circa 300 C.E., with anti-Christian sentiment growing and the Great Persecution looming, a likely date of composition.[13]

The extant fragments of *Philosophy from Oracles* come from three books, though the total number of books remains disputed.[14] Of the known books, the first concerned the worship of the gods, the second dealt with *daimones,* and the third with heroes and holy men.[15] Because he could discern no clear Plotinian influence in the text and thought that it expressed a "superstitious" concern for traditional religion, Bidez surmises that it must have been composed before Porphyry joined Plotinus's school.[16] Although Bidez's notion of developmental periods continues to exert some influence on contemporary scholarship, this method of dating Porphyry's works has been challenged. Andrew Smith, in particular, points to the inappropriateness of importing contemporary distinctions between "superstition" and "authentic philosophy" into ancient contexts.[17]

Several reshufflings of the remains of *Against the Christians* and *Philos-*

ophy from Oracles have been suggested. By pointing out important similarities in theme and content between the two works, John O'Meara argues for identifying the fragments of Porphyry's *On the Return of the Soul,* preserved only by Augustine, with the *Philosophy from Oracles.*[18] Pier Franco Beatrice has proposed that the fragments of *Against the Christians* and *Philosophy from Oracles* come from a single, anti-Christian treatise that dates to the early 300s.[19] More recently, Elizabeth Digeser has argued that *certain* fragments once ascribed to *Against the Christians* should be counted among the remains of *Philosophy from Oracles* and that the latter work was composed immediately before the persecution.[20] Yet, while the *exact* structure of each text remains difficult to discern, the fragments do fall naturally into two distinct categories: those based on the polemical interpretation of oracles and those that attack Christian texts and practices. The former represent a polemical digression within the esoteric *Philosophy from Oracles,* which was "a positive statement of the traditional religion of the Roman world."[21] The latter represent the focused attack on Christian literature, Christian intellectuals, and Christian reading practices of *Against the Christians.*

Porphyry, Lactantius's Unnamed Polemicist, and the Great Persecution

The evidence that supports a close connection between Porphyry's anti-Christian polemics and the policies of Diocletian and Galerius as well as the identification of Lactantius's unnamed polemicist with Porphyry has been addressed at several places in the main text. For the sake of clarity I muster them again here with some additional details.

1) Porphyry's declaration in his *Letter to Marcella* that "the needs of the Greeks called and the gods confirmed their request" has often been seen as a reference to Porphyry's more or less direct embroilment in the anti-Christian sentiment surrounding the outbreak of the persecution.[22]

2) Porphyry's stress on the value of ancestral traditions, both in *Against the Christians* (Harnack fr. 1) and in the *Letter to Marcella* (*Marc.* 18), has more than a passing resemblance to the rhetoric of Diocletian's, Galerius's, and Maximinus's courts (see pp. 76–78). Thus Galerius's edict of 311 connects apostasy from ancestral traditions with the disruption of order and the disorderly mixing of peoples in ways that echo and parallel Porphyry's description of Christian apostasy as a disruption of ethnic boundaries.[23] Petitions from Lycia and Pamphylia as well as Tyre to Maximinus requesting the expulsion of Christians from their cities and the emperor's

responses to them also share many features with Porphyry's rhetoric.[24]

3) Lactantius's account of an unnamed polemicist at Nicomedia accords with what is known of Porphyry and his polemics.

    a) Lactantius describes the polemicist as a self-styled 'priest of philosophy' (*antistes philosophiae*). In the *Letter to Marcella*, which dates to the same period as the outbreak of the persecution, Porphyry states that "The only [true] priest is the wise man" (*monos oun hiereus ho sophos*) (*Marc.* 16). Lactantius's phrase is not merely, as some have argued, sarcasm but a skillfull play on Porphyry's own rhetoric.[25]

    b) Against identifying the polemicist as Porphyry, some have asserted that the depraved and licentious lifestyle Lactantius ascribes to the unnamed philosopher does not square with Porphyry, who was known for his abstemious lifestyle.[26] Lactantius's description of the philosopher, however, is clearly polemical, in the same way that Porphyry's own disparagement of the moral character of Christians is polemical.[27]

    c) The strongest case against identifying Porphyry as the unnamed polemicist is Lactantius's statement that he "vomited forth three books against the Christian religion and name" (*DI* 5.2.4). *Against the Christians* was a fifteen-book treatise. Thus, some have suggested that the work presented in Nicomedia was *Philosophy from Oracles*[28] or that *Philosophy from Oracles* and *Against the Christians* were one and the same.[29] In fact, the rhetoric and practice of the court (e.g., Diocletian's and Galerius's oracular consultations; the stress laid on ancestral custom) and the focal points of Lactantius's response to the unnamed polemicist (the interpretation and merit of oracles; apostasy from tradition) reflect aspects of *Philosophy from Oracles* and *Against the Christians*. Thus I would add here that the material offered by Lactantius's unnamed polemicist (Porphyry) need not have been identical to either text.

    A number of scenarios are possible. Porphyry may have composed *Philosophy from Oracles* for the conferences at Nicomedia, *and* written *Against the Christians* at almost the same time. He may have presented an early three-book draft of *Against the Christians* at Nicomedia, a draft he later expanded into a fifteen-book treatise. Porphyry may have brought an entirely different text to Nicomedia, one that was neither *Against the Christians* nor *Philosophy from Oracles* but reflected the polemics of both.[30] Finally, Porphyry may have composed both treatises in the middle of his career, yet traveled to Nicomedia later in life to avail himself of an opportunity to directly influence imperial religious policy against his old rivals.

d) Lactantius states explicitly that the *Divine Institutes* are a response to the Nicomedian polemicists (*DI* 5.4.1). There are several additional reasons to think that Lactantius had Porphyry's polemics in mind when writing the *Divine Institutes*. First, Lactantius has a predilection for citing oracular sources as authorities for his arguments. As we saw in Chapter 2, Porphyry's *Philosophy from Oracles* laid special emphasis on oracular texts as sources of the universal philosophy. Porphyry believed that oracles were divine in origin, offering unique access to the truth if they were interpreted properly (*PO* 304F). Lactantius places a similar emphasis on oracles as records of truth, stating that he will make his defense of Christianity "from the testimonies of oracles and sacred songs" (*DI* 1.6.6).[31] Lactantius also shares Porphyry's marked interest in the oracles of Apollo. In *Philosophy from Oracles*, Porphyry uses Apollo's words to denigrate the Christian identification of Jesus as a god (*PO* 343F, 344F). It is not coincidental that Lactantius uses Apollo's pronouncements to support his apologetic explanation of Christian monotheism and Christology (see esp. *DI* 1.7.1–11, 4.13.11–15). Lactantius's use of Apollo will be discussed in more detail later, but here it is sufficient to note that Lactantius may be referring directly to one of Porphyry's anti-Christian oracles. The oracle he quotes in Book 4 of the *Institutes* may be the same oracle cited by Augustine in the *City of God* as deriving from Porphyry's *Philosophy from Oracles*.[32] In *On the Anger of God*, moreover, Lactantius quotes another Porphyrian oracle verbatim.[33] Lactantius's apologetic portrayal of Jesus also appears to owe much to Porphyry's polemical characterization of Jesus. As we saw in Chapter 2, Porphyry took an ambivalent position toward Jesus, simultaneously positioning him as a pious sage but denying him status as a god.[34] Lactantius, for his part, uses Apolline oracles to characterize Jesus as a teacher and as a divine being between the highest god and humans in an effort to quell denials of Jesus' divinity (see also above pp. 88–89).[35]

Lactantius also shares Porphyry's tendency to use the metaphor of a "way" or "path" to describe the philosophical/Christian life.[36] Porphyry's *Philosophy from Oracles* describes

the philosophical life as a "way of the blessed" that was "difficult and rough" (*PO* 323F). The same metaphor is put to
good use in Book 6 of the *Institutes*: "There are two paths . . .
down which human life must progress: one which leads to
heaven and the other which descends into the underworld"
(*DI* 6.3.1). Of course, "path" imagery had long been used to
describe the philosophical life. Lactantius acknowledges this,
writing of the paths that "the poets represent [them] in their
songs and philosophers represent [them] in their disputa-
tions" (*DI* 6.3.1). He also recognizes that his use of such a
common metaphor might lay his work open to the charge of
unoriginality (*DI* 6.2.18). Christian literature also had a long
tradition of using "path" imagery, going back at least to the
Didache.[37] As common as this metaphor was, however, there
are several reasons to think that Lactantius's use of the trope
was a retorsion of a Porphyrian concept. Lactantius calls the
path of the blessed "difficult and rough (*arduam et con-
fragosam*)" and "difficult and steep, with horrible, cruel
thorns and impeded by rocks (*difficilis et clivosa proposita est
vel spinis horrentibus aspera vel saxis extantibus impedita*)" (*DI*
6.3.2–6.4.6). Given these near verbatim echoes of *Philosophy
from Oracles*, it is difficult not to see Porphyry in Lactantius's
disclaimer: "I will ignore things which we may have in common with them, lest I seem to borrow from those whose errors I intend to reveal and refute" (*DI* 6.2.18). In addition,
Lactantius describes the road toward the underworld as a
"deceptive path," characterized by diversity and divergence
in contradistinction to the one true path to heaven (Christianity) (*DI* 6.7.1). Here again Lactantius seems to twist Porphyrian imagery. Where Porphyry characterizes the way of
the blessed as composed of "numberless paths" (*atrapitoi de
easin athesphatoi* [*PO* 323F]), Lactantius makes diversity characteristic of error. Porphyry had accused the Christians of
error (and here one cannot forget that both *planē* and *error*
connote straying and wandering), but Lactantius reflects this
charge back on his accusers.

e) Finally, Lactantius's report of the unnamed philosopher's position on persecution in Book 5 is similar to Porphyry's position on persecution as presented by Eusebius in the
Preparation for the Gospel. There are three important points of
confluence between the two passages. First, both Porphyry
and the anonymous philosopher portray the Christians as
lost travelers on a mistaken path.[38]

*kainēn de tina kai erēmēn anodian heautois suntemein, mēte ta Hellēnōn
mēte ta Ioudaiōn phulattousan.* (*PE* 1.2.2 [= Harnack fr. 1])

*professus ante omnia philosophi officium esse erroribus hominum subvenire
atque illos ad veram viam revocare id est ad cultus deorum, quorum numine
ac maiestate mundus gubernetur.* (*DI* 5.2.5)

In the passage from Eusebius, this is a "new, directionless
desert road," while Lactantius reports that the anonymous
philosopher felt "that it was the primary duty of a philosopher
to turn people away from error and recall them to the true
way." The passage from Lactantius is the logical compliment
to that preserved by Eusebius: if Christians are erring down a
directionless road, they must be redirected to the true path,
such as the one laid out by Porphyry in *Philosophy from Oracles.*
Second, both describe the Christians as turning their backs on
the gods as saviors and preservers "upon whom every people
and all cities depend" (Eusebius) and "by whose divinity and
majesty the world is governed" (Lactantius).

*Pōs d'ou pantachothen dussebeis an eien kai atheoi hoi tōn partōōn theōn
apostantes, di' hōn pan ethnos kai pasa polis sunestēken.* (*PE* 1.2.2 [= Harnack fr. 1]).

*professus ante omnia philosophi officium esse erroribus hominum subvenire
atque illos ad veram viam revocare id est ad cultus deorum, quorum numine
ac maiestate mundus gubernetur.* (*DI* 5.2.5)

These are not exact verbal parallels; however, both accounts
identify this affront to the gods' concern for human well-
being as a central feature of Christian error. In *On Abstinence*,
moreover, Porphyry expresses a traditional reverence for ancestral piety and assigns the traditional gods a place in the divine hierarchy as benevolent *daimones* responsible for the arts
and sciences and natural phenomena (*Abst.* 33, 37–38).

   Finally, both passages argue for state-sponsored coercion
as an effective means to achieve the suppression of "an impious and idiotic superstition" (Lactantius) or, in the parallel
from Eusebius, those who "have abandoned their native traditions and with idiotic and uncritical faith have taken up impious traditions considered hostile among all peoples."

*Pōs d' ou mochthērias einai kai euchereias eschatēs to metathesthai men eu-
kolōs tōn oikeiōn, alogō de kai anexetastō pistei ta tōn dussebōn kai pasin
ethnesi polemicōn helesthai.* (*PE* 1.2.4 [= Harnack fr. 1]).

> *Ut autem appareret cuius rei gratia opus illut elaborasset, effuses est in prin-*
> *cipum laudes, quorum pietas et providentia, ut quidem ipse dicebat, cum in*
> *ceteris rebus tum praecipue in defendendis deorum religionibus claruisset:*
> *consultum esse tandem rebus humanis, ut cohibita inpia et anili supersti-*
> *tione universi homines legitimis sacris vacarent ac propitios sibi deos ex-*
> *perirentur. (DI 5.2.7)*

These parallels suggest that both Lactantius and Eusebius were familiar with Porphyry's polemic, while the differences between them suggest that each came to know his polemics via different media. As Eusebius begins his list of accusations that "someone" may level against the Christians, he refers to them using pronouns and verbs in the second-person plural (e.g., "what is the strangeness and novelty in *our* way of life") but shifts to verbs and pronouns in the third-person plural (e.g., "*those* who abandon their ancestral gods").

> *Prōton men gar eikotōs an tis diaporēseien, tines ontes epi tēn graphēn par-*
> *elēluthamen, poteron Hellēnes ē barbaroi, ē ti an genoito toutōn meson, kai*
> *tinas heautous einai phamen, ou tēn prosēgorian, hoti kai tois pasin ekdēlos*
> *hautē, alla ton tropon kai tēn proairesin tou biou, oute yar ta Hellēnōn*
> *phrountas horan oute ta barbarōn epitēdeuontas. Ti oun an genoito to kath'*
> *hēmas xenon kai tis ho neōterismos tou biou? Pōs d' ou pantachothen dusse-*
> *beis an eien kai atheoi hoi tōn patrōōn theōn apostantes, di' hōn pan ethnos*
> *kai pasa polis sunestēken? ? ti kalon elpisai eikos tous tōn sōtēriōn echthrous*
> *kai polemious katastantas kai tous euergetas parōsamenous kai ti gar allo ē*
> *theomachountas . . . (ktl)?*

In all likelihood someone may first ask, who are we who propose to take up the pen, that is, are we Greeks or Barbarians, or what might there be between these? And what do we call ourselves, not with re-spect to our name, because that is evident to all, but with respect to our manner and choice of life; for they see that we neither think like Greeks nor adhere to the practices of the barbarians. Now what is foreign about us and what innovative about our way of life? How are those who reject the ancestral gods, on account of whom every peo-ple and every city has endured, not in all ways impious and atheists? Or what good can they hope for who stand in as enemies and oppo-nents of their saviors—for what else are they doing but making war against the gods . . . (etc.)? (*PE* 1.2.2 [= Harnack fr. 1])

As Eusebius moves abruptly from the questions one might put to "us" to a series of criticims of "them," he is (either un-wittingly or, as is more likely, without acknowledging it) re-porting Porphyry's words in *oratio recta*.[39] In other words, Eusebius appears to shift to the third person as he quotes di-rectly from a Porphyrian text. In contrast, Lactantius's report of the anonymous philosopher's arguments is entirely in *oratio obliqua*, giving the strong impression that he is reporting from his memory of an oral presentation rather than from any textual source.[40] This seems plausible given that Lactantius never states that he has read any text by the anonymous philosopher. Rather, as he reports immediately before recounting the philosopher's arguments, he had *heard* these arguments at public presentations at court. This would account for the significant parallels between Lactantius's account of the anonymous philosopher's arguments and the Porphyrian passage in Eusebius as well as the lack of any verbatim identity between them.

Thus, although they use slightly different terminology, both Eusebius's Porphyry and Lactantius's anonymous philosopher portray Christianity as intellectually deficient and foreign. While the passage from Eusebius does not employ deisidaimonia, the Greek equivalent of the Latin *superstitio*, the Latin term was often applied to religious traditions considered threatening because of their foreignness. Tacitus, for instance, described Judaism as a *superstitio* and applies the same term to nascent Christianity.[41] This usage continued in Lactantius's own day; Diocletian, in his edict against the Manichees, describes this new group as a "most idiotic and licentious superstitious doctrine" and explicitly identifies the Manichees as a product of Persia, Rome's sworn enemy.[42] In addition, though he does not use the term *superstitio* explicitly, Diocletian's censure of native Egyptian marriage practices is redolent with the rhetoric of "foreignness," including the labeling of traditional marriages as a practice done "through the ignorance of barbarian law" (*pro ignorantia iuris barbaricae*).[43] Lactantius is reporting the polemicist's arguments from memory. It would not be surprising, then, if Lactantius rendered the anonymous philosopher's objections to Christianity's foreignness using the term *superstitio*. Lactantius associates Porphyry's arguments so closely with the policies of the persecutors that he has assimilated Porphyry's arguments to the polemical language of the court.

Abbreviations

All translations of primary sources are my own, unless an English translation is listed here or in the notes.

For the fragmentary works of Porphyry, I reference the numbering systems used in the editions cited; where appropriate, I cross-reference the sources of the fragments, for example: Harnack fr. 1 (= Eusebius *PE* 1.2.1-4); *Reg.* 302F (= Augustine *City of God* 10.32.5—16).

Abst.	Porphyry, *On Abstinence* [*De Abstinentia*], edition: Augustus Nauck. *Porphyrii Philosophi Platonici Opuscula Selecta.* Leipzig: Teubner, 1886. Translation: Gillian Clark, *Porphyry; On Abstinence from Killing Animals.* Ithaca, N.Y.: Cornell University Press, 2000.
An.	Porphyry, *Letter to Anebo* [*Epistula ad Anebonem*], edition: A. R. Sodano. *Porfirio Lettera ad Anebo.* Naples: L'Arte Tipografica, 1958.
ANF	A Select Library of Ante-Nicene Fathers. New York: Christian Literature Company, etc., 1890–1900.
ANRW	*Aufstieg und Niedergang der römischen Welt.* Berlin: Walter de Gruyter, 1972–.
1 Apol.	Justin Martyr, *First Apology* [*Apologia*], edition: Miroslav Marcovich. *Iustini Martyris Apologiae Pro Christianis.* PTS 38 (1994).
2 Apol.	Justin Martyr, *Second Apology* [*Apologia*], edition: Miroslav Marcovich. *Iustini Martyris Apologiae Pro Christianis.* PTS 38 (1994).
CC	Porphyry, *Against the Christians* [*Contra Christianos*], edition: Harnack.
CCels.	Origen, *Against Celsus* [*Contra Celsum*], edition: *Contra Celsum.* Ed. Miroslav Marcovich. Supplements to Vigiliae Christianae 54. Leiden: Brill, 2001.
CCL	*Corpus Christianorum*, Series Latina. Turnhout: Brepols, 1953–.
CSEL	Corpus scriptorum ecclesiasticorum latinorum. Vienna: Akademie Verlag, etc., 1866–.
DE	Eusebius of Caesarea, *Demonstration of the Gospel* [*Demonstratio Evangelica*], edition: I. Heikel. GCS 23 (1913).
DI	Lactantius, *Divine Institutes* [*Divinae Institutes*], edition: S. Brandt. CSEL 19 (1890).

Ep., Epp.	Letter, Letters
fr., frr.	fragment, fragments
GCS	Griechischen christliche Schriftsteller. Leipzig: J. C. Hinrichs, etc., 1899–.
Harnack	Adolph von Harnack, *Porphyrius, "Gegen Die Christen," 15 Bücher: Zeugnisse, Fragmente und Referate.* In Abhandlungen der K. Preuß. Akad. Der Wiss., Phil. Hist. Klasse, Berlin, 1916, 1–115.
HE	Eusebius of Caesarea, *Ecclesiastical History* [*Historia Ecclesiastica*], edition: E. Schwartz, T. Mommsen, and F. Winkelmann. GCS n.f. 1999.
HTR	*Harvard Theological Review*
JECS	*Journal of Early Christian Studies*
JEH	*Journal of Ecclesiastical History*
JMEMS	*Journal of Medieval and Early Modern Studies*
JRS	*Journal of Roman Studies*
JTS	*Journal of Theological Studies*
LC/SC	*Tricennial Oration/On the Holy Sepulchre (Laus Constantini/De Sepulchro Christi)*, edition: I. Heikel. GCS 7 (1901). Translation: Harold Drake, *In Praise of Constantine: A Historical Study and New Translation of Eusebius' Tricennial Orations,* University of California Publications, Classical Studies vol. 15. Berkeley: University of California Press, 1975.
Marc.	Porphyry, *Letter to Marcella* [*Epistula ad Marcellum*], edition: Augustus Nauck. *Porphyrii Philosophi Platonici Opuscula Selecta.* Leipzig: Teubner, 1886.
Mort.	Lactantius, *On the Deaths of the Persecutors* [*De Mortibus Persecutorum*], edition: S. Brandt. CSEL 27 (1893).
NPNF	A Select Library of Nicene and Post-Nicene Fathers. New York: Christian Literature Company, etc., 1890–1900.
Or.	Constantine, *Oration to the Saints* [*Oratio ad Sanctorum Coetum*], edition: I. Heikel. GCS 7 (1902).
Orat.	Tatian, *Oration to the Greek* [*Oratio ad Graecos*], edition: *Oratio ad Graecos.* Ed. Miroslav Marcovich. PTS 43 (1995).
PA	Porphyry, *On Statues* [*Peri Agalmaton*], edition: A. Smith. *Porphyrius Fragmenta.* Leipzig: Teubner, 1993.
PE	Eusebius of Caesarea, *Preparation for the Gospel* [*Praeparatio Evangelica*], edition: K. Mras. GCS 43 (1954).
PG	*Patrologia Graeca.* Ed. J.-P. Migne. Paris: Migne, 1857–66.
PO	Porphyry, *Philosophy from Oracles* [*De philosophia ex oraculis haurienda*], edition: A. Smith. *Porphyrius Fragmenta.* Leipzig: Teubner, 1993. See also G. Wolff, *Porphyrii de Philosophia ex Oraculis Haurienda.* Berlin, 1856. Reprint, Hildesheim: Georg Olms, 1962.
PTS	Patristische Texte und Studien. Berlin: Walter de Gruyter, 1964–.
Reg.	Porphyry, *On the Return of the Soul* [*De Regressu Animae*], edition: A. Smith. *Porphyrius Fragmenta.* Leipzig: Teubner, 1993.
SC	Sources chrétiennes. Paris: Éditions de Cerf, 1943–.
SVF	Stoicorum Vetera Fragmenta. Ed. J. von Arnim and M. Adler. 4 vols. Leipzig: Teubner, 1903–24.
VC	Eusebius of Caesarea, *Life of Constantine* [*Vita Constantini*], edition: F. Winkelmann. GCS 7 (1991).

VPl.   Porphyry, *Life of Plotinus* [*Vita Plotini*], edition: P. Henry and H. R. Schwyzer. *Plotini Opera.* vol. 1. Leiden: Brill, 1951. Translation: Mark Edwards, *Neoplatonic Saints: The Lives of Plotinus and Proclus by Their Students.* Liverpool: Liverpool University Press, 2000.

Notes

Introduction

1. Lactantius, *Mort.* 10.1–4.
2. Lactantius (*Mort.* 11.3-6) reports that Diocletian and Galerius held their initial meetings in private (*cum nemo admitteretur*) and that Diocletian called upon supplemental advisors (*in consilibus multos advocabat*) only because he felt the pangs of conscience, but Lactantius's polemical intent is to paint Diocletian as a reticent persecutor while assigning the blame for persecution to Galerius's machinations.
3. *Mort.* 11.6.
4. *Mort.* 12.1: The first edict was promulgated on the day of the Terminalia, *quae sunt a.d. septimum Kalendas Martias*. The history of the Great Persecution must be reconstructed from the highly biased accounts of Christian writers, especially Lactantius and Eusebius. Modern literature on the subject is vast, but see Stephen Williams, *Diocletian and the Roman Recovery* (London: Batsford Ltd., 1985), especially chapter 14 ("The Great Persecution"); Timothy Barnes, *Constantine and Eusebius* (Cambridge, Mass.: Harvard University Press, 1981), 18–24; K. H. Schwarte, "Diokletians Christengesetz," in *E fontibus haurire: Beiträge zur römischen Geschichte und zu ihren Hilfswissenschaften*, ed. R. Günther and S. Rebenich (Paderborn: F. Schöningh, 1994), 203–240.
5. E.g., Tertullian *Apology* 30–32 (ANF 3:42–43).
6. E.g., Tertullian *Apology* 36: "If it is the fact that men bearing the name of Romans are found to be enemies of Rome, why are we, on the ground that we are regarded as enemies, denied the name of Romans?" (ANF 3:44).
7. *PE* 1.2.1.
8. *Inquiritur peragendae rei dies aptus et felix ac potissimum Terminalia deliguntur, quae sunt a. d. septimum Kalendas Martias, ut quasi terminus imponeretur huic religioni* (*Mort.* 12.1).
9. *Acts of the Scillitan Martyrs* 9, text in Herbert Musurillo, *The Acts of the Christian Martyrs* (Oxford: Clarendon Press, 1972), 88.
10. See, for example, the debate between A. N. Sherwin-White ("The Early Persecutions and Roman Law Again," *JTS* 3 [1952], 199-213) and G. E. M. de Ste. Croix ("Why Were the Early Christians Persecuted?" *Past and Present* 26 [1963], 6–38).
11. Pliny *Ep.* 10.96.1.
12. On the importance of martyrdom in the fashioning of Christian identity,

see Daniel Boyarin, *Dying for God: Martyrdom and the Making of Christianity and Judaism* (Stanford, Calif.: Stanford University Press, 1999), and Elizabeth Castelli, *Martyrdom and Memory: Early Christian Culture Making* (New York: Columbia University Press, 2004).

13. Acts 17:16-31. Thus Paul and/or Acts occupy the first chapters in many histories of apologetics, including Robert Grant, *Greek Apologists of the Second Century* (Philadelphia: Westminster Press, 1988), 19–24; Michael Fiedrowicz, *Apologie im frühen Christentum: Die Kontroverse um den christlichen Wahrheitsanspruch in den ersten Jahrhunderten* (Paderborn: F. Schöningh, 2000); and Jean-Claude Fredouille, "L'apologétique chrétienne antique: Naissance d'un genre littéraire," *Revue des Études Augustiniennes* 38 (1992), 225–26.

14. *HE* 4.2.1, 4.3.1.

15. The centrality of Eusebius's definitions in modern accounts of apologetics is stressed by Silke-Petra Bergjan, "How to Speak about Early Christian Apologetic Literature? Comments on the Recent Debate," *Studia Patristica* 36 (2001), 182–83.

16. Frances Young, "Greek Apologists of the Second Century," in *Apologetics in the Roman Empire: Pagans, Jews, and Christians*, ed. M. Edwards, M. Goodman, and S. Price (Oxford: Oxford University Press, 1999), 92.

17. Fredouille, "L'apologétique," 220.

18. "Die apologetische Literatur entstand im Leben der jungen Kirche aus der Erfahrung von Kontrast und Konfrontation" (Fiedrowicz, *Apologie*, 13).

19. "Apologetic literature emerges from minority groups that are trying to come to terms with the larger culture in which they live" (Grant, *Greek Apologists*, 9).

20. The term serves as the title of chapter 6 in W. H. C. Frend, *The Rise of Christianity* (Philadelphia: Fortress Press, 1984), 193–228. His treatment of Marcion, Gnostics, and other varieties of Christianity is representative of a tendency toward historical narratives that are constructed around an essentialized "orthodox" Christianity's contact and conflict with various "others" (especially Greco-Roman philosophy and Judaism). Karen King locates the roots of the distinction between an orthodoxy constructed as antisyncretic and heresy as syncretic miscegenation so often repeated in surveys of early Christian history and theology in early Christian heresiological discourse itself (*What Is Gnosticism?* [Cambridge, Mass.: Harvard University Press, 2003]). Rebecca Lyman points, rather, to heresiological discourse as ineluctably ambivalent, emerging from the "intractable problem of diversity together with the ideological claim of unity" ("Hellenism and Heresy," *JECS* 11:2 [2003], 209–22, 211).

21. Robert Grant, *Augustus to Constantine* (New York: Harper and Row, 1970), 112–13; Fiedrowicz, *Apologie*, 16.

22. Edward Gibbon, *The Decline and Fall of the Roman Empire* (1776–78; repr. London: Penguin Books, 1952), 262.

23. Ibid., 309–17, esp. 309–10: "There is the strongest reason to believe that before the reigns of Diocletian and Constantine the faith of Christ had been preached in every province and in all but the greatest cities of the empire; . . . our knowledge concerning the increase of the Christian name in Asia and Greece, in Egypt, in Italy, and in the West, we shall now proceed to relate, without neglecting the real or imaginary acquisitions which lay beyond the frontiers of the Roman empire."

24. Adolf von Harnack, *The Mission and Expansion of Christianity in the First Three Centuries*, trans. J. Mofat (New York: G. P. Putnam's Sons, 1908); see espe-

cially chapter 3, which traces the development of Christianity in various provinces and regions (89–306).

25. Harnack, *Mission*, 33–84.

26. Notable examples include chapter 3 of Henry Chadwick, *The Early Church* (New York: Penguin, 1967), 54–73, esp. 60–66 ("The Geographical Extension of the Church"), and the geographical arrangement of chapters and series of maps in Frend, *The Rise of Christianity* v–ix, 986–90, and endpapers; similar series of maps also appear in more recent histories, such as Bart Ehrman, *The New Testament: A Historical Introduction to the Early Christian Writings* (Oxford: Oxford University Press, 2000); the series proceeds in sequence from maps of Alexander's conquests (20) and the Roman Empire (xxviii) to maps of the progressive spread of Christianity from Paul's missions (126, 273) to 100 C.E. (45) and finally to 300 C.E. (401). As its title implies, Roderic Mullen's *Expansion of Christianity: A Gazetteer of Its First Three Centuries* (Leiden: Brill, 2004) sets out to update and expand Harnack's project.

27. Robert Markus, *The End of Ancient Christianity* (Cambridge: Cambridge University Press, 1993), 28.

28. Edward Said, *Orientalism* (New York: Vintage, 1979; reprint with afterword, 1994).

29. See, for example, Tertullian *To the Nations* 1.8, 1.20 (*tertium genus*) and *Letter to Diognetus* 1.1.

30. Clifford Geary, *The Myth of Nations: The Medieval Origins of Europe* (Princeton, N.J.: Princeton University Press, 2002), 42.

31. Bill Ashcroft, Gareth Griffiths, and Helen Tiffin, *Post-Colonial Studies: The Key Concepts* (London: Routledge, 2000), 80.

32. This is likely owing to the use of "ethnicity" in situations where the term "race" would likely have been applied in the nineteenth and early twentieth centuries. In popular usage, "ethnicity" is often used as a politically palatable substitute for "race." See Ashcroft, Griffiths, and Tiffin, *Post-Colonial Studies*, 80–84.

33. Geary, *Myth of Nations*, 42–46; Jonathan M. Hall, *Ethnic Identity in Greek Antiquity* (Cambridge: Cambridge University Press, 1997), 34–66 considers in some detail the ways in which Herodotus (and others) construe ethnicity.

34. See, for example, Timothy Whitmarsh ("'Greece Is the World': Exile and Identity in the Second Sophistic," in *Being Greek Under Rome: Cultural Identity, the Second Sophistic, and the Development of Empire*, ed. Simon Goldhill [Cambridge: Cambridge University Press, 2001], 299–303) and Suzanne Saïd ("The Discourse of Identity in Greek Rhetoric from Isocrates to Aristides," in *Ancient Perceptions of Greek Ethnicity*, ed. Irad Malkin [Cambridge, Mass.: Harvard University Press, 2001], 292), who examine the ways in which the rhetor Favorinus constructed Greekness through rhetorical performance.

35. Shaye J. D. Cohen, *The Beginnings of Jewishness: Boundaries, Varieties, Uncertainties* (Berkeley: University of California Press, 1999), 69–78.

36. Cohen (*Jewishness*, 109–10) delineates among immutable, ethnic Jewishness, political Jewishness, and "religious" Jewishness. These last two, in that they are elective and constituted by the mimesis of a set of practices, correspond to the mode of identity I have been discussing as "cultural."

37. The term is borrowed from Geary, *Myth of Nations*, 42.

38. Geary, *Myth of Nations*, 42, 49–50.

39. E. Bickermann, "*Origines gentium*," *Classical Philology* 47 (1952), 65-81; Erich Gruen, *Culture and National Identity in Republican Rome* (Ithaca, N.Y.: Cornell University Press, 1992), 6–51; Clifford Ando, *Imperial Ideology and Provincial*

Loyalty in the Roman Empire (Baltimore: Johns Hopkins University Press, 2000), 52–54.

40. Ando, *Imperial Ideology*, 58–59.

41. Peter Garnsey, *Social Status and Legal Privilege in the Roman Empire* (Oxford: Oxford University Press, 1970), 262.

42. Michael Rostovtzeff, *The Social and Economic History of the Roman Empire* (Oxford: Clarendon Press, 1957), 369–70.

43. Ando, *Imperial Ideology*, 395.

44. Garnsey, *Social Status*, 270–71.

45. See the essays collected in John Kloppenborg and Stephen Wilson, eds. *Voluntary Associations in the Graeco-Roman World*; (London: Routledge, 1996). See especially Steven Mason, "Philosophiai: Graeco-Roman, Judean, and Christian" in *Voluntary Associations in the Graeco-Roman World*, ed. Kloppenborg and Wilson, 31–58, and John Kloppenborg, "Collegia and *Thiasoi*: Issues in Function, Taxonomy, and Membership," in *Voluntary Associations in the Gareco-Roman World*, ed. Kloppenborg and Wilson, 16–30.

46. Thus Denise Kimber Buell argues that "most of the analysis of race and ethnicity in early Christian literature has focused on vocabulary, especially the use of terms such as *genos* and *ethnos*., But far more important than the presence of specific vocabulary are the maneuvers performed in a broad range of early Christian texts by rhetoric about peoplehood. These maneuvers attempt to persuade readers about what constitutes Christianness. Early Christian uses of ethnoracial concepts to make universalizing claims constitute a kind of rhetorical practice that I call *ethnic reasoning* ("Race and Universalism in Early Christianity," *JECS* 10 [2002], 429–68; idem, "Rethinking the Relevance of Race for Early Christian Self-Definition," *HTR* 94 [2001], 461–62. See also Aaron Johnson, "Identity, Descent, and Polemic: Ethnic Argumentation in Eusebius's *Praeparatio Evangelica*," *JECS* 12 (2004), 23–56.

47. Daniel Boyarin, for instance, has described how "phallogocentric notions of meaning" produced allegoresis and other discursive practices grounded in the desire for "univocity" and the suppression of "difference, whether that difference be the signifier, women, or the Jews" (*A Radical Jew: Paul and the Politics of Identity* [Berkeley: University of California Press, 1994], 16–17).

48. Alcinous *The Handbook of Platonism* 1.1, translation in John Dillon, *Alcinous: The Handbook of Platonism* (Oxford: Oxford University Press, 1993).

49. Col. 3:10.

50. Thus Jonathan Hall has traced the development of Greek identity in classical antiquity as "ultimately constructed through written and spoken discourse" (*Ethnic Identity in Greek Antiquity*, 2). Other classicists have examined the politically charged renegotiations of Greek identity in the Roman Empire (see, e.g., Simon Goldhill, *Who Needs Greek?: Contests in the History of Hellenism* [Cambridge: Cambridge University Press, 2002]; Timothy Whitmarsh, *Greek Literature in the Roman Empire: The Politics of Imitation* [Oxford: Oxford University Press, 2001]; see also the collection of essays in Goldhill, *Being Greek Under Rome*. Walter Pohl and Helmut Reimitz, eds., *Strategies of Distinction: The Construction of Ethnic Communities, 300–800* (Leiden: Brill, 1998) and Richard Miles, ed., *Constructing Identities in Late Antiquity* (London: Routledge, 1999) offer volumes of essays that consider the construction of ethnic identities in late antiquity. In the field of early Christian studies, studies such as Alain Le Boulluec, *La notion d'hérésie dans la literature grecque IIe–IIIe siècles* (Paris: Études Augustiniennes, 1985); Virginia Burrus, *The Making of a Heretic: Gender, Authority, and the Priscillianist Controversy*

(Berkeley: University of California Press, 1995); and Denise Kimber Buell, *Making Christians: Clement of Alexandria and the Rhetoric of Legitimacy* (Princeton, N.J.: Princeton University Press, 1999) have examined the production of orthodox and heretical identities by ancient Christians. Daniel Boyarin *(Dying for God* and *Border Lines: The Partition of Judaeo-Christianity* [Philadelphia: University of Pennsylvania Press, 2004]) has challenged traditional narratives of Christian and Jewish origins as based on assumptions of empirical Jewish and Christian essences, preferring instead to view the production of these religious identities as an ongoing and agonistic process of differentiation.

51. Denise Kimber Buell, *Why This New Race? Ethnic Reasoning in Early Christianity* (New York: Columbia University Press, 2005), 6–9.

52. Stuart Hall, "The Question of Cultural Identity," in *Modernity: An Introduction to Modern Societies*, ed. Hall et al. (Oxford: Basil Blackwell, 1996), 598, citing Hall, "Minimal Selves," in *Identity: The Real Me*, ICA Document 6 (London: Institute for Contemporary Arts, 1987).

53. As a general rule, however, I opt whenever possible for the more neutral translation "people/peoples," except in cases where such a translation would run counter to clarity in English or when I have used an existing translation. The few instances when existing translations have been modified are so noted.

54. Such an approach also informs Denise Kimber Buell's study of first- and second-century Christian discourse on race and ethnicity: "Foregrounding fluidity/fixity, rather than some specific content like kinship and descent, risks making ethnicity/race indistinguishable from other cultural categories, such as religion and citizenship, since both of these could also be said to share this dynamic of fixity and fluidity" (*Why This New Race*, 10).

55. For an historical account of the development of postcolonial studies, see Robert Young, *Postcolonialism: An Historical Introduction* (Oxford: Blackwell, 2001).

56. "We can conclude, then, that the word 'postcolonial' is useful in indicating a general process with some shared features across the globe. But if it is uprooted from specific locations, 'postcoloniality' cannot be meaningfully investigated, and instead, the term begins to obscure the very relations of domination it seeks to uncover" (Ania Loomba, *Colonialism/Postcolonialism* [London: Routledge, 1998], 19). "[W]e would argue that post-colonial studies are based in the 'historical fact' of European colonialism, and the diverse material effects to which this phenomenon gave rise. . . . In particular the tendency to employ the term 'post-colonial' to refer to any kind of marginality at all runs the risk of denying its basis in the historical process of colonialism" (Bill Ashcroft, Gareth Griffiths, and Helen Tiffin, eds., "General Introduction," in *The Post-Colonial Studies Reader* [London: Routledge, 1995], 2).

57. As argued, for instance, by M. Millet, *The Romanization of Britain* (Cambridge: Cambridge University Press, 1990), and Gustav Woolf, "World Systems Analysis and the Roman Empire," *JRS* 12 (1990), 223–34. See also the discussion in Jane Webster, "Roman Imperialism and the 'Post-Imperial Age,'" in *Roman Imperialism: Post-Colonial Perspectives*, ed. Jane Webster and Nick Cooper, Leicester Archaeology Monographs No. 3 (Leicester: School of Archaeological Studies, 1996), 1–17.

58. According to Bart Moore-Gilbert, "just as feminist criticism need not be confined to analysis of women's or feminist texts, or to geographical regions or socio-cultural formations in which feminism is an influence, or to the period since the technical emancipation of women (if this has, indeed, happened) in

the area under discussion, so it seems to me that postcolonial criticism can in principle be legitimately applied to any number of different contexts" (*Postcolonial Theory: Contexts, Practices, Politics* [London: Verso, 1997], 12).

59. Recent studies of premodernity that employ postcolonial theory fruitfully include the essays collected in *Roman Imperialism*, ed. Webster and Cooper; Kathleen Davis, "National Writing in the Ninth Century: A Reminder for Postcolonial Thinking About the Nation," *JMEMS* 28 (1998), 611–37; R. S. Sugirtharajah, "Postcolonial Theory and Biblical Studies," in *Fair Play: Diversity and Conflicts in Early Christianity, Essays in Honor of Heikki Räisänen*, ed. Ismo Dunderberg, Christopher Tuckett, and Kari Syreeni, (Leiden: Brill, 2002), 541–52; Calvin Troup, "Augustine the African: Critic of Roman Colonialist Discourse," *Religious Studies Quarterly* 25 (1995), 92–106; Rebecca Lyman, "The Politics of Passing: Justin Martyr's Conversion as a Problem of "Hellenization," in *Conversion in Late Antiquity and the Early Middle Ages*, ed. Kenneth Mills and Anthony Grafton (Rochester: University of Rochester Press, 2003); Boyarin, *Border Lines*; Andrew Jacobs, *Remains of the Jews: The Holy Land and Christian Empire in Late Antiquity* (Stanford Calif.: Stanford University Press, 2004); and Christopher Frilingos, *Spectacle and Empire: Monsters, Martyrs, and the Book of Revelation* (Philadelphia: University of Pennsylvania Press, 2004). See also Elizabeth Clark (*History, Theory, Text: Historians and the Linguistic Turn* [Cambridge, Mass.: Harvard University Press, 2004], 181–85], who locates postcolonial theory as one of a number of theoretical approaches useful for reevaluating premodern history.

60. In addition, some Roman historians see postcolonial discourse analysis as a means to challenge the implicit, and sometimes explicit, relationships between the study of Roman history and the ideologies of nineteenth- and twentieth-century European imperialisms; see, for example, R. Hingley, "Britannia, Origin Myths and the British Empire," *Proceedings of the Fourth Theoretical Roman Archaeology Conference* (1995), 11–23; and David Mattingly, "From One Colonialism to Another: Imperialism in the Maghreb," in *Roman Imperialism*, ed. Webster and Cooper, 49–69.

61. Thus, for instance, Athenagoras addresses his *Embassy on Behalf of the Christians* "to the emperors Marcus Aurelius and Lucius Aurelius Commodus" (Leg. 1.1 [ANF 2:129]), Tertullian directs his *Apology* to the "rulers of the Roman Empire" (*Apology* 1.1 [ANF 3:17]), and Justin addresses his *First Apology* "to the Emperor Titus Aelius Hadrianus Antoninus Pius Augustus Caesar, and to his son Verissimus the Philosopher, and to Lucius the Philosopher . . . and to the sacred Senate and Roman People" (1 *Apol.* 1.1 [ANF 1:163]).

62. Mary Beard, John North, and Simon Price, *Religions of Rome*, vol. 1, *History* (Cambridge: Cambridge University Press, 1998), 310 ("in practice the Apologies seem not to have been much read by non-Christians, their importance lying in their internal consumption within the church"), exemplify this dismissive attitude, as do Mark Edwards, Martin Goodman, and Simon Price, "Introduction: Apologetics in the Roman World," in *Apologetics in the Roman Empire: Pagens, Jews, and Christians*, ed. Edwards, Goodman, and Price, 8–9 ("the matter and style ensured that the apologists would not have been much read outside the church"). For a contrasting view, see, for instance, Frend, *The Rise of Christianity*, 234 ("The amount they wrote suggests that there was a real market for these works of popular Christian philosophy among Christians and their opponents at this time"), and Robin Lane Fox, (*Pagans and Christians* [San Francisco: Harper and Row, 1986], 305–6), who, citing the example of other petitions that did reach emperors, argues that some apologies may have reached imperial officials.

63. Edward Said points to the intimate (though sometimes obscured) relationships between intellectual discourses and imperial domination in *Orientalism*, 12, and esp. 73–92, where he considers the relationships between the rise of various European ethnographic, historical, philological, and geographical disciplines and the establishment of European colonies in the nineteenth and twentieth centuries.

64. Homi K. Bhabha, *The Location of Culture* (London: Routledge, 1994), esp. 71–72, where Bhabha highlights the inherent "alterity and ambivalence of Orientalist discourse" as a corrective to what he perceives as the overly fixed binarism in Said's conception of Orientalism.

65. Richard King, *Orientalism and Religion: Postcolonial Theory, India*, and "*The Mystic East*" (London: Routledge, 1999); Russell T. McCutcheon, *Manufacturing Religion: The Discourse on Sui Generis Religion and the Politics of Nostalgia* (Oxford: Oxford University Press, 1997), esp. chapter 2, "Autonomy, Discourses, and Social Privilege," 51–73; idem, *Critics Not Caretakers: Redescribing the Public Study of Religion* (Albany: State University of New York Press, 2001), esp. chapter 5, "'We're All Stuck Somewhere': Taming Ethnocentrism and Transcultural Understandings," 73–83; Jonathan Z. Smith, "Religion, Religions, Religious," in *Critical Terms for Religious Studies*, ed. Mark Taylor (Chicago: University of Chicago Press, 1998), 269–84.

Chapter 1

1. The literature on early Christian and Platonic "schools" is vast, but see the recent work by Edward J. Watts, *City and School in Late Antique Athens and Alexandria* (Berkeley: University of California Press, 2006). Important primary sources on Christian and Platonic philosophical circles include Gregory Thaumaturgus's *Address to Origen*, translation in Michael Slusser, *St. Gregory Thaumaturgus: Life and Works* (Washington, D.C.: Catholic University of America Press, 1998); Eusebius's account of Origen's "school" in *HE* 6.1–39; and Porphyry's *Life of Plotinus* and Marinus's *Life of Proclus*, translations of both in Mark Edwards, *Neoplatonic Saints: The Lives of Plotinus and Proclus by Their Students* (Liverpool: Liverpool University Press, 2000).

2. For a discussion of the role of texts and exegesis in late ancient philosophical practice, see Pierre Hadot, "Théologie, exégèse, revelation, écriture dans la philosophie grecque," in *Les règles de l'interprétation*, ed. Michel Tardieu (Paris: Cerf, 1987), 13–34.

3. Heinrich Dörrie, "Die Wertung der Barbaren im Urteil der Greichen: Knechtsnaturen? Oder Bewahrer und Künder heilbringender Weisheit?" in *Antike und Universalgeschichte* (Munster: Verlag, 1972), 46–175.

4. Diogenes Laertius *Lives of the Philosophers* 9.61–63, text and translation in R. D. Hicks, *Diogenes Laertius: Lives of Eminent Philosophers* (Cambridge, Mass.: Harvard University Press, 1950).

5. *Letter of Aristeas* 9, translation of R. J. H. Shutt in *The Old Testament Pseudepigrapha*, ed. J. Charlesworth (Garden City, N.Y.: Doubleday, 1985), 12.

6. Thus Herodotus famously ascribes the origins of Greek religion to Egypt; see especially *Hist.* 2.50–51. For a discussion of the place of Herodotus's theories in the development of the historiography of religions, see Arnaldo Momigliano, "Historiography of Religion: Western Views," in *On Pagans, Jews, and Christians* (Hanover, N.H.: Wesleyan University Press, 1987), 14–15.

7. Raoul Mortley, *The Idea of Universal History from Hellenistic Philosophy to Early Christian Historiography* (Lewiston, N.Y.: Edwin Mellen, 1996), 1.

8. Diodorus Siculus *Historical Library* 1.9.3, text and translation in C. H. Oldfather, *Diodorus of Sicily* (Cambridge, Mass.: Harvard University Press, 1933).

9. For Philo's *Phoenician History* see the text and translation by H. Attridge and R. Oden, *The Phoenician History*, Catholic Biblical Quarterly Monograph Series, no. 9 (Washington, D.C.: Catholic Biblical Association of America, 1981); for the text of Berossos, see G. Verbrugghe and J. Wickersham, *Berossos and Manetho, Introduced and Translated* (Ann Arbor: University of Michigan Press, 1996).

10. Text and translation of the fragments of Artapanus and Eupolemus in Carl Holladay, *Fragments from Hellenistic Jewish Authors*, vol. 1, *Historians* (Chico, Calif.: Scholars Press, 1983); see also B. Z. Wacholder, *Eupolemus: A Study of Judaeo-Greek Literature* (Cincinnati: Hebrew Union College, 1974); R. Doran, "Jewish Hellenistic Historians Before Josephus," *ANRW* II.20.1 (1987): 246–97; John J. Collins, *Between Athens and Jerusalem: Jewish Identity in the Hellenistic Diaspora*, 2nd ed. (Grand Rapids, Mich.: Eerdmans, 2000), 37–47.

11. G. E. Sterling, *Historiography and Self-Definition: Josephus, Luke-Acts, and Apologetic Historiography*, supplements to *Novum Testamentum* 64 (Leiden: Brill, 1992); Martin Goodman, "Josephus' Treatise *Against Apion*," in *Apologetics in the Roman Empire*, ed. Edwards, Goodman, and Price, 45–58.

12. Arthur J. Droge, *Homer or Moses? Early Christian Interpretations of the History of Culture*, Hermeneutische Untersuchurgen zur Theologie Bd. 26 (Tübingen: J. C. B. Mohr, 1989), 159.

13. Diogenes Laertius *Lives of the Philosophers* 3.6–7; Heinrich Dörrie, "Platons Reisen zu fernen Völkern," in *Romanitas et Christianitas: Studia Iano Henrico Waszink*, ed. W. den Boer, P. G. van der Nat, and J. C. van Winden (Amsterdam: North Holland Publishing, 1973), 99–118.

14. Persia: Porphyry *VPyth.* 6; Iamblichus *VPyth.* 19, 151, 154. Phoenicians and Chaldeans: Iamblichus, *VPyth.* 6.

15. Philostratus *Life of Apollonius* 8.7; Iamblichus *VPyth* 151.

16. Pierre Hadot, *What Is Ancient Philosophy?* (Cambridge, Mass.: Harvard University Press, 2002), 148–49.

17. Ibid., 153.

18. G. R. Boys-Stones, *Post-Hellenistic Philosophy: A Study of Its Development from the Stoics to Origen* (Oxford: Oxford University Press, 2001), 45–49. In *Ep.* 90, Seneca gives what scholars take to be a "standard" account of earlier Stoic teaching about the earliest humans in response to what he sees as Posidonius's "innovations" upon this traditional Stoic account. Posidonius's ideas will be discussed later in the chapter. On the problems associated with interpreting Seneca's letter, see Boys-Stones, *Post-Hellenistic Philosophy*, 18–20.

19. Seneca *Ep.* 90.1; *sed primi mortalium quique ex his geneti naturam incorrupti sequebantur.*

20. Seneca *Ep.* 90.

21. Seneca *Ep.* 90.10.

22. Seneca *Ep.* 90: *hanc philosophiam fuisse illo rudi saeculo, quo adhuc artificia deerant et ipso usu discebantur utilia, non credo . . . non erant illi sapientes viri, etiam si faciebant facienda sapientibus.*

23. Seneca *Ep.* 90.38–39.

24. Edelstein/Kidd fr. 284; references are to fragment and *testimonia* numbers in Edelstein and Kidd, *Posidonius I: The Fragments* (Cambridge: Cambridge Uni-

versity Press, 1972), translation in I. G. Kidd, *Posidonius III: The Translation of the Fragments* (Cambridge: Cambridge University Press, 1999).

25. Max Pohlenz, *Die Stoa: Geschichte einer geistigen Bewegung* (Göttingen: Vandenhoeck and Ruprecht, 1970), 97.

26. Galen refers several times to Posidonius's interest in "ancient/old authorities" (Edelstein/Kidd T101, T102) and mentions his interest in Pythagoras explicitly (Edelstein/Kidd T91).

27. Edelstein/Kidd frr. 285, 286.

28. Among the peoples Posidonius investigated were the Cimbri (Edelstein/Kidd fr. 272), the Celts (Edelstein/Kidd frr. 67–69, 274–76), and Jews (Edelstein/Kidd fr. 278).

29. Dalmatia (Edelstein/Kidd fr. 70); banqueting customs (Edelstein/Kidd frr. 53, 65, 283); military habits (Edelstein/Kidd frr. 54, 274); Parthian politics (Edelstein/Kidd fr. 282).

30. "on the one hand they actually blame us for not worshipping the same gods as other people, and on the other tell lies and invent absurd defamatory statements about our temple" (Edelstein/Kidd fr. 278 [= Josephus, *Against Apion* 2.7.79–96], translation in Kidd, *Posidonius III*, 352–53).

31. Edelstein/Kidd T80, translation in Kidd, *Posidonius III*, 56.

32. Kidd, *Posidonius III*, 56.

33. Edelstein/Kidd fr. 272.

34. I.G. Kidd, introduction to *Posidonius III*, 26.

35. This is pointed out by Pohlenz, *Die Stoa*, 97. Boys-Stones stresses that Stoic exegetical approaches to Homer and other ancient sources stemmed not simply from the belief that the *logos* permeated all creation but because the poets had mistakenly hidden the truths of antediluvian philosophy in their superstitious, if artful, compositions (*Post-Hellenistic Philosophy*, 36).

36. Boys-Stones has argued that these poetic allegorizations of ancient truth were unintentional and occurred despite the fictions of the poets ("The Stoic's Two Types of Allegory," in *Metaphor, Allegory, and the Classical Tradition*, ed. Boys-Stones [Oxford: Oxford University Press, 2003], 190).

37. E. Zeller and E. Wellman, *Die Philosophie der Griechen in ihrer geschichtlichen Entwicklung dargestellt* (Leipzig, 1909), 345.

38. See, for example, J. Tate, "Plato and Allegorical Interpretation," *Classical Quarterly* 24 (1930), 3; and R. Pfeiffer, *History of Classical Scholarship: From the Beginnings to the End of the Hellenistic Age* (Oxford: Oxford University Press, 1968), 238.

39. Cicero *On the Nature of the Gods* 1.41, translation in P. G. Walsh, *Cicero: The Nature of the Gods* (Oxford: Oxford University Press, 1998), 18.

40. Cicero *On the Nature of the Gods* 2.63 (Walsh 69).

41. SVF 1, n. 100, translation in Luc Brisson, *How Philosophers Saved Myths: Allegorical Interpretation and Classical Mythology*, trans. Catherine Tihanyi (Chicago: University of Chicago Press, 2004), 46, slightly modified.

42. See, for example, Cleanthes, SVF vol. 1, nn. 540, 542; Chryssipus, SVF vol. 2, nn. 1084, 1094.

43. For a discussion of the Stoics' correspondence theories of language, see Andreas Graeser, "The Stoic Theory of Meaning," in *The Stoics*, ed. John M. Rist (Berkeley: University of California Press, 1978), 77–99, esp. 97–99; Michael Frede, "Principles of Stoic Grammar," in *The Stoics*, ed. Rist, 27–76.

44. On Cornutus's allegorical reading in general, see David Dawson, *Allegorical Readers and Cultural Revision in Ancient Alexandria* (Berkeley: University of

California Press, 1992), 24–25. Glenn Most traces Cornutus's relationship to earlier Stoic exegesis. One of Cornutus's influences may have been Posidonius; according to Strabo, Posidonius also engaged in comparative etymology (Edelstein/Kidd T89). On the relationship of Cornutus's allegorical habits to those of his predecessors, see Glenn Most, "Cornutus and Stoic Allegoresis: A Preliminary Report," *ANRW* II.36.3 (1989): 2020–29.

45. Boys-Stones, *Post-Hellenistic Philosophy*, 56.

46. Cornutus *Greek Theology* (*Theologia Graeca*), ed. K. Lang, *cornuti theologiae graecae compendium* (Leipzig, 1881), 17, 26.7–12.

47. Cornutus *Greek Theology* 28, 54.12–21 (Lang).

48. Plutarch, *On Isis and Osiris* 378a text and translation in F. C. Babbitt, *Plutarch: Moralia*, vol. 5 (Cambridge, Mass: Harvard University Press, 1936), 156–57.

49. Plutarch *On Isis and Osiris* 379a–d (Babbitt 160–65) and see discussion in Brisson, *How Philosophers Saved Myths*, 68–69.

50. For exegete as priest/priestess, Plutarch *On Isis and Osiris* 2.351e; exegesis as a mystery, 378a–b (Babbitt 8–9, 156–57).

51. See also discussion in Brisson, *How Philosophers Saved Myths*, 70–71, and Christian Froidefond, "Notice," in *Plutarque: Oeuvres Morales*, vol. 5 (Paris: Les Belles Lettres, 1988), 69–70.

52. Text and French translation of the extant fragments in Édouard des Places, *Numénius: Fragments* (Paris: Les Belles Lettres, 1973); references are to fragment numbers in Des Places's collection.

53. Des Places fr. 1c (= *CCels.* 4.51).

54. Des Places fr. 1a (= *PE* 9.7.1).

55. Numenius fr. 30 (des Places) (= Porphyry *Cave of the Nymphs* 10, text and translation in *Porphyry: The Cave of the Nymphs in the Odyssey* [Buffalo, N.Y.: Arethusa Monographs, 1969]).

56. Des Places fr. 1b (= *CCels.* 1.15).

57. In des Places fr. 13 (= *PE* 11.18.13–14), Numenius describes the First God as *ho men ge ōn sperma pasēs psuchēs*, which may depend on Exodus 3:14 in the Septuagint, *egō eimi ho ōn*; see John Whittaker, "Moses Atticizing," *Phoenix* 21 (1967), 196–201.

58. Des Places fr. 1c (= CCels. 4.51).

59. Thus Michael Frede: "Hellenism in general, but in particular also in philosophy, tends to involve the conciliatory assumption that the cultural traditions of the various ancient nations involve a common core of beliefs and values, which is perhaps most readily available and accessible in its Greek articulation and formulation, but is also present in other traditions which *equally deserve respect*" ("Celsus's Attack on the Christians," in Philosophia Togata II, ed. Miriam Griffith and John Barnes [Oxford: Oxford University Press, 1997], 220).

60. For instance, Ernest Barker, "Some Foreign Influences in Greek Thought," *Greece and Rome* 5:13 (1935), 2–11; see also discussion of various approaches to philosophical eclecticism and syncretism in Pierluigi Donini, "The History of the Concept of Eclecticism," in *The Question of "Eclecticism,"* ed. J. Dillon and A. A. Long (Berkeley: University of California Press, 1988), 15–33.

61. John Dillon, *The Middle Platonists: 80 B.C. to A.D. 220* (Ithaca, N.Y.: Cornell University Press, 1977; rev. ed., 1996), 384.

62. Beard, North, and Price, *Religions of Rome*, vol. 1, 317.

63. Rebecca Preston, "Roman Questions, Greek Answers: Plutarch and the Construction of Identity," in *Being Greek Under Rome*, ed. Goldhill, 86–119.

64. Goldhill, *Who Needs Greek*, 254.

65. Thus Homi Bhabha notes that the certainty of imperial regimes in the boundaries between rulers and ruled in fact "enables a transgression of these limits from the space of that otherness" (*Location of Culture*, 67).

66. When the secure, fixed identities posited by stereotypes are threatened, these stereotypes are asserted all the more vehemently: "The *same old* stories of the Negro's animality, the Coolie's inscrutability or the stupidity of the Irish *must* be told (compulsively) again and afresh, and are differently gratifying and terrifying each time" (Bhabha, *Location of Culture*, 77).

67. On Plutarch's Platonized reading of Egyptian mythology, see Frederick Brenk, "Isis Is a Greek Word: Plutarch's Allegorization of Egyptian Religion," in *Plutarco, Platón y Aristóteles*, ed. A. Pérez Jiménez, J. García López, and R. M. Aguilar, (Madrid: Ediciones Clásicas, 1999), 227–38.

68. Des Places fr. 1a (= *PE* 9.7.1).

69. Thomas Schmidt, "Plutarch's Timeless Barbarians and the Age of Trajan," in *Sage and Emperor: Plutarch, Greek Intellectuals, and Roman Power in the Time of Trajan*, ed. Philip Stadter and Luc Van der Stockt (Louvain: Louven University Press, 2002), 57–71; idem, *Plutarque et les Barbares: La rhétorique d'une image* (Louvain: Peeters, 1999).

70. Daniel Richter, "Plutarch on Isis and Osiris: Text, Cult, and Cultural Appropriation," *Transactions of the American Philological Association* 131 (2001), 191–216.

71. Richard Alston, "Conquest by Text: Juvenal and Plutarch on Egypt," in *Roman Imperialism*, ed. Webster and Cooper, 99–109.

72. For a classic treatment of Christian research into "barbarian wisdom," see J. H. Waszink, "Some Observations on the Appreciation of 'The Philosophy of the Barbarians' in Early Christian Literature," *Opuscula Selecta* (Leiden: Brill, 1979), 272–87.

73. Lyman, "Hellenism and Heresy," 209–22, 217.

74. The most thorough study of the Hellenistic Jewish historians is Holladay, *Fragments from Hellenistic Jewish Authors*.

75. Droge, *Homer or Moses*, 136.

76. Droge, *Homer or Moses*, 159; Diodorus Siculus, commenting on the mass of sources from which he compiled his massive Historical Library, notes that "all [peoples] hold that it is they who are autochthonous and the first of all men to discover the things which are of use in life, and that it was the events in their own history which were the earliest to have been held worthy of record" (*Historical Library* 1.9.3.

77. Arthur Droge, "The Interpretation of the History of Culture in Hellenistic-Jewish Historiography," *SBL Seminar Papers* 23 (1984), 136–49; Doron Mendels, "'Creative History' in the Hellenistic Near East in the Third and Second Centuries B.C.E.: The Jewish Case," *Journal for the Study of the Pseudepigrapha* 2 (1988), 13–20. On the Erfinder motif, see also K. Thraede, Erfinder II in Reallexikon für Antike und Christentum, Bd. 5 (Stuttgart: Hiersemann, 1962), cols. 1191–1278.

78. On the presentation of Moses in Greek historiography, see John Gager, Moses in *Greco-Roman Paganism*, Society of Biblical Literature Monograph Series 16 (Nashville: Abingdon Press, 1978).

79. Diodorus Siculus *Historical Library* 1.94.

80. Diodorus Siculus *Historical Library* 1.94. There were pre-Socratic antecedents to this notion that law was ascribed to a divine source in order to force

obedience; see especially the *Sisyphus Fragment*. See also the translation in Charles Kahn, "Greek Religion and Philosophy in the Sisyphus Fragment," *Phronesis* 42 (1997), 247–62.

81. Diodorus Siculus *Historical Library* 1.94.2.

82. Josephus *Against Apion* 1.237–38, text and translation in H. Thackeray, *Josephus*, vol. 1 (Cambridge, Mass.: Harvard University Press, 1926).

83. Josephus *Against Apion* 1.249.

84. Josephus *Against Apion* 1.239–41. "Osarsiph's" laws are specifically directed against Egyptian animal worship.

85. Eupolemus at Eusebius *PE* 9.17.

86. Artapanus at Eusebius *PE* 9.18.

87. Eupolemus at Eusebius *PE* 9.26.

88. Artapanus at Eusebius *PE* 9.27.

89. On Theophilus in general, see Grant, *Greek Apologists*, 140–74; Rick Rogers, *Theophilus of Antioch: The Life and Thought of a Second-Century Bishop* (Lanham, Md.: Lexington Books, 2000); Fiedrowicz, *Apologie*, 54–55. On Theophilus's historiographic project in general, see Droge, *Homer or Moses*, 102–23.

90. Theophilus *To Autolycus* 3.16.1.

91. Theophilus *To Autolycus* 3.26.1.

92. Clement *Exhortation to the Greeks* 1 text: M. Marcovich, *Clementis Alexandrini Protrepticus*, Supplements to Vigiliae Christianae 34 (Leiden: Brill, 1995), translation, (ANF 2:173).

93. On Clement's use of Philo, see the extensive study by Annewies van den Hoek, *Clement of Alexandria and His Use of Philo in the* Stromateis: *An Early Christian Reshaping of a Jewish Model* (Leiden: Brill, 1988), and the excellent summary of David T. Runia, *Philo in Early Christian Literature: A Survey* (Minneapolis: Fortress Press, 1993), 132–56.

94. Josephus *Against Apion* 2.165.

95. Josephus *Against Apion* 2.166–71.

96. Josephus *Against Apion* 2.169.

97. On Lycurgus, see Josephus *Against Apion* 2.225; on Sparta and Crete, see Josephus *Against Apion* 2.171–72.

98. Philo *Life of Moses* 2.2, text and translation in F. H. Colson, *Philo*, vol. 6, Loeb Classical Library (Cambridge, Mass.: Harvard University Press, 1935), 451. The classic study is still E. R. Goodenough, *The Politics of Philo Judaeus* (New Haven, Conn.: Yale University Press, 1938).

99. Philo *Life of Moses* 2.2.

100. Philo *Life of Moses* 2.49–50.

101. For a general treatment of early Christian uses of Philo, see Runia, *Philo* (see note 90). Justin Martyr and Theophilus of Antioch show important affinities with the thought-world of Hellenistic Judaism, and some have argued for direct dependence on Philo. On Justin, see especially Erwin R. Goodenough, *The Theology of Justin Martyr* (Jena: Verlag, 1923); Leslie Barnard, *Justin Martyr: His Life and Thought* (Cambridge: Cambridge University Press, 1967). On Theophilus, see especially Grant, *Greek Apologists* J. P. Martín, "La presencia de Filón en el Exámeron de Teófilo de Antioquía," *Salmaticensis* 33 (1986), 147–77. Dependence on Philo is much more certain for early Christians in Alexandria, especially Clement of Alexandria and Origen; see the discussion in Runia, *Philo*, 119–83.

102. See Droge, *Homer or Moses*; Daniel Ridings, *The Attic Moses: The Dependency Theme in Some Early Christian Writers* (Göteborg: Acta Universitatis Gothoburgensis, 1995); Boys-Stones, *Post-Hellenistic Philosophy*, 176–202.

103. Theophilus *To Autolycus* 2.9.

104. *1 Apol.* 20.

105. Aristides *Apology* (Syriac) I.1–2; (Greek) I.1–2, text and French trans. B. Pouderon, et al., *Aristides: Apologie*, SC 470 (Paris: Cerf, 2003).

106. Both the Greek and Syriac versions of the *Apology* present five groups, though the exact terminology differs. The Syriac version states that "there are four races of humans: barbarians, Greeks, Jews, and Christians," but adds the Egyptians in the course of discussing the Greeks (*Apology* [Syriac] XII.1). The Greek version posits "three races of humans (*tria genēeisin anthrōpōn*) . . . those who worship those that are called gods by you, Jews, and Christians" and then subdivides the first of these into Chaldeans, Greeks, and Egyptians (*Apology* [Greek] II.2).

107. Aristides *Apology* (Syriac) II.1–VII.2.

108. Aristides *Apology* (Syriac) VIII.1–XI.7.

109. Aristides *Apology* (Syriac) XII.1–XIII.1.

110. Aristides *Apology* (Syriac) XIV.1–4.

111. Aristides *Apology* (Syriac) XV.1–3.

112. Minucius Felix *Octavius* 21 (ANF 4:185–86).

113. Clement *Exhortation to the Greeks* 4, ANF 2:184.

114. Clement *Exhortation to the Greeks* 2 (ANF 2:178).

115. Stanley K. Stowers, *A Rereading of Romans: Justice, Jews, and Gentiles* (New Haven, Conn.: Yale University Press, 1994), 97–100.

116. On points of contact between Euhemerism and the account of idolatry in *Wisdom of Solomon*, see David Winston, *The Wisdom of Solomon*, The Anchor Bible, vol. 43 (Garden City, N.Y.: Doubleday, 1979), 270–80; on Euhemerism in *1 Enoch*, see Paul D. Hanson, "Rebellion in Heaven, Azazel, and Euhemeristic Heroes in 1 Enoch," *Journal of Biblical Literature* 96 (1977), 195–233.

117. Pseudo-Philo, *Book of Biblical Antiquities* 2.9, text and translation in H. Jacobson, *A Commentary on Pseudo-Philo's* Liber Antiquitatem Biblicarum, vol. 1 (New York: Brill, 1996), 2, 91.

118. Stowers, *Rereading*, 83–85.

119. Philo *On Abraham* 40, text and translation in F. H. Colson, *Philo*, vol. 6 (Cambridge, Mass.: Harvard University Press, 1959).

120. Philo *On Abraham* 32.

121. Philo *On Abraham* 46.

122. Philo *On Abraham* 50.

123. Philo *On Abraham* 69.

124. Philo *Life of Moses* 1.3.

125. Philo *Life of Moses* 2.46.

126. Philo *Life of Moses* 2.5–6.

127. Philo *On Abraham* 47; 52.

128. See, for example, Philo *Flaccus* I.1; Philo *Hypothetica* (= Eusebius *PE* 8.6.1), text and translation in F. H. Colson, *Philo*, vol. 9 (Cambridge, Mass.: Harvard University Press, 1960).

129. Philo *On Abraham* 46, 50.

130. Clement *Stromateis* 2.9, text: O. Stählin, GCS 12 (1985), trans. ANF 2:357; *CCels.* 1.4.

131. See especially Heikki Räisänen, *Paul and the Law* (Philadelphia: Fortress Press, 1983); E. P. Sanders, *Paul, the Law and the Jewish People* (Philadelphia: Fortress Press, 1983); and Lloyd Gaston, *Paul and the Torah* (Vancouver: University of British Columbia Press, 1987).

132. Stowers, *Rereading*, 113–15.

133. Ibid., 115–16.

134. Andrew Erksine, *The Hellenistic Stoa: Political Thought and Action* (Ithaca, N.Y.: Cornell University Press, 1990), 103–10, 154–61, 192–214; see also summary discussion in Stowers, *Rereading*, 110–11.

135. Or, as Daniel Boyarin puts it, in Paul "allegoresis . . . unites both gender and ethnic identity as the secondary and devalued terms of the same binary opposition. . . . Unique to Paul is the hermeneutic shift by which the allegorized particular Israel yields the universal 'in Christ Jesus' " (*A Radical Jew*, 24–25).

136. Boyarin, *A Radical Jew*, 32.

137. Leslie Barnard, introduction to *Justin Martyr: First and Second Apologies*, Ancient Christian Writers 56 (New York: Paulist Press, 1997), 3; Grant, *Greek Apologists*, 50.

138. Justin *Dialogue with Trypho* 120.6, text in M. Marcovich, *Dialogus cum Tryphone* PTS 47 (Berlin: Walter de Gruyter, 1997).

139. Justin *Dialogue with Trypho* 29.2.

140. Justin *Dialogue with Trypho* 2.1. On Justin's philosophical education, see Goodenough, *Justin Martyr* 57–77; Mark Edwards, "On the Platonic Schooling of Justin Martyr," *JTS* 42 (1991), 17–34; Barnard, introduction, 3–5.

141. Justin recounts his testing of the schools and his conversion in *Dialogue with Trypho* 2–7. Justin hailed from Flavia Neapolis in Samaria, though he seems to have come from a thoroughly Hellenized family (Grant, *Greek Apologists*, 50–55).

142. F. Young, "Greek Apologists of the Second Century," 83–84; Grant, *Greek Apologists*, 54.

143. On the precise legal grounds for early persecutions, see the classical treatments by Sherwin-White ("The Early Persecutions and Roman Law Again" and de Ste. Croix ("Why Were the Early Christians Persecuted?").

144. *Jubilees* 11.4–5.

145. *1 Enoch* 6–11.

146. On Justin's demonology and his use of parabiblical traditions, see Annette Yoshiko Reed, *Fallen Angels and the History of Judaism and Christianity: The Reception of Enochic Literature* (Cambridge: Cambridge University Press, 2005), 161–74.

147. On Justin's doctrine of the *Logos*, see Goodenough, *Justin Martyr*, 139–75; Carl Andresen, "Justin und der mittlere Platonismus," *Zeitschrift für die neutestamentliche Wissenschaft* 44 (1952/53), 12–195; Ragnar Holte, "Logos Spermatikos: Christianity and Ancient Philosophy According to St. Justin's Apologies," *Studia Theologica* 11 (1958), 8–168; J. H. Waszink, "Bemerkungen zu Justins Lehre vom Logos Spermatikos," in *Mullus: Festschrift Theodor Klauser* (Munster, 1964), 380–90; Barnard, introduction, 14–16.

148. *Martyrdom of Justin* 2 (ANF 1:305).

149. Grant, *Greek Apologists*, 115.

150. On Tatian's distinction between "Greeks" and "barbarians," see Martin Elze, *Tatian und seine Theologie*, Forschungen zur Kirchen- und Dogmengeschichte Bd. 9 (Göttingen: Vandenhoeck and Ruprecht, 1960), 25–27, and Enrico Norelli, "La critique du pluralisme grec dans *le Discours aux Grecs* de Tatian," in *Les apologistes chrétiens et la culture grecque*, ed. B. Pouderon and J. Doré,. Théologie Historique 105 (Paris: Beauchesne, 1994), 81–87.

151. Elze, *Tatian*, 60–62.

152. Norelli, "La critique," 87–94.

153. Plato *Euthyphro* 3b: *kainotomountos . . . pero ta theia*; compare 16a.

154. Origen mistakenly labels Celsus an Epicurean. According to *Against Celsus*, the only Celsuses he could call to mind were "two Epicureans . . . the first lived in Nero's time, but the latter lived under Hadrian and afterwards" (*CCels.* 1.8). Lucian of Samosata dedicated his satirical *Alexander the False Prophet* to an Epicurean Celsus who lived during the 180s C.E. Although the date would fit Origen's Celsus, who wrote *On the True Logos* in the late 170s C.E., Origen was almost certainly mistaken in identifying Celsus as an Epicurean. None of the extant fragments of Celsus's text contains any Epicurean doctrines, and Origen, in fact, seems to question his own identification when he notes that he can discern Celsus's identity only from other texts, that is, those in which he has read of Epicurean Celsuses (*CCels.* 1.8). According to Michael Frede ("Celsus Philosophus Platonicus," *ANRW* II. 36.7 [1994], 5183–5213, and "Celsus's Attack on the Christians") Origen's apparent lack of any real knowledge of Celsus outside of the *Alēthēs Logos* itself is testimony to a rather limited distribution of the text before it fell into Origen's hands over seventy years after its composition. Everything about Celsus's treatise argues for ranking him among the Platonists of the second century. Henry Chadwick writes that "Celsus's philosophy is that of an eclectic Platonist. His affinities are with Middle Platonists like Albinus" (Chadwick, introduction to Origen: *Contra Celsum* [Cambridge: Cambridge University Press, 1953] xxvi); Frede argues that Celsus's doctrinal affinities lie, specifically, "in the anti-Aristotelian tradition like Numenius or Atticus" ("Celsus Philosophus Platonicus," 5191–92); John Dillon asserts that Celsus shares a similar polemical stance against the Epicureans and Stoics as Plutarch (*Middle Platonists*, 401). Both Frede and Dillon note that, doctrinally, Celsus offers nothing new or distinctive, yet, they add, this is precisely what makes him a perfect case study in second-century Platonism (Frede, "Celsus Philosophus Platonicus," 5187; Dillon, *Middle Platonists*, 401). Even Origen acknowledges the Platonic cast of Celsus's philosophy when he remarks that "in many instances he likes to Platonize" (*CCels.* 4.83).

155. The most systematic study of the Alēthēs Logos remains Carl Andresen, *Logos und Nomos: Die Polemik des Kelsos wider das Christentum* (Berlin: Walter de Gruyter, 1955). In French, see Pierre de Labriolle, *La réaction païenne: Étude sur la polémique antichrétienne du Ier au V^ie siècle* (Paris: L'Artisan du Livre, 1934), 111–69. For a brief but classic summary of Celsus polemics in English, see Chadwick, introduction, xvi–xxii. There have been a number of attempts to reconstruct Celsus's treatise. The most successful is that of Robert Bader, *Der Alēthēs Logos des Kelsos*, Tübinger Beitrage zur Altertumswissenschaft 33 (Stuttgart-Berlin: W. Kohlhammer, 1940). See also the English translation of R. J. Hoffman, *Celsus, On the True Doctrine: A Discourse Against the Christians* (Oxford: Oxford University Press, 1987). Various schema of the original plan of the text have been offered, but most scholars agree that, despite some shuffling, Origen preserves Celsus's arguments in essentially the same order in which they appeared in *On the True Logos* (Marcel Borret, introduction to *Origéne Contre Celse*, SC 227:33–34). Paul Koetschau divides the text into an introduction, four main sections, and a conclusion (*Origenes Werke* I–II [GCS 2: LI–LVI]). Borret argues for a similar scheme, but posits three main divisions (introduction, SC 227:118–21). Andresen's plan is a preface followed by four main divisions (*Logos und Nomos*, 32–33).

156. There are two main pieces of internal evidence that help date *On the True Logos*. First, Celsus uses the phrase *hoi nun basileuontes* (*CCels.* 8.71); this

reference to plural rulers could refer to either the years 161–69, when Marcus Aurelius ruled together with Verus, or the period between 177 and 180, when Commodus and Marcus reigned together. Second, Celsus indicates that Christians are being actively sought out and subjected to the death penalty (*CCels.* 8.69). The most intense persecutions under Marcus Aurelius occurred in the late 170s C.E., making circa 177–80 the most likely time of composition. See further Chadwick, introduction, xxvi–xxviii; Borret, introduction, SC 227, 122–29; Grant, *Greek Apologists*, 136. For a detailed discussion of Celsus as responding to Justin, see Andresen, *Logos und Nomos*, 345–72.

157. Literature on the causes and motivations behind the persecutions is vast, but for a good brief summary of the subject, see de Ste. Croix, "Why Were the Early Christians Persecuted?" James Rives has pointed out the importance of the religious proclivities of individual governors in the outbreak and severity of early persecutions ("The Piety of the Persecutors," *JECS* 4 [1996], 1–25).

158. E.g., Tertullian: "For we offer prayer for the safety of our princes to the eternal, the true, the living God" (*Apology* 30.1, translation in ANF 3:42).

159. Frede, "Celsus's Attack on the Christians," 233–34.

Chapter 2

1. The date of Porphyry's birth and the basic outline of his career can be reconstructed from the few autobiographical comments he makes in *VPl.* On the chronology of Porphyry's life see Edwards, appendix in *VPl.*, 117–19.

2. Joseph Bidez lists at least seventy-seven works (*Vie de Porphyre: Le philosophe néoplatonicien* [Ghent, 1913; reprint, Hildesheim: Georg Olms, 1964], 65*–73*), Smith an equally impressive sixty-nine (*Porphyrius Fragmenta*, ed. A. Smith [Stuttgart: Teubner, 1993], L–LIII).

3. *Marc.* 1.

4. Porphyry states that he has "combined in himself the love of father as well as husband and teacher and family, and, if you will, even native country (*tēs patridos*)" (*Marc.* 6).

5. *Kalousēs de tēs tōn Hellēn?n chreias kai tōn theōn sunepeigontōn autois* (*Marc.* 4).

6. *DI* 5.2.2. On the role of anti-Christian polemicists in the decades preceding the Great Persecution, see LaBriolle, *La réaction païenne*, 302–32, and W. H. C. Frend, "Prelude to the Great Persecution: The Propaganda War," *JEH* 38 (1987), 1–18.

7. Lactantius describes Hierocles' polemics at *DI* 5.2.12–17 and mentions him by name at *Mort.* 16.4.

8. *DI* 5.2.5.

9. See Pier Franco Beatrice, "Antistes Philosophiae: Ein Christenfeindlicher Propagandist am Hofe Diokletians nach dem Zeugnis des Laktanz," *Augustinianum* 33 (1993), 1–47, and Elizabeth DePalma Digeser, *The Making of a Christian Empire: Lactantius and Rome* (Ithaca, N.Y.: Cornell University Press, 2000). For a detailed discussion of the evidence supporting Porphyry's role at Nicomedia, see the detailed discussion in the appendix.

10. Compare especially Lactantius's account at *DI* 5.2.5–6 and the summary of Porphyry's polemics by Eusebius at *PE* 1.2.2. See also the more detailed discussion in the appendix.

11. Earlier scholarship, following Bidez, placed *Against the Christians* in the 270s C.E. (Bidez, *Porphyre*, 67). Frend situates Porphyry's polemics within a "prop-

aganda war" between Christians and conservative pagans at the end of the third century, pointing especially to Diocletian's and Galerius's consultation of the oracles in the lead-up to the persecution as evidence for the influence of *Philosophy from Oracles* and to the wide influence of *Against the Christians* in subsequent anti-Christian polemics ("Prelude to the Great Persecution"). Elizabeth De-Palma Digeser offers a strong argument for a connection between the *Philosophy from Oracles* and the oracular consultations of 302–3 ("An Oracle of Apollo at Daphne and the Great Persecution," *Classical Philology* 99 [2004], 57–77). Timothy Barnes, moreover, argues that the intolerant tone of *Against the Christians* makes the early years of the fourth century a likely date of composition ("Scholarship or Propaganda? Porphyry's *Against the Christians* and Its Historical Setting," *Bulletin of the Institute for Classical Studies* 37 [1994], 53–65). See also the discussion in the appendix.

12. *antistitem se philosophiae profitebatur* (*DI* 5.2.3); *monos oun hiereus ho sophos* (*Marc.* 16). Pier Franco Beatrice offers a detailed argument in "Antistes Philosophiae"; see also A. R. Sodano, *Vangelo di un pagano* (Milan: Rusconi, 1993), 115.

13. Socrates *HE* 1.9.30.

14. On Julian's use of Porphyry, see Socrates *HE* 3.23.

15. Cyril of Alexandria *Against Julian* 1.3 (= Harnack, *testimonium* XXIIb); Theodoret *On the Cure for Greek Maladies* 10.12 (= Harnack, *testimonium* XXIII).

16. References to Porphyry, *Against the Christians*, are to fragment numbers in the edition of Harnack.

17. On Porphyry's relationship with Middle Platonism, see Heinrich Dörrie, "Die Schultradition im Mittelplatonismus und Porphyrios," in *Porphyre*, Entretiens Hardt XII (Geneva: Fondation Hardt, 1966), 1–32; J.-H. Waszink, "Porphyrios und Numenios," in *Porphyre*, Entretiens Hardt XII (Geneva: Fondation Hardt, 1966), 35–83; Marco Zambon, *Porphyre et le moyen-platonisme* (Paris: J. Vrin, 2002).

18. E.g., Edwards, introduction to *Neoplatonic Saints*, xxx–xxxi.

19. Bhabha, *Location of Culture*, 85–92.

20. Ibid., 86.

21. "The *menace* of mimicry is its *double* vision which in disclosing the ambivalence of colonial discourse also disrupts its authority" (Bhabha, *Location of Culture*, 88).

22. On the translation and reading of this Porphyrian fragment I have been aided by the work of Elizabeth Digeser, especially her "Hellenes, Barbarians, and Christians: Religion and Identity Politics in Diocletian's Rome" (paper presented at Shifting Frontiers in Late Antiquity, Urbana-Champaign, Illinois, 2005).

23. Smith, *Fragmenta*, L–LIII.

24. References to Porphyry, *On the Return of the Soul (De Regressu Animae)*, are to the fragment numbers in the edition of Smith, *Fragmenta*.

25. *PE* 4.6.3.

26. References to Porphyry, *Philosophy from Oracles*, are to the fragment numbers in the edition of Smith, *Fragmenta*. It should be noted that this is an oracle in Porphyry's collection and not his "own" words. Nevertheless, the extant passages of *Philosophy from Oracles* give the strong impression that Porphyry only included oracles that served his "theosophy." The Porphyrian gloss that Eusebius preserves confirms that Porphyry read this oracle as evidence for "barbarian wisdom" (see also Audé Busine, *Paroles d'Apollon: Pratiques et traditions oraculaires*

dans l'Antiquité tardive (I^{te}-V^{ie} siècles [Leiden: Brill, 2005], 266–68). *Philosophy from Oracles,* like Porphyry's other exegetical texts (such as *On Statues* and *On the Cave of the Nymphs*) does consider various interpretations of texts, though he invariably prefers Platonic allegories to the "physical" allegories of the Stoics (on these differences, see Chapter 1). As I discuss in more detail in Chapter 5, Eusebius often quotes Porphyry in ways that make it appear that the philosopher advocated contradictory exegeses, but nowhere does Eusebius include an *oracle* out of which Porphyry did not extract some aspect of his "theosophy." Moreover, Porphyry states that he has edited the oracles in his collection, which strengthens the impression that he has edited the oracles to make them conducive to his Platonic exegeses. Furthermore, Robin Lane Fox has noted that Porphyry's collection of oracles was likely composed of oracles that were themselves "Platonic," much as the third-century collection of *Chaldean Oracles* was a product of later Platonism (*Pagans and Christians,* 196–97).

27. Cf. Numenius fr. 1 (des Places); see also discussion in Chapter 1.

28. Bidez, *Porphyre,* 18–19, 95–97.

29. As argued by Michael Bland Simmons, "*Via universalis salutis animae liberandae:* The Pagan-Christian Debate on Universalism in the Later Roman Empire (A.D. 260–325)," forthcoming in *Studia Patristica.* My sincerest thanks to Dr. Simmons for permission to cite his manuscript and for his helpful criticisms of this portion of this chapter.

30. Augustine *City of God* 10.32, text in CCL, translation in Henry Bettenson, *St. Augustine: City of God* (London: Penguin, 1984).

31. *Abst.* 3.5.2–3. For a detailed discussion of Porphyry's thinking on language as a marker of *logos* among humans and animals, see Gillian Clark, "Translate into Greek: Porphyry of Tyre on the New Barbarians," in *Constructing Identities,* ed. Miles, 118–21.

32. Hans Lewy, *Chaldean Oracles and Theurgy,* new ed., ed. Michel Tardieu (Paris: Études Augustiniennes, 1978), 449–59; Pierre Hadot, "Bilan et perspectives sur les *Oracles Chaldaïques,*" in Lewy, *Chaldean Oracles and Theurgy,* 711–12.

33. Hadot, "Bilan et perspectives," 712.

34. Augustine *City of God* 10.32 (Bettenson 421).

35. Smith 362T, 363T, 364aF–368F.

36. Porphyry, *Letter to Anebo,* text in A. R. Sodano, *Porfirio Lettera ad Anebo* (Naples: L'Arte Tipografica, 1958).

37. Plutarch *De Herodoti malignitate* 2.857a; note that Plutarch intends this epithet as an insult.

38. *Homeric Questions on the Odyssey* 1.42.9, 1.42.13, 2.362.4, 8.267.10; *Homeric Questions on the Iliad* 3.236.48, 20.67.56; *PO* 317F; *CC,* Harnack frr. 1 (3 times, in lines 2, 5, and 11), 39, 69; *Abst.* 1.13.25, 1.42.3, 2.51.6, 3.3.12, 3.25.13, 4.5.33.

39. Porphyry *Introduction to Aristotle's Categories* 1, text in A. Busse, *Porphyrii isagoge et in Aristotelis categories commentarium* (Berlin: Reimer, 1887), translation in Jonathan Barnes, *Porphyry: Introduction* (Oxford: Clarendon Press, 2003), 3–4.

40. Aristotle *Topics* 140a, 27–28, commented on in Porphyry *Introduction to Aristotle's Categories* 1.

41. Andrew Smith, "Porphyrian Studies Since 1913," *ANRW* II.36.2 (1987), 764.

42. G. Clark, "Translate," 120.

43. Ibid., 124.

44. Eunapius *Lives of the Philosophers* 355, text and translation in W. C. Wright,

Philostratus and Eunapius: The Lives of the Sophists (Cambridge, Mass.: Harvard University Press, 1922), 352.

45. *VPl.* 17, 21.

46. Eunapius *Lives of the Philosophers* 456.

47. Luc Brisson and Michel Patillon, "Longinus Platonicus Philosophus et Philologus," *ANRW* II. 36.7 (1994), 5214–99.

48. *VPl.* 17.

49. On Porphyry's ethnic identity and his knowledge of Phoenician language, see Fergus Millar, "Porphyry: Ethnicity, Language and Alien Wisdom," in *Philosophia Togata II: Plato and Aristotle at Rome*, ed. J. Barnes and M. Griffin (Oxford: Clarendon Press, 1997), 241–62. On his name changes and his assumption of a philosophical identity, see G. Clark, "Translate."

50. *VPl.* 1.

51. *VPl.* 3.

52. *VPl.* 3.

53. I follow David Dawson in opting for the more general term "figurative" to describe a wide range of nonliteral reading practices, including allegorical, typological, and etymological readings. As Dawson notes, concentrating on rigid distinctions between interpretive strategies runs the risk of "minimizing the extent to which different non-literal strategies inform one another" (*Allegorical Readers and Cultural Revision in Ancient Alexandria* [Berkeley: University of California Press, 1992], 5).

54. Robert Lamberton, *Homer the Theologian: Neoplatonest Allegorical Reading and the Growth of the Epic Tradition* (Berkeley: University of California Press, 1986), 19–20.

55. The Stoic exegete Cornutus, for example, is not an apologist for Homer but seeks to uncover the hidden physical and philosophical allegories contained in the epics (Dawson, *Allegorical Readers*, 38).

56. "The very tensions between literal and non-literal readings that characterized ancient allegory stemmed from efforts by readers to secure for themselves and their communities social and cultural identity, authority, and power" (Dawson, *Allegorical Readers*, 2).

57. Dawson, *Allegorical Readers*, 8–9.

58. Lamberton, *Homer the Theologian*, 22–31.

59. Porphyry *Cave* 34.

60. Porphyry *Cave* 6.

61. *VPl.* 10.

62. Porphyry, *On Statues* (*Peri Agalmatōn*); references are to fragment numbers in the edition of A. Smith, *Porphyrius Fragmenta* (Leipzig: Teubner, 1993).

63. *VPl.* 18 (Edwards 32).

64. Constantine issued the first edict, according to the Christian historians Gelasius and Socrates, at the Council of Nicaea (Gelasius *HE* 2.36; Socrates *HE* 1.9.30). The second edict was issued over a century later by the emperors Theodosius II and Valentinian III (*Cod. Just.* I 1.3). The first edict may not have been all that effective (Julian likely knew Porphyry's work in the mid–fourth century, for example), but the second may well have had the desired effect.

65. Harnack 43. The title *Against the Christians*, it should be noted, is itself a construct; Eusebius introduces quotations from the work with descriptive phrases such as *sungrammata kath' hēmōn* and *ho kath' hēmas tēn kath' hēmōn pepoiēmenos suskeuēen en d' tēs pros hēmas hupotheseōs* (*HE* 6.19.12; *PE* 1.9.20). I retain the conventional title *Against the Christians* here, however, for the sake of convenience.

66. *VPl.* 16.

67. *VPl.* 16.

68. *VPl.* 16.

69. G. Clark, "Translate," 126.

70. 1 Cor. 9:19–23.

71. Macarios Magnes, *Apocriticus,* ed. and French trans. in R. Goulet, *Macarios de Magnésie: Le Monogénès* (Paris: J. Vrin, 2003). Opinion remains divided as to the value of the *Apocriticus* as a source for fragments of *Against the Christians;* Goulet's arguments for a Porphyrian source are convincing. I have limited myself to fragments from the *Apocriticus* that seem especially likely to have come from Porphyry in that they parallel uncontested fragments and *testimonia* preserved by Jerome that show Porphyry attacking Peter and Paul (Harnack frr. 21a, 21b, 22). One fragment (Harnack fr. 28 [= *Apocr.* 3.31.4]) also contains vocabulary (*othneios*) that Goulet suggests is shared between uncontested Porphyrian fragments and the *Apocriticus* (*Macarios,* 304). R. Waelkens, *L'economie, theme, apologetique et principe hermeneutique dans l'Apocriticus de Macarius Magne: Recueil de travaux d'Histoire et de Philologie,* University of Louvain, ser. 6, no. 4 (Louvain: Bibliotheque de l'Université, Bureau du recueil, 1974), 117–34, argues similarly that fragments from the *Apocriticus* may be taken as coming from Porphyry if they can be corroborated by material outside the *Apocriticus.* For a discussion of the debate, see the appendix.

72. Acts 23:26, 25:10–12.

73. Scholars continue to disagree about the identities of the "Origens" in Porphyry's treatises. In *VPl.* 3 and 20 Porphyry identifies an "Origen" (Origen the Neoplatonist, author of a treatise titled "On Demons" that has been lost) as Plotinus's compatriot in the circle of Ammonius Saccas. Although some have attempted to identify this Origen with the Christian exegete, the two Origens are distinct. In the passage of *Against the Christians* preserved by Eusebius (*HE* 6.19), Porphyry clearly and unambiguously refers to the Christian exegete. Confusion arises because Porphyry also identifies the Christian exegete as a disciple of Ammonius (*akroatēs gar houtos Ammōniou*). Some scholars have argued that Porphyry was confused about the identities of the two Origens (Richard Goulet, "Porphyre, Ammonius, les Deux Origénes et les Autres," *Revue de l'Histoire de Philosophie et Religion* 57 [1977], 471–96), while others have argued that Porphyry conflated multiple Ammonii (Heinrich Dörrie, "Ammonios, der Lehrer Plotins," *Hermes* 83 [1955], 439–77; Mark Edwards, "Ammonius, Teacher of Origen," *JEH* 44 [1993], 1–13). Pier Franco Beatrice ("Porphyry's Judgment on Origen," in *Origeniana Quinta,* ed. R. Daly (Leuven: Peeters, 1992), 351–67), on the other hand, maintains that Porphyry has not confused two Origens but in fact had direct knowledge of Origen during a sojourn to Caesarea early in Porphyry's career. Beatrice argues that the aspersions Eusebius casts on the veracity of Porphyry's account owe more to the polemical character of Eusebius's own citation of Porphyry than to an objective critique of Porphyry's remarks. Whatever the "historical" value of Porphyry's remarks, it is absolutely clear that Porphyry intends to refer to the Christian exegete. Any "confusion" of Origens or Ammonii may well be the result of Porphyry's own deliberate polemical machinations rather than "forgetfulness" or "confusion." It is quite clear that Porphyry is mentioning both Ammonius and the Christian Origen to draw a polemical comparison between them, not to offer an objective historical commentary.

74. *HE* 6.19.5 (GCS n.f. 6:558). Among those who argue for the authenticity of Porphyry's meeting with Origen, see Beatrice, "Porphyry's Judgment on Origen," 351–67.

75. That *Philosophy from Oracles* represents anti-Christian polemic was first pointed out by Robert Wilken, "Pagan Criticism of Christianity: Greek Religion and Christian Faith," in *Early Christian Literature and the Classical Intellectual Tradition*, ed. W. Schoedel and R. Wilken (Paris: Éditions Beauchesne, 1979) and reiterated in Wilken, *The Christians as the Romans Saw Them*, 2nd ed. (New Haven, Conn.: Yale University Press, 2003), 148–56. Variations on Wilken's thesis have been argued by Pier Franco Beatrice, "Le traité de Porphyre contre les chrétiens: L'état de la question," *Kernos* 4 (1991), 119–38, and Beatrice, "Towards a New Edition of Porphyry's Fragments Against the Christians," in *Sophiēs maiētores: Chercheurs de sagesse: Hommage à Jean Pépin*, ed. M. Goulet–Cazé, G. Madec, and D. O'Brien (Paris: Études Augustiniennes, 1992), 347–55, and by Digeser, *The Making of a Christian Empire*, 93–102.

76. Wilken, *The Christians as the Romans Saw Them*, 150–51.

77. I rely here and in several subsequent quotations on the translation of Bettenson.

78. Note that Lactantius preserves the same oracle in Greek: *es de theon basilēa kai es genetēra pro pantōn, hon tromeei kai gaia kai ouranos ēde thalassa tartareoi te muchoi kai daimones errigasin* (*On the Anger of God* 23.12).

79. Compare *PO* 345aF (= *City of God* 19.23).

80. Wilken, *The Christians as the Romans Saw Them*, 152–53.

81. Michael Bland Simmons, *Arnobius of Sicca: Religious Conflict and Competition in the Age of Diocletian* (Oxford: Oxford University Press, 1995), 222–29.

82. *PO* 345aF (= *De Civ. Dei* 19.23, tr. Bettenson 886), and see Simmons, *Arnobius*, 226–27.

83. For a brief discussion of Diocletian's conservative policies, see W. H. C. Frend, *Martyrdom and Persecution in the Early Church* (Oxford: Oxford University Press, 1965), 477–81. For an in-depth discussion, see S. Williams, *Diocletian and the Roman Recovery*.

84. *HE* 8.17.6. I rely here on the translation of Norman H. Baynes, "The Great Persecution," in *Cambridge Ancient History*, vol. 12 (Cambridge: Cambridge University Press, 1939; reprint, 1989), 672.

85. *Latin Panegyric* 11.18.5, text and translation in C. E. V. Nixon and B. S. Rodgers, *In Praise of Later Roman Emperors: The Panegyrici Latini* (Berkeley: University of California Press, 1994), 102.

86. Bidez, *Porphyre*, 67–68, reiterated by Baynes, "The Great Persecution," 660, and Beatrice, "New Edition of Porphyry's Fragments," 355.

87. "The altars of God, when consecrated, do no harm, but when they are neglected, they do no good, either" (*Marc.* 18).

88. "Neither many sacrifices nor numerous offerings honor God, but the finely established god-filled intellect is joined to God, for it is necessary that like return to like" (*Marc.* 19).

89. "The general liberal consensus that 'true' knowledge is fundamentally non-political (and conversely, that overtly political knowledge is not 'true' knowledge) obscures the highly if obscurely organized political circumstances obtaining when knowledge is produced" (Said, *Orientalism*, 10).

90. *HE* 8.17.7, translation is that of Baynes, "The Great Persecution," 672.

91. On Paul: *ho polus en tō legein hōsper tēn oikeiōn logōn epilathomenos . . . (ktl.)* (Harnack fr. 28 [= *Apocr.* 3.31.1]). On Origen: *ta Hellēnōn tois othneiois hupoballomenos muthois* (Harnack fr. 39 [= *HE* 6.19.7]).

Chapter 3

1. Jerome *Illustrious Men* 83, text, G. Herding, *Hieronymus: De viris inlustribus* (Leipzig, 1879).
2. Jerome *Illustrious Men* 81.
3. Jerome *Illustrious Men* 104.
4. For brief biographical surveys, see Peter Garnsey and Anthony Bowen, introduction to *Lactantius: Divine Institutes* (Liverpool: Liverpool University Press, 2003), 1–6; Mary Francis McDonald, "General Introduction," in *Lactantius: The Divine Institutes*, Fathers of the Church, vol. 49 (Washington, D.C.: Catholic University of America Press, 1964), ix–xxiv; Fiedrowicz, *Apologie*, 84–88; René Pichon, *Lactance: Étude sur le mouvement philosophique et religieux sous le règne de Constantin* (Paris: Librarie Hachette, 1901), 1–4.
5. Jerome *Illustrious Men* 80.
6. Although Arnobius also wrote his seven-book *Against the Nations* in response to the Great Persecution, Lactantius seems to have left Africa before learning of his teacher's conversion to Christianity. Michael Bland Simmons notes that Lactantius may have mentioned Arnobius as a pagan opponent of Christianity in his letters or other earlier works mentioned by Jerome in *On Illustrious Men*, but these are now lost (*Arnobius*, 51–52). Garnsey and Bowen note that had Lactantius wanted to mention Arnobius's work, he could easily have done so in his discussion of previous Latin apologists in *DI* 5.1.21–28, 5.4.3–8 (introduction, 1).
7. Jerome *Illustrious Men* 80.
8. Timothy Barnes suggests that Lactantius was in Africa from 305 to 308 (*Constantine and Eusebius*, 13). Garnsey and Bowen suggest that this time was spent in Italy (introduction, 3).
9. Jerome (*Illustrious Men* 80) reports only that this was when Lactantius was "extremely old" (*extrema senectute*), but Barnes dates his assignment to Trier to 313 (*Constantine and Eusebius*, 13); Digeser has suggested an earlier date of circa 310 ("Lactantius and Constantine's Letter to Arles: Dating the *Divine Institutes*," *JECS* 2 [1994], 33–52).
10. Barnes, *Constantine and Eusebius*, 13, 292n99.
11. Jerome *Illustrious Men* 80.
12. On Lactantius's relationship to earlier Latin apologetic, see Pichon, *Lactance*, 33–57; Pierre Monat, introduction to *Lactance: Institutions Divines* (SC 204:45–50); Mark Edwards, "The Flowering of Latin Apologetic: Lactantius and Arnobius," in *Apologetics in the Roman Empire*, ed. Edwards, Goodman, and Price, 197–221.
13. Lactantius reports being an eyewitness to the destruction of church buildings in Nicomedia, ordered by the first persecuting edict of 303 C.E. (*DI* 5.2.2). Barnes (*Constantine and Eusebius*, 13, 291n96) argues that Lactantius must have completed the first edition of the *Divine Institutes* before 310 C.E., that is, before the deaths of any of the persecutors. Garnsey and Bowen (introduction, 3) and Digeser (*The Making of a Christian Empire*, 8) echo Barnes's conclusions. At *DI* 5.11, Lactantius reports that he saw a Christian in Bithynia give in to authorities' demands after resisting for "two years," suggesting that the apologist may have remained in Nicomedia as late as 305 C.E.
14. *ego cum in Bithynia oratorias litteras accitus docerem contigissetque ut eodem tempore dei templum everteretur* (*DI* 5.2.2). Lactantius is referring to the first of Diocletian's persecuting edicts, issued on 24 February 303, which ordered the destruction of church buildings and the burning of Christian scriptures.

15. *duo extiterunt ibidem qui iacenti atque abiectae veritati nescio utrum superbius an inportunius insultarent* (*DI* 5.2.2).

16. *Mort.* 16.4.

17. See also the detailed discussion in the appendix.

18. Lactantius's attitude toward and use of scripture has been studied in great detail by Pierre Monat, *Lactance et la Bible: Une propédeutique latine à la lecture de la Bible dans l'Occident constantinien* (Paris: Études Augustiniennes, 1982); on the authority of scripture for Lactantius, see especially 41–52.

19. Monat notes several instances, including 1.5.1, 3.1.10, 5.4.4–8, 7.5.21 (*Lactance et la Bible*, vol. 2, 19n46).

20. *CC* (Harnack fr. 4).

21. See, for example, Tertullian *Apology* 4 (ANF 3:20–21): "I shall not only refute the things which are objected to us, but I shall also retort (*retorquebo*) them on the objectors."

22. *Suscepto igitur inlustrandae veritatis officio non putavi adeo necessarium ab illa quaestione principium sumere, quae videtur prima esse natura, sitne providentia quae rebus omnibus consulat an fortuito vel facta sint omnia vel gerantur* (*DI* 1.2.1). *Sit ergo nostri opera exordium quaestio illa consequens ac secunda, utrum potestate unius dei mundus regatur anne multorum* (*DI* 1.3.1).

23. Where it is particularly significant or illustrative I have provided cross-references to the secondary sources that Lactantius quotes, cites, and alludes to. For a complete table of Lactantius's *fontes* see the edition of S. Brandt, *Lactantius Institutae Divinae*, CSEL 19 (Vienna, 1890) and the detailed footnotes in the translation of Bowen and Garnsey (see n. 4).

24. Lactantius is not adopting the Epicurean concept of *prolepsis*, which in Cicero's Latin is translated *anticipatio* (*On the Nature of the Gods* 1.44; see P. G. Walsh, *Cicero: The Nature of the Gods* [Oxford: Oxford University Press, 1998], 157–58n43), and suggests that knowledge of God is inborn and is independent of observation of the natural world. Lactantius's position is that humans were created by God to be naturally fitted for the rational observation of the order of the cosmos, thus leading them to a natural recognition of God (*DI* .2.1.14–19). This position is closer to Stoic ideas about human knowledge of the existence of the gods (e.g., *On the Nature of the Gods* 2.4).

25. See A. J. Festugière, "La doctrine des 'uiri novi' sur l'origine et le sort des âmes, d'après Arnobe, II, 11–66," in *Mémorial Lagrange* (Paris: J. Gabalda, 1940), 97–132; Pierre Courcelle, "Les sages de Porphyre et les 'viri novi' d'Arnobe," *Revue des études latines* 31 (1953), 257–71; and most recently Simmons, *Arnobius*, 13, 216–18.

26. Some of Lactantius's historical and ethnographic information comes from his reading of Cicero's *On the Nature of the Gods*: "In Cicero, Cotta the pontifex, when he is disputing against the Stoics about religions and the variety of opinions which people are wont to have about the gods, says, 'There are five Mercuries.' And after listing four in order he says, 'the fifth was he who killed Argus; for this reason he fled to Egypt and gave laws and literature to the Egyptians. The Egyptians call him "Thoth," and their first month (that is, September) is named after him'" (*DI* 1.6.2–3). To Cicero's account Lactantius joins material of uncertain provenance: "He founded a city, which even now is called 'City of Mercury' in Greek, and the Pheneatians worship him. Although he was a human, he was nevertheless most ancient and most learned in all the disciplines, with the result that his knowledge of many matters and arts gave him the cognomen 'Trismegistos'" (*DI* 1.6.3–4). The fact that there was a "City of Mercury"

in Egypt (i.e., Hermopolis) could have been taken from a basic knowledge of geography, or perhaps Lactantius had read more extensively in geography in the course of writing his own *Travels*. As with poets and philosophers, Hermetic *testimonia* are valuable insofar as they corroborate Christian doctrine.

27. Compare *Corp. Herm.* vol. 4, fr. 13, text in A. Nock and A. J. Festugière, *Corpus Hermeticum* 4 vols. (Paris: Belles Lettres, 1972–73), translation in Brian Copenhaver, *Hermetica* (Cambridge: Cambridge University Press, 1992).

28. Compare *Corp. Herm.* 5.1 and *Asclepius* 8. Lactantius notes the Greek title at *DI* 4.6.4.

29. Compare *Asclepius* 26 and *Corp. Herm.* vol. 4, fr. 12b.

30. Compare *Corp. Herm.* vol. 4, fr. 15.

31. Antonie Wlosok (*Laktanz und die philosophische Gnosis: Untersuchungen zu Geschichte und Terminologie der gnostischen Erlösungsvorstellung* [Heidelberg: Carl Winter, 1960], 180–232) argues that Lactantius owes his focus on humans' upright stance from a reading of *Timaeus* 28c, on humans' knowledge of God, mediated through the second book of Cicero's *On the Nature of the Gods*, and Hermetic traditions. Michel Perrin (*L'homme antique et chrétien: L'anthropologie de Lactance, 250–325*, Théologie Historique 59 [Paris: Beauchesne, 1981], 71) disagrees, arguing that Lactantius is simply taking the term *theoptia* as Hermes' definition of the human contemplation of the divine in a way similar to the way in which he uses Varronian etymologies to make interpretive points at other places in the *Institutes*.

32. *Corp. Herm.* 1.12 (Nock and Festugière vol. 1, 10).

33. Quoting *Corp. Herm.* vol. 3, p. 4.

34. Nock and Festugière vol. 3 II A 2.

35. See Michel Perrin's detailed discussion in *L'homme antique et chrétien*, 260–61.

36. Compare *Asclepius* 28, 25.

37. Quoting *Poimandres* 9.4; *Corp. Herm.* vol. 4, fr. 10.

38. Augustine reports that he has read Lactantius's account of Hermes in *City of God* 18.23 and he is critical of an overweening reliance on Hermes and other oracular sources in *Against Faustus* 13.1, 2, 15, 17. See also Copenhaver, *Hermetica*, xxxi.

39. Elizabeth Digeser has argued that Lactantius's interest in Hermes was part of an effort to establish an alliance between Christians and moderate "pagan monotheists" (*The Making of a Christian Empire*, 64–90). In an extensive study of the second book of Arnobius's *Against the Nations*, A. J. Festugière argues that the *viri novi* to whom the apologist directs much of his apologetic was an eclectic group that drew its philosophy from a combination of Hermeticism, Gnosticism, Neopythagoreanism, and Neoplatonism ("La doctrine des 'uiri noi'").

40. Iamblichus *On the Mysteries of the Egyptians* 1.1.2–3, text and translation in Emma Clarke, John Dillon, and Jackson Hershbell, *Iamblichus: On the Mysteries* (Atlanta: Society for Biblical Literature, 2003).

41. *VC* 2.50. Some argue that Lactantius and Constantine describe two distinct oracular consultations, while others argue that they recount the same event. Among those who conflate the accounts, see H. Grégoire, "Les chrétiens et l'oracle de Didymes," in *Mélanges Holleaux: Recueil de mémoires concernant l'antiquité grecque offert à Maurice Holleaux* (Paris, 1913), 84; Norman H. Baynes, "The Great Persecution," 665; Frend, *Martyrdom and Persecution in the Early Church*, 363; Fox, *Pagans and Christians*, 595. Among those who argue that Lactantius and Constantine describe two distinct oracles, see Averil Cameron and Stuart Hall, *Eusebius:*

Life of Constantine (Oxford: Oxford University Press, 1999), 245; Timothy Barnes originally conflated the account (*Constantine and Eusebius*, 21, 295n56) but has recently opted for the opposite view ("Monotheists All?" *Phoenix* 55 (2001), 158–59. See also Digeser, "An Oracle of Apollo at Daphne and the Great Persecution."

42. Lactantius *On the Anger of God* 23.12.

43. Augustine *City of God* 19.23.30–37 (= *PO* 344F).

44. Augustine *City of God* 19.23.17 (= *PO* 343F).

45. Augustine *City of God* 19.23.17 (= *PO* 343F) and 19.23.43–73 (= *PO* 345aF).

46. Oliver Nicholson notes similarly that Lactantius "distinguishes carefully the prophets who spoke from the Spirit of God, and so were unanimous in their utterances from the seers who have sung from the inspiration of demons" ("Broadening the Roman Mind: Foreign Prophets in the Apologetic of Lactantius," *Studia Patristica* 34 [2001], 371).

47. Porphyry expounds on the different natures of various divine beings and the sacrifices appropriate for each in *Abst.* 2.34.1–2.40.5.

48. Dionysius of Halicarnassus *Roman Antiquities* 4.62.

49. For a good introduction and translation, see John J. Collins, trans., "Sibylline Oracles," in *The Old Testament Pseudepigrapha*, vol. 1, ed. James Charlesworth (Garden City, N.Y.: Doubleday, 1983), 319–472.

50. Marie-Louise Guillaumin argues that Lactantius likely had access to the *Oracles* while still in Africa and identifies the collection of Oracles used by Lactantius as an edition dating to the third century C.E. ("L'exploitation des 'Oracles Sibyllins' par Lactance et par le 'Discours a l'assemblée des saints,'" in *Lactance et son temps*, ed. Jacques Fontaine and Michel Perrin, Théologie Historique 48 [Paris: Beauchesne, 1978], 183–202).

51. Lactantius's source for the story is the Roman historian Fenestella (Ann. Fr. 18* in H. Peter, *Veterum historicum Romanorum reliquiae* [Leipzig: Teubner, 1870–1906]).

52. Oliver Nicholson notes that Lactantius's six thousand years was common among early Christians; in particular, Cyprian argues for the same chronology in *To Fortunatus* praef. 2 ("The Source of the Dates in Lactantius's *Divine Institutes*," *JTS* 36 [1985]: 295n23).

53. Pierre Monat provides a helpful diagram of Lactantius's chronology (*Lactance et la Bible*, 280).

54. The *duoviri* (later expanded to *decemviri* and then *quindecemviri*) *sacris faciundis*. For a brief overview of their function in Roman religion, see Beard, North, and Price, *Religions of Rome*, vol. 1, 27, 62–63: for a more systematic treatment, see H. W. Parke, *Sibyls and Sibylline Prophecy in Classical Antiquity* (London: Routledge, 1988).

55. For Asclepius, see Livy, *History*, 10.47.6–7; for Magna Mater, see Livy, *History*, 29.10.4–11.8, 29.14.5. See also the discussion in Beard, North, and Price, *Religions of Rome*, vol. 1, 62–63, 69, 96–97.

56. Compare *Orac. Sib.* 8.326; *Orac. Sib.* 8.130 (trans. Collins 421).

57. "[I]n the spectacles of empire, all participants, including the audience, were on stage. To attend the shows was to take a risk, and because it was dangerous, it held great potential for the fashioning and presentation of the self" (Frilingos, *Spectacles and Empire*, 63, especially chapter 3, "A Vast Spectacle").

58. Lactantius is engaged in the same agonistic "dialectic of conflict and appropriation" that Simon Goldhill ascribes to Tertullian in his analysis of *On Spectacles*, a treatise that argues for the immorality of theatrical shows and

gladiatorial combats at the same time that it concludes with a eschatological vision of the impious suffering humiliation in a final apocalyptic spectacle ("The Erotic Eye: Visual Stimulation and Cultural Conflict," in *Being Greek Under Rome*, ed. Goldhill, 182–84).

59. "The *menace* of mimicry is its *double* vision which in disclosing the ambivalence of colonial discourse also disrupts its authority"; consequently, however, mimicry is a mode of resistance that constantly reiterates, even if only partially or metonymically, the political circumstances of its possibility (Bhabha, *Location of Culture*, 88–89).

60. Lactantius hopes that the quality of his style will help him convince his critics: (DI 5.4.8).

61. According to Oliver Nicholson, Lactantius hoped that a careful consideration of foreign wisdom would lead his readers to a Christian conception of history ("Broadening the Roman Mind," 373–74).

62. Lactantius's sources for Euhemerism are Ennius's Sacred History, a Latin translation of Euhemerus, and Cicero's *On the Nature of the Gods*.

63. Used as an anti-Christian argument, for example, by Caecilius in *Octavius* 6.2 (CSEL 2:9).

64. Lactantius acknowledges that his source is Theophilus's *To Autolycus* 3.29. See discussion in Nicholson, "The Source of the Dates in Lactantius's *Divine Institutes*," 291–92.

65. *Humanae cogitationis inventio* as opposed to *divina traditio* (DI 3.16.10).

66. *Marc.* 16.

67. *in multas sectas philosophia divisa est et omnes varia sentiunt. In qua ponimus veritatem?* (*DI* 3.4.3).

68. *Comparison of Mosaic and Roman Law* VI.4.3, text: Moses Hyamson, *Mosaicarum et Romanorum legume collatio* (Oxford: Oxford University Press, 1913).

69. *Ab hac gente* [i.e., the Canaanites, Ham's descendants] *proximi quique populi multitudine increscente fluxerunt. Ipsius autem patris* [i.e., Noah] *posteri Hebraei dicti: penes quos religio dei resedit* (*DI* 2.13.8).

70. *Nec sibi de summo deo vel Iudaei vel philosophi blandiantur: qui filium non agnovit, nec patrem potuit agnoscere* (*Epitome of the Divine Institutes* 49, text, S. Brandt, *Divinae Institutes*).

71. R. King, *Orientalism and Religion*, 37. King goes on to connect Lactantius's etymologies more explicitly with modern constructions of "religion": "The shift in the meaning of the term *religio* in a Hellenistic Christian context remains highly significant in our attempt to understand the way in which the concept of 'religion' is understood in modern Western culture. Modern discussions of the meaning and denotation of the term *religio* tend to follow Lactantius's etymology, thereby constructing a Christianized model of religion that strongly emphasizes *theistic belief* (whether mono-, poly-, heno-, or pantheistic in nature), exclusivity and a fundamental dualism between the human world and the transcendent world of the divine to which one 'binds' (*religare*) oneself. Even when Lactantius is not appealed to directly, 'religion' in a Christian (and post-Christian) context now becomes a matter of adherence to particular doctrines or beliefs rather than allegiance to ancient ritual practices" (37).

72. *Superstitiosi ergo qui multos ac falsos deos colunt, nos autem religiosi qui uni et vero deo supplicamus* (*DI* 4.28.16).

73. Jonathan Z. Smith, "Religion, Religions, Religious," in *Relating Religion* (Chicago: University of Chicago Press, 2004), 179–96, 187, originally published

Notes to Pages 106–107   217

in Critical Terms for Religious Studies, ed. Mark C. Taylor (Chicago: University of Chicago Press, 1998), 269–84.

74. Oliver Nicholson, "*Caelum potius intuemini:* Lactantius and a Statue of Constantine," *Studia Patristica* 34 (2001), 184, notes that Lactantius was "the earliest surviving Christian writer known to have been involved in the world of imperial politics."

75. This has been argued by Garnsey and Bowen (introduction, 43): "*Divine Institutes* should be read as a product of and witness to the Great Persecution, and not as a response to the turnabout in the Church's fortunes that happened under Constantine."

76. That the first edition of the text was completed before 310 C.E. can be inferred from internal evidence. In Book 5, Lactantius suggests that all of the persecuting emperors are still alive, but the first persecutor to meet his demise (Maximian) did so in 310 C.E. As he warns the persecutors (*mali principes, iniustissimi persecutors*) of their impending punishment, he does so with a future tense (*non se putent inpune laturos*) and a jussive subjunctive (*punientur enim iudicio dei*) (*DI* 5.23.1–2). On the date and circumstances of Maximian's death, see Barnes, *Constantine and Eusebius,* 34–35.

77. Several passages espousing a "dualistic" theology also made their way into some manuscripts during this period, but they do not bear on the present argument; see Eberhard Heck, *Die dualistischen Zusätze und die Kaiseranrede bei Lactanz* (Heidelberg: Carl Winter, 1972), 24–126.

78. Moreau argues that the dedication, which opens by praising Constantine for ending persecution, suggests a date after Constantine's defeat of Maxentius and the repeal of persecution by the "Edict of Milan" in 313 (J. Moreau, introduction to *Lactance: De la mort des persécuteurs* [SC 39:18]). Eberhard Heck has argued, moreover, that the first dedication, in which Constantine is addressed as imperator maxime, must have been written after the senate officially granted Constantine this title in 312 (*Die dualistischen Zusätze,* 139–40).

79. Heck concludes that Lactantius added the dedication in Book 1 during Constantine's war with Licinius in early 324 and the last dedication in Book 7 after Constantine defeated his rival later that year (DI 1.1.15). Heck, *Die dualistischen Zusätze,* 127, 141–43.

80. Heck, *Die dualistischen Zusätze,* 167–70.

81. Digeser reads Lactantius's reference to persecution "in other parts of the world" in the first long dedication in Book 1 as better fitting the situation of circa 310, when Maxentius still held Rome and Galerius and Maximinus were persecuting in the East ("Letter to Arles," 48–50). She also contends that the first dedication echoes themes presented in an official panegyric delivered in honor of Constantine in Trier in 310 (*The Making of a Christian Empire,* 134, 170). Against Heck's assumption that Lactantius could not have used the title *imperator maximus* until 312, Digeser notes that several manuscripts of the panegyric of 310 employ the title *maximus* ("Letter to Arles," 44–50; on the panegyric, see C. E. V Nixon and B. Saylor Rodgers, *In Praise of Later Roman Emperors* [Berkeley: University of California Press, 1994], 36). Digeser dates the second long dedication in Book 7 to 313, when Maximinus had been defeated by Licinius and Lactantius could declare the defeat of all the persecutors (DI 7.27.12–14; *The Making of a Christian Empire,* 134).

82. Digeser, "Letter to Arles," 35–38; The Making of a Christian Empire, 170–71.

83. Digeser, *The Making of a Christian Empire,* 134; "Letter to Arles," 51–52.

84. *Constantine imperator* (*DI* 2.1.2, 3.1.1, 4.1.1, 5.1.1, 6.3.1). In some manuscripts the dedication in 5.1.1 reads Constantine imperator maxime. For detailed discussion, see Heck, *Die dualistischen Zusätze*, 128–29.

85. *DI* 7.26.11, 14 (Heck, *Die dualistischen Zusätze*, 129–30).

86. *DI* 7.26.11 (Heck, *Die dualistischen Zusätze*, 129).

87. *DI* 7.26.11, 13 (Heck, *Die dualistischen Zusätze*, 129–30).

Chapter 4

1. Eusebius and Lactantius offer differing accounts of Constantine's vision. Eusebius (*VC* 1.28–32) reports that the emperor saw a "sign of the cross formed of light and an inscription attached to it which read, 'by this, conquer' at midday." According to Eusebius, Constantine then ordered the construction of the *labarum* based on this vision. Lactantius (*Mort.* 44) reports that Constantine was told in a dream to inscribe his soldiers' shields with the *Chi Rho*.

2. Garth Fowden, *Empire to Commonwealth: The Consequences of Monotheism in Late Antiquity* (Princeton, N.J.: Princeton University Press, 1993), 37–52.

3. Eusebius provides a lengthy description of Constantine's oratorical habits in *VC* 4.29–32.

4. *VC* 4.32.

5. "Constantine's historical memory has suffered the greatest misfortune conceivable. . . . He has fallen into the hands of the most objectionable of all eulogists, who has utterly falsified his likeness. The man is Eusebius of Caesarea and the book his *Life of Constantine*. . . . Furthermore, to say nothing of the contemptible style, there is a consciously furtive mode of expression, so that the reader finds himself treading concealed traps and bogs at the most vital passages" (Jacob Burckhardt, *The Age of Constantine the Great*, trans. Moses Hadas [New York: Dorset Press, 1949], 260–61).

6. P. Davies contends that Eusebius doctored the speech ("Constantine's Editor," *JTS* 42 [1991], 610–18). The last major study in favor of forgery was R. P. C. Hanson, "The *Oratio ad Sanctos* Attributed to the Emperor Constantine and the Oracle at Daphne," *JTS* 24 (1973), 505–11. Hanson's argument is based on the assumption that the oracle of Apollo at Daphne, referenced in *Or.* 18, was not active until the time of Julian, but this assumption has been subjected to an excellent critique by Elizabeth Digeser in "An Oracle of Apollo at Daphne and the Great Persecution."

7. Scholars who support authenticity include Timothy Barnes ("The Emperor Constantine's Good Friday Sermon," *JTS* 27 [1976], 414–23 and more recently "Constantine's *Speech to the Assembly of the Saints*: Place and Date of Delivery," *JTS* 52 [2001], 26–36); Harold Drake ("Suggestions of Date in Constantine's *Oration to the Saints*," *American Journal of Philology* 106 [1985], 335–49); Fox (*Pagans and Christians*, 627–29); and Mark Edwards (introduction to *Constantine and Christendom* [Liverpool: Liverpool University Press, 2003], xviii–xxii). Forgery is unlikely for several reasons. Eusebius's description of the emperor's oratorical habits in the *Life* does not exactly match the pattern of the *Oration*. If Eusebius had wished to forge a Constantinian speech, he would likely have used his own conception of Constantine's style as a model (Fox, *Pagans and Christians*, 629). The author of the *Oration* also espouses a Christology that Eusebius explicitly rejects (Edwards, introduction, xix–xx, and idem, "The Constantinian Circle and the *Oration to the Saints*," in *Apologetics in the Roman Empire*,

ed. Edwards, Goodman, and Price, 260–62). In addition, the *Oration* makes extensive use of Virgil, an author whom Eusebius quotes nowhere in any of his extant writings. The use of Virgil also suggests that the author of the speech was someone educated in the Latin classics—which describes Constantine but not Eusebius. Moreover, the Sibylline acrostic quoted in the speech is elsewhere quoted only by Latin authors: in particular Lactantius (Edwards, introduction, xix). As will be discussed in more detail in the chapter, the speech also deploys historical arguments that often parallel those used by Lactantius who, as was noted in the previous chapter, had been a member of Constantine's court in the years immediately preceding the *Oration*. Finally, the Greek of the *Oration* is quite different from Eusebius's style. The text was either written in Latin and translated into Greek at the court or composed in Greek initially (on these philological questions, see discussion by Fox, *Pagans and Christians*, 629–30). Problems in the Greek translation of Virgil's *Fourth Eclogue* in *Or.* 18 and other philological curiosities can be explained as the product of the official court translators who rendered Constantine's Latin text into Greek for publication (see Barnes, *Constantine and Eusebius*, 73, and Eusebius's description of the translation of Constantine's speeches in *VC* 4.29–32).

8. *Prooimion men anastaseōs . . . hē tou pathēmatos hēmera parestin* (*Or.* 1).

9. In the first of these passages, Constantine thanks God for his victories, and then addresses his audience and apostrophizes their city: "Even the great city knows it [i.e., that Constantine's victories are the result of divine favor] and applauds with praise, and the people of the most-beloved city have resolved the same, even though, when tricked into dangerous hopes she chose for herself an unworthy champion, who was immediately destroyed in a way fitting and appropriate for his recklessness" (*Or.* 22). In the second passage, Constantine recounts Diocletian's role in the persecutions. After excoriating Diocletian for savagery and impiety and noting his ignoble demise, Constantine calls attention to one of Diocletian's successors: "The whole army of the aforementioned emperor was put under the command of a worthless person who stole the rule of the Roman Empire, and when God's providence freed the great city, it was squandered in many and various wars" (*Or.* 25).

10. Timothy Barnes ("Good Friday Sermon," 421–23) once argued that these allusions point to a setting in Serdica in 317, asserting that *Or.* 22 must refer to Galerius, who resided in Serdica and was defeated nearby in 311. Barnes took the reference in *Or.* 25 as indicating Licinius; no other emperor, he argued, could legitimately be named the inheritor of Diocletian's army. Thus, he concluded that Constantine must have given the speech in Serdica after taking that city from Licinius after their first altercation in 317 C.E. More recently, Mark Edwards has advocated an even earlier date of 315 and Rome as the speech's context (introduction, xix–xxix). According to Edwards, the emperor's concern to cite Virgil and the Sibylline Oracles must presume a Latin audience. Moreover, Constantine names Rome only a few lines after apostrophizing the "most-beloved city." While others take this as drawing a clear distinction between Rome and the "most-beloved city," Edwards takes the opposite view. Edwards argues that the tyrant in *Or.* 22 is Maxentius from whom Constantine "saved" Rome at the Battle of the Milvian Bridge in 312. This would make the emperor of *Or.* 25 Maximinus, with whom Constantine claimed Maxentius had concocted a secret alliance immediately before his defeat.

11. Immediately before stating his plans to append the *Oration*, Eusebius explains that Constantine composed his works in Latin, after which translators

(*methermēneutai*) prepared them for publication (*VC* 4.32). This is almost certainly how Eusebius came by his copy of the *Oration*.

12. Fox, *Pagans and Christians*, 635–36.

13. Ibid. 638; for the letter, see *VC* 2.64–72.

14. The headings of several Constantinian laws in the Theodosian Code place Constantine in Nicomedia in late February and by June he was in Nicaea to preside over the great Council. Between these dates Fox posits a trip to Egypt that ended abortively in Antioch (*Pagans and Christians*, 638). Papyrological and numismatic evidence support Fox's reconstruction of Constantine's movements in 324–25: papyri speak of an imminent imperial visit to Egypt, while coins issued in Antioch in early 325 celebrate an *Adventus Augusti* (*Pagans and Christians*, 638, citing P. *Oxy* 1261, 1626). On Constantine, Ossius, and the Council of Antioch, see Fox, *Pagans and Christians*, 642–43.

15. Bruno Bleckman, "Ein Kaiser als Prediger: Zur Datierung der konstantinischen 'Rede an die Versammlung der Heiligen,'" *Hermes* 125 (1997), 183–202. Bleckman, however, argues a later date than either Barnes or Fox, suggesting that Constantine spoke at the synod held in Nicomedia in 328 following the deposition of Eustathius of Antioch ("Ein Kaiser," 197–200; see also discussion in Sara Parvis, *Marcellus of Ancyra and the Lost Years of the Arian Controversy, 325–345* [Oxford: Oxford University Press, 2006], 111–16).

16. Timothy Barnes, "Constantine's *Speech to the Assembly of the Saints*: Place and Date of Delivery,'" *JTS* 52 (2001), 34–36. Barnes's conclusions are based on the work of John Rist, who argues that in *Or.* 9.3 Constantine speaks of the Son as a "second god" with his own distinct *ousia* (*kai duo ousias tō arithmō dieile, mias ousēs tēs amphoterōn teleiotētos, tēs te ousias tou deuterou theou tēn huparxin echousēs ek tou prōtou*), a conceptualization of the Father and Son that would have appeared heterodox after Nicaea ("Basil's 'Neoplatonism': Its Background and Nature," in *Basil of Caesarea: Christian, Humanist, Ascetic, A Sixteenth-Hundredth Anniversary*, ed. Paul Fedwick [Toronto: Pontifical Institute of Mediaeval Studies, 1981], 155–58).

17. Barnes, "Constantine's *Speech*," 36.

18. Monotheism/monarchy (*Or.* 3, compare *DI* 1.3.18–19); sex and generation inappropriately ascribed to the gods (*Or.* 4, compare *DI* 1.16.5–6); "double-birth" and incarnation (*Or.* 11, compare *DI* 4.8.1); persecuting emperors (*Or.* 24–25, compare *Mort.* 4–7); pagan poets/Sibylline Oracles (*Or.* 10, compare *DI* 1.11.24).

19. Timothy Barnes, "Imperial Campaigns, A.D. 285–311," *Phoenix* 30 (1976), 174–93.

20. *PE* 1.2.2 (= Porphyry, Harnack fr. 1).

21. Eus. *HE* 8.17.6.

22. Michel de Certeau describes the negotiation of space as an enunciative practice homologous to other rhetorical practices and having its own grammar and figures of speech. Space is a "practiced place" homologous to reading as the operation that works over the text, and spatial practices (such as walking, standing, or, one might add, conquering) are, like writing and reading, always differential (*The Practice of Everyday Life*, trans. Steven Rendall [Berkeley: University of California Press, 1984]). In pointing to the broad homologies between speech-acts and spatial-acts, de Certeau's insights help elucidate the complexities of the "intertextual" relationships between texts (biblical, oracular, etc.) and other sites of meaning production (territorial, architectural, and so forth).

23. Numenius, des Places fr. 1a (= *PE* 9.7.1).

24. *DI* 7.16.11, 7.19.9, 7.20.3.

25. *Or.* 19.4–20.2; see apparatus in the edition for parallels to Virgil *Eclogue* 4.

26. Eusebius quotes the letter in its entirety at *VC* 2.24–44. On the authenticity of Eusebius's chapter headings, see Barnes, "Good Friday Sermon," 418–20. Eusebius says that he includes the letter, written for a pagan audience, in order to contribute to the objectivity of his history (*VC* 2.23.2). Although the letter Eusebius quotes is addressed "To the Palestinians," the closing orders publication "throughout our Oriental regions," giving this letter the same authority as an imperial edict (*VC* 2.24.1, 2.42; see also Barnes, *Constantine and Eusebius*, 208–9). Eusebius's document, which he claims is signed by Constantine himself, must be the version of the letter sent to the Roman governor of Palestine in Caesarea. Eusebius, therefore, either had access to the records of the provincial governor or collected his texts when they were posted publicly (see discussion in Andrew Carriker, *The Library of Eusebius of Caesarea*, Supplements to Vigiliae Christianae 67 [Leiden: Brill, 2003], 287).

27. The authenticity of the letter is confirmed by *P. Lond.* 878 (319–20), which preserves the letter from the end of VC 2.26 through the beginning of *VC* 2.29 (A. H. M. Jones and T. C. Skeat, "Notes on the Genuineness of the Constantinian Documents in Eusebius's *Life of Constantine*," *JEH* 5 [1954], 196–200). See also Simon Corcoran, *The Empire of the Tetrarchs: Imperial Pronouncements and Government* AD 284–324 (Oxford: Oxford University Press, 1996), 315.

28. These measures are enumerated at *VC* 2.44–45.

29. On Constantine's preference for Christians in the imperial service, see Barnes, *Constantine and Eusebius*, 210; idem, "The Religious Affiliations of Consuls and Prefects, 317–361," in *From Eusebius to Augustine: Selected Papers, 1982–1993* (London: Variorum, 1994); idem, *The New Empire of Diocletian and Constantine* (Cambridge, Mass.: Harvard University Press, 1982), chapter 9; and D. M. Novak, "Constantine and the Senate: An Early Phase in the Christianization of the Roman Aristocracy," *Ancient Society* 10 (1979), 271–310.

30. Theodosian Code 16.10.2.

31. Libanius *Oration* 30.6.

32. See especially Barnes, *Constantine and Eusebius*, 210, 246; idem, "Constantine's Prohibition of Pagan Sacrifice," *American Journal of Philology* 105 (1984), 69–72; Scott Bradbury, "Constantine and the Problem of Anti-Pagan Legislation in the Fourth Century," *Classical Philology* 89 (1994), 120–39; H.-U. Wiemar, "Libanius on Constantine," *Classical Quarterly*, n.s. 44 (1994), 522; Cameron and Hall, *Life of Constantine*, 243.

33. Eusebius quotes the letter in its entirety at *VC* 2.48.1–2.60.2. Barnes (*Constantine and Eusebius*, 377n12) argues that Eusebius presents his Constantinian documents in correct chronological sequence, against H. Dörries, "Das Selbstzeugnis Kaiser Konstantins," *Abh. Göttingen*, Phil.-hist. Kl. 34 (1954), 51, who dates the letter earlier.

34. Barnes, *Constantine and Eusebius*, 210–11.

35. See discussion in Barnes, *Constantine and Eusebius*, 210.

36. Barnes, *Constantine and Eusebius*, 210.

37. Drake, *Constantine and the Bishops: The Politics of Intolerance* (Baltimore: Johns Hopkins University Press, 2000), 199, 245–50.

38. Ibid., 284–308.

39. Ibid., 402, 532n22.

40. Ibid., 286–87.

41. See, for example, Ramsay MacMullen, *Constantine* (New York: Dial Press, 1969).

42. Drake, Constantine, 244–45.

43. Ibid., 199.

44. Holy Sepulcher: VC 3.26–32; Mamre: VC 3.51–53; Aphaca: VC 3.55.1–5; Heliopolis: VC 3.58; Didyma and Antioch: PE 4.2.10–11; Aigai: VC 3.55.5–3.56.3. Constantine's order to burn Porphyry's books has not survived, but his edict concerning Arius (Socrates HE 1.9.20 [SC 477:124]) and a later law of Theodosius and Valentinian III issued in 435 (Theodosian Code 16.5.66) offer indirect evidence.

45. Barnes, Constantine and Eusebius, 247; Fox, Pagans and Christians, 671.

46. For details, see Mort. 11–15 and in-depth discussion by Digeser, "An Oracle of Apollo at Daphne and the Great Persecution."

47. PE 4.2.10–11 (GCS 43:168–69); HE 9.3 (GCS 6:808).

48. Eusebius quotes the letter in its entirety at VC 3.30.1–3.32.2.

49. Through a careful analysis of both the archaeological record and Eusebius's account of the construction of the basilica, Annabel Wharton has shown how Eusebius's triumphalist narrative masks the "spatial agonistics" that must have accompanied the construction. The totalizing narrative of conversion through which one usually approaches the site has erased the politics of local space that leave their traces in Eusebius's and Constantine's accounts of the site's "discovery" and "rehabilitation" (Refiguring the Postclassical City: Dura Europos, Jerash, Jerusalem, and Revenna [Cambridge: Cambridge University Press, 1995], esp. 85–104).

50. Eusebius quotes the letter in its entirety at VC 3.52–3.53.4 (GCS 7:105–7).

51. Comparison of Mosaic and Roman Law VI.4.5, (Hyamson, 88–89).

52. Comparison of Mosaic and Roman Law VI.4.1 (Hyamson 87).

53. Comparison of Mosaic and Roman Law VI.4.2–3 (Hyamson 87).

54. Comparison of Mosaic and Roman Law VI.4.4 (Hyamson 89).

55. See the excellent study by Jill Harries, Law and Empire in Late Antiquity (Cambridge: Cambridge University Press, 1999), especially chapter 2, "Making the Law," 36–55.

56. Z. Rubin, "The Church of the Holy Sepulchre and the Conflict Between the Sees of Caesarea and Jerusalem," Jerusalem Cathedra 2 (1982), 79–105.

57. Eusebius may be guessing that a letter was sent and inferring its contents from what he knew of Constantine's epistolary habits and from the example of the Constantinian letters he did possess. Nonetheless, Eusebius was close enough to Phoenicia that he would likely have known that a letter was sent. Moreover, in recounting events at Aphaca, Eusebius does not say that a letter was sent and therefore appears to distinguish among the emperor's various means of communication.

58. Similarly, in her recent study of religious conversion in colonial India, Gauri Viswanathan describes the practice of census taking by British officials in terms of the construction of "narrative plots . . . in the working out of which race, caste, and religion become visible as analytical categories" (Outside the Fold: Conversion, Modernity, and Belief [Princeton, N.J.: Princeton University Press, 1998], 158).

59. Benedict Anderson describes the ways in which European imperial administration reified the identities postulated by academic discourses such as ethnography and geography. "These identities," Anderson states, "imagined by the (confusedly) classifying mind of the colonial state, . . . awaited a reification which imperial administrative penetration would soon make possible" (Imagined Communities: Reflections on the Origin and Spread of Nationalism [London: Verso, 1983, rev. ed., 1991], 165).

60. Homi Bhabha aptly describes the necessity for repetition in imperial rhetoric: "the *same old* stories of the Negro's animality, the Coolie's inscrutability or the stupidity of the Irish *must* be told (compulsively) again and afresh, and are differently gratifying and terrifying each time" (*Location of Culture*, 77).

Chapter 5

1. The *Prophetic Extracts* (*Eclogae Propheticae*) are in fact a subsection (books 6–9) of Eusebius's ten-book *General Elementary Introduction*, which is not otherwise extant (see *Ecl. Proph.* 3.1, 4.35, text, Thomas Gaisford, *Eclogae Propheticae* [Oxford: Oxford University Press, 1842]). Some scholars have sought traces of the lost books in Eusebius's other works. D. S. Wallace-Hadrill argues that the extant fragments ascribed to Eusebius's *Commentary on Luke* (*PG* 24:529–605) actually belong to the tenth book of the *General Elementary Introduction* ("Eusebius of Caesarea's Commentary on Luke: Its Origin and Early History," *HTR* 67 [1974], 55–63), but Aryeh Kofsky disagrees, citing differences in content between the fragments and Eusebius's statements in *Ecl. Proph.* 4.35 (*Eusebius of Caesarea Against Paganism* [Leiden: Brill, 2000], 51). James Stevenson argues that the first five books have made their way into the third book of the *DE* (*Studies in Eusebius* [Cambridge: Cambridge University Press, 1929], 63). Eusebius may have used the ten-book structure for his *General Elementary Introduction* in imitation and competition with similar ten-book introductions such as Anatolius's *Introduction to Arithmetic* and Iamblichus's *Introduction to Philosophy* (Barnes, *Constantine and Eusebius*, 168).

2. Tomas Hägg, "Hierocles' the *Lover of Truth* and Eusebius the Sophist," *Symbolae Osloenses* 62 (1992), 146–50, but countered by Salvatore Borzì, "Sull'autenticità del *Contra Hieroclem* di Eusebio di Cesarea," *Augustinianum* 43 (2003), 397–416.

3. For a brief but thorough summary of the text, see Elizabeth A. Clark, *The Origenist Controversy* (Princeton, N.J.: Princeton University Press, 1992), 159–63. Originally six books, only the first book of the *Apology* survives in Rufinus's late fourth-century Latin translation; text and French translation in René Amacker and Eric Junod, trans. and eds., *Apologie pour Origène*, 2 vols., *SC* 464–65 (Paris: Cerf, 2002).

4. Eusebius's *Letter to the Caesareans* represents the bishop's efforts to explain his acceptance of the Nicene Creed to his congregation; the text is available in H. G. Opitz, *Athanasius Werke*, vol. 2.1 (Berlin: Walter de Gruyter, 1940), 28–31. In the late 330s Eusebius wrote *Against Marcellus* and *Ecclesiastical Theology* at the encouragement of fellow bishops who opposed Marcellus, the bishop of Ancyra deposed in 336 C.E.

5. The centrality of Porphyry to Eusebius's apologetics has long been acknowledged by scholars such as Stevenson, *Studies*, 63; Jean Sirinelli, *Les vues historiques d'Eusèbe de Césarée durant la period prénicéenne* (Dakar: Université de Dakar, 1961), 287n1; Kofsky, *Eusebius*, 241–75.

6. Jerome *On Illustrious Men* 81. A fourteenth-century catalogue of manuscripts in the libraries of Rodosto and Mount Athos records an entry for Eusebius's *Against Porphyry*, though the text may have been destroyed in a nineteenth-century fire. See discussion in John Granger Cook, "A Possible Fragment of Porphyry's *Contra Christianos* from Michael the Syrian," *Zeitschrift für Antike Christentum/Journal of Ancient Christianity* 2 (1998), 120–21, citing Förster, *De*

antiquitatibus et libris ms. Constantinopolitanis (Rostochii, 1877) and K. J. Neumann, "Ein Bruchstück aus Kaiser Julians Büchern gegen die Christen," *Theologische Literaturzeitung* (1899), 298–304, 299.

7. Harnack dates the work before 300, arguing that it must predate the *PE/DE* (*Die Chronologie der alterchristlichen Literatur bis Eusebius* II [Leipzig, 1904], 119). Barnes sought to identify the date more securely, arguing that the work must have been written after the *Prophetic Extracts*, which give no indication of familiarity with Porphyry, and around the same time as the *Chronicle*, which makes use of chronological arguments from Porphyry's polemics. In addition, Barnes argues that the work must be later than 300, the approximate date he gives for the composition of Porphyry's *Against the Christians* (*Constantine and Eusebius*, 174).

8. Harnack argues that Eusebius's failure to mention *Against Porphyry* in any of his extant works may stem from embarrassment over what Eusebius considered a juvenile work (*Chronologie* II, 119); Stevenson (*Studies*, 36) and Barnes (*Constantine and Eusebius*, 175) agree.

9. Karl Mras suggests that the work was begun in 312, before the final end to persecution in the East, and completed in 322 (introduction to GCS 43:lv). Sirinelli argues for a slightly later dating of 312–24 (introduction to SC 206:13) and is followed by Barnes (*Constantine and Eusebius*, 178, 186). Wallace-Hadrill argues for a shorter span, from 312 to 318 (*Eusebius of Caesarea* [London: Mowbray, 1960], 57).

10. For a discussion of the passages I discuss here, see E. H. Gifford, "Introduction," in *Eusebius: Preparation for the Gospel* (Oxford: Clarendon Press, 1903; repr. Eugene, Oreg.: Wipf and Stock, 2002), xii. In *PE* 12.10.7, Eusebius writes that "even up to the present" the martyrs "have suffered" persecution; the phrase *eiseti deuro . . . peponthasin* suggests that persecution is still occurring or has ended only recently (*PE* 12.10.7). Similarly, in *DE* 3.5.78, Eusebius argues that Jesus' prediction that disciples will be put on trial before rulers and kings is being fulfilled "up to the present time" (*ho kai eiseti deuro theōrountas energoumenon*) (*DE* 3.5.78). In *DE* 5.3.11, however, Eusebius writes that the churches are flourishing, while in *PE* 1.4.1 he states that Christianity is growing after "having been harassed for so many years" (*hōs en tosoutois etōn chronois elaunomenon*), suggesting that persecution has ended and, perhaps, that he is writing in the midst of Constantine's benefactions (*DE* 5.3.11; *PE* 1.4.1). The ambivalence of this internal evidence suggests that Eusebius began the work during the last of Maximinus's persecutions (312/313) and completed it after the end of the persecutions, perhaps as late as Constantine's victory over Licinius in 324/325.

11. See Chapter 2 and the detailed discussion of Porphyry's fragments in the appendix.

12. In fact, Eusebius is quite faithful in his quotations of his sources. See Édouard des Places, "Eusèbe de Césarée juge de Platon dans la Préparation Evangélique," *Mélanges de Philosophie Grecque offerts à Mgr. Diès* (Paris: Beauchesne, 1956), 69–77.

13. Eusebius's source for Egyptian religion is Diodorus Siculus: "When the men of ancient Egypt looked up into the cosmos and wondered and marveled at the nature of it all, believed there to be two eternal and first gods, the sun and the moon, the first of which they named Osiris, the second, Isis" (*PE* 1.9.1 [= Diodorus, *Historical Library* 1.11.1]).

14. *PE* 2.2.1–61 (= Diodorus, *Bibl. Hist.* 4.2.1–4.3.2). Diodorus names Euhemerus as his source in *PE* 2.2.62 (= *Bibl. Hist.* 6.1.11). Pier Franco Beatrice has examined uses of Diodorus in apologetic literature in "Diodore de Sicile chez les

apologists," in *Les apologistes chrétiens et la culture grecque*, ed. Poudéron and Doré, Théologie Historique 105 (Paris: Beauchesne, 1998), 217.

15. See in particular Talal Asad's analysis of the politics involved in defining "religion" as a transcultural, transhistorical essence, particularly in anthropological discourses like that of Clifford Geertz (*Genealogies of Religion: Discipline and Reasons of Power in Christianity and Islam* [Baltimore: Johns Hopkins University Press, 1993], 27–54).

16. Asad, *Genealogies*, 29.

17. Zeus and Hera (*PE* 3.11.1–5); Hestia, Rhea, and Demeter (*PE* 3.11.8); Apollo (*PE* 3.11.24); Egyptian gods (*PE* 3.11.45–3.12.6).

18. Jean Pépin, "Porphyre, exegete d'Homère," in *Porphyre*, Entretiens Hardt XII (Geneva: Fondation Hardt, 1966), 231–72, on Porphyry's pluralistic method, see esp. p. 243; on the value of different exegeses, see esp. p. 245. See also Lamberton, *Homer the Theologian*, 120–21.

19. *HE* 9.2.1–9.3.1. See also the allusions to Theotecnus and his downfall at *PE* 4.2.11.

20. Porphyry elaborates on the divine hierarchy in *On Abstinence* in the course of discussing the forms of sacrifice appropriate for different divine beings: "The first god, being incorporeal, unmoved and indivisible, neither contained in anything nor bound by himself, needs nothing external . . . Nor does the soul of the world. . . . To the other gods, the world and the fixed and wandering stars—visible gods composed of body and soul—we should return thanks as has been described, by sacrifices of inanimate things. So there remains the multitude of invisible gods, whom Plato calls *daimones* without distinction" (*Abst.* 2.37 [tr. Clark 70]). Compare the hierarchy assumed in the *Letter to Anebo*: "First tell me about those called gods. I have the same questions about the sorts of superior beings that come after the gods, I mean the *daimones*, and heroes, and pure souls" (*An.* 1b–c).

21. Thus Porphyry assures the readers of *On Abstinence* that "I am not trying to destroy the customs which prevail among each people" (*Abst.* 2.33).

22. For an in-depth discussion of the polemical functions of accusations of human sacrifice in late antiquity, see J. Rives, "Human Sacrifice Among Pagans and Christians," *JRS* 85 (1995), 65–85.

23. *Abst.* 2.54–57: Porphyry cites examples from Greece, Egypt, Phoenicia, Carthage, Thrace, and Scythia.

24. The two most thorough studies of Eusebius's relationship to Judaism are Sirinelli, *Vues historiques*, 139–63, and Jörg Ulrich, *Euseb von Caesarea und die Juden; Studien zur Rolle der Juden in der Theologie des Eusebius von Caesarea* (Berlin: Walter de Gruyter, 1999).

25. On Eusebius's distinction between "Hebrews" and "Jews," see Sirinelli, *Vues historiques*, 147–63, and Ulrich, *Euseb*, 57–132.

26. This is suggested by Kofsky, *Eusebius*, 250, though he ultimately rejects such an approach.

27. *Apocr.* 3.30–31 (= Harnack frr. 27, 28), text in Richard Goulet, *Macarios de Magnésie: Le Monogénès* (Paris: J. Vrin, 2003). See also discussion in Chapter 2.

28. Aaron Johnson ("Identity, Descent, and Polemic" has pointed to the way in which Eusebius deploys "ethnic argumentation" to construct "narratives of descent" that legitimate Christianity while undercutting Greek claims to cultural superiority. To position the Hebrews as the most ancient and therefore authentic of peoples and to claim descent from them "functions as a legitimation of their rebellion against ancestral customs" (55). While Johnson's emphasis on the

importance of ethnic argumentation offers an astute unknotting of the complexities of Eusebius's genealogical arguments, it does not take account of the metaphysical problem of transcendence and embodiment that fuel them.

29. Jacobs, *Remains of the Jews*, 29–32.

30. *CCels.* 2.30.

31. *CCels.* 2.30.

32. *CCels.* 2.30.

33. Text of *LC* and *SC*: I. Heikel, GCS 7 (Leipzig: J. C. Hinrichs, 1901), translation is that of Harold Drake, *In Praise of Constantine: A Historical Study and New Translation of Eusebius's Tricennial Orations*, University of California Publications: Classical Studies vol. 15 (Berkeley: University of California Press, 1975). Following Drake, I use the abbreviation *LC* to refer to chapters 1–10 of the Tricennial Oration and *SC* for chapters 11–18. Text of *Theophany*: Samuel Lee, *Eusebius, Bishop of Caesarea on the Theophania or Divine Manifestation of Our Lord and Saviour Jesus Christ: A Syriac Version* (London: Society for the Publication of Oriental Texts, 1842), translation in idem, *Eusebius's Theophania Translated from the Syrian Version of the Original Now Lost Greek* (Cambridge: Cambridge University Press, 1843).

34. Barnes, *Constantine and Eusebius*, 253.

35. Harold J. Drake, *In Praise of Constantine: A Historical Study and New Translation of Eusebius' Tricennial Orations*, University of California Publications, Classical Studies, vol. 15 (Berkeley: University of California Press, 1975), 30–31.

36. Ibid., 31; *VC* 4.46.

37. In *SC* 11.1, Eusebius says he will "include" or "attach" (parathōmetha) to the preceding portion of the text (*tō basilikō . . . sungrammati* [i.e., the *LC*]) "revelations about solemn mysteries" (*logōn aporrētōn mueseis* [i.e., the *SC*]. See discussion in Drake, *Praise*, 39–44, 173nn1, 2.

38. Schwartz, "Eusebios," *RE* VI.1, col. 1428; Drake, *Praise*, 31. D. S. Wallace-Hadrill, however, argues that Eusebius included material from the *SC* in the speech he delivered at the Tricennalia (*Eusebius*, 185ff.).

39. G. Pasquali ("Die Composition der *Vita Constantini* des Eusebius," *Hermes* 46 [1910], 369–86) argues that Eusebius began the work as a panegyric after Constantine's death and subsequently expanded it into a narrative biography. Barnes argues that Eusebius began the narrative components first, as an addition to the *HE*, before the emperor's death ("Panegyric, History, and Hagiography in Eusebius's *Life of Constantine*," in *The Making of Orthodoxy: Essays in Honor of Henry Chadwick*, ed. Rowen Williams [Cambridge: Cambridge University Press, 1989], 110–14, and "The Two Drafts of Eusebius's *Vita Constantini*," in *From Eusebius to Augustine* [London: Aldershot, 1994], xii). Drake argues that Eusebius began compiling material for the *Life* at Constantine's request while the bishop was in Constantinople to deliver his oration in 336 ("What Eusebius Knew: The Genesis of the *Vita Constantini*," *Classical Philology* 83 [1988], 24).

40. Barnes, *Constantine and Eusebius*, 265; Pasquali, "Die Composition," 386.

41. See the extensive study by Hugo Gressman, *Studien zu Eusebs Theophanie*, Texte und Untersuchungen 23.3 (Leipzig, 1903).

42. Samuel Lee (*Eusebius, Bishop of Caesarea, on the Theophania or Divine Manifestation of Our Lord and Savior Jesus Christ* [Cambridge: Cambridge University Press, 1843], xxi) argues for a date before the *PE/DE* but is refuted by Lightfoot ("Eusebius of Caesaria," in *Dictionary of Christian Biography*, vol. 2 [London: J. Murray, 1880], 333), who notes that *Theophany* 4.37 and 5.1 declare the use of the *DE* as a source. Gressman (*Studien*, 39–42) argues for a date of 333. Wallace-

Hadrill argues for a date after the *LC*, in 337 (*Eusebius*, 52–53). Barnes is alone among contemporary scholars in opting for an early date ("shortly after 324"); his conclusion is based on an overly literal interpretation of a reference to ritual prostitution at Heliopolis in Phoenicia (*Theophany* 2.14), by which he concludes that the text must have been written before Constantine took action against the practice in 325 (*Constantine and Eusebius*, 186–87; 367n176).

43. Kofsky, *Eusebius*, 277.

44. Cf. *Th.* 3.1. Because the parallels in the Syriac translation of the *Theophany* are rendered quite literally and differ in no substantial way from the Greek of the *SC* and *LC*, I have not indicated all parallels between it and the *SC*. For a discussion of and list of parallels, see the GCS edition of the *Theophany* and Gressman, *Studien*.

45. See, for example, E. Peterson, *Der Monotheismus als politisches Problem: Ein Beitrage zur Geschichte der politischen Theologie im Imperium Romanum* (Leipzig: Hegner, 1935); N. H. Baynes, "Eusebius and the Christian Empire," in *Byzantine Studies and Other Essays* (London: Athlone Press, 1955), 168–72; Raffaella Farina, *L'impero e l'imperatore cristiano in Eusebio di Cesarea: La prima teologia politica del cristianismo* (Zurich: Pas Verlag, 1966); Francis Dvornik, *Early Christian and Byzantine Political Philosophy*, vol. 2 (Washington, D.C.: Dumbarton Oaks Center for Byzantine Studies, 1966), 611–22; Michael Hollerich, "Religion and Politics in the Writings of Eusebius of Caesarea: Reassessing the First 'Court Theologian,'" *Church History* 59 (1990), 309–25; Salvatore Calderone, "Teologia politica, successione dinastica e consecratio in età constantiniana," in *Le culte des souverains dans l'empire romain* (Geneva: Fondation Hardt, 1972), 215–61; Drake, *Praise*, 46–60.

46. Here as in the *PE*, Eusebius's sources include Porphyry's *Abst.* 2.54–56 and Diodorus's *Historical Library* 20.14.

47. The parallel passage in the *Theophany* is followed by a long ethnographic catalogue of wars and dissension among the world's peoples (*Th.* 2.65–68).

48. Thus Homi Bhabha describes the tendency of colonial education to produce threatening hybrids. This "[h]ybridity represents that ambivalent 'turn' of the discriminated subject into the terrifying, exorbitant object of paranoid classification—a disturbing questioning of the images of presences of authority" (*Location of Culture*, 113).

49. Bhahba describes the need for colonial education to be reiterated to counter the threat of hybrid mimicry of colonial acculturation: "the colonial presence is always ambivalent, split between its appearance as original and authoritative and its articulation as repetition and difference" (*Location of Culture*, 108).

50. "Such a display of difference produces a mode of authority that is agonistic (rather than antagonistic)" (Bhabha, *Location of Culture*, 108).

51. Jacobs (*Remains of the Jews*, 148) draws a connection between Eusebius's focus on the temple ruin as a Christian form of the classic Roman triumph as defeated Jews, represented by the ruined temple, are paraded as evidence of the emperor's victory.

52. Jacobs, *Remains of the Jews*, 148.

53. Porphyry, Harnack frr. 2–37.

54. Constantine's stripping of the temples, in fact, had additional (or even other) motivations besides those intimated by Eusebius. A. H. M. Jones argues that Constantine confiscated gold from temples in order to back the new *solidus* (*Later Roman Empire AD 284–602* [Oxford: Oxford University Press, 1964], 108).

Eusebius (*VC* 3.54.2–3) argues that Constantine plundered statues and other religious objects in order to display them in Constantinople to be mocked, but Cameron and Hall (*Life*, 302) note that "Eusebius has to work hard, and draw on all his linguistic resources, to turn Constantine's beautification of his city with famous statues of antiquity into an anti-pagan gesture."

55. Burckhardt, *Age of Constantine*, 301–4; Drake, *Constantine and the Bishops*, 245–50; Andrew Alföldi, *The Conversion of Constantine and Pagan Rome*, trans. Harold Mattingly (Oxford: Clarendon Press, 1948), 53–81.

56. Burckhardt, *Age of Constantine*, 292–96.

Epilogue

1. David Chidester, *Savage Systems: Colonialism and Comparative Religion in Southern Africa* (Charlottesville: University of Virginia Press, 1996), 2.

2. Ibid., 3–4.

3. Ibid., 4–5.

4. Ibid., 3.

5. "What I am attempting to bring to light is the epistemological field, the *episteme* in which knowledge, envisaged apart from all criteria having reference to its rational value or to its objective forms, grounds its positivity and thereby manifests a history which is not that of its growing perfection, *but rather that of its conditions of possibility*" (Michel Foucault, *The Order of Things: An Archaeology of the Human Sciences* [New York: Random House, 1971], xxii).

6. The years between the abdication of Diocletian and Maximian in 305 and Constantine's assumption of sole rule in 324 were marked by internal struggles for power. Constantine did lead small campaigns along the Rhine and Danube; his successes in the Balkans helped precipitate his conflict with Licinius. On the northern frontier during the early fourth century, see Michael Kulikowski, "Constantine and the Northern Barbarians," in *Age of Constantine*, ed. Lenski, 347–76. Constantine envisioned a campaign against Sassanid Persia but died before it could be realized. On Constantine and the eastern frontiers, see Elizabeth Key Fowden, "Constantine and the Peoples of the Eastern Frontier, " in *Age of Constantine*, ed. Lenski, 377–98.

7. In his dialogue *The Caesars,* Julian singles out Alexander the Great, Augustus, and Marcus Aurelius as exemplary rulers (*The Caesars* 335d, text and translation in W. C. Wright, *Julian*, vol. 2 [Cambridge, Mass.: Harvard University Press, 1913], 412–13).

8. The meaning of Julian's actions were certainly not lost on Christians. Rufinus, for instance, recognized Julian's attempt to rebuild the temple as a direct challenge to Christian conceptions of history (*HE* 10.38–40, cf. Sozomen, *HE* 5.22; Socrates *HE* 3.20; Theodoret *HE* 3.20).

9. *Relationes* 3.3, text and translation in R. H. Barrow, *Prefect and Emperor: The Relationes of Symmachus A.D. 384* (Oxford: Clarendon Press, 1973), 34–37.

10. Augustine *Epp.* 50 (Sufes), 90, 91 (Calama).

11. Rufinus *HE* 11.22 (GCS 6 n.f.:1025-26).

12. Said notes that this "textual attitude" is propagated by the "appearance of success," and offers a example: "If one reads a book claiming that lions are fierce and then encounters a fierce lion . . . , the chances are that one will be encouraged to read more books by that same author, and believe them. But if, in addition, the lion book instructs one how to deal with a fierce lion, and the

instructions work perfectly, then not only will the author be greatly believed, he will also be impelled to try his hand at other kinds of written performance" (Said, *Orientalism*, 93–94). On the relationship between the rhetoric and reality of religious violence in late antiquity, see the extensive study by Michael Gaddis, *There Is No Crime for Those Who Have Christ: Religious Violence in the Christian Roman Empire* (Berkeley: University of California Press, 2005).

13. Tomoko Masuzawa, *The Invention of World Religions* (Chicago: University of Chicago Press, 2005), 46–64.

14. Sabine MacCormack, "Gods, Demons, and Idols in the Andes," *Journal of the History of Ideas* 67 (2006), 625, and idem, *On the Wings of Time: Rome, the Incas, Spain and Peru* (Princeton, N.J.: Princeton University Press, 2006).

15. MacCormack, "Gods, Demons, and Idols," 626–28, translating and commenting on Estete in Xerex, *Verdadera relacíon de la conquista del Perú*, ed. Concepcíon Bravo [Madrid: Historia 16, 1985]), 137–38.

16. José de Acosta, *Historia Natural y Moral de las Indias*, ed. José Alcina Franch (Madrid: Cambio 16, 1987), discussed in Joan-Pau Rubiés, "Theology, Ethnography, and the Historicization of Idolatry," *Journal of the History of Ideas* 67 (2006), 590; see also Anthony Pagden, *The Fall of Natural Man: The American Indian and the Origins of Comparative Ethnology* (Cambridge: Cambridge University Press, 1982).

17. The manuscript of Bartolomé de Las Casas's *In Defense of the Indians* includes a summary of Sepúlveda's *Democrates Alter*, English translation in Bartolomé de Las Casas, *In Defense of the Indians*, ed. and trans. Stafford Poole (Dekalb: Northern Illinois University Press, 1992), 11–16.

18. "The Apostle [Paul] says, 'They knew God and yet refused to honor him as God' (Rom. 1.21). To this we answer that it is true that a common knowledge of God is naturally implanted in the minds of men, but it is very vague and universal and shows only that there is someone who puts order in things"; in the same discussion, Las Casas also draws on John of Damascus, Jerome, Augustine, and John Chrysostom (Las Casas, *Defense of the Indians*, 130–35).

19. Jean de Brébeuf, "Relation of 1636," translation in Allan Greer, *The Jesuit Relations: Natives and Missionaries in Seventeenth-Century North America* (New York: St. Martin's Press, 2000), 41–42.

20. Carina L. Johnson, "Idolatrous Cultures and the Practice of Religion," *Journal of the History of Ideas* 67 (2006), 597–621.

21. The literature on these figures is extensive, but on Ficino, see Paul Oskar Kristeller, *The Philosophy of Marsilio Ficino*, trans. V. Conant (New York: Columbia University Press, 1943); on Mirandola, see S. A. Farmer, *Syncretism in the West: Pico's 900 Theses (1486), the Evolution of Traditional Religious and Philosophical Systems* (Tempe, Ariz.: Medieval and Renaissance Texts and Studies, 1998); on Cusanus, see the essays in G. Christianson and T. Izbicki, eds., *Nicholas of Cusa in Search of God and Wisdom* (Leiden: Brill, 1991); on the Renaissance quest for the perennial philosophy in general, see Charles Schmitt, "Perennial Philosophy: From Agostino Steuco to Leibniz," *Journal of the History of Ideas* 27 (1966), 505–32.

22. Nicolas Cusanus *On the Peace of Faith* 68, text: *Nicolai de Cusa Opera Omnia*, vol. 7: *De Pace Fidei*, ed. R. Klibansky and H. Bascour (Hamburg: Felix Meiner Verlag, 1970); translation, Jasper Hopkins, *Nicholas of Cusa's De Pace Fidei and Cribratio Alkorani: Translation and Analysis*, 2nd ed. (Minneapolis: Arthur J. Banning Press, 1994), 669.

23. Pico de Mirandola, *On the Dignity of Man*, translation, *Pico della Mirandola:*

On the Dignity of Man, trans. Charles Glenn Wallis (Indianapolis and New York: Bobbs-Merrill, 1965), 23–24.

24. Samuel Purchas, *Purchas His Pilgrimage* (London, 1613), unpaginated preface, quoted and discussed in Masuzawa, *Invention of World Religions*, 51–52, emphasis added.

25. Masuzawa, *Invention of World Religions*, 107–20.

26. Chidester, *Savage Systems*, 3.

27. On the production of "religion" as a sui generis category, see especially McCutcheon, *Manufacturing Religion* and *Critics Not Caretakers*, esp. chapter 5, " 'We're All Stuck Somewhere': Taming Ethnocentrism and Transcultural Understandings," 73–83. McCutcheon argues that "not only theological and philosophical but political and social factors lie behind some scholars' reluctance to explain religion as a product of human desires, actions, and associations" (*Manufacturing Religion*, 73). To McCutcheon's insights I am suggesting here that "philosophical" distinctions between universality and particularity do not simply work together with but are conditioned by and in turn condition the "political" or "social" factors that influence knowledge about "religion."

28. Daniel Dubuisson, *The Western Construction of Religion: Myths, Knowledge, and Ideology*, trans. W. Sayers (Baltimore: Johns Hopkins University Press, 2003), 22–29.

Appendix

1. These "new fragments" include Pierre Nautin, "Trois autres fragments du livre de Porphyre 'Contre les Chrétiens,' " *Revue Biblique* 57 (1950), 409–16; F. Altheim and R. Stiehl, "Neue Bruchstück aus Porphyrios' *Kata Christianous, Untersuchungen zur klassischen Philologie und Geschichte des Altertums* 4 (1961), 23–38; D. Hagedorn and R. Merkelbach, "Ein neues Fragment aus Porphyrios gegen die Christen," *Vigiliae Christianae* 20 (1966), 86–90; Phillip Selew, "Achilles or Christ? Porphyry and Didymus in Debate over Allegorical Interpretation," *HTR* 82 (1989), 79–100; Cook, "A Possible Fragment."

2. Adolf von Harnack, *Porphyrius Gen die Christen, 15 Bücher, Zeugnisse und Referate*, Abhandlungen der koen. preuss. Akademie d. Wissenschaft, phil-hist. Klasse 1 (Berlin, 1916), 1–21.

3. Timothy Barnes, "Porphyry *Against the Christians*: Date and the Attribution of Fragments," *JTS* 24:2 (1973), 424–42. Barnes's critiques are accepted and reiterated in an influential article by Anthony Meredith, "Porphyry and Julian Against the Christians," *ANRW* II.23.2 (1980), 1126–27.

4. Elizabeth DePalma Digeser, "Porphyry, Julian, or Hierokles? The Anonymous Hellene in Makarios Magnes' Apokritikos," *JTS* 53 (2002), 466–502, argues for Hierocles; P. Frassinetti, "Sull'autore delle questioni pagane conservate nell' *Apokritico* di Macario di Magnesia," *Nuovo Didaskaleion* 3 (1949), 41–56, argues for Julian.

5. Goulet, *Macarios*, vol. 1, esp. 112–49.

6. Goulet, *Macarios*, vol. 1, 148–49.

7. Goulet, *Macarios*, vol. 1, 149n1, 304.

8. Bidez, *Porphyrye*, 67; *HE* 6.19.2 (GCS 6 n.f.:558). Porphyry went to Sicily on Plotinus's advice (*VPl.* 11).

9. This history was dedicated to the Palmyrine queen Zenobia, who conquered Egypt as part of her short-lived empire in the early 270s C.E. Extrapolating from

the amount of time it would likely have taken Callinicus to research and compose a work of history and Porphyry to acquire this text and subsequently write a fifteen-book polemic, Cameron argues that *Against the Christians* dates, at the earliest, to late 271, and may have been composed as late as 275 ("The Date of Porphyry's *Kata Christianōn*," *Classical Quarterly* 17:2 [1967], 382–84).

10. Frend, "Prelude to the Great Persecution." The argument for the connection between *Philosophy from Oracles* and the oracular consultations preceeding the persecution is strengthened by Digeser, "An Oracle of Apollo at Daphne and the Great Persecution."

11. Barnes argues that Eusebius uses the participle with the definite article descriptively, not temporally; see "Scholarship or Propaganda?," 61.

12. Harnack fr. 82; Barnes, "Porphyry *Against the Christians*," 436–37.

13. Barnes, "Scholarship or Propaganda," 65.

14. Pier Franco Beatrice notes that two early studies publish a fragment from a purported tenth book of the *Philosophy from Oracles* (Augustine Steuchus, *De perenni philosophia* III, 14 [Lugdunum, 1540], 155–57, and Angelo Mai, *Philonis Iudaei, Porphyrii philosophi, Eusebii Pamphili opera inedita* [Milan, 1816], 59–64, both cited in Beatrice, "New Edition of Porphyry's Fragments," 351nn28, 29). See also A. E. Chaignet, "La Philosophie des Oracles," *Revue de l'histoire des religions* 41 (1900), 337; H. Kellner, "Der Neuplatoniker Porphyrius und sein Verhältnis zum Christentum," *Theologische Quartalschrift* 47 (1865), 86–87; and the discussion in Beatrice, "New Edition of Porphyry's Fragments," 351–52.

15. Gustav Wolff, *Porphyrii De Philosophia ex Oraculis Haurienda* (Berlin, 1856; reprint, Hildesheim: Georg Olms, 1962), 42–43.

16. Bidez, *Porphyre*, 25–26, 28.

17. The methodologies of the late twentieth century, he notes, show that "theurgy and critical philosophy could exist side by side." A. Smith, "Porphyrian Studies Since 1913," 731.

18. John O'Meara, *Porphyry's On Philosophy from Oracles in Augustine* (Paris: Études Augustiniennes, 1959), and idem, "Porphyry's Philosophy from Oracles in Eusebius's Preparation for the Gospel and Augustine's Dialogues of Cassiciacum," in *Recherches Augustiniennes* 6 (1969), 103–39.

19. Beatrice, "Le traité de Porphyre contre les chrétiens," and "New Edition of Porphyry's Fragments," 347–55.

20. Digeser, *The Making of a Christian Empire*, 93–102.

21. Ibid., 101.

22. Pierre Benoit, "Un adversaire du christianisme au IIIème siècle: Porphyre," *Revue Biblique* 54 (1947), 552; Henry Chadwick, *Sentences of Sextus*, Texts and Studies 5 (Cambridge: Cambridge University Press, 1959), 142; Édouard des Places, ed. and trans., *Porphyre: Vie de Pythagore, Lettre à Marcella* (Paris: Budé, 1982), 89; Barnes, "Porphyry *Against the Christians*," 439.

23. For the edict in Greek, see *HE* 8.17.3–10; for Latin see *Mort.* 34.3–5.

24. See Eusebius *HE* 9.7.3–15 and discussion in Wilken, *The Christians as the Romans Saw Them*, 156–59.

25. Beatrice, "Antistes Philosophiae," 31–47; Sodano, *Vangelo*, 115.

26. First argued by Barnes, "Porphyry *Against the Christians*," 438–39, and often reiterated, most recently by Bowen and Garnsey, introduction, 2.

27. Sodano, *Vangelo*, 114.

28. Wilken, *Christians as the Romans Saw Them*; Digeser, *The Making of a Christian Empire*, 93–107.

29. Beatrice, "New Edition of Porphyry's Fragments," 348–49.

30. Sodano, *Vangelo*, 114.

31. On the question of Lactantius's knowledge of Porphyry's *Philosophy from Oracles*, see Digeser, *The Making of a Christian Empire*, 102–7.

32. Compare *DI* 4.13.11 and *City of God* 19.22.17–19.23.17 (= *PO* 343F); for a discussion, see Wolff, *Porphyrii*, 184–85, and Digeser, *The Making of a Christian Empire*, 102.

33. Compare *On the Anger of God* 23.12 and *City of God* 19.23.30–37 (= Smith 344F); for a discussion, see Wolff, *Porphyrii*, 142–43, and R. M. Ogilvie, *The Library of Lactantius* (Oxford: Oxford University Press, 1978), 24.

34. For example, in his Hecatean oracle, *Phil. ex orac.*, Smith 345F, 345aF (= Eusebius, *PE* 3.6.39–3.7.2, Augustine, *City of God* 19.23.43–73).

35. *DI* 4.13.11–15; Digeser, *The Making of a Christian Empire*, 104.

36. On this shared use of "path" imagery, see Digeser, *The Making of a Christian Empire*, 103–4.

37. *Hodoi duo eisi, mia tēs zōēs kai mia tou thanatou, diaphora de pollē metaxu tōn duo hodōn* (*Didache* 1.1, text and translation in Kirsopp Lake, ed., *The Apostolic Fathers*, vol.1 [Cambridge, Mass.: Harvard University Press, 1912], 308–9).

38. Digeser, *The Making of a Christian Empire*, 106–7.

39. Ulrich von Wilamowitz-Moellendorff, "Ein Bruchstück aus der Schrift des Porphyrius gegen die Christen," *Zeitschrift für die Neutestamentliche Wissenschaft und die Kunde des Urchristentums* 1 (1900), 101–5.

40. This is argued similarly by Sodano, *Vangelo*, 114.

41. Jews: *Annals* 4.81.2, 5.13.1; Christians: *Annals* 15.44.

42. Text of the edict in Alfred Adam, *Texte zum Manichäismus* (Berlin: Walter de Gruyter, 1969), 82–83.

43. *Comparison of Mosaic and Roman Law* 4.4.3 (Hyamson 86).

Bibliography

Major Primary Sources

Alcinous. *The Handbook of Platonism.* Trans. John Dillon. *Alcinous: The Handbook of Platonism.* Oxford: Oxford University Press, 1993.

Aristides. *Apology.* Text and French trans. B. Pouderon et al. *Aristides: Apologie.* SC 470. Paris: Cerf, 2003.

Augustine. *City of God.* Ed. B. Dombart and A. Kalb. CCL 47. Turnhout: Brepols, 1955, trans. Henry Bettenson. *St. Augustine: City of God.* London: Penguin, 1984.

Celsus. *On the True Logos.*

Clement of Alexandria. *Stromata.* Ed. O. Stählin. GCS 12. Berlin: Walter de Gruyter, 1985.

Codex Theodosianus (Theodosian Code). Text: *Theodosiani Libri XVI,* 2 vols. Ed. T. Mommsen. Berlin: Weidmann, 1934.

———— *Exhortation to the Greeks.* Ed. M. Marcovich. *Clementis Alexandrini Protrepticus.* Supplements to Vigiliae Christianae 34. Leiden: Brill, 1995.

Comparison of Mosaic and Roman Law. (Mosaicarum et Romanarum legume collation). Ed. Moses Hyamson. *Mosaicarum et Romanarum legume collation.* Oxford: Oxford University Press, 1913.

Constantine. *Oration to the Saints (Oratio ad Sanctorum Coetum).* Ed. I. Heikel. GCS 7. Leipzig: J. C. Hinrichs, 1902.

Cornutus. *Greek Theology. (Theologia Graeca).* Ed. K. Lang. *Cornuti theologiae graecae compendium.* Leipzig, 1881.

Corpus Hermeticum. Ed. A. Nock and A.-J. Festugière. *Corpus Hermeticum.* Paris: Belles Lettres, 1972–73, trans. Brian Copenhaver. *Hermetica.* Cambridge: Cambridge University Press, 1992.

Diodorus Siculus. *Historical Library. (Bibliotheca Historiae).* Text and trans. C. H. Oldfather. *Diodorus of Sicily.* Cambridge, Mass.: Harvard University Press, 1933.

Eunapius. *Lives of the Philosophers. (Vita Philosophorum).* Text and trans. W. C. Wright. Philostratus and Eunapius: The Lives of the Sophists. Cambridge, Mass.: Harvard University Press, 1922.

Eusebius of Caesarea. *Prophetic Eclogues. (Eclogae Propheticae).* Ed. T. Gaisford. Oxford: Oxford University Press, 1842.

————. *Tricennial Orations. (De laudibus Constantini).* Ed. I. Heikel. GCS 7. Leipzig: J. C. Hinrichs, 1901.

————. *Theophany.* Syriac ed. S. Lee. *Eusebius, Bishop of Caesarea on the Theophania or Divine Manifestation of Our Lord and Saviour Jesus Christ: A Syriac Version*. London: Society of the Promotion of Oriental Texts, 1842. Greek fragments and German trans. of the Syriac version in H. Gressman. GCS 11. Leipzig: J. C. Hinrichs, 1904. English trans. of the Syrian version in S. Lee, *Eusebius, Bishop of Caesarea, on the Theophania or Divine Manifestation of Our Lord and Saviour Jesus Christ*. Cambridge: Cambridge University Press, 1843.

———. *Demonstration of the Gospel. (Demonstratio evangelica)*. Ed. I. Heikel. GCS 23. Leipzig: J. C. Hinrichs, 1913.

———. *Letter to the Caesareans*. Ed. H. G. Opitz. *Athanasius Werke*. Vol. 2.1. Berlin: Walter de Gruyter, 1940.

———. *Ecclesiastical History. (Historia Ecclesiastica)*. Ed. E. Schwartz et al. GCS 6.1–3 n.f. Berlin: Akademie Verlag, 1999.

———. *Preparation for the Gospel. (Praeparatio evangelica)*. Ed. K. Mras. GCS 43. Berlin: Akademie Verlag, 1954.

———. *Life of Constantine. (Vita Constantini)*. Ed. F. Winkelmann. GCS 7. Berlin: Akademie Verlag, 1991.

Iamblichus. *De Mysteriis*. Text and trans. Emma Clarke, John Dillon, and Jackson Hershbell. *Iamblichus: On the Mysteries*. Atlanta: Society for Biblical Literature, 2003.

Jerome. *De viris inlustribus*. Ed. G. Herding. Leipzig, 1879.

Josephus. *Against Apion*. Text and trans. H. Thackeray. *Josephus*. Vol. 1. Cambridge, Mass.: Harvard University Press, 1926.

Justin Martyr. *Apologies. (Apologiae)*. Ed. M. Marcovich. PTS 38. Berlin: Walter de Gruyter, 1994.

———. *Dialogue with Trypho*. Ed. M. Marcovich. *Dialogus cum Tryphone*. PTS 47. Berlin: Walter de Gruyter, 1997.

Lactantius. *Divine Institutes. (Divinae Institutes)*. Ed. S. Brandt. CSEL 19. Vienna, 1890.

———. *Epitome Divinae Institutionum*. Ed. S. Brandt. CSEL 19. Vienna, 1890.

———. *On the Anger of God. (De Ira Dei)*. Ed. S. Brandt. CSEL 27. Vienna, 1893.

———. *On the Deaths of the Persecutors. (De Mortibus Persecutorum)*. Ed. S. Brandt. CSEL 27. Vienna, 1893.

———. *On God's Craftsmanship. (De Opificio Dei)*. Ed. S. Brandt. CSEL 27. Vienna. 1893.

Macarios Magnes. *Apocriticus*. Ed. and French trans. R. Goulet. *Macarios de Magnésie: Le Monogénès*. Paris: J. Vrin, 2003.

Numenius. Fragments. Ed. E. des Places. *Numénius: Fragments*. Paris: Belles Lettres, 1973.

Origen. *Against Celsus. (Contra Celsum)*. Ed. M. Marcovich. Supplements to Vigiliae Christianae 54. Leiden: Brill, 2001.

Pamphilus and Eusebius of Caesarea. *Apology for Origen. (Apologia pro Origene)*. Ed. and French trans. R. Amacker and E. Junod. SC 464–65. Paris: Cerf, 2002.

Passion of the Scillitan Martyrs. (Passio Sanctorum Scillitanorum). Text and trans. H. Musurillo. *The Acts of the Christian Martyrs*. Oxford: Oxford University Press, 1972.

Philo of Alexandria. *On Abraham*. Text and trans. F. H. Colson. *Philo*. Vol. 6. Cambridge, Mass.: Harvard University Press, 1959.

———. *Life of Moses*. Text and trans. F. H. Colson. *Philo*. Vol. 6. Cambridge, Mass.: Harvard University Press, 1959.

Plutarch. *On the Decline of Oracles. (De defectu oraculorum)*. Text and trans. F. C. Babbitt. *Plutarch: Moralia*. Vol. 5. Cambridge, Mass.: Harvard University Press, 1936.

————. *On Isis and Osiris. (De Iside et Osiride)*. Text and trans. F. C. Babbitt. *Plutarch: Moralia*. Vol. 5. Cambridge, Mass.: Harvard University Press, 1936.
————. *On the Pythian Oracle. (De Pythiae oraculis)*. Text and trans. F. C. Babbitt. *Plutarch: Moralia*. Vol. 5. Cambridge, Mass.: Harvard University Press, 1936.
Porphyry. *On Abstinence. (De Abstinentia)*. Ed. A. Nauck. *Porphyrii Philosophi Platonici Opuscula Selecta*. Leipzig: Teubner, 1886.
————. *To Marcella. (Ad Marcellam)*. Ed. A. Nauck. *Porphyrii Philosophi Platonici Opuscula Selecta*. Leipzig: Teubner, 1886.
————. *Against the Christians. (Contra Christianos)*. Ed. A. von Harnack. *Porphyrius, "Gegen Die Christen." 15 Bücher, Zeugnisse, Fragmente und Referate*. In Abhandlungen der K. Preuß. Akad. Der Wiss. Phil. Hist. Klasse, 1916, 1–115.
————. *Life of Plotinus. (Vita Plotini)*. Ed. P. Henry and H. R. Schwyzer. *Plotini Opera*. Vol. 1. Leiden: Brill, 1951.
————. *Letter to Anebo. (Epistula ad Anebonem)*. Ed. A. R. Sodano. *Porfirio Lettera ad Anebo*. Naples: L'Arte Tipografica, 1958.
————. *Porphyrii de Philosophia ex Oraculis Haurienda*. Ed. G. Wolff. Berlin, 1856. Reprint, Hildesheim: Georg Olms, 1962.
————. *On the Cave of the Nymphs in the Odyssey. (De antro nympharum)*. Text and trans. in *Porphyry: The Cave of the Nymphs in the Odyssey*. Buffalo, N.Y.: Arethusa Monographs, 1969.
————. *On Statues. (Peri Agalmatōn)*. Ed. A. Smith. *Porphyrius Fragmenta*. Leipzig: Teubner, 1993.
————. *On the Return of the Soul. (De regressu animae)*. Ed. A. Smith. *Porphyrius Fragmenta*. Leipzig: Teubner, 1993.
————. *Philosophy from Oracles. (De philosophia ex oraculis haurienda)*. Ed. A. Smith. *Porphyrius Fragmenta*. Leipzig: Teubner, 1993.
Posidonius. *Fragments*. Ed. L. Edelstein and I. G. Kidd. *Posidonius I: The Fragments*. Cambridge: Cambridge University Press, 1972.
Pseudo-Philo. *Book of Biblical Antiquities*. Ed. and trans. H. Jacobson. *A Commentary on Pseudo-Philo's* Liber Antiquitatem Biblicarum. 2 vols. New York: Brill, 1996.
Rufinus. *Ecclesiastical History*. Ed. E. Schwartz et al. GCS 6.1–3 n.f. Berlin: Akademie Verlag, 1999.
Sibylline Oracles. (Oracula Sibyllina). Ed. J. Geffcken. *Die Oracula Sibyllina*. GCS 8. Leipzig, 1902. Trans. John J. Collins, "Sibylline Oracles." In *The Old Testament Pseudepigrapha*. Vol. 1, ed. James Charlesworth. Garden City, N.Y.: Doubleday, 1983, 319–472.
Socrates. *Ecclesiastical History*. Ed. G. C. Hansen. GCS 1 n.f. Berlin: Akademie Verlag, 1995.
Sozomen. *Ecclesiastical History (Historia Ecclesiastica)*. Ed. J. Bidez and G. C. Hansen. GCS 4 n.f. Berlin: Akademie Verlag, 1995.
Tatian. *Oration to the Greeks. (Oratio ad Graecos)*. Ed. M. Marcovich. PTS 43. Berlin: Walter de Gruyter, 1995.
Theophilus. *To Autolycus. (Ad Autolycum)*. Ed. M. Marcovich. PTS 44. Berlin: Walter de Gruyter, 1995.

Secondary Sources

Achebe, Chinua. "Colonialist Criticism." In Ashcroft, Griffiths, and Tiffin (eds.), *The Post-colonial Studies Reader*, 57–61.

Alföldi, Andrew. *The Conversion of Constantine and Pagan Rome.* Trans. Harold Mattingly. Oxford: Clarendon Press, 1948.

Alston, Richard. "Conquest by Text: Juvenal and Plutarch on Egypt." In Webster and Cooper (eds.), *Roman Imperialism,* 99–109.

Altheim, F., and R. Stiehl. "Neue Bruchstück aus Porphyrios' *Kata Christianous.*" /j *Untersuchungen zur klassischen Philologie und Geschichte des Altertums* 4 (1961), 23–38.

Anderson, Benedict. *Imagined Communities: Reflections on the Origin and Spread of Nationalism.* London: Verso, 1983. Rev. ed., 1991.

Andresen, Carl. "Justin und der mittlere Platonismus." *Zeischrift für die neutestamentliche Wissenschaft* 44 (1952/53), 12–195.

———. *Logos und Nomos: Die Polemik des Kelsos wider das Christentum.* Berlin: Walter de Gruyter, 1955.

Asad, Talal. *Genealogies of Religion: Discipline and Reasons of Power in Christianity and Islam.* Baltimore: Johns Hopkins University Press, 1993.

Ashcroft, Bill, Gareth Griffiths, and Helen Tiffin (eds.). *The Post-colonial Studies Reader.* London: Routledge, 1995.

Barker, Ernest. "Some Foreign Influences in Greek Thought." *Greece and Rome* 5:13 (1935), 2–11.

Barnes, Timothy. "Porphyry *Against the Christians*: Date and the Attribution of Fragments." *JTS* 24:2 (1973), 424–42.

———. "Lactantius and Constantine." *JRS* 63 (1973), 29–46.

———. "The Emperor Constantine's Good Friday Sermon." *JTS* 27 (1976), 414–23.

———. "Imperial Campaigns, A.D. 285–311." *Phoenix* 30 (1976), 174–93.

———. *Constantine and Eusebius.* Cambridge, Mass.: Harvard University Press, 1981.

———. *The New Empire of Diocletian and Constantine.* Cambridge, Mass.: Harvard University Press, 1982.

———. "Constantine's Prohibition of Pagan Sacrifice." *American Journal of Philology* 105 (1984), 69–72.

———. "Scholarship or Propaganda? Porphyry's *Against the Christians* and Its Historical Setting." *Bulletin of the Institute for Classical Studies* 37 (1994), 53–65.

———. "Constantine's *Speech to the Assembly of the Saints*: Place and Date of Delivery." *JTS* 52 (2001), 26–36.

———. "Monotheists All?" *Phoenix* 55 (2001), 158–59.

Baynes, Norman H. "The Great Persecution." In *Cambridge Ancient History.* Vol. 12. Cambridge: Cambridge University Press, 1939. Reprint, 1989.

Beard, Mary, John North, and Simon Price. *Religions of Rome.* 2 vols. Cambridge: Cambridge University Press, 1998.

Beatrice, Pier Franco. "Un oracle anitchrétien chez Arnobe." *Mémorial Dom Jean Gribomont.* Studia Ephemeridis "Augustinianum" 27 (1988), 107–29.

———. "Le traité de Porphyre contre les chrétiens: L'état de la question." *Kernos* 4 (1991), 119–38.

———. "Towards a New Edition of Porphyry's Fragments Against the Christians." In M. Goulet-Cazé, G. Madec, and D. O'Brien (eds.), *Sophiēs Maiētores: Chercheurs de sagesse: Hommage à Jean Pépin.* Paris: Études Augustiniennes, 1992, 347–55.

———. "Antistes Philosophiae: Ein Christenfeindlicher Propagandist am Hofe Diokletians nach dem Zeugnis des Laktanz." *Augustinianum* 33 (1993), 31–47.

———. "Diodore de Sicile chez les apologists." In Poudéron and Doré (eds.), *Les apologists chrétiens*, 217–35.

Bergjan, Silke-Petra. "How to Speak about Early Christian Apologetic Literature? Comments on the Recent Debate." *Studia Patristica* 36 (2001), 182–83.

Bhabha, Homi K. *The Location of Culture*. London: Routledge, 1994.

Bidez, Joseph. *Vie de Porphyre: Le philosophe néoplatonicien*. Ghent, 1913. Reprint, Hildesheim: Georg Olms, 1964.

Bishop, Alan J. "Western Mathematics: The Secret Weapon of Cultural Imperialism." In Ashcroft, Griffiths, and Tiffin (eds.), *The Post-colonial Studies Reader*, 71–76.

Bleckman, Bruno. "Ein Kaiser als Prediger; Zur Datierung der konstantinischen 'Rede an die Versammlung der Heiligen.'" *Hermes* 125 (1997), 183–202.

Boyarin, Daniel. *A Radical Jew: Paul and the Politics of Identity*. Berkeley: University of California Press, 1994.

———. *Dying for God: Martyrdom and the Making of Chrisitanity and Judaism*. Stanford, Calif.: Stanford University Press, 1999.

———. *Border Lines: The Partition of Judaeo-Christianity*. Philadelphia: University of Pennsylvania Press, 2004.

Boys-Stones, G. R. *Post-Hellenistic Philosophy: A Study of Its Development from the Stoics to Origen*. Oxford: Oxford University Press, 2001.

——— (ed.). *Metaphor, Allegory, and the Classical Tradition*. Oxford: Oxford University Press, 2003.

———. "The Stoic's Two Types of Allegory." In Boys-Stones (ed.), *Metaphor, Allegory, and the Classical Tradition*, 189–216.

Bradbury, Scott. "Constantine and the Problem of Anti-Pagan Legislation in the Fourth Century." *Classical Philology* 89 (1994), 120–39.

Brenk, Frederick. "Isis Is a Greek Word: Plutarch's Allegorization of Egyptian Religion." In Pérez Jiménez, García López, and Aguilar (eds.), *Plutarco, Platón y Aristóteles* Madrid: Ediciones Clásiras, 1999), 227–38.

Brisson, Luc. *How Philosophers Saved Myths: Allegorical Interpretation and Classical Mythology*. Trans. Catherine Tihanyi. Chicago: University of Chicago Press, 2004.

Brisson, Luc, and Michel Patillon. "Longinus Platonicus Philosophus et Philologus." *ANRW* II.36.7 (1994), 5214–99.

Buell, Denise Kimber. *Making Christians: Clement of Alexandria and the Rhetoric of Legitimacy*. Princeton, N.J.: Princeton University Press, 1999.

———. "Rethinking the Relevance of Race for Early Christian Self-Definition." *HTR* 94 (2001), 461–62.

———. "Race and Universalism in Early Christianity." *JECS* 10 (2002), 429–68.

Burckhardt, Jacob. *The Age of Constantine the Great*. Trans. Moses Hadas. New York: Dorset Press, 1949.

Burrus, Virginia. *The Making of a Heretic: Gender, Authority, and the Priscillianist Controversy*. Berkeley: University of California Press, 1995.

Carriker, Andrew. *The Library of Eusebius of Caesarea*. Supplements to Vigiliae Christianae 67. Leiden: Brill, 2003.

Castelli, Elizabeth. *Martyrdom and Memory: Early Christian Culture Making*. New York: Columbia University Press, 2004.

Chadwick, Henry. *Sentences of Sextus*. Texts and Studies 5. Cambridge: Cambridge University Press, 1959.

———. *The Early Church*. New York: Penguin, 1967.

Christianson, G., and T. Izbicki (eds.). *Nicholas of Cusa in Search of God and Wisdom.* Leiden: Brill, 1991.

Clark, Elizabeth A. *The Origenist Controversy.* Princeton, N.J.: Princeton Unviversity Press, 1992.

———. *History, Theory, Text: Historians and the Linguistic Turn.* Cambridge, Mass.: Harvard University Press, 2004.

Clark, Gillian. "Translate into Greek: Porphyry of Tyre on the New Barbarians." In Miles (ed.), *Constructing Identities,* 112–32.

Collins, John J. *Between Athens and Jerusalem: Jewish Identity in the Hellenistic Diaspora.* 2nd ed. Grand Rapids, Mich.: Eerdmans, 2000.

Cook, John Granger. "A Possible Fragment of Porphyry's *Contra Christianos* from Michael the Syrian." *Zeitschrift für Antike Christentum/Journal of Ancient Christianity* 2 (1998), 113–22.

Corcoran, Simon. *The Empire of the Tetrachs: Imperial Pronouncements and Government AD 284–324.* Oxford: Oxford University Press, 1996.

Courcelle, Pierre. "Les sages de Porphyre et les 'viri novi' d'Arnobe." *Revue des études latines* 31 (1953), 257–71.

Davies, P. "Constantine's Editor." JTS 42 (1991), 610–18.

Davis, Kathleen. "National Writing in the Ninth century: A Reminder for Postcolonial Thinking About the Nation." *JMEMS* 28 (1998), 611–37.

Dawson, David. *Allegorical Readers and Cultural Revision in Ancient Alexandria.* Berkeley: University of California Press, 1992.

De Certeau, Michel. *The Practice of Everyday Life.* Trans. Steven Rendall. Berkeley: University of California Press, 1984.

De Ste. Croix, G. E. M. "Why Were the Early Christians Persecuted?" *Past and Present* 26 (1963), 6–38.

Den Boer, W., P. G. van der Nat, J. C. van Winden (eds.). *Romanitas et Christianitas: Studia Iano Henrico Waszink.* Amsterdam: North Holland Publishing, 1973.

Des Places, Édouard. "Eusèbe de Césarée juge de Platon dans la Préparation Évangélique." In *Mélanges de Philosophie Grecque offerts à Mgr. Diès.* Paris: Beauchesne, 1956, 69–77.

Digeser, Elizabeth DePalma. "Lactantius and Constantine's Letter to Arles: Dating the *Divine Institutes.*" *JECS* 2 (1994), 33–52.

———. "Lactantius and the Edict of Milan: Does It Determine His Venue?" *Studia Patristica* 31 (1997), 287–95.

———. *The Making of a Christian Empire: Lactantius and Rome.* Ithaca, N.Y.: Cornell University Press, 2000.

———. "An Oracle of Apollo at Daphne and the Great Persecution." *Classical Philology* 99 (2004), 57–77.

Dillon, John. *The Middle Platonists: 80 B.C. to A.D. 220.* Ithaca, N.Y.: Cornell University Press, 1977. Rev. with afterword, 1996.

Dillon, John, and A. Long, A. (eds.). *The Question of "Eclecticism": Studies in Later Greek Philosophy.* Berkeley: University of California Press, 1988.

Donini, Pierluigi. "The History of the Concept of Eclecticism." In J. Dillon and A. A. Long (eds.), *The Question of "Eclecticism."* Berkeley: University of California Press, 1988, 15–33.

Doran, R. "Jewish Hellenistic Historians Before Josephus." In *ANRW* II.20.1 (1987), 246–97.

Dörrie, Heinrich. "Ammonios, der Lehrer Plotins." *Hermes* 83 (1955), 439–77.

———. "Die Wertung der Barbaren im Urteil der Greichen: Knechtsnaturen?

Oder Bewahrer und Künder heilbrigender Weisheit?" In *Antike und Univer-salgeschichte.* Munster: Verlag, 1972, 46–175.

———. "Platons Reisen zu fernen Völkern." In den Boer, van der Nat, and van Winden (eds.), *Romanitas et Christianitas*, 99–118.

Drake, Harold. *In Praise of Constantine: A Historical Study and New Translation of Eusebius' Tricennial Orations.* University of California Publications, Classical Studies, vol. 15, Berkeley: University of California Press, 1975.

———. "Suggestions of Date in Constantine's *Oration to the Saints.*" *American Journal of Philology* 106 (1985), 335–49.

———. "What Eusebius Knew: The Genesis of the *Vita Constantini.*" *Classical Philology* 83 (1988), 21–38.

———. *Constantine and the Bishops: The Politics of Intolerance.* Baltimore: Johns Hopkins University Press, 2000.

Droge, Arthur J. *Homer or Moses? Early Christian Interpretations of the History of Culture.* Hermeneutische Untersuchungen zur Theologie Bd. 26. Tübingen: J. C. B. Mohr, 1989.

Dubuisson, Daniel. *The Western Construction of Religion: Myths, Knowledge, and Ideology.* Trans. W. Sayers. Baltimore: Johns Hopkins University Press, 2003.

Dunderberg, Ismo, Christopher Tuckett, and Keri Syreeni (eds). *Fair Play: Diversity and Conflicts in Early Christianity, Essays in Honor of Heikki Räisänen.* Leiden, Brill, 2002.

Dvornik, Francis. *Early Christian and Byzantine Political Philosophy.* 2 vols. Washington, D.C.: Dumbarton Oaks Center for Byzantine Studies, 1966.

Edwards, Mark. "On the Platonic Schooling of Justin Martyr." *JTS* 42 (1991), 17–34.

———. "Ammonius, Teacher of Origen." *JEH* 44 (1993), 1–13.

———. "The Flowering of Latin Apologetic: Lactantius and Arnobius." In Edwards, Goodman, and Price (eds.), *Apologetics in the Roman Empire*, 197–221.

———. "The Constantinian Circle and the *Oration to the Saints.*" In Edwards, Goodman, and Price (eds.), *Apologetics in the Roman Empire*, 251–75.

Edwards, Mark, Martin Goodman, and Simon Price (eds.). *Apologetics in the Roman Empire: Pagans, Jews, and Christians.* Oxford: Oxford University Press, 1999.

Ehrman, Bart. *The New Testament: A Historical Introduction to the Early Christian Writings.* Oxford: Oxford University Press, 2000.

Elze, Martin. *Tatian und seine Theologie.* Forschungen zur Kirchen- und Dogmengeschichte Bd. 9. Göttingen: Vandenhoeck and Ruprecht, 1960. Erksine, Andrew. *The Hellenistic Stoa: Political Thought and Action.* Ithaca, N.Y.: Cornell University Press, 1990.

Farina, Raffaella. *L'impero e l'imperatore cristiano in Eusebio di Cesarea: La prima teologia politica del cristianismo.* Zurich: Pas Verlag, 1966.

Festugière, A. J. "La doctrine des 'uiri novi' sur l'origine et le sort des âmes, d'après Arnobe, II, 11–66." In *Mémorial Lagrange.* Paris: J. Gabalda, 1940, 97–132.

Fiedrowicz, Michael. *Apologie im frühen Christentum. Die Kontroverse um den christlichen Wahrheitsanspruch in den ersten Jahrhunderten.* Paderborn: Ferdinand Schöningh, 2000.

Fontaine, Jacques, and Michel Perrin (eds.) *Lactance et son temps.* Théologie Historique 48. Paris: Beauchesne, 1978.

Foucault, Michel. *The Order of Things: An Archaeology of the Human Sciences.* New York: Random House, 1971.

Fowden, Elizabeth Key. "Constantine and the Peoples of the Eastern Frontier." In Lenski (ed.), *Age of Constantine*, 377–98.

Fowden, Garth. *Empire to Commonwealth: Consequences of Monotheism in Late Antiquity*. Princeton, N.J.: Princeton University Press, 1993.

Fox, Robin Lane. *Pagans and Christians*. San Francisco: Harper and Row, 1986.

Frede, Michael. "Principles of Stoic Grammar." In Rist (ed.), *The Stoics*, 27–76.

———. "Celsus Philosophus Platonicus." *ANRW* II.36.7 (1994), 5183–5213.

———. "Celsus's Attack on the Christians." In Griffith and Barnes (eds.), *Philosophia Togata II*, 218–40.

Fredouille, Jean-Claude. "L'apologétique chrétienne antique: Naissance d'un genre littéraire." *Revue des Études Augustiniennes* 38 (1992), 219–34.

———. "L'apologie chrétienne antique: Métamorphe d'un genre polymorphe." *Revue des Études Augustiniennes* 41 (1995), 201–16.

Frend, W. H. C. *Martyrdom and Persecution in the Early Church*. Oxford: Oxford University Press, 1965.

———. *The Rise of Christianity*. Philadelphia: Fortress Press, 1984.

———. "Prelude to the Great Persecution: The Propaganda War." *JEH* 38 (1987), 1–18.

Frilingos, Christopher. *Spectacle and Empire: Monsters, Martyrs, and the Book of Revelation*. Philadelphia: University of Pennsylvania Press, 2004.

Gaddis, Michael. *There Is No Crime for Those Who Have Christ: Religious Violence in the Christian Roman Empire*. Berkeley: University of California Press, 2005.

Gaston, Lloyd. *Paul and the Torah*. Vancouver: University of British Columbia Press, 1987.

Geary, Patrick J. *The Myth of Nations: The Medieval Origins of Europe*. Princeton, N.J.: Princeton University Press, 2002.

Gibbon, Edward. *The Decline and Fall of the Roman Empire*. 1776–78. Repr. London: Penguin Books, 1952.

Goldhill, Simon (ed.). *Being Greek Under Rome: Cultural Identity, the Second Sophistic, and the Development of Empire*. Cambridge: Cambridge University Press, 2001.

———. "The Erotic Eye: Visual Stimulation and Cultural Conflict." In Goldhill (ed.), *Being Greek Under Rome*, 154–94.

———. *Who Needs Greek?: Contests in the History of Hellenism*. Cambridge: Cambridge University Press, 2002.

Goodenough, Erwin R. *The Theology of Justin Martyr*. Jena: Verlag Frommannsche Buchhandlung, 1923.

Goodman, Martin. "Josephus' Treatise *Against Apion*." In Edwards, Goodman, and Price (eds.), *Apologetics in the Roman Empire*, 45–58.

Goulet, Richard. "Porphyre, Ammonius, les Deux Origénes et les Autres." *Revue de l'Histoire de Philosophie et Religion* 57 (1977), 471–96.

———. *Macarios de Magnésie: Le Monogénès*. Paris: J. Vrin, 2003.

Graeser, Andreas. "The Stoic Theory of Meaning." In Rist (ed.), *The Stoics*, 77–99.

Grant, Robert M. *Augustus to Constantine*. New York: Harper and Row, 1970.

———. "Porphyry Among the Early Christians." In den Boer, van der Nat, and van Winden (eds.), *Romanitas et Christianitas*, 181–87.

———. *Greek Apologists of the Second Century*. Philadelphia: Westminster Press, 1988.

Grégoire, H. "Les chrétiens et l'oracle de Didymes." In *Mélanges Holleaux: Recueil de mémoires concernant l'antiquité grecque offert à Maurice Holleaux*. Paris, 1913.

Gressman, Hugo. *Studien zu Eusebs Theophanie.* Texte und Untersuchungen 23.3. Lepzig, 1903.

Griffith, Miriam, and John Barnes (eds.). *Philosophia Togata.* Oxford: Oxford University Press, 1989.

———. *Philosophia Togata II.* Oxford: Oxford University Press, 1997.

Guillaumin, Marie-Louise. "L'exploitation des 'Oracles Sibyllins' par Lactance et par le 'Discours a l'assemblée des saints.'" In Fontaine and Perrin (eds.), *Lactance et son temps,* 183–202.

Hadot, Pierre. "Bilan et perspectives sur les *Oracles Chaldaïques.*" In Lewy, *Chaldean Oracles and Theurgy,* 711–12.

———. "Théologie, exégèse, revelation, écriture dans la philosophie grecque." In Michel Tardieu (ed.), *Les règles de l'interprétation.* Paris: Cerf, 1987, 13–34.

———. *What Is Ancient Philosophy?* Cambridge, Mass.: Harvard University Press, 2002.

Hagedorn, D., and R. Merkelbach. "Ein neues Fragment aus Porphyrios gegen die Christen." *Vigiliae Christianae* 20 (1966), 86–90.

Hägg, Tomas. "Hierocles' the Lover of Truth and Eusebius the Sophist." *Symbolae Osloenses* 62 (1992), 146–50.

Hall, Jonathan M. *Ethnic Identity in Greek Antiquity.* Cambridge: Cambridge University Press, 1997.

Hall, Stuart. "The Question of Cultural Identity." In Stuart Hall et al. (eds.), *Modernity: An Introduction to Modern Societies.* Oxford: Basil Blackwell, 1996.

Hanson, Paul D. "Rebellion in Heaven, Azazel, and Euhemeristic Heroes in 1 Enoch." *Journal of Biblical Literature* 96 (1977), 195–233.

Hanson, R. P. C. "The *Oratio ad Sanctos* Attributed to the Emperor Constantine and the Oracle at Daphne." *JTS* 24 (1973), 505–11.

Harnack, Adolf von. *The Mission and Expansion of Christianity in the First Three Centuries.* Trans. J. Mofat. New York: G. P. Putnam's Sons, 1908.

Harries, Jill. *Law and Empire in Late Antiquity.* Cambridge: Cambridge University Press, 1999.

Heck, Eberhard. *Die dualistichen Zusätze und die Kaiseranrede bei Lactanz.* Heidelberg: Carl Winter, 1972.

Hingley, R. "Britannia, Origin Myths and the British Empire." *Proceedings of the Fourth Theoretical Roman Archaeology Conference* (1995), 11–23.

Hollerich, Michael. "Religion and Politics in the Writings of Eusebius of Caesarea: Reassessing the First 'Court Theologian.'" *Church History* 59 (1990), 309–25.

———. *Eusebius of Caesarea's Commentary on Isaiah: Christian Exegesis in the Age of Constantine.* Oxford: Oxford University Press, 1999.

Holte, Ragnar. "Logos Spermatikos: Christianity and Ancient Philosophy According to St. Justin's Apologies." *Studia Theologica* 11 (1958), 8–168.

Jacobs, Andrew. *Remains of the Jews: The Holy Land and Christian Empire in Late Antiquity.* Stanford, Calif.: Stanford University Press, 2004.

Johnson, Aaron. "Identity, Descent, and Polemic: Ethnic Argumentation in Eusebius's *Praeparatio Evangelica.*" *JECS* 12 (2004), 23–56.

Johnson, Carina L. "Idolatrous Cultures and the Practice of Religion." *Journal of the History of Ideas* 67 (2006), 597–621.

Jones, A. H. M. *The Later Roman Empire: AD 284–602.* Oxford: Oxford University Press, 1964.

Jones A. H. M., and T. C. Skeat, "Notes in the Genuineness of the Constantinian Documents in Eusebius's *Life of Constantine.*" *JEH* 5 (1954), 196–200.

Jones, Roger Miller. *The Platonism of Plutarch and Selected Papers.* Menasha, Wisc.: George Banta, 1916. Reprint, New York: Garland, 1980.

King, Karen. *What Is Gnosticism?* Cambridge, Mass.: Harvard University Press, 2003.

King, Richard. *Orientalism and Religion: Postcolonial Theory, India, and "The Mystic East."* London: Routledge, 1999.

Kloppenborg, John, and Stephen Wilson (eds.). *Voluntary Associations in the Graeco-Roman World.* London: Routledge, 1996.

———. "Collegia and *Thiasoi*: Issues in Function, Taxonomy, and Membership," in Kloppenborg and Wilson (eds.), *Voluntary Associations in the Graeco-Roman World,* 16–30.

Kofsky, Aryeh. *Eusebius of Caesarea Against Paganism.* Leiden: Brill, 2000.

Kulikowski, Michael. "Constantine and the Northern Barbarians." In Lenski (ed.), *Age of Constantine,* 347–76.

LaBriolle, Pierre de. *La réaction païenne: Étude sur la polémique antichrétienne du Ier au V^ie siècle.* Paris: L'Artisan du Livre, 1934.

Lamberton, Robert. *Homer the Theologian: Neoplatonist Allegorical Reading and the Growth of the Epic Tradition.* Berkeley: University of California Press, 1986.

Larson, Charles. "Heroic Ethnocentrism: The Idea of Universality in Literature." In Ashcroft, Griffiths, and Tiffin (eds.), *The Post-colonial Studies Reader,* 62–65.

Le Boulluec, Alain. *La notion d'hérésie dans la literature grecque IIé-IIé siècles.* Paris: Études Augustiniennes, 1985.

Lenski, Noel (ed.). *The Cambridge Companion to the Age of Constantine.* Cambridge: Cambridge University Press, 2006.

Lewy, Hans. *Chaldean Oracles and Theurgy.* New ed., Michel Tardieu (ed.). Paris: Études Augustiniennes, 1978.

Lightfoot, J. B. "Eusebius of Caesarea." In *Dictionary of Christian Biography,* vol. 2. London: J. Murray, 1880, 308–48.

Loomba, Ania. *Colonialism/Postcolonialism.* London: Routledge, 1998.

Lyman, Rebecca. "The Politics of Passing: Justin Martyr's conversion as a Problem of 'Hellenization.' " In Kenneth Mills and Anthony Grafton (eds.), *Conversion in Late Antiquity and the Early Middle Ages.* Rochester: University of Rochester Press, 2003.

———. "Hellenism and Heresy." *JECS* 11:2 (2003), 209–22.

MacCormack, Sabine. "Gods, Demons, and Idols in the Andes." *Journal of the History of Ideas* 67 (2006), 623–47.

———. *On the Wings of Time: Rome, the Incas, Spain and Peru.* Princeton, N.J.: Princeton University Press, 2006.

Markus, Robert. *The End of Ancient Christianity.* Cambridge: Cambridge University Press, 1993.

Mason, Steven. "Philosophiai: Graeco-Roman, Judean, and Christian." In Kloppenborg and Wilson (eds.), *Voluntary Associations in the Graeco-Roman World,* 16–30.

Masuzawa, Tomoko. *The Invention of World Religions.* Chicago: University of Chicago Press, 2005.

Mattingly, David. "From One Colonialism to Another: Imperialism in the Maghreb." In Webster and Cooper (eds.), *Roman Imperialism,* 49–69.

McCutcheon, Russell T. *Manufacturing Religion: The Discourse on Sui Generis Religion and the Politics of Nostalgia.* Oxford: Oxford University Press, 1997.

———. *Critics Not Caretakers: Redescribing the Public Study of Religion.* Albany: State University of New York Press, 2001.

Miles, Richard (ed.). *Constructing Identities in Late Antiquity*. London: Routledge, 1999.

Millet, M. *The Romanization of Britain*. Cambridge: Cambridge University Press, 1990.

Momigliano, Arnaldo (ed.). *The Conflict Between Paganism and Christianity in the Later Roman Empire*. Oxford: Basil Blackwell, 1963.

———. *Alien Wisdom: The Limits of Hellenization*. Cambridge: Cambridge University Press, 1971.

———. *On Pagans, Jews, and Christians*. Hanover, N.H.: Wesleyan University Press, 1987.

———. "Historiography of Religion: Western Views." In *On Pagans, Jews, and Christians*, 11–30.

———. "The Origins of Universal History." In *On Pagans, Jews, and Christians*, 31–57.

Monat, Pierre. *Lactance et la Bible: Une propédeutique latine à la lecture de la Bible dans l'Occident constantinien*. 2 vols. Paris: Études Augustiniennes, 1982.

Moore-Gilbert, Bart. *Postcolonial Theory: Contexts, Practices, Politics*. London: Verso, 1997.

Mortley, Raoul. *The Idea of Universal History from Hellenistic Philosophy to Early Christian Historiography*. Lewiston, N.Y.: Edwin Mellen, 1996.

Most, Glen. "Cornutus and Stoic Allegoresis: A Preliminary Report." *ANRW* II.36.3 (1989), 2014–65.

Mullen, Roderic. *The Expansion of Christianity: A Gazetteer of Its First Three Centuries*. Leiden: Brill, 2004.

Nautin, Pierre. "Trois autres fragments du livre de Porphyre 'Contre les Chrétiens.'" *Revue Biblique* 57 (1950), 409–16.

Nicholson, Oliver. "The Source of the Dates in Lactantius's *Divine Institutes*." *JTS* 36 (1985), 291–310.

———. "Broadening the Roman Mind: Foreign Prophets in the Apologetic of Lactantius." *Studia Patristica* 34 (2001), 364–74.

———. "*Caelum potius intuemini:* Lactantius and a Statue of Constantine." *Studia Patristica* 34 (2001), 177–96.

Norelli, Enrico. "La critique du pluralisme grec dans le *Discours aux Grecs* de Tatian." In Poudéron and Doré (eds.), *Les apologists chrétiens*, 81–87.

Novak, D. M. "Constantine and the Senate: An Early Phase in the Christianization of the Roman Aristocracy." *Ancient Society* 10 (1979), 271–310.

Ogilvie, R. M. *The Library of Lactantius*. Oxford: Oxford University Press, 1978.

O'Meara, John. *Porphyry's On Philosophy from Oracles in Augustine*. Paris: Études Augustiniennes, 1959.

———. "Porphury's *Philosophy from Oracles* in Eusebius's *Preparation for the Gospel* and Augustine's *Dialogues of Cassiciacum*." *Recherches Augustiniennes* 6 (1969), 103–39.

Pagden, Anthony. *The Fall of Natural Man: The American Indian and the Origins of Comparative Ethnology*. Cambridge: Cambridge University Press, 1982.

Parke, H. W. *Sibyls and Sibylline Prophecy in Classical Antiquity*. London: Routledge, 1988.

Parvis, Sara. *Marcellus of Ancyra and the Lost Years of the Arian Controversy, 325–345*. Oxford: Oxford Unviversity Press, 2006.

Pasquali, G. "Die Composition der *Vita Constantini* des Eusebius." *Hermes* 46 (1910), 369–86.

Pépin, Jean. "Porphyre, exegete d'Homère." In *Porphyre.* Entretiens Hardt XII. Geneva: Fondation Hardt, 1966, 229–72.

Pérez Jiménez, A., J. García López, and R. M. Aguilar (eds.). *Plutarco, Platón y Aristóteles.* Madrid: Ediciones Clásicas, 1999.

Perrin, Michel. *L'homme antique et chrétien: L'anthropologie de Lactance, 250–325.* Théologie Historique 59. Paris: Beauchesne, 1981.

———. "Lactance et la culture grecque: Esquisse d'une problématique." In Poudéron and Doré (eds.), *Les apologists chrétiens,* 297–313.

Peterson, E. *Der Monotheismus als politisches Problem: Ein Beitrage zur Geschichte der politischen Theologie im Imperium Romanum.* Leipzig: Hegner, 1935.

Pfeiffer, R. *History of Classical Scholarship: From the Beginnings to the End of the Hellenistic Age.* Oxford: Oxford University Press, 1968.

Pichon, René. *Lactance: Étude sur le mouvement philosophique et religieux sous le règne de Constantin.* Paris: Librarie Hachette, 1901.

Pohl, Walter, and Helmut Reimitz (eds.). *Strategies of Distinction: The Construction of Ethnic Communities, 300–800.* Leiden: Brill, 1998.

Pohlenz, Max. *Die Stoa: Geschichte einer geistigen Bewegung.* Göttingen: Vandenhoeck and Ruprecht, 1970.

Poudéron, B., and J. Doré (eds.). *Les apologistes chrétiens et la culture grecque.* Théologie Historique 105. Paris: Beauchesne, 1998.

Preston, Rebecca. "Roman Questions, Greek Answers: Plutarch and the Construction of Identity." In Goldhill (ed.), *Being Greek Under Rome,* 86–119.

Räisänen, Heikki. *Paul and the Law.* Philadelphia: Fortress Press, 1983.

Rawson, Elizabeth. "Roman Rulers and the Philosophic Advisor." In Griffith and Barnes (eds.), *Philosophia Togata,* 233–57.

Reed, Annette Yoshiko. *Fallen Angels and the History of Judaism and Christianity: The Reception of Enochic Literature.* Cambridge: Cambridge University Press, 2005.

Richter, Daniel. "Plutarch on Isis and Osiris: Text, Cult, and Cultural Appropriation." *Transactions of the American Philological Association* 131 (2001), 191–216.

Ridings, Daniel. *The Attic Moses: The Dependency Theme in Some Early Christian Writers.* Göteburg: Acta Universitatis Gothoburgensis, 1995.

Rist, John (ed.). *The Stoics.* Berkeley: University of California Press, 1978.

Rives, James. "Human Sacrifice Among Pagans and Christians." *JRS* 85 (1995), 65–85.

———. "The Piety of the Persecutors." *JECS* 4 (1996), 1–25.

Rogers, Rick. *Theophilus of Antioch: The Life and Thought of a Second-Century Bishop.* Lanham, Md.: Lexington Books, 2000.

Rougier, Louis. *Celse Contre les Chretiens la réaction païenne sous l'empire romain.* Paris: Copernic, 1977.

Rubiés, Joan-Pau. "Theology, Ethnography, and the Historicization of Idolatry." *Journal of the History of Ideas* 67 (2006), 571–96.

Rubin, Z. "The Church of the Holy Sepulchre and the Conflict Between the Sees of Caesarea and Jerusalem." *Jerusalem Cathedra* 2 (1982), 79–105.

Said, Edward. *Orientalism.* New York: Vintage, 1979. Reprint with afterword, 1994.

Saïd, Suzanne. "The Discourse of Identity in Greek Rhetoric from Isocrates to Aristides." In Irad Malkin (ed.), *Ancient Perceptions of Greek Ethnicity.* Cambridge, Mass.: Harvard University Press, 2001.

Sanders, E. P. *Paul, the Law and the Jewish People.* Philadelphia: Fortress Press, 1983.

Schmidt, Thomas. *Plutarque et les Barbares: La rhétorique d'une image*. Louvain: Peeters, 1999.

———. "Plutarch's Timeless Barbarians and the Age of Trajan." In Stadter and Van der Stockt (eds.), *Sage and Emperor*, 57–71.

Schmitt, Charles. "Perennial Philosophy: From Agostino Steuco to Leibniz." *Journal of the History of Ideas* 27 (1966), 505–32.

Schott, Jeremy M. "Founding Platonopolis: The Platonic *Politeia* in Porphyry, Iamblichus, and Eusebius." *JECS* 11 (2003), 501–31.

———. "Porphyry on Christians and Others: 'Barbarian Wisdom,' Identity Politics, and Anti-Christian Polemics on the Eve of the Great Persecution." *JECS* 13 (2005), 277–314.

Schwarte, K. H. "Diokletians Christengesetz." In R. Günther, and S. Rebenich (eds.), *E fontibus haurire: Beiträge zur römischen Geschichte und zu ihren Hilfswissenschaften*. Paderborn: F. Schöningh, 1994, 203–40.

Selew, Phillip. "Achilles or Christ? Porphyry and Didymus in Debate over Allegorical Interpretation." *HTR* 82 (1989), 79–100.

Sherwin-White, A. N. "The Early Persecutions and Roman Law Again." *JTS* 3 (1952), 199–213.

Simmons, Michael Bland. *Arnobius of Sicca: Religious Conflict and Competition in the Age of Diocletian*. Oxford: Oxford University Press, 1995.

Sirinelli, Jean. *Les vues historiques d'Eusèbe de Césarée durant la period prénicéenne*. Dakar: Université de Dakar, 1961.

Smith, Andrew. "Porphyrian Studies Since 1913." *ANRW* II.36.2 (1987), 717–73.

Smith, Jonathan Z. *Map Is Not Territory*. Chicago: University of Chicago Press, 1978.

———. *Relating Religion*. Chicago: University of Chicago Press, 2004.

Sodano, A. R. *Porfirio Lettera ad Anebo*. Naples: L'Arte Tipografica, 1958.

———. *Vangelo di un pagano*. Milani Rusconi, 1993.

Stadter, Philip, and Luc Van der Stockt (eds.). *Sage and Emperor: Plutarch, Greek Intellectuals, and Roman Power in the Time of Trajan*. Louvain: Louvain University Press, 2002.

Sterling, G. E. *Historiography and Self-Definition: Josephus, Luke-Acts, and Apologetic Historiography*. Supplements to *Novum Testamentum* 64. Leiden: Brill, 1992.

Stevenson, James. *Studies in Eusebius*. Cambridge: Cambridge University Press, 1929.

Stowers, Stanley K. *A Rereading of Romans: Justice, Jews, and Gentiles*. New Haven, Conn.: Yale University Press, 1994.

Tate, J. "Plato and Allegorical Interpretation." *Classical Quarterly* 24 (1930), 142–54.

Troup, Calvin. "Augustine the African: Critic of Roman Colonialist Discourse." *Religious Studies Quarterly* 25 (1995), 92–106.

Ulrich, Jörg. *Euseb von Caesarea und die Juden: Studien zur Rolle der Juden in der Theologie des Eusebius von Caesarea*. Berlin: Walter de Gruyter, 1999.

van den Hoek, Annewies. *Clement of Alexandria and His Use of Philo in the Stromateis: An Early Christian Reshaping of a Jewish Model*. Leiden: Brill, 1988.

Viswanathan, Gauri. *Outside the Fold: Conversion, Modernity, and Belief*. Princeton, N.J.: Princeton University Press, 1998.

Wacholder, B. Z. *Eupolemus: A Study of Judaeo-Greek Literature*. Cincinnati: Hebrew Union College, 1974.

Wallace-Hadrill, D. S. *Eusebius of Caesarea*. London: Mowbray, 1960.

———. "Eusebius of Caesarea's Commentary on Luke: Its Origin and Early History." *HTR* 67 (1974), 55–63.

Warmington, B. H. "Did Constantine Have 'Religious Advisors'?" *Studia Patristica* 19 (1989), 117–29.

Waszink, J.-H. "Bemerkungen zu Justins Lehre vom Logos Spermatikos." In *Mullus: Festschrift Theodor Klauser.* Munster: Aschendorff, 1964, 380–90.

———. "Porphyrios und Numenios." In *Porphyre.* Entretiens Hardt XII. Geneva: Fondation Hardt, 1966, 33–84.

———. *Opuscula Selecta.* Leiden: Brill, 1979.

———. "Some Observations on the Appreciation of 'The Philosophy of the Barbarians' in Early Christian Literature." In *Opuscula Selecta,* 272–87.

Webster, Jane and Nick Cooper (eds.). *Roman Imperialism: Post-Colonial Perspectives.* Leicester Archaeology Monographs No. 3. Leicester: School of Archaeological Studies, 1996.

———. "Roman Imperialism and the 'Post-Imperial Age.'" In Webster and Cooper, *Roman Imperialism,* 1–17.

Wharton, Annabel. *Refiguring the Postclassical City: Dura Europos, Jerash, Jerusalem, and Ravenna.* Cambridge: Cambridge University Press, 1995.

Whitmarsh, Timothy. *Greek Literature in the Roman Empire: The Politics of Imitation.* Oxford: Oxford University Press, 2001.

Whittaker, John. "Moses Atticizing." *Phoenix* 21 (1967), 196–201.

Wilamowitz-Moellendorff, Ulrich von. "Ein Bruchstück aus der Schrift des Porphyrius gegen die Christen." *Zeitschrift für die Neutestamentliche Wissenschaft und die Kunde des Urchristentums* 1 (1900), 101–5.

Wilken, Robert Louis. *The Christians as the Romans Saw Them.* 2nd ed. New Haven, Conn.: Yale University Press, 2003.

Williams, Rowan, ed. *The Making of Orthodoxy: Essays in Honor of Henry Chadwick.* Cambridge: Cambridge University Press, 1989.

Williams, Stephen. *Diocletian and the Roman Recovery.* London: Batsford, 1985.

Winkelmann, Friedhelm. *Euseb von Kaisareia: Der Vater der Kirchengeschichte.* Berlin: Verlags-Anstalt Union, 1991.

Wlosok, Antonie. *Laktanz und die philosophische Gnosis: Untersuchungen zu Geschichte und Terminologie der gnostischen Erlösungsvorstellung.* Heidelberg: Carl Winter, 1960.

Woolf, Gustav. "World Systems Analysis and the Roman Empire." *JRS* 12 (1990), 223–34.

Young, Frances. "Greek Apologists of the Second Century." In Edwards, Goodman, and Price (eds.), *Apologetics in the Roman Empire,* 81–104.

Young, Robert. *Postcolonialism: An historical Introduction.* Oxford: Blackwell, 2001.

Zambon, Marcel. *Porphyre et le moyen-platonisme.* Paris: J. Vrin, 2002.

Zeller, E., and E. Wellman. *Die Philosophie der Griechen in ihrer geschichtlichen Entwicklung dargestellt.* Leipzig, 1909.

Index

Acknowledgments

I could not have completed this book without the support of numerous mentors, colleagues, and friends.

I presented early versions of several chapters at the annual meetings of the Society of Biblical Literature, the American Academy of Religion, the North American Patristics Society, the Society for Late Antiquity's Shifting Frontiers conference, and the International Patristics Conference. An earlier version of Chapter 2 first appeared as "Porphyry on Christians and Others: 'Barbarian Wisdom,' Identity Politics, and Anti-Christian Polemics on the Eve of the Great Persecution," *JECS* 13 (2005), 277–314. The audiences at each of these conferences and the editors and reviewers at *JECS* offered many useful insights.

I have been fortunate to be part of vibrant and creative scholarly communities at Duke, UNC-Chapel Hill, and UNC-Charlotte. I owe special thanks to Elizabeth Clark; much that is of value in this project I owe to her patient criticism and mentoring. I also thank those who have read or commented on this book at various stages: Adam Becker, Mary Boatwright, Ann Burlein, Catherine Chin, Gary Crites, Elizabeth Digeser, Andrew Jacobs, Joanne Maguire-Robinson, Sean McCloud, Zlatko Plese, Carrie Schroeder, Tina Shepherdson, Randy Styers, Kristi Upson-Saia, and Lucas Van Rompay. Two teaching assistants, Jeremy Absher and Chad Day, tolerated many hours in front of photocopiers and my conversations about Porphyry and Eusebius. Special thanks are due to Ginger Stickney for helping to prepare the index. I am also grateful to the editors of the Divinations series and to the editors and staff at the University of Pennsylvania Press. I would especially like to thank the two anonymous reviewers who offered many helpful comments on the manuscripts; Jennifer Backer, whose excellent copyediting saved me from a number of errors (any that remain are, of course, my own); and Derek Krueger and Jerome Singerman for shepherding this book (and me) through the publication process.

I thank my mother and late father for teaching me that "how" and "why" are more interesting than "what," and my grandparents, whose support has been instrumental in my education. I am also grateful to Janice and Dennis Powell, who have been like second parents. Thanks also to my feline "children," Buttercup and Henrietta, for keeping me company and for helping to interrupt me when I needed it.

I owe my greatest debt to my best friend and partner, Michelle Powell. The pages that follow have benefited immeasurably from her insight, kindness, and love. She has always supported and encouraged me, often at great personal sacrifice. For this, and for so much else, I dedicate this book to her.